CHARLESTON

CHARLESTON

RACE, WATER, AND THE COMING STORM

SUSAN CRAWFORD

Foreword by Annette Gordon-Reed

PEGASUS BOOKS

NEW YORK LONDON

CHARLESTON

Pegasus Books, Ltd.
148 West 37th Street, 13th Floor
New York, NY 10018

First Pegasus Books cloth edition April 2023

Interior design by Maria Fernandez

Library of Congress Cataloging-in-Publication Data is available.

ISBN: 978-1-63936-357-5

10 9 8 7 6 5 4 3 2 1

Printed in the United States of America
Distributed by Simon & Schuster
www.pegasusbooks.com

*For Mitchell, and for everyone who has looked
at a coastline and wondered*

Contents

Foreword

The first decades of the twenty-first century will likely be remembered as a time of extreme political divisiveness in the United States. Efforts to address major problems through concerted action by government and other entities have been hampered by a degree of social polarization that some historians suggest rivals the decade of the 1850s and the lead up to the American Civil War. The dream of effective—and bipartisan—efforts to address problems that touch people all along the political spectrum seems elusive.

Political polarization has spilled over into science, with people taking sides on scientific issues based upon their political views. This has profoundly shaped the discourse about one of the most serious issues facing not just the United States, but the entire world: climate change. The consensus among the vast majority of scientists who study the issue is that the Earth is undergoing, and will continue to undergo, changes in climate that will transform agriculture, spur emigration from areas burdened by higher temperatures, create recurring catastrophic weather events, and flood cities built along coasts as ocean levels rise. Some, usually considered to be on "the right," see talk of climate change and exhortations to try to do something as overblown and anti-economic growth. The charge that human beings may be the cause of, or are in some ways exacerbating the problem, is especially anathema to many in this group. They strenuously object to efforts to change human behavior with the goal of slowing down or arresting climate change. On the other side are environmentalists and those who are often designated as part of "the left." They believe that drastic steps should be taken immediately to deal with what they see as an existential crisis.

As Susan Crawford makes plain in *Charleston: Race, Water, and the Coming Storm*, planet Earth has experienced extreme changes in climate for many millennia—ice ages, changes in sea levels, land masses disappearing beneath oceans. But what is different about those situations and today is that we human beings have a greater awareness of what is happening, and actually have the chance to take measures to minimize the suffering that extreme conditions can cause. Our knowledge and predictive capacity allow for preparation. But how is this done in a society so riven by political partisanship and culture warring that people cannot, will not, agree on what constitutes "knowledge." Moreover, efforts to prepare for the looming crisis are expensive. It is always difficult to get people to pay for future benefits at the expense of what they see as their current and immediate needs.

How does all of this play out in the context of America's tortured racial history? *Charleston* raises this especially appropriate question because that history has been a significant source of the divisions that exist within American society today. The circumstances of Charleston, South Carolina are instructive on this point. Charleston was one of the major conduits for enslaved Africans brought to what would become the United States. It is estimated that nearly half of the captives passed through its historic port. Over the years, South Carolina became home to large numbers of African Americans. Indeed, by the time of the Civil War, there were three Black people for every one white person in the state. Of course, to protect the institution of racially based slavery,

South Carolina led the Southern states out of the United States, pre-cipitating the Civil War. After a brief period in Reconstruction when Black men participated in the government, the state's legacy of resisting equal citizenship for Black people, through violence and legalized segregation, continued well into the twentieth century.

Now, as Charleston faces the prospects of sinking land and a rising sea level, Crawford's *Charleston* shows how important it is to consider the ways in which the legacies of slavery and racism have shaped and continue to shape the city's response (and nonresponse) to its precarious environmental position. For many white and well-off residents, Charleston's predicament is a real estate investment problem: do they sell now or remain? The questions are different for residents who are poor and do not own their homes—renters and residents of public housing. The story that unfolds in these pages reveals a history of second-class treatment of Black residents who, for generations, have lived burdened by recurrent flooding with little significant help from the city. Who have struggled to be heard despite great efforts by their community. All available evidence indicates that the problem of flooding will grow worse and worse, and the most economically and socially vulnerable people will be in ever more dire straits. Will the government authorities be able to rise above historical patterns and take action on behalf of the marginalized people in the city? It is a question for the local, state, and federal governments, and it is one that will be asked about other American coastal cities. The nation deserves a good and right answer.

Annette Gordon-Reed
Carl M. Loeb University Professor
Harvard University
Cambridge, Massachusetts

1

Charleston and
Its Global Cousins

We believe the map of the world's coastlines is drawn by human occupation. In the mind's eye, teeming masses of people stand on the edge of what they believe to be solid ground, gazing outward at the sea, their places taken seamlessly, endlessly, by younger versions of themselves. Some of those people, lucky and well-organized, supported by the societies in which they live, build structures whose windows look seaward as well, heaps of them, great clotted tangles of mud, steel, glass, and iron pressed, more or less, up against the water. From above, all these people and buildings together make up dark, comfortably solid shapes marking where land ends and liquid begins.

In reality, this map is not drawn by us. Over millions of years, sea levels have gone up and down. During the last ice age, tens of thousands of years ago, global shorelines extended miles beyond current land masses and sea levels were about 400 feet lower than they are now.[1]

About 20,000 years ago, much of the watery area we now know as the North Sea was dry land. Imagine a continuous mass about the size of Denmark, plunked down between Britain and Holland. Now add gentle hills, valleys, streams, lakes, fish, birds, and ample quiet. Humans, too; in fact, people had likely been living there for almost a million years at that point, as far as we can tell. It must have been delightful—there was beauty, and there was plenty to eat. Historians call this place Doggerland.

Then, about 8,500 years ago, ice lakes started to melt into the North Sea.[2] The waters surrounding the residents of Doggerland began to rise. The richness of the land they lived on gradually started to change, as trees and vegetation were swallowed by wetlands, and as firm ground morphed from soil to sand to marsh. High places that had been linked by land became islands. New water channels gradually emerged. It was a slow process, but it was inexorable. The people of Doggerland would have had to change their ways over time, do things differently than their ancestors had done, in response to the rising waters.

We can't tell much about the lives of the people who lived in this area because there is water there now.[3] Sand carried by the rising waters across Doggerland, left behind on top of all those lovely hills and valleys when the inundation ended, reveals nothing, no human remains or artifacts. But archaeologists guess from evidence found on the still-dry margins of Doggerland—particularly in present-day England—that the Doggerlanders lived in society, in groups. They weren't wandering around aimlessly. They weren't hopelessly in transition on some kind of land bridge. They settled when and where they could. They must have been attached to Doggerland, with its waving grasses and abundant wildlife. But eventually, after a few generations of living in a gradually wetter place, they had to move away.

As an invitation to imagination, the story of the inundation of Doggerland is a treasure. It's the last time that modern man experienced significant sea level rise. Vincent Gaffney, a professor of landscape archaeology at the University of Bradford, speaks with enormous warmth about the contours of Doggerland. He knows what it looked like because vast seismic data sets have been gathered by companies looking to extract oil and gas from beneath the North Sea. "We are looking at totally unexplored countries," he says. "Where else in the world could you find complete rivers, lakes, hills, and valleys, that've never been mapped before? That had human occupation. And what does it mean for us at the moment?"

Gaffney is convinced that Doggerland was one of the most economically productive areas in Europe. When it went under, 20 percent of Europe's land mass vanished. He told the BBC's Melvyn Bragg in 2019 that a large Mesolithic house built in Howick, on the coast of Northumberland, had probably been put together by people coming off the North Sea Plain onto the still-solid ground—something like New York City retirees building a house in the Berkshires. Once those Mesolithic men and women walked away from their old, prosperous haunts, they settled firmly into a relocated residential life, bringing with them their sociable, comfortable existence. That Howick house was a substantial place. It was lived in for a hundred years and featured a number of hearths for nut roasting.[4]

The lesson from Doggerland is that beaches, wetlands, and marshes historically have moved with changing sea levels without difficulty and rewritten the boundaries of continents. We humans have adapted to this movement in the past, shifting location to keep our collective feet dry while continuing to live in friendly clumps. But this time there is an obstacle in the way: forgetting the power of oceans, and believing that we should by rights get to live wherever we want, forever, people have built up our global coastlines and plopped concrete in places where water would otherwise be going. This time the change, driven by human activity, is happening very quickly.[5]

◆

Each coastal city has an origin story. A trading post, a landing point, or a fishing haven was established long ago, took root, and sprawled outward and upward. These stories feel both obvious and irrelevant to each city's current occupants, if they know them at all. Each coastal native witnesses part of a century, notices decay and growth, and gives up his or her place to more recent arrivals. Those lucky few who build may imagine with some satisfaction that their imprints will remain beyond their lifetimes, if only for a while. Those who live in rooms that were built by generations before may imagine that generations to come will find their homes there, too.

The consequences of the rapidly accelerating sea level rise and other heat-related water woes the globe is now experiencing will abruptly change these patterns for the 800 million people who now live near water on coasts around the world.[6] Someday, not too long from now, the stories of many current coastal and riverside cities will include sudden plot twists as well as new beginnings, as edges that had seemed solid liquify and become indistinguishable from the seas around them. Some coastal areas will have to be abandoned altogether. Water sources that few among us consider in our daily lives will suddenly become intensely interesting. There is water beneath our feet (groundwater) that is beginning to bubble upwards, pressed towards and then through the surface of streets as prolonged wet periods cause underground water tables to rise. At the same time, increasing human demands for fresh groundwater—for drinking water, irrigation, and the cooling of data centers—is causing those coastal aquifers to shrink, which gives salty water, pushed onward by rising seas, room to intrude. The withdrawal of huge quantities of fresh water for humans to drink also causes land to subside, increasing sea level rise (relatively speaking) further. It takes a tiny amount of salt to make water undrinkable.

There's more: slower-moving heavily intense rainstorms (sometimes called rain bombs or, more colorfully, frog-drowners) are becoming more frequent, as ever-more water is soaked up by ever-warmer air and the strength of the winds that used to push those storms along their paths diminishes. Those winds are calming because the poles are warming much more quickly than the tropics. The differences between the two that used to generate those winds are shrinking. Increasingly intense hurricanes and extreme river flooding are being joined by daily high tides made higher by sea level rise, as increasingly warm ocean water is taking up more space and encroaching on land. All this will render many low-lying areas profoundly uncomfortable and eventually uninhabitable. In many places, these challenges will be piled on top of more frequent stretches of ever-more-extreme heat. For many people, there will not be enough water to drink.

The people of Doggerland had hundreds of years to get used to sea level rise as the globe warmed. Even then, those who didn't move up to the highlands—present-day Britain—still had an island left to stand on. Until they didn't. Several thousand years ago, a sudden underwater landslide off the coast of what is now Norway triggered a wall of water that flooded what remained of Doggerland.[7] The place slumbered for eighty centuries beneath the North Sea until scientists began to explore its past.

Given the brittle instability of what we have created along global coastlines, we have far less time than the Doggerlanders did to adapt safely to the changes to come. Because of the level of carbon already in the atmosphere, beginning in the early 2030s, the rate at which the seas are rising will accelerate at a rapid pace.[8] Between 2020 and 2050, we will see as much sea level rise as we did over the last century.[9] Even if emissions decrease, sea level increases of as much as 8 feet between 2050 and 2100 cannot be ruled out.[10] "Then we are talking about situations that are not adaptable," says Dr. William Sweet of the National Oceanic and Atmospheric Administration (NOAA).[11] Dr. Sweet means that many coastal residents will not be able to stay where they are.

It is not a question of whether these changes will happen, but when. There are strong indications that this transition is coming quickly for

coastal cities around the globe: NASA's satellite and buoy data show
the Earth is heating at unprecedented speed;[12] most of the last ten years
have set records, one after the next, for the hottest ever, and the world
will likely experience a 2° to 3°C increase over late-1800s temperatures
by the end of the century.[13] Several climate tipping points that will
trigger *additional* nonlinear increases in sea level rise, including the
melting of Antarctic and Greenland ice sheets, are becoming likelier
as emissions and temperatures continue to increase.[14]

◆

Charleston, South Carolina is one of many cities around the globe
that will be deeply affected by rising waters in the years to come. Its
geography is that of a small New York City, with a central peninsula
surrounded by outer boroughs. That peninsula, perched between the
Ashley River on the west and the Cooper River on the east, has been
the site of an important Atlantic port for nearly 350 years. The city also
has a history of racial immorality, often ignored by its contemporary
boosters. About 40 percent of all the enslaved people who were forcibly
brought to America first stepped ashore there, and after the importation of enslaved people was banned by the nation in 1808, Charleston
was a center of the country's domestic slave market. Enslaved people
were the basis of Charleston's economy and development for two hundred years, planting and harvesting the rice and extracting the indigo
that the region exported, filling the marshy margins of the peninsula
with trash, rubble, and human waste. The city of Charleston took on
the function of whipping enslaved people on behalf of their owners.
It was the place where America's Civil War, fought over the issue of
slavery, began.

Today, its historic peninsula is a magnet for seven million mostly
white tourists a year. For its visitors, the peninsula's bars, restaurants,

and luxury hotels are sites for care-free indulgence and relaxation, a chance to enjoy the feeling of well-attended wealth while forgetting all the tensions of everyday life. The place has an amnesiac, ahistorical quality that is highly attractive to white celebrants, who drowsily pad along its pretty streets before tucking into their next big meal; they are enjoying the suggestion of moneyed graciousness around them, not thinking too hard about where that money came from. Tourism, centered on Charleston, is one of South Carolina's largest industries, contributing more than $10 billion annually to the region's economy.[15] But these visitors are spending and drinking and shopping in a place with a baleful past that, by most objective measures, is living on borrowed time.

In September 1989, midway through the forty-year incumbency of Charleston Mayor Joseph P. Riley, Hurricane Hugo made landfall up the Atlantic coast in McLellanville, South Carolina. Hugo's winds did great damage to Charleston, but the storm also brought national attention to the city, and Mayor Riley was able to harness substantial public funding to develop and improve its historic peninsula. Over the next few decades, Charleston became the most rapidly gentrifying city in America and one of the most expensive in the southeast in which to live. It also spread outward across marshes and sea islands. A majority Black city in the 1970s, it has become majority white. Today it is a place of crushing traffic, suburban sprawl, astounding economic inequality, and ongoing racial discrimination as well as touristic charm; it is, in fact, an extreme example of these urban characteristics.

For all these reasons, the story of Charleston's reaction to the rapidly increasing risks of sea level rise has global implications. Although Charleston's role in American history is uniquely disturbing and its low-lying, sandy topography is particularly vulnerable to the ravages of sea level rise, its lack of planning for the involuntary displacement of its Black and low-income residents by rising sea levels is not unusual. Few global cities are doing enough to plan ahead for what is coming.

What is special about Charleston is that its global reputation for charm and hospitality contrasts so vividly with the risks its poorest residents now face as the waters rise.

◆

A good deal of change has already occurred, worldwide, because of climate change. Jakarta, Indonesia is swiftly sinking and almost the entirety of Bangladesh is in crisis. Heavy rains in Bangladesh and India in 2022 left two million people stranded and killed dozens.[16] The eighty-mile-an-hour winds of Hurricane Ida in September 2021 were accompanied by three-and-a-half inches of rain that landed in one hour on New York City, drowning people living in illegal basement apartments when overloaded sewers backed up and overflowed.[17] Some 1,700 people died in Pakistan from extreme flooding over the summer of 2022, and tens of millions were displaced.[18] About half a million people live in the Maldives on 1,200 very low coral islands and their homes—along with those of anyone else living on a Pacific island—are already at great risk.[19] Tens of millions of people in China live in risky coastal regions, and hundreds of people died in Henan province when more rain fell there over four days in July 2021 than usually falls in a year.[20] Ft. Myers, in southwest Florida, was devastated by Hurricane Ian in September 2022.

Hurricanes today are stronger, rainstorms are heavier, storms move more slowly, groundwater tables are rising rapidly, and rivers are overflowing in catastrophic ways. Hurricane Harvey was a rain bomb during which sixty inches of rain fell over four days in 2017 in southeast Texas.[21] Heavy rain turned deadly in the Côte d'Ivoire in June 2020 when it triggered a landslide.[22] More than two million people in Lagos, Nigeria were affected by flooding during 2020.[23] Alexandria, Egypt, surrounded by water, has experienced intense rain and flooding each year since 2015.[24] During the summer of 2021, two months' worth of rain fell over Western Europe in two days, causing death and destruction in Germany, Belgium, and several other countries.[25] Major flooding in Australia in March 2021 caused billions of dollars of damage over the wettest week coastal New South Wales had ever seen.[26] Western Canada, India, Japan, and Northern South America all experienced exceptional rainfall and flooding that year. Flash flooding struck Zion National Park and much of southern Utah during that same summer.

Predictions about how much water is coming, and when, vary greatly. In 2019, Prime Minister Lee Hsien Loong announced that Singapore would prepare for about thirteen feet of sea level rise by 2100.[27] Some scientists say we should be planning on three feet of rise by 2050, six feet by 2070, and ten feet by 2100.[28]

The timing of sea level rise is uncertain because how and when ice sheets in Antarctica and Greenland will melt is uncertain.[29] If the Thwaites Eastern Ice Shelf in Antarctica fails, which may happen as soon as five or ten years from now, and the glacier it is holding back slides or calves into the ocean, sea levels will rise about two feet from that effect alone; if the West Antarctic Ice Sheet collapses, the world will see an increase of between ten and a half feet and fourteen feet; if *all* the ice on Antarctica and Greenland melts, sea levels will be more than two hundred feet higher than at present, drowning New York City, Shanghai, and Tokyo.[30] We know that the rate of this rise can accelerate very quickly; it did before, when great ice sheets collapsed thousands of years ago, even without human encouragement forcing the process along.[31] We also know that beginning in about 2025 the moon's 18.6-year cycle that is currently suppressing the rate of increase in global sea levels will go into its next phase, amplifying the rate of rise.[32] (This is called the "moon wobble" cycle.)[33] All told, given continued high emissions (which we hope will be mitigated somehow) and the already-observed melting of glaciers, it is beyond dispute that sea level rise is happening almost three times faster than scientists had thought it would as recently as 2011,[34] and that there is now a substantial chance that there will be *more* than six and a half feet of global sea level rise by 2100.[35] This amount of sea level rise is not spread evenly around the world: Charleston gets more than the global average.[36]

We know that storms and floods in the United States and around the world disproportionately harm Black and low-income communities whose residents are involuntarily permanently displaced, rendered homeless, or ground more deeply into poverty.[37] Of the people who lived in the neighborhood in Houston that sustained the worst damage during Hurricane Harvey in 2017, nearly half were people of color.[38] Hurricane Katrina, in New Orleans in 2005, hurt Black neighborhoods the most.[39] Hurricane Ida in 2021 devastated low-income communities south of New Orleans.[40] Affordable housing in America, largely occupied by low-income Black people, is at very high risk of being damaged or destroyed by coastal flooding over the next few decades.[41]

These same patterns will play out in Charleston. The city is in the Lowcountry region in South Carolina, and it is very, very low: more than a third of the houses in the city are at ten feet above sea level or less.[42] It is a many-layered place whose history runs deep but where solid ground is scarce. The first settlers saw mostly marsh when they arrived in 1640, stepping gingerly over scores of muddy creeks. High ground is almost nonexistent in Charleston.[43] Much of the city was built on fill—trash, oyster shells, wooden pilings, human waste, loose dirt—over centuries, and now Nature wants her land back. Its residents have already become accustomed to frequent high-tide flooding on days when the sun is shining.

A hundred years ago, the city flooded less than once a year. Forty years ago, the city flooded ten times a year. The city flooded eighty-nine times in 2019, almost once every four days, sixty-eight times in 2020, and forty-six times in 2021.[44] Beginning in about 2032 the number of days a year Charleston floods will start climbing rapidly. By 2050, damaging flooding will be happening ten times more frequently than it did in 2020. In the chapters ahead, you will hear a great deal about what this will be like for the people who live there, and particularly for Charleston's Black residents. There are large areas of damp, filled land within the city's surprisingly far-flung limits, including chunks of suburban sprawl that tourists never see, that are suddenly at very high risk of chronic inundation over the next few decades.

◆

Given that peoples' safety is at issue and that scientists are becoming confident that a rise of about 3°C is likely by 2100, it seems reasonable that governments at all levels should be planning for the worst outcomes now. The message that climate change is happening, and happening quickly, is acknowledged by national governments around the world. But the translation of that message into action at the local level is not yet, really, happening.

The trouble is that sea level rise is taking place relatively slowly compared to the human attention span—which is, let's face it, gnat-like, and made even shorter when other crises (a global pandemic, the threat of world war, domestic political instability, rising inflation) are on our minds. City leaders, occupied with running for reelection, prioritize continued growth and expanding the tax base over protecting against future doom. And, although each increasingly intense hurricane or rainstorm is terrifying taken alone, people often forget that fear with the passage of time. Awareness is smoothed over by the common cognitive bias toward believing that anything awful is anomalous. Humans are not by nature long-range planners, particularly when they are focused on simply surviving. Boosterism and denial are at work in Charleston, as they are everywhere.

Cities may also believe that their state or national governments will ride to their rescue should they suffer a cataclysmic storm or begin to experience unlivable levels of sea level rise. Spending money now on moving people or planning ahead for new, safe communities may feel imprudent when someone else is likely to pay to save you later, and so cities continue encouraging floodplain development near rivers and coasts. To the extent they do plan ahead, cities with scarce resources focus on protecting the highest-value properties first, reasoning that their limited money is best spent where it will have the highest payoff. This approach is not altogether their fault: In the US, a platoon of state and federal policies work the same way. This kind of analysis causes real cruelty to those not lucky enough to be wealthy. In Charleston, many of those less lucky residents are Black, and this cost-benefit optimization amplifies and entrenches historic patterns of racism and segregation.

There are cities facing similar risks in America that are farther along in planning for the changing world, but even those more advanced planning efforts suffer from the some of the same gaps when it comes to the risks of displacement for vulnerable residents. Boston, itself built half on landfill, has a "Climate Ready Boston" master plan that calls for elevating streets, building berms, turning parks into water storage receptacles, and adding watertight doors to subway entrances. But notwithstanding the city's rhetorical focus on equity, it maintains its "Coastal Resilience Solutions for Dorchester" plan separately from its overall strategic plan for the city. The city's primary focus is adapting to challenges that affect property values for downtown real estate and white Boston. More than two-thirds of Boston's Black residents live in Dorchester and the nearby neighborhoods of Roxbury and Mattapan; the average white household's wealth in Greater Boston is $247,500 while the average Black household's wealth is $8. There are no sea walls where Boston's poorest residents live, no plans to resettle them, and no clear source of funding to do so.

Similarly, the Commonwealth of Virginia has unveiled a sweeping plan called the "Virginia Coastal Master Planning Framework" that acknowledges the vulnerability of its low-income and minority coastal residents and recognizes that "protecting every component of the built environment exactly where it stands today is not realistic" and "some homes, businesses, roads, and communities will become uninhabitable as sea level rises." But although the document does require that equity issues be taken into account by municipalities while those cities are seeking input from residents, it does not provide planning directions or resources for cities that want to assist those low-income and minority residents to move away from the rising waters. Miami is taking the same approach, claiming that protecting high-value coastal real estate is both possible and appropriate and refusing to plan for ceding land or paying low-income renters to move to higher, safer ground. Charleston's story reveals a general blind spot that will become more visible as at least thirteen million people are expected to have to retreat from swamped American coastlines. Americans will learn, if they did not know already, that some lives count and some do not.

◆

And so as the earth warms and the waters rise, coastal cities everywhere have an incentive to keep quiet about the range of accelerating risks confronting them and are paying little attention, most of the time, to the risks faced by their poorest residents. These risks are so sweeping, and the changes likely to come sooner rather than later will be so disruptive, that thinking broadly about what is owed to every city resident *right now* is beyond the capacity of most leaders, including those in Charleston.

Their plans may be changed for them by the insurance, banking, and real estate industries now propping up coastal land values, who are capable of long-term actuarial assessments. They will begin raising their prices, exit completely, or collapse quickly, and millions or billions of people will be in distress.

Insurance companies and teeming coastal megacities were not part of the picture when humans lived on Doggerland. This is why Rachel Bynoe, a lecturer in archaeology at the University of Southampton, thinks gradual adaptation might have been just fine with Doggerland's residents. "Where we see sea level rise as something that's very negative and terrifying, because we're very sedentary, and we have really high population densities—in the past, where those two things weren't quite so strong. . . it could've been catastrophic at points, perhaps, but generally speaking, this would've been a slow process that would've just changed the affordances of these areas," she told the BBC in mid-2019. "So it's not necessarily something to be seen in a negative light." "Affordances" is a quilt of a word, covering a range of novel things to do that are made possible by a changing world.

There are things coastal city leaders could be doing now that would take advantage of new affordances made possible by our more advanced capacities to plan. Imagine gradually making it more expensive to live in dangerous places while simultaneously providing time-limited incentives and subsidies supporting moving away—a multidecade plan, for example, to gradually phase out the mortgages on properties that will be eventually returned to nature, and to subsidize future rent payments if made in higher, drier places. Imagine planning for a multidecade, gradual move, in consultation with each community, to new and welcoming locations well-connected to transit and jobs.[45] Imagine caring for the least well-off among us, ensuring that they have a voice in this

planning and choices about whether, when, and how to leave, while firmly setting an endpoint on human habitation in the riskiest places, or, at least, making it clear that these places will be repurposed for other uses.

Without this kind of vision, the coming transition will be a cliff rather than a slope, casting millions into sudden misery.

Governments at all levels need to understand that the riskiest response of all would be to do nothing, or to act only incrementally, in the face of already accelerating threats that may at any moment abruptly begin accelerating even more quickly, robbing us of our ability to plan.[46] Would you get on an elevator if you knew there was a substantial chance of the cables holding the car snapping just before you reached your floor? Would you have your city's residents collectively get on that elevator? I don't think so. And if elevators don't worry you, think airplanes.

◆

Around the world, nations are spending tens of billions of dollars on coastal protection. In the United States, we spend it with almost no planning as to how it is prioritized or allocated. Congress gives money to the Army Corps of Engineers and essentially asks that the Corps come back and tell Congress later what it did. The $15 billion wall the Corps built after Hurricane Katrina has been hailed as a tremendous success, but the wall did not protect communities of people living south of New Orleans when Hurricane Ida hit in September 2021. The wall was not designed to reach them because their properties were not considered valuable enough by the Corps to merit protection.

There are substantial lessons here: There is no chance that we can afford to wall off the entire coast of the country or all populations living along rivers. It is also far from clear that the walls we are building now will be sufficient ten or twenty years from now.

More unplanned spending: On a somewhat random basis, the
Federal Emergency Management Association (FEMA) will buy out
houses that chronically flood, but the payments are low, take years for
suffering homeowners to access, and so far have addressed just 45,000
homes out of the millions that should probably be vacated.[47] We spend
billions dumping sand on beaches that are shrinking or moving. The
truth is we will never have enough sand or enough money to keep
the status quo in place.

The reason some beachfront homeowners, but not all, get that sand
dumped on their beaches, and the reason that some portions of cities,
but not all, get federal funds for building walls, is that the one rule of
thumb for all these expenditures is that they be made subject to a cost-
benefit analysis. But that means the only thing that is valued is the price
of the property being protected. Lower-income people, or renters, do
not get protected or rescued. "We are spending the money where we get
the biggest bang for our buck," says James D'Ambrosio, a spokesman
for the Army Corps in New York. "It may sound hardhearted, but to be
fiscally responsible and to be stewards of taxpayer money, we have to
abide by the greater benefit of the public good."[48] Surely we have values
that rise above mere dollars and cents. Surely we are interested in
everyone thriving, not just those who have the highest land values.

Few are talking about how America is going to get through the rapid
rise in sea level that is coming. Like most other countries, we have no
national plan. There is an intuitive sense that building walls and pumping
sand on beaches is the right thing to do, because it will protect existing
property interests and keep things as they are. But is that wise?

◆

There are hints that the omertà that has kept leaders from openly planning to address the threats facing them is beginning to crack. Ever

since a fearsome North Sea storm drowned thousands of its people in 1953, the Netherlands has been armoring its coastline. Dutch engineering prowess shields Amsterdam and Rotterdam, building seawalls to block surges of water driven by storms and deploying pumps to dry city streets, busily moving water from rainstorms and riverine flooding back over those walls into the sea. The Dutch were already expert in building dikes by 1953, but that storm prompted them to redouble their efforts and become global experts in keeping water away from their people. They're proud of this armoring and market it effectively around the globe, including in Charleston, as we will learn.[49]

This self-presentation, this global Dutch image, is based on the implicit promise that the massive Dutch building and designing effort—and expertise that is made available at a price to American cities—has rendered the Netherlands *safe*, including, importantly, the densely populated Randstad area of Rotterdam, Amsterdam, Utrecht, and other major delta cities. As landscape architect and proud Dutchman Steven Slabbers says, "Deltas are the best places to live in the world if you know how to deal with the water."

Back in 1986, the national Delta Project team of the Netherlands published a technical report on what would happen if extreme water levels suddenly appeared to be likely. They said, stoically, that they'd be capable of pumping the entire flow of the Rhine upwards and out into the sea, creating a giant, sunken "polder"—a low area constantly pumped to keep dry—of essentially the entire Randstad. They could raise their walls and dikes by twenty-one feet, everywhere—an enormous task. All technically possible! All comically, *cosmically*, expensive. And they hadn't taken the possibility of rapid ice glacier melting into account.[50] Retreat was certainly not on the table as an option.

Some elements of the Dutch government have now begun to realize that a wall high enough to protect against the very worst storms that are coming soon will be too expensive and difficult to build and maintain.

Not only that, life behind those very high walls would be unpleasant; the water left trapped behind them would turn brackish as flora and fauna died. They are starting to admit that even they can't pump away a relentlessly rising North Atlantic and all the country's inland rivers forever in any cost effective way. And if they do pump all the water from the Rhine, Meuse, Scheldt, and Ems rivers over those enormous dikes, the heavier salt water from the sea will form an underground wedge and seep beneath any wall, which will be disastrous for agriculture and drinking water.[51] At some point, it will make sense to begin moving businesses and people away from the frayed, wet western edge of their country towards the east and safety.

Retreat, or planned abandonment, of their soft-soiled delta region is not an attractive concept for Dutch landscape architects in the business of providing armoring services. Slabbers again: "We are not going to give up on [the Randstad conurbation]. It's the same as New Orleans. New Orleans is in big trouble, but the value is too big to say, 'Okay, ocean, it's all yours. Here is your bride.' No, no way."[52]

According to Professor Simon Richter of the University of Pennsylvania, things began to change in the Netherlands in 2017 when Deltares, one of the country's leading engineering and water research institutes, published the results of a policy exercise entitled, "What If Sea Level Rises More Rapidly." For the first time, Deltares included the uncertain contributions from melting ice in Antarctica in its risk assessment. That study said that the existing armoring lining the coast of the Netherlands would be adequate only until 2050. It was necessary to begin planning for higher sea levels, Marjolijn Haasnoot, a senior researcher on climate and water at Deltares, announced, because otherwise the speed of change might make it difficult to plan at all.[53]

A 2019 article in Dutch by climate journalist Rold Shuttenhelm called "Sea Level Rise Is Bigger Than We Think, and The Netherlands

Doesn't Have A Plan B" was the first public discussion in the Netherlands of the possibility of accelerated sea level rise prompting retreat from the Dutch coast.[54] It quoted Kim Cohen, a physical geographer at Utrecht University, saying that Dutch schools should consider "German as a mandatory second language," and describing a scenario in which "we join the Federal Republic of Germany as a federal state." It was illustrated by a sketch showing coastal Dutch cities as a series of islands joined by causeways arcing across a lagoon.

Then, in 2019, Deltares presented four pathways for the Netherlands' adaptation to accelerated sea level rise.[55] Three of these scenarios involved even stronger armoring designed to keep the water at bay. The last, "meebewegen," or "accommodate," involved retreat. The appealing cartoonish drawing accompanying this last scenario showed the low-lying west of the Netherlands as completely inundated, with the Hague, Amsterdam, and Rotterdam preserved as floating islands joined to the distant mainland by bridges. The implication was that everyone not standing on those islands would have moved to the east, which was indicated as a playful cross-hatched line labeled "DUITSLAND" (Germany). This was new.

According to Haasnoot, the country's options in a time of accelerating sea level rise are swiftly narrowing to two: "either you close [the water] off completely and live with the consequences, or you say: maybe we should just give it back to nature and focus on other areas to live in."[56] She coauthored a 2021 report in *Science* that argued there was "an urgent need to keep coastal retreat on the table as an option to adapt to sea-level rise."[57] In particular, the report suggested that keeping retreat in mind could help "avoid increasing investments that eventually become higher sunk costs." Buying time with incremental measures might trigger greater risk exposure and make the problem worse, because developers would rely on the reduction of risk promised by these steps.

Finally, in December 2021, the Dutch government pivoted: the Dutch Delta Commissioner, Peter Glas, directed the part of the Dutch government responsible for planning housing to assume at least two meters, or more than six feet, of sea level rise by 2100.[58] That department had planned to build 820,000 houses in vulnerable areas. Glas told them not to build in places where water was already pooling during extreme rain events or where drainage wasn't working. (The Netherlands has a long history of water governance that is independent of ordinary municipal government, and Glas as Delta Commissioner is an independent advisor and coordinator of flood safety and adaptation efforts who is responsible for taking on board the most recent data and setting policy. He gets unquestioned respect in his country. As Dutch landscape architect Steven Slabbers puts it, "There are two professions in the world from which there is only one person. That's the pope. And that's the Delta Commissioner. . . . And when he says, 'We are going to do it this way,' we *are* going to do it this way.")[59] In response to a specific plan to build thousands of new homes in Nieuwerkerk aan den IJssel, an area of the Netherlands just a few miles northeast of Rotterdam that is almost seven meters below sea level, Glas pointed out that building there would be a particularly bad idea. If a rainstorm similar to those that flooded Germany and Belgium in July 2021 arrived, the city's pumps would not be capable of draining the area for at least two weeks.[60] It's a horrifying vision: modest houses would be completely submerged, and there aren't adequate evacuation routes.

Although Glas confirmed that the current dikes and walls along the Dutch coast that protect the Randstad from inundation would be adequate until 2050, he noted that the speed of sea level change meant that it wouldn't be safe after that to rely on those walls. And, Glas politely suggested, noting the need for additional housing in the Randstad, "For the more distant future, the Delta Commissioner therefore also advises central government to investigate how urbanization can be distributed differently across the Netherlands in the long term." It was time, the Dutch were finally saying publicly if subtly, to plan ahead for a new reality away from the coast. Even they wouldn't necessarily be able to engineer their way out of the rapidly rising water to come.

◆

Charleston, with its miles of flat, interconnected watersheds, is even more threatened by sea level rise than the Netherlands. An equitable, well-planned relocation might be a better solution than attempting to smooth out the wealthier portions of the city's coastline with complex gates and walls.

That relocation will be difficult. It will take intense and often frustrating work. It is not a technical problem, or a financial problem. It is a problem of trying to figure out how relocation can be done—let's call it "strategic withdrawal" if you don't like the words "relocation" or "retreat"—in a way that actually improves peoples' lives and allows their communities to continue, if that is what they or their children want. In the middle of this complexity is the history of race in Charleston, in South Carolina, and in the United States. The challenges that Charleston and its Black and low-income residents face in confronting the transition to come go on and on. Laura Cantral, former executive director of the Coastal Conservation League in Charleston, who moved away from Charleston at the end of 2021, says that the multi-dimensional intersections between water and race are the story. "It [race] can only be addressed by awareness and understanding this complexity that most people aren't interested in. It's hard. This is why we haven't done more on climate change as a country. Because it's hard. And it's abstract. It has felt abstract and too big to wrap any one brain around. Now it's not abstract any more."[61]

◆

Although the rate at which the seas will rise is uncertain, we already know what our worst natures will bring about if left unchecked. In 2007, Dutch experts from government, the private sector, and academia were brought into a scenario-planning exercise nicknamed the "Atlantis Project." They were asked to predict the consequences of the collapse of the West Antarctic Ice Sheet.

The Dutch interviewees sketched out a timeline of likely reactions: First, it would take a while for a sense of urgency to develop. Only after some very surprising floods would government action be taken, and only if politicians thought those steps were high priorities in relation to other issues that were important to them at the time. Meanwhile, large companies would be acting on their own, relocating their plants and headquarters to the eastern, inland, edge of the Netherlands, or even to other countries. People would choose to follow those companies, particularly highly educated, mobile people. This movement would undermine the historical willingness of the Netherlands to defend its land against water at all costs. At first, only the areas of relatively low economic value—the southwestern and northern parts of the country—would be abandoned. Later, the Randstad region of Amsterdam and Rotterdam in the western part of the Netherlands would be allowed to vanish as well once their well-off residents had left. In general, the interviewees expected puny and belated actions by a government beset by short-termism and incrementalism, and not enough public support for relocation of poorer people. This sounds about right. London experts were also interviewed, and they suggested that it would be similarly abandoned, with great suffering experienced by its poorest residents.[62]

Newspaper reporters have praised the prescience of the president of Indonesia, Joko Widodo, who in 2019 announced that his government would abandon sinking, flooding Jakarta and move its capital to higher ground hundreds of miles away in Kalimantan, in eastern Borneo.[63] What went unnoticed was that the government's plans to move *did not include* the eleven million people who live in Jakarta, much less the thirty-one million who live in its metropolitan area of Jabodetabek.[64] The architect who won the design contest for the move of the capital city, Sibarani, was asked to plan for *between 9,000 and 15,000 people.* His eventual plan was a bit more generous, and called for a city of about 56,000. These days, the government is saying that somewhere between 1.8 and 5.5 million Jakartans will be moving to the new capital by 2045.[65] Whatever the final capital in Borneo will look like, it is clear that Indonesia is planning to relocate only a portion of the population of Jakarta. Many of those who will remain live extraordinarily precarious lives. Will moving to Kalimantan save Jakarta? It will save the government. It might save the people who can afford to and want to move. But it will not save millions of Indonesians.

◆

Charleston's regional population has roughly doubled over the last fifty years, and is on track to reach one million people by 2040. The city's footprint has also grown enormously over the last few decades, from nine square miles in 1960 to 140 square miles today. Development in low-lying Charleston has proceeded at a breathtaking rate, as the city's heavy reliance on commercial and rental property taxes—overwhelmingly its primary source of revenue—has led it to encourage extraordinary construction in the form of large apartment buildings and hotels.

The problems that this congested, complicated city faces are not problems of the future. They are problems for today. The city already has all the information it needs, all the visualizations and data it could possibly require, to work with other cities in its region to implement concrete plans designed to help its Black and lower-income citizens. At the moment, however, there is no real plan to help them.

Instead, the city's current "plan"—born of hope, defiance, and resignation—appears to be to allow the city to suffer through a hurricane that will trigger a national focus on its plight and open the gates to federal disaster recovery funding. Such federal funding may include, city leaders hope, support for an Army Corps of Engineers plan to build a twelve-foot-tall concrete wall around the historic peninsula that would shield tourist areas and the city's large Medical District from storm surges. But the planned wall (for which such federal support is entirely hypothetical) would take decades to build, would likely be outmoded in a decade or so, and wouldn't by itself protect the city from the chronic tidal flooding and drainage problems that now make life miserable for so many of its residents. Nor, obviously, would it help resettle the city's poorest residents in safe, dry, dense places of dignity and opportunity. Every week, month, and year that goes by without city leaders pushing for major planning aimed—at least in part—at helping Charleston's poorest residents move away from the rising waters only further threatens their safety.

This issue has become increasingly urgent in recent years. Enormous storms battered Charleston in 2015, 2016, 2017, 2018, and 2021. Hurricane Ian, one of the strongest storms to hit the US in decades, missed Charleston by a whisker in September 2022.

Charleston, like other global cities, should be confronting the risks it faces and planning on a regional basis for a drastically changed future that may include strategic withdrawal. But working regionally will be very difficult: Within Charleston County alone, there are seven separate governmental entities (the City of Folly Beach, the Town of James Island, the Town of Sullivan's Island, the Town of Mount Pleasant, and the City of North Charleston), as well as the city of Charleston and the county itself, all competing for resources.

The city of Charleston has a patchwork presence in the boroughs of Johns Island and James Island, where several communities refused to be annexed into the city. There is no visible cooperation among the thirty local governments in Charleston's region. Jurisdiction is a tangled mess in the Charleston region, as it is everywhere. Charleston's failure to plan regionally does not make it unique, but its many-layered history of racism taken together with more than three decades of out-of-control gentrification and development makes that failure particularly glaring. Black residents of Charleston have barely been consulted by the city officials leading its spray of uncoordinated planning initiatives.

If Charleston had the leadership, vision, money, and planning capacity it needed, it would, today, stop development in vulnerable areas and let everyone (of all skin colors) who wanted to leave those areas leave. It would pay property owners for the property they had left—or otherwise subsidize residents to leave—and turn those areas into marshy, soft, water-absorbing places. It would plan ahead, in collaboration with nearby cities and counties, for attractive, higher-ground areas near Charleston's metro region that would be both affordable and well-served by public transit, so that people who loved Charleston's culture could resettle there. It would ensure that those new places included both public and affordable housing so every Charlestonian could find a welcoming place to live, and jobs so they could work. It would close its constantly flooding public housing units on the peninsula and compassionately help resettle the people living there in those new, safe, connected, dense, economically diverse areas. It would dismantle its hospital district—now floating uneasily above loose, trash-filled land—and move those functions to far safer places. It wouldn't build a blank twelve-foot storm surge wall around the peninsula, which would destroy the historic city's beauty while leaving the rest of the city's residents to take their chances. If Charleston were to make this vision a reality, it could found its future on its best essential qualities and serve as a key example for other coastal cities. And it might become a more equitable, more welcoming place in the meantime. But there isn't much time, even if city leaders were willing. And if it will take a major storm to draw attention to the region's precarious position and cause money to flow its way, all indications are that such a reckoning may come sooner rather than later. Charleston's luck, long history, and trust in Providence cannot protect the city forever.

When slow-to-change racial structures, a profound respect for white history, an inborn dislike for government intervention, an overwhelming focus on growth, and a reluctance to act with urgency meet hurricanes, rising waters, and sinking land, what happens? In all its bravura, complacency, and cruelty, Charleston's relationship with its current and future flooding woes expresses much about the underside of American life: an obsession with development and property rights above all else, undergirded by centuries of racism. When the crisis happens—when a major storm hits or the frequent floods become undeniably chronic—the region's minimal, haphazard, and shockingly underresourced efforts to plan ahead will be revealed, and its particularly immoral treatment of its Black and poorer residents will be laid bare. Unless Charleston changes its ways with substantial leadership and assistance from our national government, the waters to come will have ruinous consequences—for the city, certainly, and for Charleston's Black and low-income residents most of all. And what is likely to happen in Charleston is likely, absent a substantial shift in attitude, to happen in many other coastal cities around the globe.

2

Charleston's Natural Environment

On a warm summer evening, the water is black and rippling. It fills the broad street and runs up past the doorsills of the well-lit stores, glistening in the light of lamps and neon signs. It isn't raging, it is simply *there*, out of place, and rising quickly. In its thinnest advancing layers, visible against marble steps, it carries leaves and twigs; the debris from the last street it filled, and the streets and alleys before that. There is unseen muck swirling through the growing depths below the streetlights. The water came from the sky in buckets, pouring down at a rate of six inches an hour. It also came from the rivers lining the peninsula, and before that from the sea; it is endless. At an invisible intersection the water laps over the base of a stop sign. An abandoned white minivan stands beyond the sign, emergency lights flashing, its wheels covered by the water's darkness. Two white tourists, the man holding the woman's hand stiff-armed up above the water, are making their way down the nonexistent sidewalk and into the vanished intersection of Church and North Market Streets. He's holding a red shopping bag above the water in his other hand while he pushes through the thigh-deep wetness. Perhaps those two had been hoping for a dinner out; the lights are on in Queology Barbecue, three blocks to the east, but there is an unexpected foot of water inside.

A handful of blocks north, there are fewer streetlights and no stores. The water seems fiercer here and less constrained as it rises, running over the soft dimpled asphalt and cascading beneath ragged doors into the living rooms of low-slung houses. Refuse is floating everywhere in the dark murk running through the streets, because trash cans holding remnants of every imaginable meal have tipped and spilled into the rush of muck. The windows of long, battered cars are still visible, marking the edges of the blocks, but the cars themselves seem to be sagging into the borderless darkness. Few people are outside; most know better than to expose themselves to the toxic stew that is running through their neighborhood and into their cramped living quarters. One older Black resident is out, a man in high dark rubber boots that rise to his thighs; he is poking with a long wooden pole at a place where rising ripples are circling near the front bumper of an abandoned car. There is a drain below where he is standing, but it is having little effect. The nineteenth century storm drain system under the peninsula's streets was designed to take water from the higher land, the inner spine of the peninsula, out to the lower rivers on either side, using gravity to drain the city streets, but the rivers are no longer lower and the drains stay full. The rivers and the streets are indistinguishable in rainstorms and on dry days when the tides are high. The tourists are experiencing this tonight as they wade through the streets. It is a Saturday night in June in Charleston, South Carolina.

The flood lasts for hours. The tourists will have a story to tell when they get home. In the end, they will forget this wet, confusing evening and remember instead the colorful mansions and still quiet streets of the Charleston peninsula in the midday sun. It is just one nighttime disruption; a seam between two peaceful days in the 350-year history of the city. But the seam is loosely sewn. Visible through its threads are all the moments that came before.

◆

Thousands of years ago, most of the Charleston region was under the ocean. The water covering Charleston carried sand, and when the waters receded, about 8,200 years ago, they deposited sand and marsh on the 150-foot-thick layer of mud and clay that had been below the sea. From a geological standpoint, the Southern coast down from Charleston to past Savannah is an enormous valley on which the Santee River had deposited sediments over millions of years, filling it up with sand and dirt. That sandy sediment had been refreshed from time to time. Some of the sand was left in the form of the barrier islands that lie along the Atlantic near the Charleston Peninsula—Kiawah, Folly Beach, Johns Island, James Island, Sullivan's Island, and Isle of Palms—and some underlies the Charleston Peninsula itself. The layer of mud below the sand is called the "marl." Although there is rock below that marl—it's called Santee Limestone—the firmer, drier land in the region is not very firm, nor very dry. The groundwater right below the sand is often between three and ten feet underground.

It is 1669, August. An expedition sets off from London in three vessels—the two-hundred-ton frigate *Carolina*, the ship *Port Royal*, and the sloop *Albemarle*, a single-masted vessel. It is a rough journey: the sloop is wrecked at Barbados and the ship is wrecked in the Bahamas. Eventually, the repaired frigate *Carolina*, carrying twenty-nine white English settlers, all male, sixty-three white indentured servants, both men and women, and at least one enslaved African, arrives on the coast of what will be known as South Carolina.

Seeing muddy marsh abutting the sea, the vessels turn inland, following a river to a more solid stopping point upstream. Looking out from their craft, those on the *Carolina* would have seen waves of marsh grass and Spanish moss-draped oak trees. They call their disembarkation point Charles Towne Landing (now in the West Ashley portion of Charleston, which is across the Ashley River from downtown). Charles Towne, up on a bluff, is an island settlement, a port for boats to call as part of long journeys from England, to the West Indies, and then up the East Coast. There are no roads from Charles Towne to Virginia or the other colonies that exist at the time. These men have arrived in very low country, a world of marshes, tidal creeks, and swamps; they need to march ten miles inland to reach the coastal plain, where the land is higher.

The captain of the *Carolina*, Henry Brayne, knows the river they have just traveled up: he had been on an earlier expedition that had named it for Lord Anthony Ashley Cooper, the 1st Earl of Shaftesbury who is one of eight Lords Proprietors of what will become the Province of Carolina. Cooper is looking to invest in a colony in the new land.[1] It is now April 1670, and the muddy marsh next to the Ashley River will be known someday as Charleston. Right now, the initial arrivals are relieved to be on solid ground after seven months at sea.

Five months later, another boat arrives from Bermuda, bearing more white servants and at least three Black enslaved people: John Sr., Elizabeth, and John Jr.[2] Alone among the new English settlements, enslaved people are introduced in this colony from the very beginning.[3]

◆

The Lord's Proprietors, the seven men who, along with Lord Cooper, are investing in the new colony, beg the settlers to move thirty miles inland to firmer ground. Creeks are everywhere. Marsh grasses wave. What is now West Ashley is one big marsh, called Bear Marsh, and what is now John's Island is essentially three sandbars running parallel to each other, like rows of corduroy, next to which there is more marsh.

But those early ambitious settlers want a deepwater port for trade with Barbados. They find a narrow finger of forested land next to the Ashley River that has heaps of oyster shells on its tiny fingernail. The shells were likely left by Indigenous people.[4] It is a promising spot, with another river (later named the Cooper) to the east. They call it Oyster Point and decide to settle there. There is a spine of relatively higher sandy ground on that peninsula—less than ten feet above sea level—that will someday be today's King and Meeting Streets.

What there is of land in the region is mostly sand and mud plopped on clay. Sand dunes, essentially. A backhoe could dig through it pretty easily. Sand is terrible at absorbing water, so when water lands on it, it will just begin to float or flood lower places nearby. There are wide swaths of marshland, interconnected by watersheds sitting on top of that sand and mud. Watersheds in "normal," higher, harder regions have predictable paths, following divides; water will be understood to choose a side and come out a single outlet, somewhere. Norfolk, Virginia, yet to be settled, has uplands and watersheds that exit out of a single outlet, for example. Not so in the Carolina Lowcountry: here, watersheds interconnect at multiple points. You simply cannot block water from moving freely around the Lowcountry, because it is essentially a giant, interconnected floodplain.

Charleston's topography is not simple. Salt marshes cut through by tidal creeks are everywhere, their surfaces dry at low tide and under-water at high tide, the tides pulsing twice a day. Spartina grasses, or cordgrass, the sentinels of southeastern marshes, play an important role in the creation of those marshes. They hang on to sediment when it rolls through, driven by the tides that ebb and flow through one another across the region. Today, there are some 43,000 mapped streams in Charleston County alone.

◆

In April 1673, John Culpeper is instructed by the Lords Proprietors to measure the metes and bounds of a possible settlement on Oyster Point "in a square as much as Navigable Rivers will permit."[5] There isn't much room. The rivers encroach everywhere. But the lookout of the site is attractive, allows better access to the Atlantic Ocean's shipping lanes, and will be (the settlers earnestly hope) breezy. By December 1679, Oyster Point is the preferred location for the English investors in the new colony. Lord Anthony Ashley Cooper and the other Lords Proprietors direct that all parts of the fledging colonial government are to relocate there, and that the place is to be called Charles Towne—a name chosen to flatter England's king, Charles II, in continued hopes that the Crown will support the enterprise.[6] They lay out thirty-three lots on Oyster Point by 1681. East Bay is an early north-south street, running from a creek where present-day Market Street lies to another creek near where Water Street is today. Lots of creeks. Lots of marshes. Present-day Meeting Street marks the western edge of the settlement.[7]

Boat after boat from the West Indies, from Barbados, arrive at the new flood-prone, marshy settlement with its small grid of straight streets between waterways. There are threats: a Spanish attack on the settlement moving east from present-day Beaufort made it to within twenty miles of Charles Towne. But the city was rescued on August 26, 1686 by "a Hurrican wonderfully horrid and distructive," which terrorized the Spanish forces and sent them back to Florida.[8] Many more hurricanes would follow. The settlers love the luxury of elaborate furnishings and they live short lives of drinking and spending supported by canny trade and, later, the production of sugar by huge numbers of enslaved people.[9] Early arrivals, exhausted by their journeys, often fall ill from miasmic diseases prevalent in Charles Towne, and many die before they are forty.[10]

Those who stay enslave swarms of Indigenous people and work them and trade them as well as the Black enslaved workers they have imported from Barbados. Charleston initially strongly resembles the West Indies both politically and socially, with a large population of enslaved people of color and a class of white aristocrats anxious to leave their pasts as the second sons of Barbadian planters and make their fortunes, their livelihoods made possible by enslaved labor. Sails dot the harbor in large numbers. The port of Charles Towne and its trade are thriving by 1683.[11]

Charleston is mostly water at its start. Look at this map from Edward Crisp in 1704.

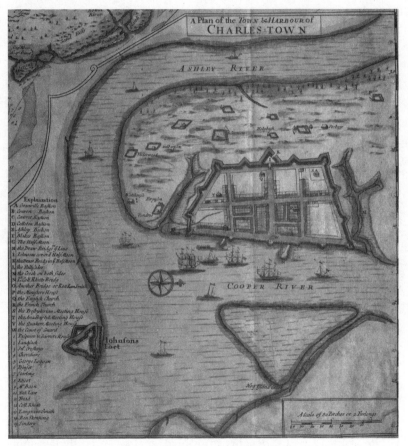

A complete description of the Province of Carolina in three parts:
1st, the improved part from the surveys of Maurice Mathews & Mr. John
Love; 2nd, the West part by Capt. Tho. Nairn; 3rd, a chart of the coast from
Virginia to Cape Florida by Edward Crisp, Thomas Nairne, John Harris,
Maurice Mathews, and John Love has been modified (cropped).

It shows a settlement behind a wall—by 1706, there are about 3,500 people jammed into that settlement—with creeks everywhere around it. Creeks penetrate nearly half of the peninsula.

◆

To create land where there is marsh, you have to cover the water. That is what the successors of these original settlers do, for three centuries. To create smooth continuous surfaces, they fill in the creeks and marshes that lie next to the old sand dunes that make up Charleston's "high" ground. For fill, they use trash, rubble, dirt, offal, and whatever else is at hand. Generations of savvy Charleston developers solve the problem of real estate scarcity by simply creating more land. Until after the Civil War, enslaved people do most of the work. Dragging junk and wood and household refuse into wet areas and waterways and covering them up with sawdust, sand, and dirt is a clever fix. A large portion of Charleston is at some point the original Charleston city dump.[12]

Charlestonians become expert at filling land.[13] The narrow peninsula of colonial days is substantially expanded. Marshes are filled in. Bridges are built. During the 1720s, the wall west of the settlement is taken down and the already-existing east-west roads of Tradd and Broad are extended westward. Bridges are built to connect the former Oyster Point (now called White Point) with the settlement on the Cooper River. More extending and filling follows, with East Bay Street extended northward. Over the years, city fathers strongly favor upper-class areas of Charleston when it comes to both filling and drainage; Oyster Point, later renamed White Point Gardens, benefits from high-quality, carefully laid inorganic fill (ballast stones, sands, shells), where lower-class neighborhoods are left with trash and offal. This poses health risks to poorer areas but allows elite, slaveholding property owners to avoid the taxation expense of city-wide improvement projects.[14]

The 1949 Alfred O. Halsey map of the Charleston peninsula
("Showing Original High Tide Water Lines, Fortifications, Boroughs,
Great Fires, Historic Information, etc.") shows where creeks and
marshes once were that have been filled over time.

*"Historic Charleston on a map, showing original high tide
water lines, fortifications, boroughs, great fires, historic
information, etc.," by Alfred O. Halsey, 1949.*

Today, much of Charleston is sitting on landfill. Floating on trash.

◆

To understand the story of Charleston's current water risks, you need
to spend time with a map. The city of Charleston, greater Charleston,
is at once a highly typical as well as a highly unusual American city.
It is much, much larger than that downtown peninsula; there are four
other boroughs of the city of Charleston, separated by water from the

peninsula, that extend out in sprawling, car-centric blotches from downtown: West Ashley, Johns Island, James Island, and Daniel Island on what is called the Cainhoy Peninsula. The peninsula is walkable and slow. Outer Charleston is low-slung and definitely not walkable or bikeable, with crushing traffic, harrowing commutes, lots of concrete, big box stores, fast food outlets, and endless cul-de-sac neighborhoods that connect only to roaring boulevards. These outer suburbs are a far cry from the peninsula, the Charleston of which white tourists dream. Even the mention of Charleston invokes visions of still, graceful courtyards, shaded and manicured, barely visible behind high gates. Noble, lofty former planters' houses, close together, lining long, silent streets. Warm breezes and endless numbers of fine restaurants. Biscuits. Hospitality. These visitors, or potential visitors, are thinking of the lower peninsula if this is their image of Charleston. For many years' running, it's been the top American city to visit, according to *Travel + Leisure* and several other luxury travel magazines.

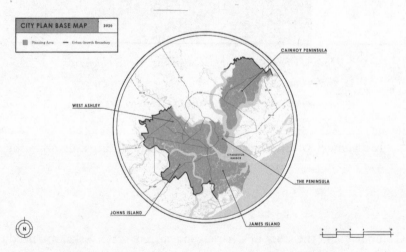

Charleston City Plan map, designed by Mary Mac Wilson.

Like New York City, Charleston is a city of neighborhoods. The peninsula, discussed in Chapter 5, is the original downtown, today's tourist destination, the place where the early colonists built their first dwellings, wharves, and port. Over decades, it was filled in to the south and west from the original fort, all the way to the Ashley River. Charleston grew northward of Boundary Street (now Calhoun Street) later, just as Manhattan grew north.

The East Side, discussed in Chapter 6, was once outside the city's borders, and was incorporated into the city of Charleston only in 1850.[15] It is very low and wet, and although rapidly gentrifying, it is the place where most of the peninsula's Black residents still live.

The Neck, the subject of Chapter 7, is the area at the top of the peninsula originally squeezed by creeks across which Indigenous traders walked on the Broad Path (now King Street) to markets north of Charleston. What is called "The Neck" has changed as landfilling and development has moved north.

Much of the upper western edge of the peninsula, discussed in Chapter 8, used to be rice mills and lumber mills. It was a marshy area that became home to hundreds of Black families. Today it is the site of the hospital district, Brittlebank Park, the new WestEdge development, and the Gadsden Green Homes, a public housing complex that floods routinely.

James Island, West Ashley, and Johns Island are described in Chapter 9. They are all different: West Ashley, the largest and most populated area, was once Bear Swamp, and is the site of enormous subdivision development that began in the 1950s; its population grew 23 percent between 2010 and 2019. Johns Island is still the most rural area of the city and has been a place where Black farmers have made their livings. It has become the site of development, particularly along its Maybank Highway which runs along one of the very few high ridges in the region. Maybank Highway sits on an old dune structure that runs parallel to the coast. Johns Island's population more than doubled between 2010 and 2019; during those same years, Black households on Johns Island declined by 31 percent while white households grew by 64 percent.[16] James Island is now thickly populated with housing and is mostly white. Daniel Island, on the Cainhoy Peninsula, includes most of the highest land in the city and has been the site of planned recent development.

Since Hurricane Hugo hit in September 1989, the number of housing units in the region has more than doubled. If a similar storm arrived on the same track today, it would cause at least $16 billion in damage—60 percent more than Hugo.[17]

Now let's layer above the map of the city of Charleston the elevation of these areas. Less than 5 percent of the land in the city is thirty feet or more above sea level, and just about fifteen of Charleston's overall 120 square miles is more than twenty feet above sea level. At least half of the city's land is no more than ten feet above sea level.[18] Most of the city would be swamped by a Category 3 storm today, and most of it will be chronically inundated by high tides by 2050.[19]

The Cainhoy Peninsula has the highest percentage of higher land (more than ten feet), with about twelve square miles. Johns Island comes in next, with about seven square miles of higher land. But the peninsula, West Ashley, and James Island are all very, very low, with very little land more than ten feet above sea level.[20]

This means that most of the lands and buildings in the city are now subject to risks from both tides and storms. As sea levels rise, where development does not exist salt marshes around the region will drown and marshland will naturally migrate upland and become new habitats for birds, fish, and vegetation. Left to its own devices, that's what would happen to much of the Charleston region.

At least 70 percent of the city of Charleston, which means at least 100,000 structures, is in a floodplain as defined by FEMA, meaning that FEMA believes there is a 1 percent chance in any given year that a storm (called a "100-year storm") will flood these places. (About

70 percent of the city's square miles is *both* in the current FEMA floodplain *and* would be covered by water in the event of a Category 3 storm; about 90 percent of the land in Charleston that is fifteen feet above sea level would be swamped by such a storm.)[21] FEMA's maps are out of date, are created by a raft of private entities across the country whose methodologies are not standardized, and do not reflect the accelerating risks of climate change.[22] Rainfall events of very high intensity are happening more often these days, and what is currently understood by FEMA as a 500-year storm is becoming the 100-year storm[23]—which means that FEMA's maps likely vastly understate the current risks to the region. FEMA's maps also look backward at historical risks presented by past storms, rather than forward to future sea level rise or increased rain. But more about that later.

In July 2019, visiting Dutch landscape architects strongly advised the city of Charleston not to allow anyone to live or work in areas below six feet in elevation, saying that those "wet zones," as they called them, should instead be used as living shorelines or buffers. In talking about this recommendation, Yttje Feddes, a distinguished former Dutch National Landscape Architect, said the sandy soil in these zones was not capable of storing water. "So it's also important not to build and to live there," Feddes said. She went on to recommend that there be "very few buildings" in the "ecological zone," between six and ten feet in elevation, as well as in the "transitional ecological zone," between ten and fifteen feet—in other words, in most of the rest of the city's land area. Just single houses on stilts, widely separated from other houses, and leaving half the acreage for trees and bioswales that could carry water, are appropriate for that "transitional ecological zone," she said. No landfill should be allowed there, and all the roads should be elevated.

Feddes also said she knew "we are talking about someone's property." She went on to suggest that development rights should be transferred across the entire region as part of an "integrated watershed master plan." Dense development should be allowed only on the historic sand ridges, like Maybank Highway.

Feddes had been asked to look at still-rural Johns Island in making these recommendations, but the entire region has the same topography. King Street, on the peninsula, is one of those historic sand ridges. These compacted ridges are stronger and safer ground, but they are also much smaller ground—perhaps a third or less of the city's overall acreage.[24] The Dutch team was the strongest the Netherlands could have fielded, landscape architect Steven Slabbers (also Dutch) says. "They are all very much respected, internationally respected, well known in the Netherlands," according to Slabbers.[25]

By the time the written report of these suggestions was transmitted to the public a few months later, Feddes's elevation-related building recommendations had been softened to remove the strong ideas that no one should *now* be living in the wet zone, and very few buildings should be allowed *now* below fifteen feet in elevation. It read instead, "We recommend prohibiting future development in the wet zone," and said that because "The ecological zone carries substantial flood risk. . . . Those living in this zone should be fully aware of the risk they assume by living there." It said that, between ten and fifteen feet, the "coastal forests in this zone should not be further degraded." And the report did not make crystal clear that the very low topography of Johns Island is replicated across the region. It did state that land that was "once naturally wet, will be again."[26] The city had already begun work with the Army Corps of Engineers on a perimeter wall for the historic peninsula, about which we'll learn much more in Chapter 4.

◆

The geography and topography of Charleston is internalized by its residents. Michelle Mapp, a longtime community development advocate now working with the ACLU of South Carolina to help prevent eviction and displacement of low-income and Black households, has noticed the flooding getting worse in recent years. Before law school, she was running the South Carolina Community Loan Fund out of an office in West Ashley. Her commute there from her home on the North Charleston/Summerville line usually took fifteen minutes. But by 2018, rainfall could delay her for an additional hour or more. "There's places that are flooding in Charleston that never flooded when I was growing up," Mapp, who is Black, says. "It is scary. If we have any bit of rain, it's like all of a sudden it all just falls apart."[27] She sees what the future holds for Johns and James Island: "Twenty years from now, twenty-five years from now, we're not going to have the population on James and Johns Island that we have [now]. I mean, Mother Nature is going to dictate that. We can have all the arguments we want, but the writing's on the wall."[28] We will spend more time with Mapp in Chapter 7.

David White, a young socially minded Black entrepreneur in Charleston who grew up on Line Street on the East Side, says, "Water's always been an issue for me." He remembers visiting his grandmother in a public housing apartment on South Street on the East Side, and having his route there be "always flooded." Flooding just happened. "If we wanted to play or walk up the street we would have to go around [flooded streets] or get soaked." Going to and from his elementary school, Wilmot J. Fraser Elementary, which closed in 2010, "was just a mess," White says. "I think it [the flooding] was always just a problem and I just got, I wouldn't say used to it, but I just was numb to seeing it. I knew what streets were probably flooded. I knew how to navigate around, I think that's sad."

He now lives on the west side of the peninsula on Sans Souci Street, and he's noticed that there are streets around him that flood now that didn't flood when he was a child. Recently he was taking his father to the hospital on the west side, down a main thoroughfare called Rutledge Avenue, and Rutledge was impassable.

Flooding on the East Side has also gotten worse in recent years. White runs a nonprofit providing laundry services to people experiencing homelessness on the East Side, called Laundry Matters. "I used to think that I knew what streets I could navigate through," he says. "But now it's like, there are streets that didn't flood that are flooding now. So I have to think strategically, how do I get to Laundry Matters?" He's frustrated: "I also think about the population we serve, they aren't able to get to the laundromat if the streets are flooded. They're mostly walking. You can't walk through the water with bags of clothes." He does after-school tutoring and coding classes, and he always has to plan around rain and flooding in Charleston. "It affects everything," White says.[29]

Rev. Joseph Darby, an AME minister in Charleston who is vice-chair of the NAACP's Charleston office, remembers encountering flooding in Charleston in 1999, when he was serving as pastor for Morris Brown AME. One day, on his way to Morris Brown, driving in from west of the peninsula, he'd noticed the street in front of him was backed up. He couldn't figure out why. He kept going. And then he saw cars moving even more slowly. He had begun to pray as he realized he was about to drive through a river. "Oh, Lord, don't let this thing flood, don't let this car get ruined." He'd looked out the window of his car and had seen water surging about halfway up the vehicle. He had promised himself and his God that when he traded in his car he would be buying SUVs from then on. No more low-slung cars for Rev. Darby, pastor of Charleston.[30]

Over the years Rev. Darby has grown accustomed to the flooding as it has become more frequent and more severe. During the summer of 2019, there were pictures of the flooding on national television and in the newspapers, and major news outlets got in on the story. "Oh, this massive flooding in Charleston, this is terrible!" Darby's raised voice mimics the hysteria. One of the pictures looked familiar to him. It had been the street where Nichols Chapel, his current church, is—Bogard Street. The newscaster said, "Look how high the water is!" and Darby's thought had been, "Big deal. It's only up to the second step of the church."[31] Sunny day flooding these days creates little rivers on all the streets around Nichols Chapel.

John Tibbetts, a white science journalist who has been living and working in Charleston for thirty years, sold his house on James Island during the summer of 2022 to move to Minneapolis. He remembers commuting from James Island to the peninsula during the early 1990s and seeing flooding on the way, particularly around the medical district on the west side of the peninsula. "But it just seemed very, very mild and usual, and you could get around it in the early '90s," he remembers. "It is like that old frog in the [boiling] water thing," he says. He started to notice flooding often making his commute unworkable around the 2010s. And then the significant storms that struck the region in 2015, 2016, and 2017 shocked him and changed his view of the entire water situation in Charleston. One of the reasons Tibbetts and his wife Kitty, a science writer for NOAA, moved is the increasing risk of disaster and flooding in the region. "We see where things are going," he says. "I'm sixty-six, I could live twenty years. I don't want to be an older person here" dealing with the consequences of flooding.[32]

A thrum of dread lies behind many waking moments in Charleston during hurricane season, year after year. The water, glimpsed from afar, becomes unfriendly, animate. Televisions stay on even more than

usual, and every named storm that forms out in the Atlantic is anthro-
pomorphized. *He's getting closer. She missed us this time.* Both Black and
white Charlestonians talk about the anxiety they experience during
hurricane season. "Even if the storm doesn't come this way, everybody
still has this cortisol built up from stressing the whole week before
as you slowly watch it come in and prepare, and imagine what would
happen," environmental advocate Jenny Brennan says.[33] Charlestonians
who were around for Hugo have vivid memories of the devastation a
storm can wreak: the flying trees, the ripped-off roofs, the absence of
electricity for weeks afterwards. Says Tibbetts, "We are also burned
out on a constellation of problems here. Every hurricane season we
watch the tropical Atlantic with dread. We are tired of evacuating."[34]

It isn't just increasingly intense storms and chronic flooding that
Charleston is worried about. The city is an all-hazards place: it also
sits on a seismic fault. Small earthquakes have recently been rumbling
through the area around Columbia, upstate from Charleston. No one
knows when or if the big one is coming.

After a cataclysmic 1886 earthquake, the Charleston city fathers
took all the rubble and pushed it on top of millponds and rice fields to
help create more land. When San Francisco suffered an earthquake in
1909, consultants from Charleston went out to teach the people of San
Francisco how to similarly make new land using rubble.[35] This area is
today called the Marina District. We now know that made land shakes
really well, especially when it has a high water content. And that's why
the Marina District, built on that earthquake-sourced fill, is now the
most dangerous zone in the city for any future earthquake: in that area
the ground will fail and become liquid when the earth shakes intensely.
Buildings and infrastructure will shatter. When an earthquake strikes,
the land beneath Charleston's red-hot real estate market will similarly
turn to cake batter. Both Charlestonians and the successors of their
former clients in San Francisco are worried about this.

◆

Out in the tropical reaches of the Atlantic, a tiny swirl of air and water, spinning and rising, is forming. The water is bathtub warm, heated by the sun during long sultry days. Water vapor meets cooler, drier air above—only slightly cooler air, because this year is one of the ten hottest years on record around the globe, and only slightly drier—but the difference is enough to cause movement. The tiny swirl is rising because the denser, cooler air above is sinking below the hotter, less dense, wetter air below: nature is seeking equilibrium, and to get there takes motion and change, the push of gases from pockets of high pressure to low. Our tiny swirl is growing quickly, the vapor forming into droplets that whirl and rise, wind-rushed and unguided. It gathers strength and width, the ever-warmer air able to take in ever-more water vapor, but hardly moves along the ocean's surface. Our swirl knows nothing of this, has no intention other than to reach equilibrium, somewhere; it is all potential, a gathering of wetness and wind, and it seeks to release its differences in some form. If it does this by dumping its cargo of water and fierce gales over land it will be disastrous; the Bahamas experienced this in 2020, when slow-moving Hurricane Dorian flattened habitations and lives over dozens of hours. If our swirl dumps over Charleston at the same time that a high tide lands, it will be a cataclysm.

Our swirl is traveling slowly now, on its way to meet up with the schedule of the tides at the edge of land. That schedule is set by the moon, and so high tides are arriving on time on Charleston's shores. Nothing, so far, has changed about the moon. The tides themselves, however, are changing rapidly, slapping ever higher. Our swirl, all potential, may dump from above at the same time a high tide, now very high, rushes in from the sea.[36]

Water vapor, drawn out by the sun, rises, cools, forms droplets, forms clouds. All of this is expected, but in the tropics the weight of the resulting whirling clouds of wind and rain and the intensity of the torrents that fall from them is ever mightier as the 2020s tick by. More monstrous. All this activity is accelerating, bringing more frequent and larger storms and higher tides at the same time that the thin layer of sand covering the Charleston peninsula is settling. Over the decades, all the rivers in the region, the Savannah as well as the Santee, have been fully harnessed and engineered to serve the region's interests. This means that the sediment that used to travel down them to the Lowcountry no longer does.[37] As a result, under the weight of development and with the withdrawal of underground water aquifers, the coastal area is slowly subsiding: subsidence accounts for about 40 percent of the sea level rise currently being experienced by the Charleston region. The groundwater is rising as well, bubbling up into the streets.

Imagine that time runs forward, one month per second. The storms arrive as steady snare drum ratatats, with a rimshot here and there: the comings of cataclysms. We will need more words to describe these punctuations. The rain falls and puddles, moment after moment. The rivers swell. The pulse of the rivers' tides washes higher across the peninsula and its outlying boroughs, like an incoming sea undermining a child's sandcastle. Plump planes packed with tourists arrive and depart in swarms. Restaurants slam their doors closed, one after the next, heavy footfalls on a wooden floor. New ones take their place, but they are flimsier and temporary—inflatable rafts propped on a beach. The wealthy white people who own houses on the lower peninsula put up "For Sale" signs and are driven to the airport to take up residence in other, safer places. The buzz of their departures is initially mild, a background thrum that is difficult to hear, but then swells to become a cicada-like chorus. Beginning in about 2032—say two minutes from now—the pace of flooding on the peninsula becomes nearly constant. The blue on the God's-eye map that shows where water is in the city of Charleston stays in place, almost unblinking, merging with the surrounding sea.

Against all this rising movement and noise, there is a barely audible tenor line. There are those who have nothing to sell and nowhere to go. They are mostly Black residents of Charleston, living compressed in areas of intergenerational poverty on the East and West sides of the peninsula that are all firmly in the wet zone. They are also thousands of not-rich people, white and Black, living in the outer boroughs in subdivisions slapped up towards the end of the twentieth century who cannot afford to move. They are hanging on in swampy conditions, staying in place as long as they can. This singing line starts calmly—they have been through so much over so many centuries in Charleston. Then it changes to an all-out scream.

That's time for you, when it comes to rising, heating water and the city of Charleston. It disrupts things. It makes life in the wet and ecological zones identified by those Dutch landscape engineers unpleasant and ultimately impossible. It cannot run in the other direction to keep the antebellum dream of Charleston in place, to command the mansions to stay upright, to keep the plates of shrimp and grits coming, or to keep the placid tone of suburban life at a steady state, any more than you can put a shattered piece of crystal back together. It's irreversible.

All the arrows are going sharply upward: the danger of a damaging storm surge in Charleston is increasing, and average storms are getting more intense, as warming oceans make it more likely that a hurricane will develop into a Category 3 storm with winds of 100 miles per hour or higher.[38] The wave of water that would pummel the city in the event of a Category 3 hurricane would flow over essentially all of it. Meanwhile, flooding frequency is drastically accelerating.

About a quarter of all flooding events recorded between 1922 and 2021 in Charleston happened in the last five years. The National

Oceanic and Atmospheric Administration (NOAA) has predicted that the increase in high-tide flooding along the Atlantic coast will be extraordinary, and that current (2020) numbers of flood days will double or triple by 2030—double the eighty-nine floods in 2019, the sixty-eight floods in 2020, the forty-six floods in 2021, each one of which made some roads in Charleston impassable and undermined structures.[39] By 2050, the agency says, the number of days of more serious flooding could be five to fifteen times as great as it was in 2020.[40] Backing up this prediction, data drawn from the tide gauges four miles out in Charleston Harbor are showing, if extrapolated, that the city will have 200–240 flood days a year by 2040. When sea levels rise, more land becomes inundated and is lost to water, groundwater levels rise, and salt water intrudes into freshwater aquifers. With just three feet of sea level rise, much of the city will be chronically inundated; only those sand ridges on Johns Island, the spine of the peninsula, and parts of the Cainhoy Peninsula will be reliably dry.

◆

There are slower processes rolling along that may have an additional outsize impact on Charleston by the end of the century. In Western Antarctica, there is a hunk of ice that people call the Doomsday Glacier.[41] One of the largest glaciers in the world, it is already having a substantial impact on global sea levels: its loss of more than fifty billion tons of ice each year due to global warming accounts for about 4 percent of annual sea level rise.[42] Right now, the Doomsday Glacier is connected to land by a large ice shelf that acts as a kind of safety band, holding back the mass of the giant West Antarctic Ice Sheet, which is as big as two Alaskas.[43] The ice shelf has historically been grounded on an underwater mountain on the bottom of the sea. Now it is essentially melting from below, and it is gradually fracturing.[44] When the ice shelf eventually gives way, the whole Doomsday Glacier will become one with the water.[45]

Because the Doomsday Glacier, also known as the Thwaites Glacier, plays a central role in holding back the rest of the West Antarctica Ice Sheet, which contains enough water to raise sea levels by between ten and sixteen feet, the demise of its protective ice shelf, and the uncertainty as to the timing of that demise, is particularly important to Charleston and other East Coast cities.[46] Right now, Antarctica is putting a significant gravitational tug on water, pulling liquid towards itself.[47] (The earth truly is not flat.) But as Antarctica loses mass due to melting, the gravitational signature of the whole earth will change. There will be less gravity near the ice sheets, and there will be a kind of gravitational release that will cause a greater-than-global-average sea level rise at larger distances, including along the entire East Coast.[48] If this melting happens, it will cause at least two more feet of sea level rise in Charleston and the rest of the East Coast over decades, not centuries.[49]

This process, this breaking up of the ice sheet holding back the Doomsday Glacier, cannot be stopped or reversed; it is already baked in by the rate of change in the level of emissions that has taken place.[50] At the same time, the uncertainty as to when this melting will happen is very high, and we should certainly not give up on mitigating emissions that are driving the changes around us. We are on course at the moment, though, to blow well past the international climate targets that have been agreed to as of 2022. As warming continues, the probability of exceeding six feet of global sea level rise by the end of the century—and quite a bit more than that along the East Coast—also rises substantially.[51] Some scientists estimate that the fracturing of the ice sheet holding back the Doomsday Glacier could take as little as five to ten years to happen, although others say that it's more likely to happen toward the end of the century and beyond.[52] NOS, the Dutch public broadcast outlet, said in early 2022, "The process appears to be accelerating, potentially causing some ice shelves [holding back the Thwaites Glacier] to shatter within five to ten years."[53]

A tipping point, as defined by the Intergovernmental Panel on Climate Change (IPCC), is a "critical threshold beyond which a system reorganizes, often abruptly or irreversibly." The Thwaites Glacier is called the Doomsday Glacier because it is susceptible to a tipping point. When a threshold is reached in the melting of that ice shelf, it will abruptly change its state.[54] The ice shelf and the Doomsday Glacier are systemically brittle: they will be one thing, ice, until they are very suddenly another thing—a lot of water, as it melts quickly. (The glacier's status as a tipping point for the impact of global climate change on tens of millions of people has been known since at least 2008, when Tim Lenton, a professor of climate change and earth system science at the University of Exeter, wrote in Proceedings of the National Academy of Sciences [PNAS], a peer reviewed journal of the National Academy of Sciences, about the possible abrupt changes that might occur caused by global warming.)[55]

We do not have great data about this tipping point; it is very hard to estimate the threshold beyond which a remote and difficult-to-access ice shelf abruptly becomes water and allows part of a giant glacier to flow into the sea. Airplanes cannot land there, because the ice is full of cracks and divots. Helicopters can't get there either, because it is too far away. But unmanned submarines can probe under the friable ice shelves, and scientists from around the world are doing their best to figure out what is happening.[56] There are signs that the risk of this tipping point tipping is escalating. Geophysicist Rob Larter told climate author Jeff Goodell in late 2021 that "The net rate of ice loss from Thwaites Glacier is more than six times what it was in the early 1990s." The IPCC told policymakers in 2021, "The probability of low likelihood, high impact outcomes," which is another name for tipping points, "increases with higher levels of global warming."[57] In other words, the potential impact of this melting on society, which could be very high indeed, is becoming more likely.

The melting of the Doomsday Glacier is not the only tipping point that is becoming more likely to cause catastrophic flooding in the Charleston region on top of accelerating sea level rise. A second slowly arriving tipping element will likely cause a substantial change in the ocean dynamics affecting Charleston: the slowdown of the Gulf Stream. Charleston and the Gulf Stream have always been intertwined. The city's founders chose its location in the seventeenth century because they viewed it as a perfect spot for a trading post between England and the Caribbean islands. The Gulf Stream, a wide swath of current fifty miles offshore transporting warm water up from the tropics to the North Atlantic, allowed ships to make good time on the way back to England. Charleston's subtropical climate comes from its low latitude, low-lying elevation, and proximity of that warm current; people go out to the Gulf Stream to fish for red snapper and swordfish.

It's a wide, cobalt-blue stream, part of a giant clockwise ocean oscillation driven by the flux of water with different densities: salty, colder water in the North Atlantic, dense and heavy, drops deep into the ocean (because it is cold, it is heavier) and moves along the bottom until it rises to the surface near the equator. Then that colder water, warmed by the sun and made even saltier through evaporation, rises (warm water is less dense) and is carried northward from the Gulf of Mexico around the Florida peninsula, encouraged along by winds, as the Gulf Stream. It accelerates up the East Coast until it gets to Newfoundland, where it stretches across to Western Europe, releasing heat that helps make that region more temperate; once it's done that and arrives in the frigid climate near Greenland, it becomes cold and dense again and sinks to the depths, beginning its cycle anew. The whole majestic rollercoaster is called the Atlantic Meridional Overturning Circulation, or AMOC.[58]

Looking out at the Atlantic from Charleston, you can think of the Gulf Stream as a kind of linear bubble moving quickly from south to north offshore that is made of high, warm water. On the east side of the Gulf Stream, away from the coastline, the sea is something like five feet higher than it is on the western, landward side of that current.[59] In other words, by rushing past with enormous momentum, in all its warmth and width, the Gulf Stream is holding seawater back from flooding Charleston further. But as ice melts into the North Atlantic from a rapidly warming Arctic and as rainstorms increase in the north, that northern water is becoming fresher. That means the density differences driving the Gulf Stream are lessening; less water is sinking and less warm water is being drawn from the south. (There is already a "cold blob" southeast of Greenland that seems to indicate that less warm water is reaching the region from the Gulf Stream.)[60]

As areas of global water come into more of an equilibrium, the forces driving the motion of this giant current will weaken.[61] The Gulf Stream will slow and then, possibly, stop; it has already become 15 percent weaker than it was in the mid-twentieth century.[62] A weaker Gulf Stream will be a less effective guardian of the southeast coastline. As it slows down, coastal water levels in South Carolina are going to go up by at least three feet or so, on top of the already accelerating sea level rise that NOAA is extrapolating from its observations plus whatever happens with the Doomsday Glacier. As with the ice sheet melting in Antarctica, scientists think it is more likely that the Gulf Stream slowing will happen towards the end of this century rather than right now. But it's another tipping point, another process whose critical moment we're not very good at anticipating.

Charleston is a golden, squawking canary in the coal mine. Seas are rising faster there than in other global locations: the extrapolated level of sea level rise expected in Charleston, based on direct observations of tide gauges in Charleston Harbor, is greater than that across the globe as a whole because of differences in ocean currents, water density, and subsidence.[63] We also know that Charleston's sea level rise will be worse than that in its neighbor North Carolina. Right offshore of South Carolina, there is a wide flat shelf followed by another flat shelf that helps to focus and pile water on Charleston. It's essentially a long zone of shallowing water right next to the region. That is why we are seeing more buildup and faster accumulations of water along the coast of Charleston than in North Carolina. The official name of these shallow shelves is the Blake Plateau; Norman Levine of the College of Charleston calls it the "Charleston bump."[64] But the whole East Coast is experiencing levels of sea level rise that are greater than the global mean.

"The numbers can be scary," says Billy Sweet, a scientist at NOAA. "The long-term projections aren't necessarily the types of information a citizen would want to hear or think about."[65] Both these dynamics, the melting of the Doomsday Glacier and the slowdown in the Gulf Stream, are potentially game-changing in terms of the consequences they may have for human lives. The places affected by these events will move suddenly from Status Quo X to Status Quo Y; a different state, a different equilibrium. Status Quo Y could be an extreme: a chronic and likely complete inundation of, say, eight feet of sea level rise over decades, not centuries. The chances of these tipping points being reached in the next thirty years are highly uncertain. But scientists are quite certain that flooding is going to get much, much worse over that same period. As Norm Levine puts it, "Are you going to plan for the one in ten chance that a plane is going to crash on landing?" Where peoples' lives are concerned, when we're talking about infrastructure, the whole point is to plan for safety.

What will happen to the residents of Charleston, South Carolina if five feet of water arrives by 2070? Or six or eight or ten feet by the end of the century? We have the opportunity, right now, to reject both pollyannish optimism *and* wails of despair. Governments at all levels, federal, state, and local, should be planning. They can decide, pushed forward by their constituents, that it is worthwhile to act with compassion and dispatch, to spend the money and allocate the resources that are needed to help everyone lead a thriving life in safety. We can do better, and we must. The voices of those Charlestonians who see the storms ahead can provide a guide.

Chapter 3
Rev. Joseph P. Darby and the History of Charleston

n November 1805, today's intersection of Church and North Market Streets on the Charleston peninsula was a meandering waterway called Market Creek. That month, the City Council of Charleston issued a strongly worded ordinance:

> WHEREAS since the importation of slaves from Africa, several instances have occurred, of dead human bodies having been thrown into the waters of the harbour of Charleston. And whereas such practices are extremely disgraceful, and ought to be prevented by the severest penalties, that can be inflicted by the City-Council:
>
> I. Be it therefore ordained by the Intendant and Wardens of Charleston, in City-Council assembled, and it is hereby ordained by the authority of the same, That in future no person or persons whatsoever, shall throw, or cause or order to be thrown, any dead human body or bodies, into any of the rivers, creeks, or marshes, within the harbour of the city, on pain of forfeiting for each and every such offence, the sum of one hundred dollars.[1]

Charleston's City Council was under pressure in 1805. After a series of booms and busts in the business of importing enslaved people to Charleston, the advent of the American Revolution in 1774 seemingly brought this practice to a temporary end as a legal matter: the South Carolina delegates to the Continental Congress, along with those from the other colonies, pledged to give it up.

But, reconsidering, South Carolina representatives ensured that the successful conclusion of the Constitutional Convention of 1787 would require a deal. In exchange for supporting the new union of states, the delegates from the Carolinas and Georgia extracted a pledge from their colleagues that Congress would not interfere with the African slave trade until 1808. Meanwhile, the South Carolina legislature, worried that the importation of enslaved people would make it difficult for white residents of the state to find decent jobs and thus undermine the state's already flagging economy, banned importing slaves until at least 1804. Then the Louisiana Purchase and the acquisition of the Mississippi Territory opened enormous amounts of land as potential cotton fields, making cheap labor a higher priority. The South Carolina legislature had a change of heart: beginning in late December 1803 the slave importation trade began again in the state. South Carolina was the only southern state to reopen trade in importing enslaved people.[2]

With just four years to go before the Constitutional compromise would end the sanctioned transatlantic slave trade forever, the slavers went into a frenzy. They had no time to waste. They packed shackled human bodies into ships on the west coast of Africa, 300 to 400 at a time, with no room to move and little air. Sickness in these horrific conditions was common, and many West Africans died on the way to Charleston; many others tried to kill themselves by refusing to eat or drink, and some were force-fed by their captors. Slave traders played the odds as long as possible, hoping to sell any captive who still retained a breath of life. At the last moment, at the nearest possible interval to the point of a chance of a sale, the slave traders took their inventory. The last dead bodies were cleared away, rolled overboard just before the remaining sickened, terrified human cargo arrived for purchase in the city of Charleston.

It is this mad dash to the importation finish line that annoyed the leaders of the city of Charleston by the fall of 1805, not the sale of Black humanity itself. Commerce was commerce; nothing wrong with that, they seemed to say. But dumping those bodies was unseemly. It was impolite.

◆

Just as a map can help you get your bearings in an unfamiliar city without giving you a guide to every brick, there are a few historical moments that help in understanding the forces that have shaped multi-layered, touristic Charleston. What is playing out in Charleston is not just the risk of extinction of the historic sections of a seaside city built on wetlands—similar things will happen to Boston, which will lose its seaport and its Back Bay rowhouses; New York City, which will lose its outer reaches and the winding narrow streets of its first downtown; Norfolk, which will lose its Chrysler Museum and Opera House; and Shanghai and Jakarta, which will lose their entire urban areas. It is also the result of hundreds of years of unchanging, patronizing, blind mistreatment of Charleston's Black and low-income residents, veiled in politeness and bolstered by an unflagging belief in the primacy of commerce.

Charleston, along with Boston, was one of America's first two great, prosperous cities—but its people made different choices than Boston's citizens right from the beginning. Rice plantations made possible by slave labor dominated Charleston's economy, beginning in 1690—just as sugar had dominated Barbados—and the rule of law in both Barbados and Charleston was initially organized around keeping slavery in place. Charleston became one of the richest cities in the colonies, deploying a complex tag system to keep track of enslaved people, raising taxes on the sale and ownership of enslaved people within its boundaries, and using enslaved labor to fill in its creeks and build its buildings—as well as to tend outlying plantations. Bostonians also owned slaves in the eighteenth century, but their role in the city's economy was far more limited, mostly because large-scale agriculture was not part of the city's way of life. On the other hand, Boston played a central part in the slave trade from the 1630s through the 1760s, importing slaves from Africa and then sending them to the West Indies to be traded for sugar.[3] Slavery in Massachusetts was abolished in the 1780s, and after that Boston made different choices—the city became one of the centers of the abolitionist movement in the nineteenth century.

All the trade made possible by the water around the narrow peninsula, particularly of the rice Charleston planters started exporting in the mid-1690s, made Charleston the richest and largest American city south of Philadelphia by the mid-eighteenth century. But those riches depended completely on uncompensated enslaved labor. Nearly 200,000 enslaved people captured in Africa and brought to America in shackles were imported through Charleston.[4]

Rice supplied by South Carolina fed Europe and South America, and after the transatlantic slave trade was abolished in 1808, Charleston was a crucial center of America's domestic trade in enslaved people through the Civil War.[5] Frustrated by the large crowds that attended auctions of enslaved people and blocked traffic, the city's leaders decreed in 1856 that public sales would no longer be allowed.[6] These transactions did not cease—they were moved inside to slave-trading offices and marts. Politeness, again.

Most of Charleston's residents from the early 1700s until the 1850s were Black, and Black Charlestonians worked in a wide variety of professions, both skilled and unskilled; before the Civil War, Charleston was home to a large population of free Black people.[7] Denmark Vesey, a Black man who was literate and had worked for years in ports throughout the world, had bought his freedom and sought to free his wife and other family members but had been frustrated in the attempt. In 1822, Vesey drew up a plan for a large-scale insurrection. His plans were leaked and Vesey was executed.

Vesey's planned rebellion lived on in the memories of white Charlestonians. The city became a center of support for slavery and, later, for secession from the Union. In the mid-1850s, Robert Bunch, who had just come to Charleston to be the British consul there, reported that "it is most difficult for anyone not on the spot to form an adequate idea of the extreme sensitiveness and captious irritability of all classes of this community on the subject of Slavery."[8] Charlestonians rallied behind pro-slavery advocates like John C. Calhoun in their efforts to ensure the "peculiar institution" on which their economy depended would not be constrained. And that is why Calhoun plays an important role in the history of the city, although he was not himself a Charlestonian.

◆

John Caldwell Calhoun, sunken-eyed and thin-lipped, had always wanted to be president. He had more than paid his dues, distinguishing himself in both the House of Representatives and the Senate as an elegant and forceful speaker on behalf of his native state of South Carolina, modernizing the War Department under James Monroe following the War of 1812, serving two different presidents—John Quincy Adams and Andrew Jackson—as vice president, and serving another, John Tyler, as secretary of state. For almost forty years, he had been the unchallenged ruler of South Carolina politics. A one-time supporter of a strong, centralized army, improved federally funded roads, and a strong national bank, he became a fervent supporter of states' rights—in particular, the "peculiar and local power" to enforce slavery in Southern states, an institution Calhoun identified as a "positive good." Calhoun's views were (and are) outrageous. His analysis of the 1840 census claimed that "the African is incapable of self-care and sinks into lunacy under the burden of freedom."

Calhoun had calculated much of his career to increase his odds of becoming president. He did not succeed, however, and a photograph taken of him by Matthew Brady in 1849—the year James K. Polk ceded the presidency to Zachary Taylor—depicts a cadaverous and grimly outraged man, set-mouthed and shaggy-haired, gripping his cloak with two bony crossed hands.

Photograph of John C. Calhoun by Matthew Brady, 1849.

Calhoun's last speech on the floor of the Senate in March 1850, read out by Sen. James Mason of Virginia, urged the nation to ensure that all new western territories were open for slavery and that the

South would be given a veto when necessary to protect its peculiar interests. Otherwise, disunion would result. Later that same month, Calhoun—the ideological figurehead of the Confederate cause—died of tuberculosis at age sixty-eight in Washington, DC.

Calhoun was buried in the leafy, pleasant churchyard of St. Philip's in downtown Charleston. To get there, his coffin was carried by Charlestonians along Boundary Street, which was promptly renamed Calhoun Street in his honor. He did not live to see his state become the first to secede from the Union following the 1860 election of Abraham Lincoln. Nor was he present to applaud the overthrow of Reconstruction in 1876. But Calhoun vividly returned to the imaginations of white Charlestonians in 1887, when a nostalgic fever for the supposed honor and values of the antebellum South (and a thinly veiled desire to suppress and repeal the rights of Black citizens) led the Ladies' Calhoun Monument Association to erect in Marion Square—the home of The Citadel, the military college that had been established to protect white Charleston following that failed 1822 slave rebellion by Denmark Vesey[9]—the most expensive monument to the Lost Cause in the entire state: a statue honoring Calhoun in the act of rising from his chair to speak while pointing outward with his right index finger. Calhoun seemed to be standing up for Charleston's interest in protecting the racial structure of the Old South.

That 1887 statue, one of hundreds of Confederate and white supremacist monuments erected around the same time, was justly seen by outraged Black Charlestonians as a symbol of slavery meant to intimidate them. Placed near the Neck neighborhood of the peninsula, in which most of the city's free Blacks had lived and where their descendants still had houses, it was regularly defaced: "We used to carry something with us," Mamie Garvin Fields, born in Charleston in 1888, explained in a Smithsonian publication, "if we knew we would be passing that way, in order to deface that statue—scratch up the coat, break the watch chain, try to knock off the nose." The unnamed female figure sitting at the base of the monument—Justice, the only allegorical figure installed of the four that had been planned to sit below Calhoun—prompted Black locals to derisively call the monument, in Gullah dialect, "Mr. Calhoun an' he Wife."

The Ladies' Calhoun Monument Association, likely reacting to this campaign of guerrilla defacement and mockery by Black Charlestonians, decided in 1896 to remove the 1887 statue and build a new, taller one. They probably thought height would protect John Calhoun from abuse. They were wrong. The defacement continued, directed at the base of the new monument, even though it was extremely difficult to see Calhoun's face from the ground. The scarecrow figure of John C. Calhoun spookily towered over the city for another 120 years, 115 feet above Marion Square, more totemic than ever—not a man but the very idea of white supremacy, in columnar form.

◆

As of the 1850s, the city of Charleston reached from the former Oyster Point, now called the Battery, to just north of newly renamed Calhoun Street (then called "the Neck"), as well as east to the Cooper River and west to the Ashley River over filled creeks and marshes.

Plan of the City and Neck of Charleston, S.C., 1844.

The city's white upper class erected grand mansions on the Battery, and although the parties were lavish, the economy of the city was sagging. Sleepiness was setting in as Charleston resisted industrialization and continued its reliance on rice and, later, indigo.

The Civil War was rooted in Charleston. The election of Abraham Lincoln in November 1860 was the tipping point. Not long before, Rev. Richard Furman of Greenville, South Carolina, had laid out his views of the inevitable consequences of Lincoln's ascendancy for his white listeners: If Lincoln were to be elected, "every negro in South Carolina and every other Southern State will be his own master; nay, more than that, will be the equal of every one of you. If you are tame enough to submit, abolition preachers will be at hand to consummate the marriage of your daughters to black husbands."[10] If Black South Carolinians were given the right to vote, they would vastly outnumber whites in two-thirds of the state's districts. White Charlestonians were aghast—they feared Lincoln would make white workers compete with Black residents for jobs and, most fundamentally, cause the races to mix in social life. Lincoln's election was, for them, a cataclysm.

The state's Secession Convention began its meetings in the capitol city of Columbia in December 1860 but then decamped to Charleston, where pro-secession fever was running even higher and the food and hotels were better. On December 20, by a unanimous vote taken in Institute Hall downtown, South Carolina left the Union, the first state to do so. Celebrations broke out in Charleston's streets. Four months later, the first shot of the war was fired at Fort Sumter, the federal outpost located in Charleston Harbor atop an artificial island built of rock and stone, by Brigadier General P. G. T. Beauregard of the newly formed Confederate States of America.

Charleston was a majority Black city by the time the war ended. Large numbers of freemen had moved to Charleston to seek work, many of them living along the docks on the Cooper River in desperate circumstances.[11] Union Major General Daniel E. Sickles, who was appointed military commander for the Carolinas in order to oversee the Reconstruction of the South, worried about the bitterness of white Charlestonians towards the Union and the idea of social life with Black residents.[12] His worry was well-founded. Although more Black Charlestonians than white residents were elected to public office between 1869 and 1876, white Charlestonians were rankled that Black residents were allowed to go to theaters and restaurants under the new South Carolina nondiscrimination laws. After Reconstruction collapsed in 1876, federal troops left the state and control over the state legislature was retaken by ex-Confederate Democrats; Charleston swiftly followed suit. Meanwhile, the city's prosperity continued to diminish, segregation advanced, and Black Charlestonians who could not afford to move elsewhere were relegated to the unhealthiest, wettest neighborhoods on the East Side while wealthy white residents clustered south of Broad street.

Beginning in the late 1920s, elite white Charlestonians, worried about preservation of their increasingly dilapidated, somnolent city, founded a series of institutions aimed at marketing Charleston to the rest of the country as a golden, charming destination. You could call it the Antebellum Industrial Complex. They created a network of cultural institutions focused on chosen portions of the city's past; not the late unpleasantness of the Civil War, not the violent truths of its slave-owning history, but the timeless graciousness of warm Southern hospitality served up by Black hands.[13]

White members of families who could trace their lineage back to colonial days founded the Society for the Preservation of Negro Spirituals and danced at St. Cecelia Society Balls. As historian Stephanie Yuhl has vividly documented, Charleston was shaped by these white Charlestonian institutions—the Society for the Preservation of Old Dwellings, the Poetry Society of South Carolina, the Gibbes

Museum—to become in the 1930s a magnet for people seeking a "romantic," "historic," "quaint," and "old-worldly" atmosphere, whose stage was peopled by a "noble" white gentry and "picturesque" Black working class. Charleston sold itself as "America's Most Historic City." By the mid-twentieth century, Charleston had been transformed from a dilapidated, backwards town into a tourist destination,[14] a place portrayed in memory and day-to-day performative behavior where the Civil War was downplayed and whites were paternalistically affectionate toward a subservient Black population.

The elite, white Society for the Preservation of Negro Spirituals, founded in 1922, played a particularly jarring role in this history-creation. This was not vaudeville minstrelsy in blackface. These performers, giving concerts in Boston and New York City in the late 1920s and early 1930s to large and enthusiastic audiences, dressed as slaveowners as they earnestly sang dozens of spirituals about which they were viewed as authorities by other white Americans.[15] Most of them actually were the descendants of slaveowners, as members of the Society were required to be "Charleston people who were born and reared on plantations nearby or who were reared under plantation traditions."[16] They conveyed on stage a genteel Old South aura as well as an ideal of premodern, rigid racial hierarchy; they proclaimed that their purpose was to protect Black spirituals "sung in slavery days" from corruption and celebrate "the slave's love for this Master and our undying love for our Maumas."[17] The Society asserted that their members "all know and understand the negro character, probably as well as any white man ever does."[18] Slavery was reframed as a benevolent antebellum reverie, and the singing of these songs was presented as a gentle homage by patrician whites to the heartfelt native hymns that had been sung by their loyal Black retainers; all of this, in the imagination of their listeners, lit by moonlight and heard near wide-leafed magnolia trees. In this collectively conjured, highly selective history, Black Charlestonians were present only as stereotypes—as domestic help and street vendors, for example.

Charleston's charms drew in Frederick Law Olmsted Jr. (the son of the famous civic designer), who made a professional surveying visit to Charleston in mid-January 1940 at the request of some of those leading Charlestonians. Olmsted sent them a report that attempted to capture the "intangible values" that made up the "peculiar and distinctive" aesthetic of the southern portion of the Charleston peninsula:[19]

> Though [these values are] very difficult to describe they are widely, if somewhat vaguely, recognized and appreciated as summing up into a distinctive and extraordinarily charming amenity characteristic of certain physical aspects of Charleston and definitely associated with certain kinds of old physical objects and conditions . . . which happen, through the accidents of Charleston's peculiar history, to have been inherited in various states of preservation and alteration from periods prior to 1860.

Those leading citizens combined forces in service of the marketing of extraordinary charm, setting gears in motion that led to extraordinary displacements of Black Charlestonians. Northerners, including President and Mrs. Franklin D. Roosevelt, ate this stuff up. The Charleston Chamber of Commerce was delighted at the "good advertisement" the Society for the Preservation of Negro Spirituals generated for the city. It was all so American, so redolent of shared values of nobility and romance.

CENTRAL CONSIDERATIONS.

Whatever else the Committee is concerned with
it is very centrally concerned with some intangible values peculiar to Charleston, which are of much present
importance and of still greater potential importance if
the physical things and conditions that give rise to them
can be adequately safeguarded, but which are exceedingly
liable to progressive diminution and irrecoverable loss.

Though very difficult to describe they are
widely, if somewhat vaguely, recognized and appreciated
as summing up into a distinctive and extraordinarily
charming amenity characteristic of certain physical as-
pects of Charleston and definitely associated with certain kinds of old physical objects and conditions (not-
ably certain kinds and arrangements of buildings, walls,
fences, gates etc. and of trees, gardens and other open-
spaces etc.), which happen, through the accidents of
Charleston's peculiar history, to have been inherited in
various states of preservation and alteration from periods
prior to 1860.

These intangible assets are primarily esthetic;
directly valuable to many people of Charleston and elsewhere for the personal enjoyment derivable from them; indirectly of much economic value, present and potential,
through the willingness and ability of appreciative people to pay substantial economic prices for the privilege
of enjoying them under sufficiently favorable conditions,
either as residents of the city or as passing visitors.
Their esthetic value is due in part to the time-tested
artistic excellence of some of the individual physical
units. It seems, however, much more generally due to
the cumulative effect of many adjacent physical units
more notable for a picturesque harmoniousness and self-
consistency in the pleasant impressions they produce than
for any breath-taking beauty in most of the component
units. This in turn seems to be due primarily to two
historic facts.

In the first place, these physical units (residential and otherwise) were created, to an extent that
is extraordinary considering the size of the city, to
meet the practical needs and satisfy the esthetic desires
of people who were for the time being very prosperous and
whose preferences were directly or indirectly much influenced by some of the finer cultural traditions of England
and America, at periods when the prevailing fashions happened to be such that the general run of design and construction (apart from any masterpieces) could readily be
done, and was done, with a workmanlike understanding of
what was attempted, so that at worst it seldom fell below

Scan of Olmsted Associates Records
by Olmstead Associates.[20]

Along these same lines, Charleston planned in 1931 for its population's "ultimate racial distribution" through the first city Historic Zoning Ordinance ever adopted in this country. A proposed "general city plan" by Morris Knowles, Inc., used as the basis for that ordinance, mapped out "white residence districts" and "colored residence districts" as well as proposed roads and business districts, and used pale dots (representing "ten white people" each) and dark dots (representing "ten negro people" each) to indicate who would eventually live where.

II - Estimated Ultimate Distribution of Population

The design of municipal utilities and facilities depends upon the population they are intended to serve. The most desirable information to have on hand in the study of any area, whether ward, city or region, is the population of the area in question when ultimately developed in a reasonable manner. Population data, on the basis of ultimate development, have been determined and utilized for the planning studies at Charleston. This determination has been made by ascertaining the use to which property within the present city limits best may be put, and its probable type of development, as provided in the zoning plan and ordinance. On this basis, it is found that within the present limits of the city, approximately 75,000 people may be accommodated in a reasonable way. It is estimated that about 45,000 of these would be white persons.

Plate I, page 11, shows the present distribution of population, and Plate II, page 12, the probable ultimate distribution of population within the present city limits. The latter information forms the basis for the design of the school and the park and playground plans.

Attention is called to the estimated distribution of white and colored populations in wards 5 and 7, particularly in the sections immediately adjoining Calhoun Street. The future development within these two wards is difficult to determine and there is more chance for an inaccurate

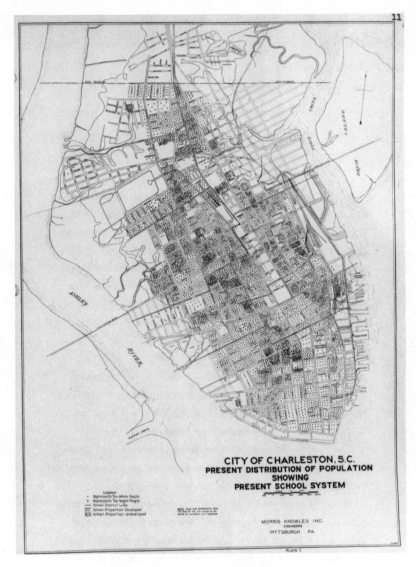

*Excerpt from Morris Knowles plan, showing "white
residency districts" and "negro residency districts."*

The swampy East Side was planned to be populated entirely by Black
residents, as was the area around what is now the Gadsden Green
Houses on the west side, while the plan suggested that "undeveloped

sections adjoining the Ashley River [where the medical district is now] will be reserved as white residence sections by developers through the use of deed covenants."

First, West of King Street residence sections are indicated as likely to be occupied by white persons, with the exception of the areas in the vicinity of the Burke and Simonton Schools and the area located approximately between King Street, Spring Street, Rutledge Avenue and Line Street. It is felt that these three negro sections are definitely established. Moreover, population studies show that these areas will probably continue to be necessary to house a portion of the future estimated negro population.

The negro section in the vicinity of the county jail has deteriorated into a slum area. It is decidedly to the advantage of the city and property owners interested in this section to eliminate this condition and this has been anticipated in making the general plan.

It is believed that undeveloped sections adjoining the Ashley River will be reserved as white residence sections by developers through the use of deed covenants.

Second, with a few minor exceptions, it is probable that residence property east of King Street and north of Laurens Street may ultimately become negro sections. Such development generally will be advantageous and should be encouraged when and as necessary. North of Mary Street the present tendency already is toward negro occupancy.

Regarding this section of the city, attention is called to the present development and the existing predominant white occupancy of the area between Mary Street and Laurens Street. In view of the results of the last two

United States census returns which successively show a decided decrease of negro population, it seems desirable to preserve as long as possible, the present character of this section. In other words, it is believed desirable that reasonable efforts be exercised to keep this a white section as long as negro population continues to decrease. This reasoning has prompted the suggestion that the Buist School be converted, in the near future, into a white elementary school. Previous mention of another possibility to improve this general section has been made in the discussion of "Estimated Ultimate Distribution of Population".

Existing School and Present Enrollment

The locations of existing schools, school properties and school districts are shown on Plate I, previously referred to as showing the present distribution of white and negro population. The schools also are listed in Tables Nos. 3 and 4, together with the grades for each school; the number of class rooms; the total seating capacity; the enrollment of each school for April, 1931, and for the year 1930; the population of each school district, and the present ratios between enrollment and population. Table No. 3 is for white schools and Table No. 4 for colored schools. For convenience of reference, a number has been given to each school, as listed in Tables Nos. 3 and 4, and a corresponding number noted on Plate I. Tables Nos. 5 and 6 show the total enrollment for the system of white schools, classified as to grades for alternate years from 1920 to 1930; and the enrollment

Morris Knowles, Inc., Report of the City Planning and Zoning Commission, upon a Program for the Development of a City Plan with Specific Studies of Certain Features Thereof, 2 July 1931. "[U]ndeveloped sections adjoining the Ashley River will be reserved as white residences sections by developers through the use of deed covenants. . . . [R]esidence property east of King Street and north of Laurens Street may ultimately become negro sections. Such development generally will be advantageous and should be encouraged when and as necessary."

And, says Rev. Joseph Darby, the well-regarded longtime AME minister, the Civil War has never really ended in Charleston. The slick, well-marketed, ahistorical reproduction of Charleston's past trumpeted across the country by the Society for the Preservation of Negro Spirituals is still going strong, and Morris Knowles's contemplated distribution of the population worked out exactly as planned. Slavery wasn't just "back then," Darby says, because it still frames the way the citizens of Charleston—particularly the long-timers—relate to one another. "Charleston is Confederate Disneyland," he adds.

◆

Rev. Joseph A. Darby is a soft-spoken man in his seventies with sloping shoulders and a deliberate, gentle manner. His voice frequently rises with soft, teasing humor, mimicking without anger the incredulous reactions and unthinking statements of some of the white Charlestonians he has known over the years. Darby was born in Columbia, South Carolina. His mother, Eloise Janerette Darby, who adored him, was a teacher. He remembers her as gracious and strong, someone who was noble and humble at the same time. He has only foggy memories of his father, Joseph Anthom Darby Sr., who died when Darby was three years old. Both sets of grandparents were South Carolinians: Joseph Darby Sr.'s parents came from Fort Motte, in Calhoun County; Eloise's parents came from Eastover, about thirty miles outside Columbia.

Darby's great-great-great-great-grandmother's last name was Singleton. "I know that her place of birth was West Africa, and that she was brought as a slave to South Carolina and named for her owner," Darby says. That ancestor's daughter, Molly Singleton Smith, was born in 1830 and lived until 1911. She was buried in the churchyard of Saint Philip AME Church in Eastover, where Darby was pastor in the 1990s. "Molly Singleton Smith is the matriarch of many Black families in Eastover," he says.

Two of his great uncles and a great-grandfather, all on his mother's side, were preachers, which makes Darby a fourth-generation minister. That great-grandfather, Ivy W. Johnson, had come out of slavery, building a reputation as a passionate minister in his twenties after the Civil War. By all accounts, Ivy Johnson was a heck of a preacher. Once he roared, "If you don't get right, God's going to do something," and an earthquake struck, right on time. His nickname forever after had been Earthquake Johnson.

Darby grew up in Wheeler Hill, a diverse, close-knit, middle-class neighborhood in Columbia. "It had the obligatory two Jewish grocery stores," says Darby. It had good schools within walking distance: the Florence C. Benson Elementary school and Darby's beloved high school, Booker T. Washington, "a wonderful institution with talented teachers." There were three churches then on Wheeler Hill, all within about five or six blocks of each other. "There was the traditional system of community control wherein if you did not belong to one of those churches, you pretty much didn't belong on Wheeler Hill," Darby says. He remembers how fun it was to see folks who you knew had been raising holy hell on Saturday night sitting up in church on Sunday morning. "They might not have had their heads on straight, but they knew enough to be there every Sunday morning," he says.

Eloise did not let Darby get involved in the civil rights movement in the mid-1960s. She wasn't going to have Joe locked up or arrested or killed. He'd been upset, but had complied; as a result, he didn't get to feel what it was like to be at those protests.

Eloise Janerette Darby was ninety pounds of fierce determination. Back when Rev. Darby was in elementary school on Wheeler Hill, a purse snatcher once ran past his house after pulling a lady down. When his mother called the thief's name out, the purse snatcher stopped and came back. Eloise chewed him out for about five good, solid minutes, then made him go back, check on the lady, pick her up, dust her off, and return her purse. Then Eloise Darby told the purse snatcher, "You know I'm going to call your mama by the time you get home because you know better than this."

After college at South Carolina State, Darby, newly married, worked as a part-time minister in Columbia for more than a dozen years while he held down a job as a social worker with the state of South Carolina's juvenile justice system. He prepared for his final ordination in the AME ministry by attending the Lutheran Theological Southern Seminary in Columbia. Lutheran, one of the only choices in the city for Darby at a time when the AME church required a master's degree in divinity for ordination but had no active nearby AME seminary of its own, required a reading knowledge of Greek. The school offered a six-week summer course in Greek but about half the students (all Black bivocational ministers) routinely failed.

The Lutheran Church eventually began admitting part-time AME pastors while having them take a semester-long course in Greek at the same time. The students celebrated the decision with much pomp and ritual, but "AME Bishop Frank Reid was unimpressed," Darby remembered. Reid said, "This is nice, but it's nothing new." He had seen wonderful new initiatives pop up, and had seen that everybody enjoyed the step being taken, had sung Kumbaya, had held hands. Reid predicted that this initiative, like the others, would die soon. "You need to make radical change, not just incremental change," Darby remembered Reid telling younger people. Sure enough, the change didn't last ten years.

At the time, Darby thought Bishop Reid was speaking unduly harshly. Now he knows better. "It was age speaking," he says. That was wisdom.

Darby later learned that the reason half the Black students failed the six-week summer course in Greek was because they were being treated differently by the faculty. The white students had been allowed to treat the final test as a take-home exam and, by studying good published translations and working together, passed in large numbers. The Black students sat in a room in the seminary in the presence of the professor to take the test and failed in large numbers. To Darby's mind, any change in the treatment of Black people had to be radical, not incremental. It was age speaking.

Eventually, Darby says, "God liberated me from state government," and he took on his own full-time church near Columbia. "When I ceased to be dependent on the state government for a job I found I could shoot off my mouth," he says. He was "being paid by a bunch of Black folk, most of whom agreed with me." He had freedom.

It is not in Darby's nature to brag, but he rose. He was asked to join innumerable committees and lead statewide ecumenical endeavors. He was a committed, caring, and well-organized pastor of each of his flocks as he moved to different church homes. Along the way, two sons had been born to Darby and his wife Mary Bright Darby. Wags in town noticed both times that sons were coming to Joseph and Mary and routinely suggested that the child be named Jesus Christ. "We went along with it," Darby says. Both boys were given J. C. initials, and Jason Christopher Darby and Jeremy Christian Darby have since grown up to have children of their own.

By December 1998, fifteen years after he left college, Darby had pastored three churches in the Columbia area and become a leader of the Columbia ministerial. The Bishop then assigned him to AME's "first church" in South Carolina, Morris Brown AME in Charleston. "Morris Brown is the first church because it is the largest in the state," Darby says. Moving to Charleston was a big adjustment; the boys were in school in Columbia and Mary was teaching nearby. But Darby had been summoned and it was time to go.

Morris Brown was "historic, large, and complicated," he remembers. Darby thrived there for fifteen years. He became the presiding elder in the Beaufort AME district, responsible for thirty-three churches in the southern part of the state. Then Mary fell ill.

"The road between Beaufort, Charleston, and Georgetown got very long," Darby says. Mary had several minor strokes and began to show symptoms of vascular dementia. Darby needed to be with her to care for her. When he returned to work, his bishop put him back in the pulpit, this time at Nichols Chapel, which Darby politely calls "a nice place to be," signaling that it is small. "It is enough work, but not too much. It is not Morris Brown level of work or Beaufort district level of work, but it is a good church," Darby says. He thinks he might slow down eventually. No time soon. Retirement is mandatory at seventy-five in his church. Otherwise, "I will just keep chugging right on," Darby says.

◆

Darby remembers his presiding elder in Columbia, Alonzo Middleton, preparing him for the contrast between the state capital and Charleston: "Okay, now, you need to understand something. You ain't in Columbia any more. You're in Charleston now, so whatever you see or hear, you can be shocked, you can be stunned, you can be amazed, but don't ever be surprised."

Darby chuckles at the memory. "That was good advice," he says. "I have seen things in Charleston that have shocked, stunned, and amazed me, but I have learned not to be surprised," Darby says. He has come to understand over the years that Charleston is a place where "there is still a great deal of antebellum complication." At the same time, it is a city that prides itself on politeness. "Raging politeness," Darby calls it. "People are so relentlessly polite," Darby says, "that they can't talk about anything uncomfortable." That raging politeness comes into play when they talk about race and class in Charleston, and when those subjects lead to conversations about public education, transportation, runaway gentrification, and rising waters.

Not only did raging politeness still reign, but the old Charleston way of "Black mitigation" still exists, says Darby. "The city wants to do X, so what is the least the city can do when doing X that will appease the Black folks and not cause too much friction?" he says. When the big, beautiful Arthur J. Ravenel Jr. Bridge forming the background to the opening credits of the Bravo reality TV show "Southern Charm"[21] was built over the Cooper River, its construction between 2001 and 2005 on the Charleston side of the bridge uprooted the Black community there. A lot of East Side people were displaced and never got the opportunity to move back. "The city," Darby says drily, "created a few college scholarships to compensate for that." The six-lane Crosstown Expressway, first opened in 1968, cut a gash through a mostly Black neighborhood, destroying about 150 houses and creating a wall between Black areas to its north and the mostly white lower peninsula to its south. The city called it the Septima Clark Parkway in honor of a Black civil rights heroine who was forced to teach on Johns Island because she was not allowed to instruct children in Charleston's schools, but did nothing to help the neighborhood and the lives that its construction destroyed.

In Columbia, "there was a greater willingness to be frank on the part of both Black and white people," Darby thinks. In Charleston, "there is more emphasis on going along with the flow." In his view, when the city has historically done the least it can get away with to help the Black community, there has been little uproar from Black people, who maintain a "deep desire to get along." More so than Darby has seen in any other city, "Black Charlestonians seem to have an inordinate desire to please the powers that be."

Darby tells a story about political organizing in Columbia. A ministerial alliance made up of the NAACP, the Urban League, Black

business leaders, and Black elected officials got together for breakfast
to strategize and mobilize voters to get a racist sheriff out of office. "It
worked," he says. The informal group, which didn't even have a name,
spoke with one voice again when the big fight over the South Carolina
statehouse Confederate flag came to a boil in 2015.

But when the NAACP tried to do the same kind of informal
convening in Charleston, by the time of the third breakfast meeting
bureaucracy and worry had crippled the work of the group. Members
asked what their mission statement should be. "Who would be spokes-
person? What would the group be called? Who would respond to
reporters?" Darby remembers. Something, whether fear or accultura-
tion, tangled people in knots. "So many Black Charlestonians have a
strong instinct to avoid rocking the boat," Darby thinks. Darby knows
that bishops in the Black church have avoided sending pastors from
Charleston to the biggest pulpits in Charleston. They figure those are
the pulpits that need to be filled by advocates, and do not think they
are going to find advocate pastors in Charleston.

Columbia's region had been full of Historically Black Colleges and
Universities (HBCUs): Allen University, Benedict College right down
the road, South Carolina State in Orangeburg, Voorhees College in
Denmark. The Charleston region didn't have a single HBCU. Darby
thinks that absence has allowed an insular community in Charleston,
both Black and white, to hold to old traditions. In Columbia there was
much less of a caste system among Black residents and only a mild sense
of caste discrimination, because local institutions of higher learning
had elevated Black and white people alike to academic success. "That
didn't happen in Charleston," Darby points out. The status quo, Darby
thinks, is extraordinarily powerful in Charleston, among both its Black
and white residents. "Charleston is still the Old South," Darby says.
Columbia has had a Black mayor, a Black police chief, a Black fire
chief, a Black council chair, a Black school board chair, and a Black

school superintendent. Even in 2022, "Charleston has had very little of that," Darby says. The city's senior staff is overwhelmingly white, as is the mayor.

"There is no Black professional class in Charleston," Darby believes. His younger son, Jeremy, lives in Raleigh, North Carolina, because he couldn't get a job in Charleston. Jeremy is a graduate of the University of South Carolina who won multiple awards in college for his graphic design abilities. But better opportunities led him elsewhere. Darby's older son, Jason, a marketing and communications professional who had been named to the inaugural "Top 40 under 40 South Carolinians" list in 2014, worked at Trident Technical College in Charleston for a while but then had been very glad to get out of Charleston. He had moved to Columbia, Darby says, because there was no core of "young Black people who got together for recreation, advocacy, or anything else in Charleston."

"The Black kids with the most potential move away; those who move to Charleston often don't stay very long because there is very little to do," Darby says. The local corporations, like Boeing, "know how to schmooze pleasantly about diversity and other cosmetic discussions about race in Charleston," he says, "but don't open their mouths much on the social issues at all." If there had been a cadre of "young Black people who had been able to get the jobs they needed and stick it out in Charleston," he says, they could have kickstarted real change in the city. Instead, the Black community had become largely indigent and isolated in segregated low-lying areas like the West Side and the East Side, among the poorest census blocks in the region.

Darby tells a bitter joke: "Where do Charleston's young black professionals get together?" Answer: "In Columbia."

Darby sees that throughout Charleston, when it comes to road relocation, when it comes to the people the city will disturb, when it comes to whose houses the city will let flood—"it is always the Black community that suffers." That happens, he knows, because a lot of those in the Black community don't have the luxury of making noise. But as the wearer of several official and unofficial hats in Charleston, Darby does. He can drop an op-ed into the *Post and Courier* or get quoted by national media whenever he wants. When he writes columns, one of his Black friends will always come up to him and say, "Thank you for saying what you said. You said just what I wish I could say." Other Black people get afraid that the boss might read something they wrote. "They might end up unemployed. Some folks probably fear physical harm," he says. But Darby knows he can be unafraid and frank.

He knows there is no hall of power that he cannot access in Charleston. "Except," he admits wryly, "maybe a white private club." Back in 2018, the all-white Charleston Rifle Club admitted thirteen of fourteen proposed members. The fourteenth was a respected Black emergency room doctor, Dr. W. Melvin Brown III.[22] In Charleston, a few private clubs still do not admit women as full members, and at least two have no Black members. "Charleston is just slow," says Darby.

Rev. Darby was a close friend of Clementa Pinckney, who was murdered during the 2015 Mother Emanuel massacre. When he heard there had been a shooting, he picked up the phone and got Clementa's voicemail. Then he texted, and called again. But the voicemail box was full. "Clementa never let his voicemail box fill up like that," Darby says. Then the Deputy Chief called. "It's a bloodbath at Emanuel," he told Darby. "And Pinckney's gone, too."

Darby witnessed the weirdness of Fox News trying to figure out how to report on the killings. At first they framed it as an attack on religious freedom, but then Dylann Storm Roof was identified and everyone saw his Confederate flag and his desire to start a race war. That was a problem for Fox: "Oh, my God, what are the Black people going to do?" Darby mimics. Then a couple of the families of the victims said,

"We forgive you." "Not all the families said that," Darby remembers, "but a couple did." And the response was, "Oh, thank God. The Black people forgive us."

"And it was all holding hands across the Ravenel Bridge, and remembrance after remembrance, all still rolling along," Darby says. "Charleston is still overplaying its racial unity, and it just is not there."

Darby says that Black people in Charleston, in order to survive and go on with their own lives, have gotten used to simply waving away unfeeling and astonishing behavior on the parts of the whites around them. The "forgiveness" expressed by Black worshippers at Mother Emanuel AME church following the 2015 massacre was completely misunderstood by so many. "Forgiveness doesn't mean everything is okay," Darby says. "It means that you've got people whose faith was nurtured in slavery, people whose ancestors were slaves, people who, for the most part, unless they could escape, had to endure a life that was filled with brutality, with rape, with division of family, with beatings. How do you endure that and not strangle the person who's doing that and know that you're going to get strangled in turn? You learn to say, 'I'm going to leave you in God's hands.' And you move on. That's what the people at Mother Emanuel were saying. They were not saying just, 'I forgive.' They were saying, 'I'm going to leave you in God's hands and let God deal with you.'"

Darby explains that they are commanded by God to love, and so no matter how angry many Black residents get, or how disenfranchised or inequitably treated they feel, they believe they are called at all times to avoid mentioning how they are feeling. White Charleston hasn't understood that yet. All that politeness on the Black side is shielding whites from Black rage.

"All that shared mourning after Emanuel was good," Darby says. "The grief was good. I appreciated all of that," he says. "But at some point in time you can't just say, 'Isn't it wonderful that we shared this moment of forgiveness.' At some point in time you have to ask why this kid, Dylann Roof, felt obliged in twenty-first century America to be crazy enough to get a gun and decide to go kill folks," Darby says.

Roof was himself a tourist, who drove eighty miles from rural mid–South Carolina to visit Sullivan's Island and the Charleston Peninsula. He wrote in his manifesto that he had come to Charleston because "it is [the] most historic city in my state, and at one time had the highest ratio of blacks to Whites [sic] in the country."[23] The forces that shaped Roof, like the ones that caused Officer Michael Slager in 2015 to shoot fifty-year-old Walter Scott eight times in the back as he ran away from Slager's traffic stop in North Charleston, were still potent.[24]

In fact, Darby says that the backdoor Jim Crow character of the peninsula was the strangest thing he had ever seen. Since Charleston's roaring gentrification began in the early 1980s, Black residents of the region had felt they should not be downtown after dark. Black twenty-somethings often experienced the indignity of being refused entrance to clubs and restaurants on the lower peninsula; even today, it is well-known that bouncers and owners use contrived "dress codes" to exclude them. Dance club managers would tell DJs that it was "too dark in here," and that they should change the music they were playing to ensure Black customers are not interested in staying, or that they will be fired if the percentage of Black guests remained high.

Darby enjoys trying to make a difference in Charleston. If his mother was still alive, he would want her to know that he understands she was trying to protect him by not letting him go to protests during the civil rights era. And he would want her to know that he hasn't missed the movement. It is still going on in Charleston.

◆

Charleston's geographic and racial history are intertwined. As we've learned, filling frequently flooded, marshy land was a constant process on the peninsula, from the 1680s forward. The place was initially a tiny quagmire, just a few blocks running down the Cooper River and two blocks running west toward the Ashley. There were creeks and marshes everywhere. Colonial era visitors describe a hot, wet, low, sandy, pestilential town, with rivers flowing over two-thirds of the place most of the time. Wetlands, tidal creeks, marshes, and mudflats, with low stands of trees and brush, gradually gave way to filled-dirt streets. Even in the early 1970s, Charleston was mostly just that peninsula, the five or so square miles of sandy low ground between the Cooper and the Ashley, about half of which had been filled in by dirt and trash dumped over creeks and wetlands. Although the peninsula had been home to about 71,000 people in the 1940s, decades of white flight out to the suburbs in search of white schools and neighborhoods had left the peninsula depopulated by the 1970s, with just about 40,000 people left, the majority of whom were Black. There were no restaurants to speak of; certainly none worth exclaiming over. Charleston had become dilapidated. Mayor Palmer Gaillard, who ran Charleston between 1959 and 1975, worried about his exiting tax base and moved to annex part of West Ashley, on the other side of the Ashley River, into the city. Gaillard tripled the size of Charleston to eighteen square miles.[25] Then Joe Riley took over.

◆

Joseph P. Riley, mayor of Charleston between 1975 and 2015, was frantic about annexation. Obsessed. Over his years in office, he increased the land area of Charleston twenty times over, to 128 square miles. By the time he left office at the end of 2015, the peninsula accounted for just 4 percent of the city's sprawling size, and just a quarter of its population.[26] "Today," says local developer Vince Graham, "the city is 72,000 acres. It's bigger than Washington, DC and Boston combined."[27]

Riley's annexation campaign was not an altogether smooth process. Residents of James Island, to the west, resisted—hard. They didn't trust the Charleston of the 1980s, perhaps out of racism or sheer dislike for anything urban. They tried to form their own towns, on the fly, to avoid being folded into Charleston. Three times, James Islands advocates went all the way to the Supreme Court of South Carolina to stave off annexation. Each time they got thrown out of court, Mayor Riley went on a speedy annexation spree, getting developers to buy up land that then could be annexed into the city of Charleston—before the James Islanders tried to incorporate themselves again. In the end, an independent Town of James Island was pulled together, but it was much smaller than the islanders had initially planned. An array of subdivisions had been quickly built out, fast and loose, stormwater infrastructure unclear, drainage ditches unclear, leaving an extraordinarily fractured area looking something like a half-cooked pancake right before it's flipped over, its surface marked by innumerable tiny bubbles. Those bubbles were the houses or small areas that had not been annexed into the city. You could tell which house was part of what city only by the colors of the garbage cans nearby. The same thing had happened in West Ashley, right across the Ashley River from the peninsula, except with less citizen pushback, where Riley had fought with North Charleston to annex land. Riley's strenuous annexation efforts brought in an extraordinarily large swath of territory, reaching from the enormous Cainhoy Peninsula to the east of the peninsula to Johns Island, James Island, and West Ashley in the west.

All of this increased the city's tax base and access to federal support, and thus its ability to bring new businesses, residents, and tourists to the jewel-like peninsula. Without a tax base, Charleston couldn't be run;

the city couldn't provide the services that people need. So Charleston grew swiftly: between 2013 and 2018 alone, 127 new subdivisions and nearly 4,500 lots were built in the city.[28]

In the end, astonishing development throughout the now-sprawling city ran ahead with few rules. The city at times either ignored existing conditions or failed to enforce the development rules it had adopted.[29] During Mayor Riley's tenure, the city's Board of Appeals let a development go through on James Island that was built several feet below FEMA's minimal height requirements.[30] Individual developers in the suburbs, throwing up hundreds of single-family, widely spaced homes, were nominally charged with handling the runoff created by their new houses. But the city was not checking anyone's homework very carefully. It wasn't just houses: the Bon Secours Hospital, part of the Roper St. Francis Healthcare company—the second largest employer in the region in 2016—had been built in a low floodplain area; it stood on Henry Tecklenburg Road. (Henry Tecklenburg was the current mayor's father; he was a developer in this region as well.)

Building in "special flood hazard areas" (defined by FEMA as an area that will be inundated by "[a] flood event having a 1 percent chance of being equaled or exceeded in any given year") was routine in the city of Charleston; as of 2018 at least sixty percent of the city's parcels, and probably more like seventy percent, were in these areas. More than 100,000 structures in Charleston are sited in FEMA's notoriously inaccurate floodplains.[31] The city had the highest number of "repetitive loss" buildings in the state—754 of them—meaning that owners of the property had filed at least two claims totaling $1,000 within a ten-year period—which amounted to a quarter of all of South Carolina's repetitive loss sites. Most buyers didn't know about any of this.[32] It was fair to say that there had been a general lack of coordination across these conditions, and that the chaotic outgrowths of many incremental developments had not been planned to work in concert with the watersheds nature had established—not that the city had known, exactly, where those watersheds were.

Over time, and particularly beginning in the 1970s, Charleston moved into its marshes. Because of Mayor Joe Riley's energy in the 1970s and 1980s, the city of Charleston now includes huge amounts of suburban sprawl in West Ashley (72 percent white), James Island (83 percent white), Johns Island (77 percent white), and Daniel Island (almost all white, but geographically part of the former Cainhoy Peninsula where descendants of freed slaves still live). Both the city and the developers shared incentives not to check too rigorously for drainage issues created by the building of thousands of new subdivision homes. When you're building an empire, you're not concerned with ensuring the new development you're encouraging—so as to lengthen your tax rolls and secure the future of the crown jewel, the peninsula—is actually appropriate for the topography on which it's built. Particularly when many of the people who will live in those houses will be only modestly wealthy, if white. Michael Miller, the first Black recorder of deeds in Charleston County, gives Riley credit for transforming Charleston from, he says, "a city that nobody knew unless you happened to have family that lived here," to one of the most visited places in the world. "But, in doing that," Miller continues, "in my humble opinion there was a lot of neglect that went on when it comes to the flooding issues in Charleston," as well as sea-level rise in general. Miller believes these issues weren't given sufficient priority under Riley, and that "now it's almost too late to build a wall."[33] Vince Graham agrees, saying that during Riley's annexation binge, "we've not thought about flood-prone areas."[34]

◆

Following his initial election in 1975, Mayor Riley's overriding goal was revitalizing the peninsula. Annexation of territory had been part of that plan. Additional development on the peninsula itself was a central element as well. Riley survived years of attacks from old Charlestonians, including litigation by preservationists, and succeeded in wrestling a large combination hotel-convention center into being in the heart of Charleston's decaying downtown business district.

In September 1989, Hurricane Hugo brought a monstrous surge of nearly thirteen feet of water onto the peninsula along with sustained 140-mph winds.[35] The storm also brought opportunity: Riley harnessed the insurance money, federal attention, and national media focus flowing into the still-sleepy, beloved city after the disastrous storm—Oprah Winfrey brought a film crew to Charleston—to land additional private sector investment in Charleston. Hugo had helpfully demolished some eyesores and left more of the peninsula available for commercial development.[36] Between 1992 and 2011, about a third more land was covered by development in Charleston than had been the case before Hugo.[37] Over the years, Riley brought into being a new $140 million performing arts center,[38] a giant aquarium, a global shipping port, a minor-league baseball stadium, a beautiful waterside park, and many other attractions. Charleston became a foodie paradise.

Mayor Riley achieved his goal of revitalizing Charleston over his forty years in office, and along the way Charleston also became the nation's fastest-gentrifying city. Neighborhoods on the Charleston peninsula that had been full of working-class Black citizens became far whiter and far richer, as home prices soared and Black residents were pushed out or sold out, retreating to the separate city of North Charleston or to West Ashley.

Michelle Mapp, the former housing trust fund director and a current lawyer with the ACLU of South Carolina, remembers being told by Bill Saunders, a Charleston community and civil rights advocate in Charleston whose grandfather had been born enslaved, that Black people who occupied land at different times in the United States were always displaced once it became valuable. Or they were unable to hold on to land they owned once it became valuable, because they couldn't afford the repairs or maintenance or hiked-up property taxes the land required. "Even though their property may be worth $500,000, that average Black resident can't go take out a home equity line on that property because they probably don't have the income to then support being able to pay that back," says Mapp. "And so, it becomes a cycle. Someone comes to the door and says, 'Hey, we'll give you X for that piece of property.' How can that person, that Black family, hang on in the face of an amount of money that will immediately improve their lives?"

Meanwhile, the area became known by people across the country as a great place to retire to. The vibrant restaurant scene on the Peninsula whose growth Riley had encouraged, plus the warm climate and glorious natural vistas of the region—mossy oaks! endless marshes!—proved irresistible to aging northerners. Rev. Darby believes Mayor Riley basically has a good heart. But he also recognizes that Mayor Riley, like all of us, "got a lot wrong": the former mayor did nothing to tame the resulting raging gentrification or temper its consequences for the city's poorer Black residents.

Since 2010, the Charleston region has become one of the most expensive places to live in the southeast—second only to Washington, DC, and ahead of Atlanta. Charleston was the nation's fastest-growing apartment market in 2020.[39] But the median household income in Washington is about 30 percent higher than in Charleston. At the same time, the gap between median Black incomes in Charleston and median White incomes in Charleston is large and growing: $33,468 compared to $78,000 as of 2018. The high cost of living combined with large income disparities has led to a dramatic departure of Black families; some 1,200 Black households left the Peninsula between 2010 and 2020 alone. Black Charlestonians and white people who grew up in Charleston in the 1970s and 1980s remember a city that was mostly made up of Black residents. Over these same years of rampant development, the peninsula portion of a city that had been mostly Black flipped to being mostly white. When Riley became mayor, there were seven majority African American high schools on the peninsula. Forty years later, just one Black high school was left, with fewer than 300 students. Charleston County lost the most Black residents of any county over the past decade.[40] After decades of local policies and tax benefits aimed at supporting pro-growth, preservation-minded development, the population of the peninsula is at most 15 percent Black, and falling.

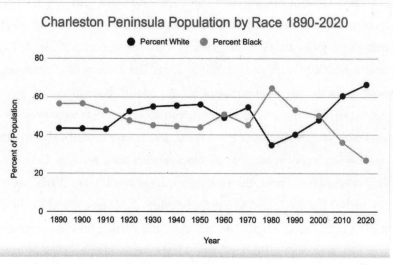

Summary of population by race on Charleston's peninsula, 1890-2020[41]

Bernard Powers, now an esteemed professor at the College of Charleston, was a graduate student there in 1976. At that time, Powers says, "All this area above Calhoun Street, this is the Black community up here. And below [Calhoun Street] there were examples of scattered Black residents who owned their houses." Even in the early 1990s, Powers recalls, when white college students went to the College of

Charleston's housing office, they were told, "Don't look at anything above Calhoun Street. Look at anything below Calhoun, but don't go above Calhoun Street."[42] All that changed, and the College of Charleston was involved.

The College of Charleston, founded in 1770 to keep the sons of planters at home rather than traveling off to Oxford or Harvard (where they might learn abolitionist ideas),[43] whose main buildings were built by enslaved people, has played a key role in the absence of affordable housing on the peninsula. Initially a municipal college with an enrollment of about 500 at its peak, it took its ownership back into private hands in 1949 to avoid having to enroll Black students. It remained a segregated institution, still with about 500 students, until 1966, when its board finally voted to admit Black applicants. In 1970, it returned to being a public institution. Its growth became explosive: 1,500 by 1972, nearly 5,000 by 1979, and 10,000 in 2021. The College of Charleston, now one of the largest public universities in South Carolina, didn't have dormitories for most of its students, and those students were typically well-off. New residences being erected near it have tended to be luxury apartments built by national developers with deep pockets. Students and parents were price-insensitive; students would say, "Well, we're taking out student loans" to pay for housing, or "Mommy and Daddy's paying it," driving a high-end luxury rental market on the peninsula that displaced poorer Black renters. Maybe better planning would have created a college-housing market off the peninsula, but the complete lack of public transit stymied that kind of thinking, if it ever existed.

Mayor Riley's ambitious forty-year tenure created a vibrant tourist economy, a great place to retire, and a great place for students to go to college. Charleston also became a place where young people of all colors, but particularly its Black residents, struggled to make a living, had to work multiple jobs, if they could find them, and couldn't afford to live anywhere near the charming peninsula.

◆

Tourists love experiencing the serenity of the foot of the Charleston peninsula. In European cities tourists visit large civic monuments: the Brandenburg Gates, the Colosseum, the Eiffel Tower. In Charleston it's the leafy lower peninsula neighborhoods. People come to Charleston to see the Battery houses, the Rainbow Row, to walk down Church Street, or take a horse-drawn carriage up and down the lanes. The grand houses they have come to see are stately and grave, many standing sideways to the narrow streets, their expansive porches—some call them "piazzas"—in silhouette. Some of those porches have baby-blue ceilings, painted that way to ward off evil spirits, and they front on graceful side-gardens shaded by trees. Old brick, worn stucco in gentle golden tones, grand proportions: the closely set houses below Broad Street radiate quiet residential glamor. The white tourists come in squads, in battalions, clumping through the lanes and snapping pictures, strolling in anticipation of a giant, colorful feast at some famous (or unknown) restaurant nearby.

◆

Nationwide protests following the murder of George Floyd in Minneapolis included a protest in Charleston's business district that turned violent, damaging more than 150 buildings on the night of May 30, 2020. About two weeks after that nighttime protest Michelle Mapp's pastor, Rev. Nelson B. Rivers III, stood in Marion Square dressed in a blue pinstriped double-breasted blazer, a white-and-blue striped tie, and a fedora, and spoke into a microphone attached by a wire to a small speaker.[44] Rivers had grown up in Charleston, on Rutledge Avenue. He said, "On this corner, maybe 60 years ago, [I] was told that Black people could not cross Calhoun Street. And that's when the name 'Calhoun' began to mean so much to me."[45] Calhoun Street, in those days and beyond, had been considered the boundary between white Charleston and Black Charleston.

Rivers was standing next to the base of the statue of John C. Calhoun that towered more than a hundred feet above the square. He was flanked by several Black leaders and politicians, and he was there to spur Mayor Tecklenburg to action. Rivers said he had called the mayor the week before, and had told Tecklenburg that the time had come for him, as mayor, to take steps to remove the Calhoun statue, "this monument to hate." The mayor, he reported, had replied that he was sworn to uphold the law, implying that the state's Heritage Act prevented him from moving the statue. Rivers, moving into a rhythmic speaking cadence, said he had told the mayor that Martin Luther King had said "An unjust law is to be opposed." And today, Rivers was calling on the mayor, the City Council of Charleston, and the South Carolina General Assembly to remove the statue. It was about to be the fifth anniversary of the Emanuel massacre, and John C. Calhoun was the symbol of the Confederacy whose flag Dylann Roof had loved. "John C. Calhoun was Dylann Roof for Black Charlestonians," Rivers said.

Rivers had been calling for the removal of the statue for years. But now, following the visibly pure evil of George Floyd's murder by Derek Chauvin, there were people marching all over the world to attest that Black lives mattered. "These voices of outrage are on a different level," Rivers said. Now the time had come to take action, not just to acknowledge the city's racist, evil, wicked past, or convey thoughts and prayers in the general direction of Charleston's Black residents.[46] "Don't act like Charleston is not exactly what made John C. Calhoun possible," Rivers said indignantly. "The time has come for us to find the courage and the moral center to remove this odious symbol of hatred. And we ask it be done not next month, not next year, but right now." Here, now. It was a short, strong speech.

What legal barrier was Mayor Tecklenburg pointing to? The Heritage Act is a South Carolina law from 2000, passed in response to efforts to get the Confederate Flag flying over the state capitol taken down, that forbids removing or changing any war monument or memorial that is on public property.[47] It also forbids renaming public property—like Calhoun Street. Changing anything covered by the Heritage Act requires a two-thirds vote of the state legislature. But the Calhoun monument stood on *private* property. The Washington Light Infantry and the Sumter Guard are both remnants of state National Guard units that have owned Marion Square since 1832, when the city sold the park to local militia for use as a drilling practice ground. The city leases the park and maintains it. The Light Infantry had objected to removal of the statue in the past,[48] but it was not theirs. The monument had been deeded to the city of Charleston's City Council in 1898 by the Ladies' Calhoun Monument Association.[49] And the Heritage Act covers war memorials, but the Calhoun statue wasn't one.

So the law didn't apply. It never had.

Miraculously, the City of Charleston reconsidered its legal position following Rev. Rivers's call to the mayor.[50] The mayor announced on June 17, the day after Rivers's press conference, that the City Council would be considering relocating the statue the following week. City Council voted unanimously to have it removed.

Mika Gadsden, a leading local Black activist and founder of the Charleston Activist Network, a Gullah Geechee descendant, and the daughter, in her words, of "Jim Crow refugees from Charleston," was scornful about the mayor's sudden action on the fifth anniversary of the Mother Emanuel massacre. For years, the city government hadn't said who actually owned the monument or why they couldn't bring the monument down. Gadsden said on her online broadcast, "You [Tecklenburg] lied to us since your first term. You said you couldn't bring it down. I'm not going to give you kudos for dragging your feet and doing something you could've done on day one, something that has been divisive."[51]

Calhoun, that tough old bird, did not go easy.

Twelve hours after crews started work, the statue was still connected to its towering pedestal; workers hacking away at the statue with power tools were making no progress, and the crowds that had gathered to celebrate the removal of the statue at midnight the night before had long since drifted away. It was just too hot to stick around under the pounding sun. A diamond-toothed chainsaw managed to cut through the granite, but it was hard to get water up that far in the air to cool the saw's chain. It took another five hours to take John Calhoun down, after nearly 124 years atop his stone column. It turned out that epoxy and a metal rod had been, under the statue's surface, holding Calhoun firmly in place all those years. Weeks later, workers toppled the column; the base of the monument still remained.

Much else about Charleston has stayed locked in place, similarly invisibly, over the last 150 years. Calhoun would have no trouble recognizing the charming lower peninsula of Charleston, and would likely be delighted by how supremely white it has become.

Mika Gadsden said during her online livestream broadcast in 2021 that the tourist culture of "partying, and having a good time, and Instagram, and Instagram-able streets laden with the vestiges of slavery" had nothing to do with "what it really feels like to live in Charleston, especially if you're a member of a marginalized community." Gadsden had sharp words to say about Riley, who she said had displaced "generations" of Black people from the peninsula in the "pursuit of erecting all of these monuments to just pure, utter greed, and luxury, and capitalism." She added, "We've prioritized tourists and out of state developers, shit, out of the country developers. We prioritized them over our own people here. So this is a city to visit. This is not a city where we can live and enjoy, and that's a shame."[52]

4
Charleston and Water, 2016–2022

B ecause the historic peninsula and much of the outlying suburban area of Charleston is so low, gravity-driven systems designed to drain water away from where people live are often ineffective. There isn't enough height difference between the source of the water and where it needs to go (into the Ashley or Cooper Rivers) to encourage the water to get there on its own. Water pools and remains on the surface, and the pipes designed to carry it fill with muck. Much of the fill deployed by builders over centuries to cover marshland and creeks has been organic, which means it decomposes and sinks over time, leaving more low places for water to gather.[1] The city's history is full of reports of miasmic fevers, putrid ponds, and filthy streets.

Charleston owes a great debt to engineer Charles Parker, who in the 1850s made a minute study of the city's drainage problems and pushed the City Council to install underground arched brick-lined drainage tunnels that would be large enough, and sloped enough, to carry water off the streets of the peninsula. Those brick tunnels are still there, and parts of the system still function.

In 1984, Mayor Riley commissioned the city's first-ever comprehensive stormwater master plan. It reported that the 1850s gravity-driven system was no longer adequately draining the streets of the peninsula, 90 percent of which was by then covered by development. The 1984 plan confirmed that the parts of the peninsula most prone to flooding corresponded perfectly with the outlines of land that had been artificially created over centuries. It recommended a bristling list of projects designed to add pumps connected to much larger concrete drains. The pumps would move as much as 34,000 gallons of water a minute into the tunnels, and the wider drains, placed 120 feet down into the stiffer mud of the Cooper Marl (the clay/mud layer below) instead of in the sandy soil, would allow large amounts of water to flow through the system rather than backing up onto the streets.[2]

The $500 million list of plans in the 1984 document (in today's dollars) prompted work on several drainage projects.[3] Riley often said he was proud of what his administration had accomplished. But as of 2018, less than half of the projects had been carried out.[4] Much of the problem was money: Riley had raised property taxes before he left office to increase the amount targeted for drainage (from $16 to $32 per year on a $200,000 home) and had imposed a higher stormwater utility fee on water and sewer bills ($6 per home per month instead of $2),[5] but the gap was enormous.[6] Hundreds of millions of dollars were still needed to implement Riley's thirty-five-year-old plans. A large portion of the western portion of the peninsula, from Calhoun Street south to the Low Battery, needed dramatic drainage infrastructure, but there was no obvious source of funding for it. So too for the Crosstown Freeway area on the east, and no major water infrastructure project had been implemented for the constantly flooding East Side.[7]

The other problem was perspective. Riley had thought of his water problem as drainage. Keeping the water at bay, moving it off the streets, had been his focus—to the extent it had been prioritized among the blizzard of projects he simultaneously pressed forward at all moments during his time as mayor. That 1984 report had been a master drainage plan, not an adaptation plan, entirely aimed at getting existing levels of water off the land, not shifting or eliminating development or moving people to higher and drier places.[8] It largely targeted the tourist areas of the peninsula, although several small projects had been aimed at the suburbs.[9] And it had been based on early 1980s thinking, before people were as focused on sea level rise.

In 2007, a city committee staffed by volunteers produced a 187-page report calling for a blue-ribbon commission to draft a sea-level rise adaptation plan. Nothing happened. The City Council, wholly controlled by Mayor Riley during this era, merely "received" the report and didn't implement the recommendation to create an adaptation blueprint. Not until late 2014 did he create a staff committee—a far cry from the top-level experts group that had been called for by the 2007 report—to look at water's effects on the city of Charleston.[10] That staff committee produced the first Charleston sea level rise strategy in 2015, weeks before Riley left office. The brief strategy, just fifteen pages long, assumed a 1.5 to 2.5 foot level rise in 50 years. Laura Cabiness, the Public Service Director for the city, said that looking out across decades at a six foot sea level rise would have dampened buy-in to the plan.[11]

The 2015 strategy wasn't awful, but nor was it detailed. It identified, in broad terms, a set of initiatives aimed at, as Mayor Riley's cover note put it, improving "our ability to withstand these [tidal flooding] effects." It softened any alarmist message, saying only that "the current data indicates the expected increase in sea level is more gradual initially, but may accelerate over time." It made no recommendations about existing or future developments other than noting that the city had recently adopted an ordinance requiring new structures to be built one foot above FEMA's base flood elevation—a level Houston found wholly inadequate just two years later. Most of the plan's attention was on drainage improvement. There was, essentially, no comprehensive plan under Mayor Riley to confront and adapt to rapidly accelerating sea level rise; there was certainly no plan to move vulnerable populations out of the way to high, dry, and dense locations.

"I don't blame Riley," science journalist and longtime chronicler of the South Carolina environment John Tibbetts says. "At the time they were still dealing with councilmembers who didn't believe sea level was really rising. And they didn't believe climate change was real. So even if Riley had been on top of it, it would've been tough to get City Council behind it."[12]

In South Carolina, if you appeared to believe in human-caused "climate change" in the mid-2010s, you were allying yourself with former Vice President Al Gore—to many, the very devil, someone who believed in Big Government and wanted to destroy private enterprise. Scientists at the state Department of Natural Resources had spent a year in 2011 drafting a comprehensive report sounding the alarm about the effects of climate change on South Carolina—including substantial risks to Charleston's drinking water as saltwater pushed along by sea level rise seeped its way further up the estuaries and freshwater aquifers contracted as groundwater was pumped out to be treated, as well as increased flooding where people were living.[13] But the report had been squelched in 2012 by the private sector board overseeing the agency.[14] The chair, a man named John Evans who ran a family construction business, said that the report would embarrass then-Governor Nikki Haley.[15]

Even the words "sea level rise" could not safely be uttered in South Carolina politics if their use carried the implication that mankind had had something to do with it. Pressed during a 2018 debate to comment on the cause of global warming, Gov. Henry McMaster laughed helplessly. "The water's coming up," he said. The crowd watching the debate laughed along with him. They knew he couldn't use the words.

ANDY SHAIN: "Do you believe in global warming, and if so, what do you think the cause is?"

MCMASTER: "I think it's getting warmer. Whether that fits your definition of global warming I don't know, but it is getting warmer. And I know that the water's coming up."

SHAIN: "Well, why do you think that is?"

MCMASTER: "The water's coming up."

SHAIN: "Well, OK. Because?"

MCMASTER: "Must be something melting somewhere, I guess."

SHAIN: "And it's melting because . . . ?"

MCMASTER: "Because it's warmer."[16]

In this context of denial, Mayor Riley had threaded the needle: he concentrated on drainage solutions on the peninsula and achieved some minor drainage victories to which he frequently pointed. Nonetheless, Mayor Riley knew when he was mayor that increasingly rising waters were a major challenge for the city. Fixing the problem would be very expensive; that wasn't something he relished, because Riley liked to not be beholden to anyone and he liked to control his budgets.[17]

It was also in Riley's nature to be optimistic and hopeful. Asked by an interviewer on the PBS NewsHour during his last year of office about sea level rise, he had said confidently that "Climate change is not going to remove Charleston from the landscape." Tourists were arriving in droves. "There's no cause for despair," he said. "The incremental improvements will protect this beautiful, historic city." He went on, talking about fortifying the Battery and improving drainage. But when pressed by the interviewer, he was unable to say what amount of sea level rise over the coming decades his city was planning on.

JACKIE JUDD: Are you planning on a one-foot rise? Is that the working assumption?

JOSEPH RILEY: We're planning on a range. It's incremental. We—and each year or decade, you will further calibrate that.

JACKIE JUDD: What is the range?

JOSEPH RILEY: Well, the range, you need to ask our resiliency people, but we're—we see some—some a foot, some less than a foot, some more than a foot.

This was an embarrassing exchange for the mayor, a rare slip. His own 2015 Sea Level Rise Strategic Plan had assumed a range of 1.5 feet to 2.5 feet of rise over the following fifty years.[18]

As Riley approached the end of his forty-year incumbency in 2015, though, no one was raising hell about rising waters—a silence that was good for tourism.[19] There hadn't been a major storm since Hugo in 1989. Riley left office a nationally celebrated mayor who had transformed Charleston into one of the most famous cities in the world.

◆

About a month before the election that brought Mayor Riley's former staffer John Tecklenburg into office as Riley's successor, a massive rainstorm hit Charleston. As Mike Seekings, a city councilmember, remembers it, "A cloud literally sat over the top of Charleston and drove rain straight down, 36 inches of it in 72 hours." Seekings is exaggerating—it was more like twenty inches—but the storm was a monster, and it combined with high tides and onshore winds to produce significant flooding across Charleston.[20] "The flooding is unprecedented and historical," Dr. Marshall Shepherd, a meteorologist and director of the atmospheric sciences program at the University of Georgia, told the Associated Press. "You could have brought a tugboat down the street," says Seekings. Riley told the press that he'd never seen flooding as bad in his forty years as mayor. In the record books, the storm is known as the Historic Flooding of Oct. 1–5, 2015. Gov. Nikki Haley said parts of South Carolina were deluged with rainfall that would be expected to occur once in 1,000 years, and urged everyone to stay inside.[21]

A year later, Hurricane Matthew, a Category 1 hurricane with 75 mph winds, traveled thirty miles offshore from Charleston and made landfall near McClellanville.[22] It also produced astounding flooding in Charleston.

One year after that, Hurricane Irma weakened to a tropical storm before generating the third highest ever peak storm tide in Charleston Harbor. Then came Tropical Storms Michael and Florence (2018), severe coastal flooding in November 2018, and Hurricane Dorian (2019). Michael, Florence, and Dorian veered away from Charleston, but not before they triggered mandatory evacuations and enormous economic losses in the region.

These storms, and particularly the three supposedly once-in-1,000-year storm events, one after the other in 2015, 2016, and 2017, rocked Charleston. Tibbetts says, "I had been yelling about this to people for years and years, but it deeply shocked me that the weak side of a hurricane [2016's Hurricane Matthew] could create that kind of flooding downtown. I thought that it would take a direct hit." He was also "surprised" by the 2015 storm, which he called a "super flooding event." Before these storms, his take on the situation was, he says, "That the flooding was [a] nuisance and the city was working on it. And it was a terrible hassle for the people living downtown and commuters." He continues, "It was a nuisance, but it just seemed something that the city was reacting slowly to, but wasn't unmanageable." Following the storms, "It seems unmanageable now."[23]

◆

John Tecklenburg came into office in January 2016 thinking that his major issue was going to be traffic congestion. He had devoted a good portion of his inauguration speech to praising Joe Riley (the "best Mayor in America," maybe even "the whole world").[24] Then, in his words, "a storm or two coming along" forced him to focus on the reality of sea level rise.

Tecklenburg is the mild-mannered, affable son of two formidable parents, Esther and Henry Tecklenburg. Both were civic stars in Charleston and the state, Henry as a successful developer and businessman who had chaired the State Ports Authority, and Esther as a city councilmember in the 1980s with Riley. Henry died suddenly at sixty-five in 1993, on the day he was going to accept an appointment in the Clinton Administration as an Undersecretary of the US Department of Commerce.[25] The confident, loud-voiced Henry, the power broker, was the political mastermind behind Ernest F. "Fritz" Hollings's successful career as one of South Carolina's senators, which eventually lasted for thirty-six years. Sen. Hollings described Henry Tecklenburg after his death as a "one-man kitchen cabinet to me and other prominent Democrats" in South Carolina.[26] Henry Tecklenburg had also been a successful businessman, running the Shell Oil distributorship his father-in-law had founded for decades.

John Tecklenburg, in appearance a softer-faced man than his father and a person that no one would describe as a power broker, was also a businessman before going into public service. He took over the family oil distribution business in 1980 and ran it until 1995, when he sold it. He was a commercial real estate agent, and he built and ran a general store on Daniel Island. His operational experience with politics before running for mayor in 2015 was under Mayor Riley, for whom he served as Charleston's director of economic development in the 1990s as the city's extraordinary growth marched along.

Tecklenburg is not an unintelligent man, but there is something performative about him. This quality is hard to put your finger on. It is as if he is constantly *playing the role* of mayor, his hands splayed out in planned, beseeching gestures, all the fingers moving together in a flipper-like motion, as his mild tenor voice calls for others' attention. At the drop of a hat on almost any occasion if there is a piano nearby, he will sit himself at its keyboard and roll through a spiritual or a soft rock anthem or a jazz tune, as if the music could do the forceful talking for him. He is a sincerely religious man; he said in January 2019 that he had been "called to run for Mayor of Charleston," and that rather than this being a "calling to run to follow somebody who had been there for forty years," he had been "called to share God's message of love and forgiveness" for Charleston's dark history of slavery and racism. He believes, he said, his voice breaking, "Charleston was called to a special place to be able to share that message."[27]

The mayor does not appear to have the gift of making other people work with him, at the same time that he does seem to have some mild ethical weaknesses. Tecklenburg borrowed $80,000 from the accounts of an elderly woman for whom he was acting as a conservator. He paid the money back with interest by the time the matter was brought to

Charleston County Probate Judge Irvin Condon's attention in May 2018. Condon removed Tecklenburg as conservator, saying, "This court cannot start a precedent of allowing conservators who broke the law by self-dealing, make risky investments, who obscure transactions, who disclose publicly private information, who misstate what had transpired, to stay on as conservator."[28] In 2019, an audit found that Tecklenburg had used his city credit card to pay for travel for his wife (later reimbursed), to increase funding to two nonprofits his wife is involved in, and other things—small stuff, but continual.[29] On the whole, though, the general view of Tecklenburg is that he is not a bad or selfish man. Far from it. He is a genuinely earnest fellow. But he is not a strong leader; he is no Joe Riley.

Structurally, Tecklenburg came into office with real leverage: Charleston, unlike the many American cities that hire professional city managers to run things, operates within a "strong mayor" context. The fulltime mayor of Charleston has the power, on paper, to hire staff and set budgets. Mayor Riley's practice had been to provide the council with a single budget figure for each department of the government—"here's the total budget amount"—for up-or-down approval, no editing, no detail, and the answer had always been "Yes." Riley had been the model "strong" mayor, in action as well as on paper, with complete control over City Council and every detail of city operations by the end of his many decades in office. He had known what every vote tally would be before the vote was taken. Tecklenburg has not been able to wield those structural powers effectively following Riley's departure. In fact, the City Council in 2018 managed to claw control over the budget entirely away from him, and Tecklenburg, always one to want to achieve consensus, let this happen. An ad hoc committee now goes line by line through each department budget, calling in city staff to explain what is going on, asking about each expenditure. His first term in office was rough: several members of City Council ran against him and were openly impolite to him during meetings.

In January 2018, Tecklenburg went to the Winter Meeting of the United States Conference of Mayors in Washington, DC. He met the Dutch ambassador, Hendrik Schuwer, over what he coyly calls "a couple of adult beverages."[30] Tecklenburg knew that leading Dutch water engineers had gone to New Orleans, Norfolk, Virginia, and New York after Hurricane Sandy for what were called "Dutch Dialogues," brainstorming sessions designed to introduce American cities to Dutch water expertise.[31] He invited Ambassador Schuwer to come to Charleston to facilitate a similar engagement. Succeeding with this invitation, he said, "reminded me of my dad. He had a very large personality, much larger than mine, but I got a little piece of it."[32] Henry Tecklenburg, advisor to scores of South Carolina politicians and swashbuckling utility owner, evidently still had a grip on his son's imagination.

A top-flight group of Dutch landscape architects and engineers trooped around the city during July 2019. Tecklenburg played the piano and sang for them at a reception in a downtown gallery. His choice of entertainment had possibly been intentionally ironic, although he is not an ironic man: the mournful Randy Newman ballad "Louisiana 1927." It's about the colossal devastation caused by the Mississippi River flood of 1927, and the sentiment that the North (and all of government, really) didn't care about the people whose lives were destroyed ("Loo-eez-ee-ann-a, they're tryin' to wash us away"). It's a song that became an anthem in New Orleans following Katrina. Tecklenburg sang with emotional gusto and clearly enjoyed the polite applause that followed.[33]

At the closing session where the Dutch experts made the recommendations described in Chapter 2, Mayor Tecklenburg had the last word. He was vaguely optimistic. He had worn a brightly colored Van Gogh tie in honor of the Dutch engineers in attendance. He said he had to admit, "Just a few years ago, with storm after storm, I was feeling like, where are we going to go with all this?" But now, with all these people in the room together, he saw "real hope for the future of Charleston." It was as if, to him, the mere presence of a crowd was enough to make progress inevitable. He cracked Southern-wise, "Nothing ain't gonna happen. Somethin' is going to happen." But it wasn't clear what would actually be done to protect Charleston's residents. "We see the light at the end of the tunnel. God bless you," the mayor concluded, smiling. Perhaps Providence would do the job.

Rev. Joe Darby thinks John Tecklenburg is a decent guy. "Sometimes too decent," says Darby. "He got tickled with me once," says Darby, "because I told him, after five or six months of witnessing his extreme decency, that he needed to change his ways." Darby continued: "Number One, the mayor needs to appear to be an SOB sometimes. That comes with the territory of being mayor. He shouldn't please everybody." And, Darby had said to him, "Number Two, every time you make a public appearance, you ain't got to play the piano. We all know you can play the piano." Tecklenburg plays "way more than he should," in Darby's view.[34]

◆

Tecklenburg's time in office has been punctuated by the introduction of a number of plans and processes aimed at addressing Charleston's flooding problems. Luckily for him, and for the city's residents and visitors, no hurricane has directly hit Charleston so far during his mayoralty. There have been some near misses: Torrential flooding brought the city to its knees right at Christmas in 2019, Category 1 Hurricane Isaias skirted Charleston just offshore in August 2020, flash flooding and Tropical Storm Elsa hit downtown Charleston in June and July 2021, respectively, and Hurricane Ian made landfall just north of Charleston in September 2022.

The planning process that has recently grabbed most of the city's attention was introduced by the Army Corps of Engineers in October 2018. The Army Corps proposed to foot the bill for a three-year, $3 million Coastal Flood Risk Management Study.[35] As of late-2022, that study is still ongoing. The basic idea, if Congress goes along with the proposal, is that over thirty or forty years the Army Corps will build a wall around the peninsula of Charleston. Applicable law allows the Corps to build protections only against catastrophic hurricane surges—not floods caused by rising tides or punishing rainstorms or rising groundwaters. The wall would be twelve feet high, made of concrete, and interrupted by an elaborate network of floodgates.[36] It's a competitive process to get funding for Army Corps projects, and Charleston's leaders have said they hope the city's high "benefit-cost ratio" will make the wall attractive to Congress: the Corps is supposed to protect high-value commercial and historic areas from storm surge, and has asserted that this ratio is "11:3" for Charleston—Dale Morris, the city's Chief Resilience Officer, and a former employee of the Dutch embassy, says "the benefit cost ratio of the Charleston peninsula project is the highest of its kind in the nation"—a very confident number, given all the indeterminacy necessarily involved.[37]

Congress would cover 65 percent of the cost of planning and building the wall, while the city would be on the hook for the remaining 35 percent.[38] If the city wanted to make any changes to the Army Corp's eventual plans, for example, to tie them into the peninsula's drainage system or to be more aesthetically pleasing, the city would have to pay for those changes itself. Just the peninsula, and not the rest of the city of Charleston, would be addressed by this wall, because only there is the property valuable enough to make the project worthwhile. Not even all of the peninsula would be covered by the wall, which will not reach two areas primarily inhabited by hundreds of Black Charlestonians: Rosemont and the Bridgeview Apartments, in the current Neck area (discussed in Chapter 6). There, the properties are not valuable enough to merit protection by the wall; in the Corps's terms, the benefits they would get from storm damage reduction will not be greater than the cost of the project. Those properties will be bought out or perhaps raised instead.[39]

So far, the Corps is estimating that planning and building the wall will cost $1.1 billion. Charleston's share would be $385 million.[40] The current plan is for the wall to sit on land, walling in the peninsula. It is far cheaper to build on land than in the marsh.

The wall idea has been assailed on several different grounds. It won't be high enough to protect against the walls of water that will sweep ashore during the most damaging storms.[41] It won't stretch all the way around to the East Side for decades.[42] It won't reach those Black settlements on the Neck. And it won't do anything about the nuisance flooding, rainstorms, and rising groundwaters that are rapidly getting worse. To cover the city's share, hundreds of millions of dollars would somehow need to be found by a city whose entire annual budget is about $200 million—all of which is routinely allocated and spent each year.[43] And the wall will be ugly and will block any view of the water.

But at least the city is planning for the peninsula. The rest of the city of Charleston—almost 90 percent of its residents—will not be protected by the Army Corps wall, if and when it is ever built and whatever storm surge harm it manages to deflect.[44]

In late May 2022, NOAA predicted that for the seventh year in a row the coming hurricane season would probably feature above-normal activity in the form of fourteen to twenty-one named storms, six to ten hurricanes, and three to six major hurricanes.[45] As of the preparation of this text, the same number of debilitating floods have arrived so far in 2022 as in 2019, which was the record high flooding year in Charleston.

◆

Prof. Norman Levine of the department of geology and environmental geosciences of the College of Charleston is a round, bearded, balding man in his late fifties with a friendly, open face. Levine is South Carolina's earthquake and preparedness director as well as the editor of one of the state's geology journals. He wears wire-rimmed glasses and polo shirts, with cardigans added during the mild South Carolina winter. On the shelves of his small office, stacks of premade supermarket lunches are perched in front of piles of papers and books, and more heaps of papers have found their way onto the floor. There's a small whiteboard with student names and projects on it; a caricature of Levine has been tacked to a nearby wall showing him smiling widely, surrounded by piles of paper, with a Big Gulp tumbler close at hand. He has an easygoing manner but at the same time seems wildly busy and distracted. Students stick their heads into his office frequently ("Can I borrow a mouse from someone?" "People are looking for you, but you look busy.").[46] He is fiercely proud of the work he has done and has a healthy self-regard in general. But he has frequent difficulty actually pulling up the data or slide he wants to show to illustrate a point he's making: so many slides, and so much data, flow through his office. His underresourced Lowcountry Hazards Center is a hub of research and reporting, much of it necessarily driven by student work, about all the risks faced by the Charleston region; his office is also the Santee Cooper Geographic Information System (GIS) and Remote Sensing Center.

In May 2019, at a preparation meeting held for the Dutch landscape architects who would be making recommendations to the city of Charleston, Levine stood in a conference room that had once been part of a cigar factory on the East Side of the peninsula of Charleston. The room was packed with Dutch professionals, Charleston city officials, and developers, and Levine was invited to give a presentation about Charleston's geomorphology and water flows. There were very few Black people in the room. Levine put on a rumpled blazer and serious shoes for the occasion.

"Well," he had said towards the end of his presentation, "now sea levels are coming back, folks, and so these features," the old waterways and marshes, "are reconnecting with the water." The Atlantic would eventually become indistinguishable from the Charleston region; the situation, he said, was different and worse even than in Norfolk, Virginia. The room fell silent. Everyone listened intently to him. He seemed to enjoy casting terror.

Levine said that day in 2019 that given the pace at which sunny day flooding was increasing in Charleston, after 2032, Charleston would lose the ability to make changes that would keep life going in the region. Following that year, the frequency of flooding that would affect businesses and roads would leap up suddenly, in a hockey stick of accelerating activity. By 2050, there would be 319 days a year of flooding, up from 38 in 2020 and 240 in 2040. Levine emphasized that 2032 was the inflection point, the moment right before the slope of change would become unmanageable. "We have to work to live with water, not just engineer against it," he concluded. "We have to look at our options." Then he walked to the side of the room.

◆

Not only were there very few Black Charlestonians in the room for Levine's presentation, there were also very few present for the final recommendations from the Dutch team two months later. Those recommendations included a dramatic and transformative reworking of the East Side neighborhood to accommodate water, including moving public housing, building greenways, raising roadways, increasing the availability of permeable surface areas, and bringing old creeks to the surface as part of an overall stormwater storage strategy.

Although he is a prominent Black leader and although the NAACP office in Charleston was located on the East Side in 2019, Reverend Darby was not consulted during the Dutch Dialogues. The public meetings held as part of the Dialogues attracted no more than a handful of African Americans. The strong recommendations made by the Dutch about the East Side in their initial reports were later watered down by City Hall before becoming public, and there was little real outreach. "There should be some significant Black participation in that because some of those flooding problems really hit the Black community hard," Darby said about the Dutch Dialogues.[47] He was disappointed in the city's efforts to work with Black residents. "If you look at executive staff, it's still not reflective of the demographics of the city at all," said Darby.[48] Darby hopes the city will get its act together before the high waters come that will flood the city most days. That time is coming. The city hasn't been tested yet.

◆

The city was tested in a different way in late May 2020. The news of the murder of George Floyd on May 25 came on the heels of the killings of Ahmaud Arbery (in coastal Georgia) and Breonna Taylor, triggering protests nationwide. Charleston was no exception. Protests were planned for May 30, a Saturday. Michelle Mapp's two teenagers, Seth and Jordan, wanted to join the protest—just as Darby had wanted to join in during the 1960s.

Mapp's husband Marquette laid down the law. "Not going to happen," he said to Seth and Jordan, firmly. "You have got to figure out other ways to participate." Both the kids were upset about that ruling, and it led to a lot of conversations that weren't quiet. "It is safety," Marquette said to them all. He told them, "The City of Charleston police have riot gear. Things can get out of hand quickly. And they're likely to let loose with some response that is way out of proportion." The Charleston police, who accounted for fully a quarter of the city's overall budget, had a reputation for disproportionately interfering with young Black people using trumped-up excuses.[49] Driving while Black and dancing while Black were both risky pursuits in Charleston, and it was obvious to Mapp and her husband that protesting while Black would be a problem.

Jordan and Seth kept it up, arguing that they wanted to be there. "It's right now, it's happening," they said. Marquette was unmoved. "Right now, I'm responsible for you," he told them. "Seth, when you're on campus next year, and Jordan, when you go off to college, if you want to get out and protest, you can go right ahead. And I can only hope and pray that I've instilled in you what you need and that you're going to act in a sensible manner." But not now, he made clear, not while they were under his roof. That got their attention; Michelle saw respect in Seth's and Jordan's faces. He was worried something would happen to them.

On Saturday night, May 30, they all watched the local news together, tracking protests in downtown Charleston. A number of the protesters seemed to be white. There were a lot of Black protesters, too, but Mapp knew that many Black parents of young adults had acted to protect their kids from being harmed or unfairly arrested by making them stay home. The protests went on for hours in a mostly peaceful way, with marchers gathering around the Confederate Defenders of Charleston monument at the tip of the peninsula and then listening to speeches in the City Market. They heard speaker after speaker talk about the need for structural changes in America and in Charleston. But after dark tensions rose: hundreds of people surged from the City

Market into upper King Street, and began to break windows and set dozens of fires, damaging about 135 businesses.[50]

Astonished tourists were hustled away from their dinners by restaurant staff members as the chaos and destruction outside accelerated. Anger that was spilling across the country over the callous killing of Black people by police had finally made it to Charleston, where it was accompanied by the local pain of decades of unfair treatment. It was the worst melee the city had seen in more than a hundred years,[51] and most of the people that were arrested that night were from the Charleston region. By 3 A.M., it was over.

Mapp watched those scenes play out without surprise. "Of course there were riots in Charleston," she says. "All the issues we're grappling with as a country, in terms of race, have their roots here." The slave trade, the slave codes, the policing that was set up to control the slaves, all of that came from Charleston. The city was still a profoundly unfair place, and the "Kumbaya" moments that had unfurled in Charleston following Walter Scott's murder and the Mother Emanuel Church massacre had been, in some sense, coverups. The continual pain and hurt and intimidation evoked by the symbols of the confederacy that were still present—she remembered hearing about the vote in 2015 to take the Confederate flag down from the state capitol when her family was driving from Atlanta back to Charleston, and crying in disbelief—that always-present threat of violence made talk about moving forward on policies that would help Black people in Charleston lead thriving lives meaningless. As of the time of the protests, John C. Calhoun, the voice of slavery, was still towering 115 feet up in the air in Marion Square, and Black people had hated that statue for a hundred years because they knew it stood for intimidation. Of course there had been riots in Charleston. Mapp was relieved that Jordan and Seth had not been involved; that relief was now mixed with a small hope that Charleston might finally be waking up.

Other cities had already awakened and seemed to believe in the humanity of people of different races. Mapp felt mostly fairness in Atlanta before they moved back to Charleston in November 2001. But she wouldn't get lost in the negativity; there was a lot of work to be done in Charleston, and it was so important not to give up. "Giving up on South Carolina and moving away would be," she says, "giving up on America." There needed to be a representation of what could be, right here in Charleston. Maybe the riots would nudge the city in that direction.

◆

The violence associated with the May 30–31 riot, unprecedented in Charleston's modern history, was extraordinarily jarring to those white people who hadn't been paying attention to the cruelty of life for Black Charlestonians or who had come to believe that Charleston had achieved some kind of post-racial serenity best expressed by high-quality food and well-tended houses. It resulted in significant damage to a number of King Street restaurants and shops. An official report later determined that the police had been dramatically underprepared and outmaneuvered and had used gas and pepper balls on protesters.

The next day, the head of the Charleston tourist association, Helen Hill, urged member businesses to put a good spin on things. She wanted to ensure that the tourists kept visiting, and that would require that downtown kept its golden image: "Please remind your staff who handles social media to post only uplifting and positive content. Remember our audience is bigger than local!"[52] she said. A columnist in the *Post and Courier*, Edward Gilbreth, declared that he was shocked by the violence: "After all, we [whites and Blacks in Charleston] know each other—at least those of us who have been around here for a while.

We love each other, and many local families have interconnections that go back generations, if not centuries. . . . [M]any Charlestonians pride themselves on a sense of meaningful progress in recent decades and to some degree a shared understanding of things. . . . In Charleston, though, we get along well and have amazed the rest of the country and the world by doing so . . ." Gilbreth asked, "[T]o what extent was it instigated and agitated by fringe left and anarchist groups such as Antifa?"[53]

This was Old Charleston in written form, the blind and deaf expression of a benevolent relationship that had never existed in reality. Mapp's pastor at the Charity Missionary Baptist Church in North Charleston, Reverend Nelson B. Rivers III, who grew up on Rutledge Avenue on the peninsula, found the idea that outsiders had to be behind the protests insulting: "This notion that we've gotten a special bunch of Black folk here who won't protest is part of this denial by the white majority that hearkens back to the 'good negro' on the plantation."[54]

The drumbeat of tension and despair in Charleston was beginning to sound more like large sets of cymbals clashing to anyone who cared to listen. Something was brewing in Charleston: A large Black Lives Matter sign went up on June 5 right next to I-26, the major Charleston freeway that brings tourists directly from the airport in North Charleston to the lower peninsula on a concrete ribbon set far above the worn houses of Black residents. The city imposed a curfew for the peninsula for that same night, to protect the tourist district.

Turmoil and anguish over George Floyd's death roiled Rev. Darby's congregation, and he could sense that people were wanting to become politically engaged and active. "That was good," Darby says. "That needed to happen." The Black church might have lost some influence, he had to admit, but it was still a rallying point, still a place of safety and security. "The civil rights movement of the '50s and '60s . . . was spearheaded by the Black church," he told the Associated Press a few months before the Charleston protests.[55] "Now you've got Black Voters Matter and Black Lives Matter. They don't have that same connection to the church, because it's not seen as a spiritual battle as much as it is a social-political battle." Still, advocacy had to be part of the church's role; not everyone got that, but Darby knew that the hard-earned progress of the Black residents of Charleston would be lost if the church didn't stay relevant and keep fighting.[56] Entrenched and powerful entities didn't change without a push.

◆

Mika Gadsden, speaking on her twitch.tv broadcast, pulled the threads together a year later about Charleston. She sharply criticized the benevolent tourist narrative surrounding the city and, in particular, the powerful Charleston Area Convention and Visitor Bureau's failure to acknowledge the daily pain experienced by the city's Black residents.[57] "No, it's [Charleston is] home to citizens, to real families," she said on her livestream broadcast. "The laws and the policies around me need to act like this is more than just fucking Disney World."[58] She thought the city should be figuring out *why* there was violence on King Street. "And I would argue," she said, "much like some of the environmental issues that Charleston's contending with, I would argue that when you push people and forces so far, that there's a reverse reaction." King Street and Charleston's wild gentrification had not been hospitable to Black people, and the sense that Black people were stuck in low-wage jobs, didn't have opportunities, weren't heard, didn't have places to go where they felt safe or appreciated, and didn't own the businesses in Charleston that could take advantage of the city's wealth and billion dollar tourism industry, all of that had been bubbling below the surface and was now erupting in unrest. "I know y'all want to make it an antebellum Disney World," she said on her livestream broadcast. "I know y'all do."

Then she continued: "I know it's about to be SeaWorld, right? Because y'all not really doing what y'all need to do with climate change, but I know y'all want to make it the happiest place on earth, but this is a real ass city. We're real ass people."[59]

5

The Lower Peninsula and Jacob Lindsey

The Charleston peninsula is like a tongue. There is a line across the tip of that tongue, Broad Street. "South of Broad" is the shorthand for the lower peninsula's lofty antebellum mansions and their now-very-expensive owners.

Map of the lower peninsula.

There is another line nine blocks north of Broad and parallel to it, Calhoun Street. (In the 1970s, north of Calhoun was considered "the Black neighborhood.") The main shopping street, King Street, extends north from Broad in a perpendicular line. On the east side of the lower peninsula, there is a flat-topped wall about 1,400 feet long called the High Battery that tourists can walk on; it runs south to a Confederate memorial at White Point Garden where there are steps that go down to street level. Those steps connect to a lower wall, the Low Battery, that marches along the foot of the South of Broad neighborhood and up the Ashley River side of the peninsula.

The imagined Old South of the first half of the nineteenth century in Charleston has its ruling class, the planters, who built great houses South of Broad. Today's passersby gaze at these mansions and picture silver and carriages, courtliness, and refined hospitality, lit by candles and swept by refreshing seaside breezes. The more romantic of the tourists may people these houses and their lush gardens with their aristocratic owners, arriving in January for the social season from their plantations upriver, readying themselves for a whirl of horse races and balls. Exclusivity, dissolute behavior, wealth, and old names—Alston, Manigault, Rutledge, Vanderhorst, and even the fictive Rhett Butler—all of this is catnip for white visitors, and has been for more than a century. It is a place of eighteenth century urbanity. Local developer Vince Graham talks about the original "walled city" of the lower peninsula, the oldest neighborhood in the Carolinas, whose sixty-two acres today include "760 homes of all kind of different shapes and sizes," five churches, City Hall, and beautiful streets. "That was the DNA of wonderful urbanism," says Graham.[1]

What preserved the lovely South of Broad houses in Charleston was economic failure and a series of calamities. Following the planters' era, Charleston never made money again, until recently. There was either an economic panic or the Civil War, or a world war, or a financial collapse, or a great fire, or a great earthquake in 1886, some disaster showing up every decade or so. The city got thrown back on its heels over and over again, and never had a chance to blossom or have great prosperity of its own. The preoccupation of the Charlestonians that lived South of Broad, many of them very proud of their genealogy, became fixing up their old houses. By the 1930s, Charleston had become a decaying town, the place DuBose Heyward describes in his book *Porgy and Bess*, with a fairly integrated downtown—integrated not because of some transcendent ideal of racial equality, but because everyone was broke.

White women living South of Broad became desperate to shore up their ancestors' special role in their dying city. When the owner of the John Stuart House at the corner of Orange and Tradd Street sold off the drawing rooms of his house to northerners to raise money in the 1930s, the old ladies were horrified. This was the house, these were the very rooms, from which a Revolutionary War hero, Francis Marion (the "Swamp Fox"), had jumped out the window and broken his leg![2] These women basically invented the historic preservation movement in America, declared the whole downtown a historic site, and commissioned zoning and marketing plans aimed at keeping their perceived world, leaving Black Charlestonians in concentrated neighborhoods.

Not all the houses South of Broad are mansions. Joe Riley grew up in a modest place on Gibbes Street in the 1950s. By that time, Charleston was in decline and some of those mansions had been divided into apartments. The Rileys lived on the first floor of that Gibbes Street house and rented out the second until the family moved to a bigger house on Murray Boulevard when Riley was twelve.[3] He told his biographer, Brian Hicks, that he remembered running through the streets South of Broad with his friends; those streets were Riley's playground.[4] A white child in the 1970s would have had the same experience, riding bikes freely through the streets. There would have been lots of kids running around. There were no restaurants to speak of then, except maybe a Hardee's or a Burger King. The one exotic foreign restaurant in the city at the time, LaBrasca's Pizzeria, was way uptown on King Street near Hampton Park and served spaghetti as well as the first slices of pizza ever sold in Charleston.[5]

That child of the 1970s would have seen perhaps five flood days a year. On those days, streets of the lower peninsula would fill with water, and the child might get the chance to sail in a little dinghy up Colonial Street on the lower west side of the peninsula right into Colonial Lake. It was a joke; it was fun; it was a rare treat.

Western edge of lower Charleston peninsula,
including Colonial Lake.

By 2019, after Charleston had become the fully gentrified, hyper-expensive, tourist-pummeled place it is today, South of Broad was facing eighty-nine days of flooding a year. The basements and lower floors of the antebellum Georgian and Federalist homes, for which their owners had paid enormous sums as Charleston's real estate market boomed, were getting wet and damaged. Rot and mold marched through those houses. South of Broad had changed completely. John Tibbetts moved to the peninsula in 1992. "When we moved here, there were kids playing in the street, in the neighborhood South of Broad, and you just don't see it [now]," he says. "And people who live there seem to be mostly people who live there temporarily, part-time. Or they're older people from New York who can afford to go and live there. And so that sense of a coherent community, it changed slowly over time. Charlestonians don't live there."[6]

◆

From its beginning as an incorporated city in 1783, Charleston largely relied on private owners to fill, drain, and level their own lots. But because the city has always focused its spending on areas where it felt the costs would be worthwhile, South of Broad, and in particular the waterfront area now called the Battery—so ideal for strolls and vistas—has been an exception. As the health risks of using trash and organic waste for fill materials became more widely known, for example, the city used higher-cost, inorganic materials (sand, shells, ballast stones) to fill land near today's Battery.[7] The High Battery was built (essentially out in the Cooper River at the time) at great expense between 1808 and 1818 out of granite blocks brought from the north.[8] Charles Parker, the same city engineer who came up with the brick tunnel drainage system in the 1850s, successfully encouraged the city to raise the height of the Battery walls in 1855.[9] Lower-class areas up the east side of the peninsula got garbage for fill, and workers lived next to noxious tanneries and mills on the north west side of the peninsula.

Today's City Council is repeating this pattern, acting to protect the area South of Broad while doing little for poorer, Blacker areas elsewhere.

Murray Boulevard, Joe Riley's teenage Charleston street, runs along the foot of the peninsula beside the Ashley River. It was built on top of mudflats by the city at the beginning of the twentieth century and protected by a concrete seawall (built on a timber deck supported by timber pilings) now called the Low Battery.[10] The landfill placed behind the protection of the Low Battery between 1909 and 1919 allowed the city to divide the mudflats into 191 residential lots. The Depression ended the project at Tradd Street.

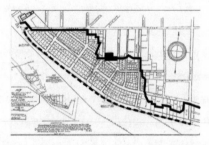

Map with overlays by the City of Charleston; black line shows reclamation of 47 acres and division into 191 lots; dotted line is the Low Battery.[11]

Eventually, under the onslaught of storms and rain, the concrete of the Low Battery began to crack and erode. In 2013, the city spent more than $3 million improving the "turn" area that connects the High and Low Batteries. But when Tropical Storm Irma crashed over the walls in September 2017 bringing the Atlantic into White Point Park, it became clear that more shoring up was needed.

Photo of Low Battery flooding. Photo taken September 11, 2017.

In 2019, the city embarked on a $70 million project to put the wall on piles driven seventy feet down into the firmer Cooper Marl, raise the 4,800 foot long Low Battery by two feet, to essentially the height of the High Battery, install larger storm drains and outfalls for water to encourage it to exit to the Ashley River, add a promenade lined by a granite curb to its inside flank, and build new sidewalks and "parklets" next to the repaved boulevard.

As Charleston historian Nic Butler puts it, "Both the High and Low Battery seawalls were designed to create high land out of underwater real estate."[12] The new Low Battery now looks terrific, crisp and clean, and will drain and protect the mostly white residential area behind it much more effectively than the old one did—at least for a while. Some South of Broad homeowners are taking matters into their own hands, paying to elevate solid masonry houses, lifting *whole houses* up out of the pluff mud on which they are sitting and dropping them back on top of hundreds of piers anchoring the houses in the Cooper Marl 80 feet below.[13] (They have persuaded the historic preservation people, still very powerful in Charleston, to allow them to take these steps.) What ordinary person could afford this?

In contrast, Latonya Gamble, the president of the Eastside Community Development Corporation, and a Black woman who grew up in East Side public housing that was built on top of the city dump, wants her community to be included in the city's plans and walls. She told Daron Calhoun of the Avery Research Center in May 2021, "our people have been dealing with the flooding [on the East Side] for as long as I can remember." The problem was particularly awful for the poorer people living in public housing, Gamble said. "I can't tell you how many times they have to start over, because there's mold in the house or it flooded and they have to throw away their stuff," she said. Gamble wants the East Side's concerns to be focused on by the city. "And as we see them make plans all over the city for walls and other areas, we just want to be included in that plan to make sure that you're not leaving us out of that plan," she says.[14]

One of the speakers during the late June 2020 City Council meeting at which the vote was taken to remove the Calhoun monument, a white woman named Audra Rhodes, spoke in support of having the statue come down. Then she continued: "I want to remind us that narratives are also used as a tool of distraction. For example, right now, what we should be talking about as Charlestonians is properly funding Black schools in Charleston. Why the most vulnerable communities [that] are seeing rising sea levels and the rising level of the flooding in Charleston are typically Black neighborhoods and why their—" Rhodes's time was up; her microphone was cut off. But she had landed on a crucial weakness in the city: symbols seem to get more time than action. Mayor Tecklenburg said, "Thank you, Ms. Rhodes. We appreciate that. We got your drift."

◆

Meet someone who used to live on the lower peninsula: Jacob Lindsey, Charleston's city planner from 2015 to 2020. Lindsey, a thin, fast-talking, bearded white man in his forties, is as taken with the still charm of the downtown peninsula as anyone: the massive white steeple of St. Michael's at the corner of Meeting and Broad soaring above the stately mansions; the White Point Garden, with its walkways, gazebo, and thick old oak trees; the pleasant evening hum of the bar at Husk that he passed each evening on his quick walk home from his office in the dim light to the corner of King and Queen Street. When he was the city planner, he lived on the lower peninsula so that he and his wife Martina, and their baby girl Nora, could feel like they were in a city and walk everywhere they needed to go. Their tiny house downtown was all they could afford on the extraordinarily expensive Charleston peninsula. The supermarket, it turned out, was too far away to walk to, and they were surrounded by tourists most of the time.

Lindsey was brought to Charleston by Mayor Riley in 2012 as the thirty-four-year-old director of the city's Civic Design Center, an organization that served as an interface among city-led projects, private developers, and nonprofits. Later Mayor Riley had made him an "Urban Design Lead" (a vague title with uncertain responsibilities) for the city, and then, right before the 2015 election that had brought Tecklenburg in as Riley's successor, the outgoing mayor had appointed Lindsey the city's Planning Director. Riley had wanted to avoid abuse by any very strong leader of the structural powers that Riley had invested in the mayor's office over the course of his forty years in that role, and had seen Lindsey as a good steward who would have a steady, moderating hand, whoever the new mayor would be. "The Riley Way," Lindsey says, "was a very much command and control government. It was very successful in that regard. The benevolent dictator gets a lot of things done." Lindsey survived the transition from Riley to Tecklenburg and spent endless hours at the job, wrangling and working and talking away; he never stopped thinking about how to improve Charleston, never unplugged.

Lindsey thought the effort was well worth it. He had initially found the city inspiring, an extraordinary urban environment that he had felt lucky to live in. The cultural renaissance of Charleston under Riley, led by a booming hospitality industry, had given the city an astonishing Condé Nast label: "The #1 City in the World to Visit." He saw Charleston playing at the same level as other mid-size global cities like Zurich, Melbourne, or Copenhagen, and the idea of making the city he lived in even better appealed to him. Mayor Riley, America's Favorite Mayor, had inspired him, too; he shared his sense of the importance of design, and had been a mentor and a friend to him.[15]

The young Lindsey, as an intern and then a newly minted college graduate, had bubbled continually, speaking at a breakneck pace, making connections among the possibilities of everything. Why cars, why not streetcars everywhere? Why not prioritize bicycles? Why not make it very difficult for cars to travel on King Street? Make it a pedestrian haven instead! Why not ensure that storefronts were narrow and rents were low? Why not plan neighborhoods that were vibrant, walkable, and well-stocked with the retail and community elements everyone needed to live a good life? He had traveled widely, always with his sketchpad, studying European places like Paris, Zurich, and Copenhagen; he had been overwhelmed and delighted by the bicycling culture of Amsterdam and the infrastructure there that made that lifestyle possible.

The older Lindsey, the city planner, fully comprehended the extreme risks that the city faces in the form of extraordinarily rapidly advancing sea level rise and increasing wet blasts of heat.[16] He saw the gaps that are making things difficult for the city—its absence of leadership, the region's fractured governance, and the city's lack of funds—and understood that things were not going to get better any time soon. He was still capable of being wildly enthusiastic about the possibilities of cities, dropping New Urbanist names (designers interested in walkable neighborhoods and public transit) into his speeches. But in his role as city planner, Lindsey never let his guard down in public, never strayed into public negative talk about Charleston's future, and never talked about the possibility of disaster.

Life under Tecklenburg was different, although Lindsey was careful not to say exactly why. By 2020, Lindsey had become increasingly expressionless, navigating the endless meetings and glacial pace of Charleston's City Hall with pale, tightlipped politeness. One of his friends from college visited and laughed at him, saying Jacob was dying inside. He laughed along with his friend, but he remembered the moment.

In July 2020, midway through drafting Charleston's Comprehensive Plan that was due at the end of that year, Lindsey applied for a job as the city planner in Boulder, Colorado. By the end of October, Lindsey announced that he had accepted the planning job and would be moving in early November. This was a sudden and untimely departure from the city's perspective. Lindsey told the press that he found the decision to leave Charleston "gut-wrenching." At the same time, his father Ronny Lindsey, a tinkerer with bicycles and cars who still lives in Washington, Georgia, where Lindsey grew up, was "relieved." "Charleston's situation shocked him," Lindsey says. The city was so very vulnerable, so precarious. Ronny Lindsey was thrilled for his son that he was moving to Boulder, and very proud.

◆

Personnel come and go. Things keep changing in Charleston. A large private developer, Lowe, plans to transform seventy-four acres of the

state-owned port acreage on the Cooper River (the east side of the
lower peninsula, north of Broad but south of Calhoun) into a giant
residential complex.[17]

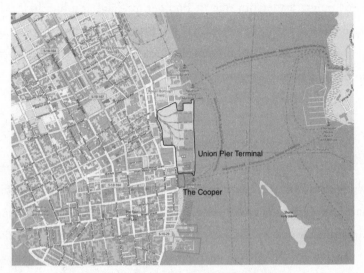

Map of Union Pier Terminal and The Cooper.

What's truly odd about the project, called the Union Pier
Redevelopment, is that the city is trumpeting it as a huge opportunity
at the same time that it is buying out frequently flooded houses in
the suburbs. With one hand, the city is encouraging and celebrating
building on land that once was indistinguishable from the Cooper
River—and may be again in a matter of decades. With the other hand,
the city is admitting that it allowed building in unsafe areas. Although
these actions seem contradictory, they are actually part of the city's
overall plan, such as it is, to survive into the future: The city hopes to
keep its property tax revenues growing steadily as it plans to somehow
build a wall around the lower peninsula that will protect the Union
Pier project and the highest-value properties in the tourist area against
storm surge, at great public expense. People in lower-value areas will
be left to their own devices or, at best, bought out at pennies on the

dollar. There is no plan to help all of Charleston's residents make the transition to a thriving future life in a dry place.

Jacob Lindsey's story is firmly intertwined with this narrative. He left his public leadership role in Boulder, managing a hundred other people, to return to Charleston after just thirteen months. Now Lindsey is wearing a different hat: he is working with Lowe to smooth the Union Pier permitting process with the city of Charleston.

◆

For all its hymns to the supremacy of private enterprise, for all the ways it crystallizes the ascendance of the private over the public, Charleston is home to a fully state-operated port. (Usually state ports authorities lease facilities to terminal operating companies that manage and run the port.)[18] This public operation was set up in order to avoid union labor when the State Ports Authority took over the port's operation from the city of Charleston in the 1940s.[19] That's why, in a city and a state that has historically resisted the idea of public education and public transit, a public authority wields such power in Charleston.[20]

Although most of the Union Pier acreage owned by the South Carolina Ports Authority—and therefore, nominally, by the public—is officially labeled wetlands, Lowe, the private developer that wants to buy the land, believes about twenty-five acres of it can potentially be developed.[21] Lowe is already building The Cooper, a six-story, luxury 225-room waterfront hotel with ground-floor retail and restaurant spaces next to those seventy acres, although it had to pause work for several months in 2021 because of what it described as a "piling issue."[22] Lowe now plans to create office, retail, residential, and commercial buildings that will be propped on the soft sand that had been plopped on top of filled waterfront marsh decades before to create Union Pier.[23]

The Union Pier Redevelopment Plan that Jacob Lindsey has been hired to shepherd, announced by the State Ports Authority in 2020, serves a number of interests. For the state, it is a well-timed bid to get out from under the risk of Union Pier losing value with the waters' rise as well as an opportunity to privatize a substantial public asset. The South Carolina Ports Authority (SCPA) is looking to make a handsome profit on the deal: "The values in the city have risen significantly since we first started thinking about it," Jim Newsome, then the South Carolina Port Authority's CEO, said in 2020. "So we think it's the right time. All the sort of components, all the pieces of the puzzle are sort of aligning where we can do this."[24] Real estate values, Newsome confirms, "probably changed the calculus" for the decision to sell off the property.[25] David Wren of the *Post and Courier* wrote in May 2022 that the Ports Authority would be making "tens or even hundreds of millions of dollars" on the deal.[26] For its part, the city is already imagining a "tremendous amount of economic value and housing and other things for the city," in the words of Chief Resilience Officer Dale Morris, that would come out of the redevelopment of Union Pier.[27]

The city has more focused reasons to support redevelopment of Union Pier. To get The Cooper done, the other project next to Union Pier, Lowe promised to pay $2.1 million for an additional pipe to drain water from thirty acres of downtown Charleston and carry it out to the Cooper River. The city's share of that pipe was $300,000. The city no doubt believes that it will get a similar deal out of the redevelopment of Union Pier. The SCPA doesn't pay taxes to the city; a new private owner of the property would. As another plus for both sides of the transaction, any incremental increases in property tax revenues experienced after the land was rezoned could be devoted in advance to the new roads and other pieces of infrastructure that the large parcel would require, rather than be made available to the city of Charleston as a whole.[28]

It's a win-win, according to CEO Newsome: "It opens up the entire eastern side of the waterfront to the people of South Carolina and Charleston," Newsome told the *Post and Courier* in May 2022. "We really would like to move this along, and we believe the city will be quite cooperative on that front. I think our interests are aligned to get it done as quickly as we can."[29] Newsome sounds confident. It is now Jacob Lindsey's responsibility to get the Union Pier project done.

After his abbreviated stint as Boulder's city planner, Lindsey was hired in November 2021 as a Lowe Vice President, responsible for "development entitlement and master planning activities,"[30] meaning he would guide the project through the layers of city processes necessary to get the huge parcel of made land rezoned from its permitted use for industrial, one-story warehouses to far higher density, far taller buildings, and residential buildings as quickly as possible.

It isn't just rezoning that is needed; Union Pier was an industrial area as well as a dumping ground for waste of all kinds. Old landfills polluted the waters nearby with a colorful variety of chemicals. Untreated sewage had been pumped into the Cooper River until the early 1970s.[31] Businesses operating on the Union Pier site before 1981 had "stored and transported fuel and chemicals that could have seeped into the soil and groundwater," there were at least five above-ground gas storage tanks on the property,[32] and coal tar produced by an old gas works, a coal processing plant that had been in business from 1855 to 1957 along the Cooper River, are still being monitored.[33] Lindsey is in charge of getting this mess cleaned up.

Once Lowe finishes building its multiuse commercial development on top of Union Pier, the buildings will then, with any luck, be promptly sold off. Developers' loans are paid off on a much shorter timescale than a typical thirty-year home mortgage.[34] It is a game of musical chairs in which some sap, someone who has fallen in love with Charleston and who doesn't believe the waters will be rising quickly, will be stuck owning highly risky waterfront property that may cease to exist. That someone will be paying high rates of property taxes to the city of Charleston that will then be dedicated solely to shoring up the tourist area around Union Pier.

What a plan! Union Pier is "going to be a place where there's going to be lots of people living," Councilmember Mike Seekings, who represents the South of Broad neighborhood on City Council, represents real estate developers in his own private legal practice, and ran against Mayor Tecklenburg in 2019, said during a City Council meeting in June 2021.[35] The developer is estimating that the new property will add more than $1 billion to the city's tax base and create more than 2,000 jobs.[36] Lowe has every incentive to puff: not only is it being paid $50,000 per month to get the property permitted for sale, it also has a right of first refusal to buy the site for development. And if another developer buys the Union Pier site, Lowe will get 9.5 percent of the final price.[37]

Lindsey told the *Post and Courier* in 2022 that coming back to Charleston to work for the developer on the Union Pier project was a "once-in-a-lifetime opportunity."[38] For his lifetime, maybe. For the next generation's lifetimes, not so likely, unless something extraordinary happens to protect the project.

The outline of today's Union Pier, if superimposed on a 1788 map of the area, shows that almost all of it was then sitting in the Charleston Harbor.[39] Part of the Cooper River. Tide flats. Marsh. It will be again, sooner rather than later.

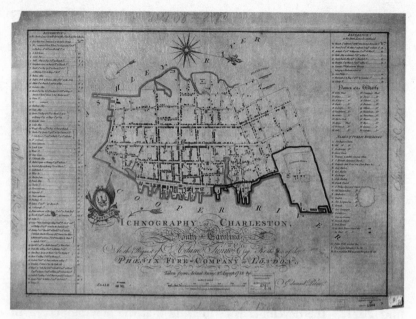

Outline of Union Pier Redevelopment Project superimposed on
1788 "Ichnography of Charleston, South-Carolina: at the request
of Adam Tunno, Esq., for the use of the Phœnix Fire-Company
of London, taken from actual survey, 2d August 1788."

Already, high tides are regularly swamping the entrance to Union Pier.[40] But if you are Charleston, and you want the state authorities to have the time to sell off land, the developers to develop it, and the city to reap the tax revenues, you'll do anything you can to avoid a panic while developing Union Pier.

No one—not the state, the developer, or the city—has an incentive to face facts about the mid-century water crisis to come. They have invested too much in the idea of making money from Union Pier to stop now, in 2022. The project represents a gigantic bet on Charleston's ability to stay dry.

The Union Pier dream has been around for decades. It was a key element of Mayor Riley's plans for the area, beginning in the 1980s. After his initial proposal for a mixed-use "Festival Marketplace" on part of Union Pier failed,[41] Riley brought the idea back in his 1996 Downtown Plan. Riley always wanted to bring more tourists and activity to the Cooper River waterfront, even though the area had already been—*by 1996*—designated a floodplain by FEMA.[42] FEMA's maps, in Riley's late-1990s view, were barriers to development that needed to be overcome, not guides to safety. Riley viewed Union Pier as a great opportunity for the city but also a very difficult site to redevelop.[43] He kept emphasizing that the redevelopment would provide an aesthetic bonus to the city: the Cooper River would once more be glimpsed down streets running from the spine of the peninsula through the new development to the water, rather than blocked completely from view by chain-link fencing and the solid sides of railcars surrounding the port, as it had been for almost a hundred years.[44] Enhanced public access to the waterfront would be a big plus.[45] Councilmember Mike Seekings called the Union Pier redevelopment project "the most important and probably the most valuable 30 acres on the East Coast of the United States today."[46] Similarly, the former state port authority CEO, Jim Newsome, says Union Pier "is one of the most valuable properties on the East Coast."[47]

For the developer, Lindsey's new employer, Union Pier is a massive, head-scratchingly tricky project that will require both up-front capital and political deftness. But the payoff will be great. And once the grand plans are implemented and the buildings are up, Lowe will be free to sell them and wash its hands of the entire enterprise. The company has no plans to actually manage the resulting development.

◆

Perhaps the city's plan, and by extension Lindsey's plan as the project's privately hired shepherd, is that the proposed Army Corps perimeter wall will protect the Union Pier parcel from harm deep into the future. But when the Army Corps of Engineers in Sept. 2021 announced its tentative plan, it left Union Pier outside its proposed wall. The SCPA objected sharply to the placement proposed for the wall because it would leave the artificial land under Union Pier unprotected from storm surges. According to Seekings, with apparently just a few phone calls from the SCPA, the Army Corps agreed to redraw the wall, moving it sharply east towards the Cooper River, to accommodate the Ports Authority and bring Union Pier within the wall's coverage. There was no process, no reporting, no City Council meeting about this. It simply happened.[48] That's how powerful the unaccountable SCPA is. It's all about economic benefit to the planners; after all, something like one out of every twenty jobs in the Charleston region can be attributed to the SCPA's operation of one of the nation's top ten seaports.[49]

What's odd, though, is that the wall won't reach the port for decades. Planning for Phase 1 will happen before construction of Phase 1, and all that will be finished before Phase 2 planning begins. Phase 1 is to plan and build the structure protecting the Medical District, a wall running from the Coast Guard station up the Ashley River to behind the Joe Riley Stadium. Phase 2 will be the Lower and Upper Batteries. Only in Phase 3 will the port get protection from any wall.[50] Because the city won't want to pay its share of design and construction costs for any later phases unless it absolutely has to, and because design of later phases won't start until construction of all the previous phases is done, it will be decades before the city will get to any later phases of the project beyond protecting the Medical District and the Batteries, the most valuable areas of the peninsula.

Also, the wall will be built only to protect against medium surges from medium storms, not against high tides, rainstorms, or river flooding. It won't include the structures needed to drain the Union Pier development of water. It can't: the Army Corps's remit covers only protection against storm surge.

Weirdly, the city's hope seems to be that the first phase of the wall, or maybe all of it, will be overtopped by a big storm, and *then* the Army Corps will be allowed to work on—and pay for—draining and pumping solutions; Morris suggested exactly this to City Council in February 2022. The idea is that those drainage solutions would be nominally targeted at remediating the overtopping problem and thus within the Army Corp's legal and financial jurisdiction. Water slopping over the wall in a storm will be identified as a "design exceedance"— a problem with the wall's initial design—whose fixes can be funded 65 percent by the federal government.[51] Where on earth the city would get the hundreds of millions of dollars to fund its 35 percent of the construction of that wall remains unclear.

A wall that would not be built for decades, whose construction was unfunded, and that, if things went well, would prove to be inadequate for its single purpose: That was the slim reed of hope on which protecting any development of Union Pier had to be based.

Because if that wasn't the plan, given the risks of sea level rise to the Charleston region, the city's rationale for moving forward with the redevelopment of Union Pier was uncertain. Either the city didn't believe that the waters were rising, or it did but also believed there was time to make as much money as possible before handing its problems over to others—or before the problems became too obvious for Union Pier's new buyer to ignore.

◆

Beyond these issues, the SCPA is hoping to avoid unionization of its piers by exiting the city of Charleston and moving all its activities to its nonunion North Charleston port. Some of the proceeds from selling off Union Pier will help cover the $1.5 billion in debt the SCPA took on to build that new container facility and support its expansion.[52] "I believe it's safe to say that it's a transformational amount of money. . . . We're a capital-intensive business, so getting a proper return from what is likely the most valuable property on the East Coast of the United States is a really a good thing for our core business, which is growing our container business, our cargo business, and really bringing economic benefit to the state of South Carolina and the region," Newsome told the *Post and Courier* in May 2022.

This part of the story leads us to a mostly Black union, Local 1422 of the International Longshoreman's Association, also known as the ILA.

◆

Local 1422 has historically staffed the State Ports Authority's unloading and loading of the enormous ships that dock at the Port of Charleston. It is a robust organization of dockworkers whose predecessor union was organized right after the end of the Civil War and chartered in 1869 by permission of a state legislature to which Black men had been elected in large numbers.[53] After the collapse of Reconstruction in 1876, that predecessor union's charter was not renewed and Charleston's port itself fell into disrepair.[54] The revival of the port under the ownership and operation of first the city of Charleston (from 1920 to 1940) and then the state, under the newly formed South Carolina State Ports Authority, also fueled the union's revival in the 1940s.[55]

The union has been effective ever since in fighting for its members' interests.[56] When containerized shipping arrived in the 1970s, the union exacted a per-ton container royalty from shippers that was paid out to working union members, whose numbers had been cut down by automation but who now had skilled jobs as crane operators.[57] The result: far fewer longshoreman union members were needed for loading and unloading containerships that arrived at Charleston's Columbus Street Terminal (just south of Union Pier), but those who remained were far better paid and supported by healthcare and pension benefits. Leon Bailey, an ILA member, told the *Post and Courier* in September 2021 that these waterfront jobs were "one of the best ways that a working man can provide, not just a decent living, but a good living for his family."[58] All of the ILA union's leaders had gone to college. The union's strength in South Carolina, the country's least-unionized state,[59] was a source of pride for many Black residents of Charleston.[60]

The port's fortunes and the union's strength grew together: As Charleston became the nation's fourth busiest container port in the 1990s,[61] politicians running for election sought the union's influence with its members, along with that of the Black church and the NAACP. In the lead-up to the 2008 presidential election, Barack Obama came to town and met with a small group of ILA officials. Obama tapped into an emotional connection with them by having a conversation about fatherhood.

Then those Columbus Street Terminal cranes became outdated and the State Ports Authority took them out. Container ships began calling at another State Ports Authority facility on the other side of the Cooper River, in Mount Pleasant. The Ports Authority changed the function of the Columbus Terminal, making it the jumping-off spot for thousands of Volvos and BMWs that had been brought to Charleston by rail from South Carolina manufacturers (and couldn't be safely put into containers) to be loaded onto ships along with other goods[62] for export to 125 countries.[63]

The union persisted, its members working as mechanics and clerks for the shippers that arrived at the port, moving cargo and cars around both the Columbus and the Mount Pleasant terminals alongside the largely white, nonunionized employees of the SCPA. Meanwhile, the Authority spent $2 billion to build the new Hugh K. Leatherman terminal in an altogether different city: North Charleston.[64]

Many displaced Black residents of the city of Charleston moved up to North Charleston after they left the peninsula. Michelle Mapp points out how painful the SCPA expenditure is for low-income people in North Charleston, noting that the state "built a billion dollars in infrastructure on new roads [to serve the North Charleston port], but [North Charleston is] also home to some of the poorest performing schools" in the country.[65]

The planned opening of the Leatherman terminal in March 2021 gave Local 1422, the largest and oldest Black union in South Carolina, a chance to ensure that crane driver and yard worker jobs there would be assigned to union members under their master contract with the United States Maritime Alliance, a trade association representing container carriers, direct employers, and port associations on the US East and Gulf Coasts.[66] But there is a basic legal issue: Although the Maritime Alliance includes the SCPA as well as shipping companies, the SCPA never actually *signed* the master contract,[67] and takes the position that the new terminal is not covered by that agreement. (In other words, paraphrasing: "We're not a party to that agreement, and even if we were North Charleston wouldn't be part of it.") It was clear that the SCPA is willing to bluster its way through the conflict: the union's master contract is due to expire on September 30, 2024 and the union will then lose a lot of leverage. The SCPA has dug in its heels and is asserting those 400–500 jobs at the Leatherman terminal will be nonunion.[68] Meanwhile, major shipping companies, not wanting to get caught in this dispute, are refusing to use the North Charleston port, which remains quiet.

At the same time, the union is participating in the overall move to North Charleston, in a sense: it is planning to sell its former union hall on the peninsula and has moved its headquarters to North Charleston.[69] There are still ILA jobs at the Columbus Street Terminal, directly up the Cooper River from Gadsden's Wharf, where Charleston's boisterous participation in the nation's traffic in enslaved people centered,[70] but those jobs are also on the chopping block. Dale Morris, the city's Chief Resilience Officer, has said publicly that the SCPA may be moving out entirely: "Who knows what the future of transportation looks like in 25 years? Will we be exporting BMWs and Volvos from that facility? No one knows."[71] Either water or the combined forces of the city and the State Ports Authority will gradually squeeze out the ILA's role in the city of Charleston.

◆

The city is investing in its relationship with its South of Broad residents, and in league with the State Ports Authority has plans for a gleaming new multipurpose development next to the Cooper River on the lower peninsula. Jacob Lindsey, former walkable-city enthusiast and determined public servant, has switched hats and is now a key part of these plans. These moves will, in the end, squeeze the role of a strong Black union even further, as the entire port operation shifts to North Charleston. That's a good move for the port—it's safer there. But none of this is part of any holistic plan to make the city a better place for all Charlestonians to live. The Union Pier story on the lower peninsula encapsulates Charleston in a shiny nutshell: Prioritize development, to hell with the risks. The idea that the former city planner has returned to make money from the project adds to the picture.

You can't make Charleston up. It's amazing enough on its own.

6

The East Side and David White

T he East Side of the Charleston peninsula, lying roughly between Meeting Street on the west, East Bay on the east, Stuart on the north, and Mary on the south, is the convergence point for many of the city's issues: it is swiftly gentrifying and low-lying, has no grocery stores or public transit to speak of, is the site of powerful racial tensions, and is a place where Black people are living in frequently flooded public housing.

The East Side.

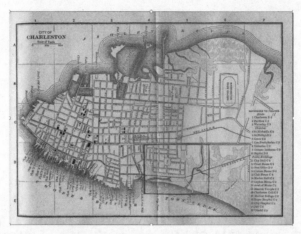

Appletons' general guide to the United States and Canada. Part II.
Western and Southern States, marked to show location of present-day
East Side, New York: D. Appleton and Company, Charleston 1885.

The lower-income residents of the East Side will have nowhere to go
when the slow-rolling cataclysm of sea level rise eventually hits. Absent
dramatic interventions, much of the East Side will return to marshland.

The East Side began in the 1760s as a planned development, surrounding a marshy public square, for affluent merchant families—a
sort of gated community, bounded by Vardell's Creek and Marsh to
the north and the Cooper River to the east, outside what was then the
city boundary of Charleston. Its imaginative developer, Henry Laurens,
called it Hampstead Village, and claimed that ships with a ten-foot
draft could navigate Vardell's Creek at high tide.[1] By the time of the
Civil War, the large homes of Hampstead Village had been destroyed
twice—during the Revolutionary War and again during the War of
1812—and the village had morphed into a densely populated neighborhood of small lots and rented buildings housing a wide variety of
mostly Black laborers, both enslaved and free, jammed next to factories,
machine shops and, beginning in 1882, a massive cotton mill that
became a cigar factory in 1912.[2]

The twentieth century saw more changes as white residents left
for the newly developing suburbs west of the Ashley River and Black
residents moved into Hampstead after being priced out of the lower
Charleston peninsula. The East Side was the place where the city put
most of its public housing—the Wraggborough Homes, the Cooper
River Court, the Meeting Street Manor, and other scattered public
housing units.[3] By the early 1960s, when the census showed that
Hampstead Village had become mostly Black for the first time, it
was viewed as a ghetto by "Old White Charleston." Its houses lacked
modern water and sewage facilities. The area began to be called,
unkindly, the East Side.[4] "And that's pretty much when the city gave
up on the neighborhood," historian Nic Butler told the *Post and Courier*
in October 2019.[5] Some East Side residents were forced out in the
1960s to make way for a new Cooper River Bridge and never found a
way to return.[6] "People are still waiting," Latonya Gamble, president
of the East Side Community Development Corp., said of community
expectations for new housing in 2021. "Remember when they removed
the [old] Cooper River Bridge, and they said that they were going
to; 'Oh, we're going to replace these homes, and we're going to have
people come back' and stuff like that. I've had a community meeting
last year sometime. And somebody was all, 'so when are they going
open to people to come back?' . . . People are still waiting to come back
from the Cooper River Bridge."[7] Constructing ramps to the new bridge
in the 1960s displaced many residents, and during that same decade the
building of the Crosstown Freeway severed the northern part of
the neighborhood from the south.

Today, most of the residents of the East Side are still Black, as are
nearly all the residents of its public housing complexes,[8] but the population of the East Side is becoming whiter. The most recent census
divides the East Side into two and shows that south of Lee Street, the
population of Black residents has declined to 39 percent, the population

of white residents has increased to 52 percent, and the overall area has grown by 10 percent since 2010. The northern part of the East Side, which includes a large housing project, is 58 percent Black residents and 36 percent white—a 94 percent increase in white residents since 2010.[9]

Nonetheless, most of the Black Charlestonians who still reside on the peninsula live on the East Side, and most live below the poverty line. The unkindness and lack of fairness with which the East Side has been treated for decades—underresourced, ill-served by transit or grocery stores—is now amplified by the growing number of fetid floods that afflict the area. The dimpled asphalt of the low streets of the East Side lies on top of garbage and human waste that was dumped there for decades. In the 1880s alone, tens of thousands of pounds of refuse were dumped on Hampstead's streets.[10] During that same decade, Vardell's Creek, which had formed the northern border of Hampstead Village when it was laid out, where Blake Street intersects East Bay today, was filled with garbage and offal. Why such dumping? Because the trash had to go somewhere, and because this odorous fill dirt allowed new land to be developed and property tax to be collected. Beneath the slowly settling garbage and human waste underlying the streets of the East Side, water still flows, influenced by tides that ever-more-frequently break through the surface of the roads, carrying the stink and miasma of that old garbage with it in the form of atmospheric levels of E. coli bacteria as well as other potential pathogens like tuberculosis, staph, and cholera.[11] Drainage problems continue to afflict the East Side.[12] Latonya Gamble, president of the East Side Community Development Corporation, is frustrated with what she sees as the city's failure to prioritize the flooding, housing, and other concerns of the East Side. "We're all frustrated," she told the *Post and Courier* in August 2018. "I think the East Side has been patient for too long. . . . [I]t just seems like we're always put on the back burner. That may not be true, but that's how it feels to us."[13]

◆

At the same time, the East Side is steadily gentrifying, as rich white people move back into an area other white people left years ago, buying scores of properties in a very short time from Black homeowners. Older Black residents of the East Side have been the subject of predatory practices by house-flippers and developers, who hand over letters that offer up-front cash in exchange for a quick signature.[14]

From Rev. Joe Darby's perspective, the idea that the East Side is becoming a magnet for new, richer populations is truly strange. "The word that comes to mind is weird," he says. "I would not see how any-body would want to move, even into a gentrified area, if you know it's chronically flooded and built on poop."

New white residents of the East Side memorably clashed with the Black community there during the summer of 2019, when Timothy Haman Jr., a forty-one-year-old white chef who worked in a downtown restaurant, was murdered outside his new East Side apartment by a Black teenager. The teenager wasn't himself an East Side native; he'd come in from West Ashley (likely looking for drugs, in Rev. Darby's opinion). Most crime on the East Side, Darby believes, is perpetrated by outsiders. But other white residents of the East Side immediately held a vigil and called for a community meeting with the Charleston police. The vigil irritated Black Charlestonians living on the East Side, Darby remembers. "How many Black folks had been killed in Charleston," he recalls them asking, "without you folks holding a vigil?"

The community meeting was an evening of high tension—one of the most contentious sessions in Charleston that Rev. Darby ever saw. White East Side residents, while justifiably outraged by the murder, essentially tried to take over the neighborhood association, calling for an enhanced and more punitive police presence on the East Side. The existing Black neighborhood association members were profoundly affronted. The Black community association members essentially shut out the whites who were seeking to take things over and made clear that they were interested in stronger police-community relationships, not greater punishment. Darby, watching and listening, was concerned. "Racial tensions are likely to get worse," he says. And he is worried that the tensions will quickly lead to violence rather than effective advocacy for change. Younger Black people are impatient with institutions of any kind—meaning the NAACP and the Black church are unlikely to be able to counsel them about how best to proceed.

Rain and race intersected on the East Side in May 2020 when wind, flooding, hail, and rain in the form of a severe thunderstorm pummeled the Charleston area. More than twenty-two streets were closed on the peninsula and water poured into the East Side. Two new white residents pulled out floaties—a pink flamingo, a blue whale—and filmed themselves cavorting in the water covering President Street. Mika Gadsden, a young Black activist, pointed out on Twitter that Black homes filled the background of the video, and tweeted, "Imagine how tired they [Black residents] must be of all this 'nuisance flooding.' But, sure, enjoy the floaties and bacteria, Chad." King Street, the relatively high spine of the peninsula, was flooded for blocks; local news captured video of a car floating down Bee Street; East Side residents struggled through hip-deep water on the streets.

◆

Eric Jackson, a middle-aged Black man whose childhood was spent in public housing on South Street on the East Side, remembers being kept inside for days when it flooded back then. "Kids got hookworms from walking through the water," he says. "You get locked in, you get blocked in, your parents can't move the car or whatever the case may be, so your day is stopped. It's raining now, you got to stay in the house."

Jackson attended Burke High School on the peninsula. He's seen the gentrification on the East Side. Between the time he left for the military in 1985 and returned in 1998, the place changed enormously. Jackson wasn't able to afford living on the peninsula when he moved back and had to move to West Ashley. Now, decades later, he thinks the city should build public housing away from the water. "That's just something that they know they have to do," Jackson says. Charleston's City Plan, adopted in late 2021, acknowledges that the lowest lands in the city will someday again be covered in water or marsh, but so far the region's plan (one echoed across the country) is to have private developers use tax credits to transform existing public housing. The developers will be responsible for renovating or replacing the buildings where they are.[15] (New units will be "affordable," but that label raises more questions than it answers. Rents have gone up more than thirty percent over the last two years in Charleston.[16]) There does not appear to be a strategy aimed at moving low-income public housing residents to higher ground.

◆

David White, Jackson's nephew, is an energetic, smiling, early-thirties entrepreneur and Black native of the East Side who got his MBA at South Carolina State more than a decade ago. Now he works for the state of South Carolina in social services, supervising a unit that has placed about five hundred kids in foster homes across ten counties. As we already learned, a few years ago, uncle and nephew opened Laundry Matters, a laundromat that also provides homeless and low-income people with free laundry service. White wants to help others, and finds the work satisfying. "Just knowing that they have that satisfaction of something as simple as getting their clothes washed" feels good to White. He and his uncle also run a youth organization on the East Side, offering after-school tutoring and coding classes.

White's mother has worked her entire career in the canteen at The Citadel, Charleston's military college founded to protect the city from slave rebellions in the early nineteenth century, and White grew up visiting his beloved grandmother, Roberta Jackson, in the projects on South Street on the East Side—the same place where Eric Jackson grew up. As a child, White remembers noticing that America Street flooded frequently, and that "Drake Street was probably the worst street" when it came to water. People got used to flooding on the East Side. "I don't think we thought about it, oddly, as a problem," says White. "I think it was only a problem when we realized we couldn't do what we wanted to do." He says he was "numb to seeing it" as a child. "I knew what streets were probably flooded. I knew how to navigate around," he says. Going to and from his elementary school on Columbus between Drake and America was just a mess when it flooded. "We didn't have a choice," says White, who adds, "I think that's sad." He says he just wanted the flooding to be fixed. "I never really understood the problem or why it is taking so long to be fixed. It's been a long time," he says. "I think it mainly affected those low-income areas," White adds.

White says he understands growth and expansion, but says "it just seems unfair" when people are displaced "that can't necessarily afford to move to Summerville." One of his uncles was forced out of his house to move to North Charleston because they were expanding I-26, this was years ago, but the project never happened. "Now," he says, "in front of his house sits a brewery."

He is dumbfounded by what is "technically called affordable housing" in the region. It's too expensive. The East Side used to have a Piggly Wiggly grocery store on Meeting Street when White was growing up, but now it's just an empty building and the East Side is a food desert. The closest grocery store is an expensive Harris Teeter more than a mile away from White's former (now closed) elementary school. "It's not really walkable because East Bay Street I don't think has much sidewalk," White says. East Bay also floods. There's a Food Lion on the west side of town, but its parking lot has terrible flooding.

White says there are streets on the East Side that flood as of late 2020 that didn't flood during his childhood. "I used to think that I knew what streets I could navigate through," he says. But that has changed. "So I have to think strategically. How do I get to Laundry Matters?" The uncertainty troubles him. "I also think about the population we serve," he says. "They aren't able to get to the laundromat if the streets are flooded. They're mostly walking, so you can't walk through the water with bags of clothes," White says. He's clearly pained by the thought. "It is frustrating," he says. "We do free wash days. But because of the weather, the rain, they can't get there." Same with the kids coming for tutoring. "We have to plan around rain, plan around flooding in Charleston."

Water and racism in Charleston connect for White. "Just growing up here in Charleston I guess I can speak on race," he says. "I think it [indignities of racism] goes along for me, along with the flooding thing. As a child, I didn't see much of it, but now it's kind of more blatant. And as an adult you can recognize and realize that there are several businesses downtown that say just really bad things about Black people and Black folk." His voice is lowering; he's stopped laughing. He knows different businesses don't want Black customers: "There are too many Jamaals in this club or this bar, let's change the music," White explains, they will say. They'll use dress codes to limit the number of Black people who can get in and tell a DJ he'll be fired if there are too many Black people on the dance floor.[17]

"I'm not surprised by it," White says. "I think leaving Orangeburg [where he went to college], coming back to Charleston I realized it is very racist. Just prejudiced and racist." He says clubs and restaurants in Charleston want the Southern Charm clientele. "And I just think that it's their loss, because there are so many amazing Black people that are doing so many great things," White says. He's spent a lot of time on the lower peninsula, and so he thinks he's "more used to it, or numb to it." He goes on: "But I have friends that don't live downtown, [if] they come downtown, they say, 'Hey, why can't we go there?' Or 'Why we don't feel comfortable being here?'" After that kind of experience, his friends "would maybe feel more comfortable going to North Charleston where there are more Black-owned restaurants, bars, venues. So now they're just, like, 'I don't want to go downtown because we don't feel comfortable down there.'" White falls silent.

He misses his favorite Black-owned business on King Street, a clothing store on Mary and King that closed in 2017. A Black-owned restaurant called LJ's serving soul food on King between Cannon and Spring also closed. Martha Lou's on East Bay is closing its doors. "In my younger days I just felt more comfort being on King Street," White says. Now, he says, it's uncomfortable "to walk up and down King Street now and have to think about, 'Oh, they probably have a dress code, we probably can't get in.'" He grew up in the Boys and Girls Club on Mary Street, says it was his "saving grace," and is sad that it is now closed, as are his East Side elementary and middle schools. "A lot of my memories are gone," says White.

When White was growing up, he knew the police officers that were mentors in the kids' programs that he and his friends were part of. Now, today, he thinks you have to think twice about police on the East Side. It's the uncertainty: "'What do they want? What did I do? Who do they think I am? How am I going to get treated if they get out of their car? What could happen?' . . . That's a real feeling for a lot of people here. We grew up on the East Side, [but] now we can't necessarily walk from the corner store to Mall Park on Columbus Street without thinking, 'There's a cop down there, what could happen?'" The overwhelming uncertainty of racism is like the overwhelming uncertainty of water for White. "It's the unknown. It's scary. I think the best we could do is just knowing, 'I didn't do anything wrong.' But sometimes that's not enough."

White can't imagine that the city of Charleston would make the tough choices necessary to help the people of the East Side resettle. "It's been so long," he says. "The low income population that's been moving and displaced for some time now, I don't think that's going to stop," White says. "Where are the people going?"

White himself is not planning to leave. "Through all that I still love Charleston," he laughs. It's home. "My dream is to have that community feel again," the feeling of the thriving little East Side village he had as a child. "And that doesn't necessarily mean all Black or all white, just for everybody to feel comfortable." He continues, "Probably won't get that going up and down King Street any more, but just, like, within the neighborhoods on the East Side. I want it to be safe, yes. But I also want it to feel like everybody's welcome. And not feel like they're being pushed out, pressured or anything like that."

These days, David White lives on the west side of the peninsula. He says he doesn't spend time outside his house unless he has to, and he never varies his running route through mostly Black neighborhoods where he believes he is recognized as a consistent presence. "I would not feel comfortable going down a different route," he says. Because then things would be uncertain. "Then I'm running with my headphones in, and have to think about this family looking at me, like, 'Who are you? Are you new? Why are you here?'"[18]

Michael Miller, now in his early fifties, is the Register of Deeds for Charleston County, the first Black man to hold that role in the 239 years the title has existed. He grew up in the Goose Creek area but played soccer every week on the peninsula as a child near where the Charleston Aquarium is today. A housing project called the Ansonborough Homes used to be where the parking garage for the aquarium is now, and there was a sports field in front of the project. Condos are there now. "Once

I became an adult," Miller says, "they said the field was contaminated. They tore down the projects, moved the families, and then subsequently built a park across the street, a parking garage on that same location, and then built the Charleston Aquarium across the street."[19] Laura Cantral, the former Coastal Conservation League director, agrees: "There's plenty of history in this city, putting aside the current crisis of climate and sea-level rise, and more water, of low-income African American communities being displaced because they were told 'This is a risky place to be. There's creosote, chemicals. We need to relocate you.' And now there are very high-end condos sitting on that property."[20]

Miller is interested in gentrification on the Charleston peninsula. "Anytime there's growth, or what people like to call gentrification, taking place," he says, "somebody has to be displaced. Typically, because the land is so valuable, because it is surrounded by water, unfortunately it's been my experience that those folks who are impacted the most tend to be people who are disenfranchised and people of color." He remembers confronting Mayor Riley about what happened to the people who lived in Ansonborough Homes, "And how convenient it was for him to say that the land was contaminated, then you tear down the property, relocate the families, remove fields of play for children—and then you turn around sometime later and say that the land's no longer contaminated after you've already torn the building down." He remembers feeling shock in the room, crowded with young Black professionals who had been brought in to talk to Riley about one of his reelection bids. "You would have thought that I asked just a vile question to the mayor," Miller says. "Everybody was just so afraid for me, like, 'Michael, how can you dare ask that question?'"

In Charleston, Miller has learned, even the word "gentrification" is taboo, he says. "Somebody said, 'That's not the term we use,' and I said, 'Well, what's the term?' And, they said, 'The term is we want to preserve our *historical integrity*.'" Using the word gentrification "sounds bad," he says. His view is that although making neighborhoods better and more vibrant is a good thing, "I think it becomes a bad thing, or not so positive, when the same folks who are in those communities cannot get access to the lifting up, to being empowered to be better and be more in the same community they grew up in."

He's still angry that Mayor Riley used money that would otherwise have gone to the Charleston County school board to build Waterfront Park along the Cooper River. (The building of Waterfront Park in turn led to the State Port Authority's ability to sell off part of its land to Lowe for the building of the Cooper luxury hotel.) Riley had gone to the school district and borrowed money cheaply, saying he'd repay it in twenty-five years. "The Charleston County School District budget is larger than the City of Charleston's budget, is larger than the County of Charleston's budget. It is the largest budget in the tri-county area"—of Berkeley, Dorchester, and Charleston counties, says Miller. Then Riley spent that money on building Waterfront Park. The school district was paid back after thirty years, following a five-year extension of the loan, and the development of the parking lot that became Waterfront Park was accompanied by a host of other hotel and restaurant projects that, in their totality, produced a peninsula on which Black residents no longer lived. "I did not feel that the school district should be the financier of rebuilding the city," says Miller. He points out that Riley's terms in office coincided with a time during which the peninsula lost many public schools that had been educating Black children and many small Black-owned businesses. In Miller's view, "Mayor Riley systematically used the money of taxpayers, of Black folk, to displace Black folk from the peninsula." And yet, he points out, "They still voted for him blindly. It was almost like a blind leadership. Blind faith."

Miller says Black Charlestonians are wary of speaking freely around white people for fear of losing their jobs or way of life. He says his dad told him when he was a little boy that "words have meaning," and that it was important to make sure people understand exactly what he is saying. "You never forget the smell or the stench or the sight of racism," Miller says. "You never forget it when you see it in somebody's eyes or in their face, and whether it's subtle or it's overt, you know it and you recognize it." It was around him in Charleston: "Sometimes, the sting of racism on the peninsula was as clear and in your face as somebody passing gas," Miller says. "And then sometimes, it was as subtle as a soft handshake and a 'Good morning, how are you?'"

He is confident that the gentrification of the East Side is part of an overall pattern of displacement. He had several friends whose grandparents owned homes on the East Side; after the grandparents died, the children could not afford to renovate those homes or pay the taxes, so they sold. "That's not the fault of any one person or one administration or philosophy of gentrification," Miller acknowledges. "It's more of the word 'lack.' Lack of resources, lack of opportunities, lack of knowledge, lack of education on some point in some respects. But more importantly, it's financial. I mean, if I can't afford to pay the taxes on my mother's home, I'm going to be forced to sell it." Was this racism in action? "It just so happens that the people don't have any money, and it just so happens the people happen to be Black," says Miller. "Or, it just so happens that they happen to be poor and happen to be Black. Either way you look at, it still smells the same way."

He sees the East Side as emblematic: "I think the East Side is a cliché of what's happening on the peninsula in other places. Charleston is becoming, and has become, a city of the well-to-do," Miller says. It is a cruel place, he says. "But embedded in its cruelty is this quasi, pseudo-southern charm that draws a lot of Caucasians to this town and they love Charleston. They love what Charleston represents. But once you start to unpeel the layers of that onion, and that's probably true of anything, it's not as it appears," says Miller.

The city's racial past has not ended for Miller. "Charleston is the Ellis Island for Black people," he says. "Caucasians have the College of Charleston. They've got The Citadel. The city has everything white folk would want, and it offers little to young Black professionals."

Nonetheless, Miller is staying. Black friends who have left Charleston come back and shake their heads at the ongoing racism and strangeness of the place, saying, "Man, Charleston ain't changed." Miller's response, he says, is "How could it be changed, when you are one of our best natural resources. You left us." He continues: "You're like LeBron James. You left Cleveland and went to South Beach. You went to Miami, and then you wonder why Charleston isn't growing. Because people like you left."

◆

Just as the city's focus for the lower peninsula is the potential economic windfall of the development of Union Pier, its focus for the East Side is the development of the Lowcountry Lowline Park, named to evoke the success of the High Line park in New York City, that would run over an old Norfolk Southern railroad bed under I-26 overpasses in the middle of the peninsula—right along the western edge of the East Side. Land for the Lowline, which is currently in a blighted state, was bought by the city and a nonprofit private group, the Friends of the Lowline, in 2017.[21] The idea is that the Lowline will be both a walking area and a park, with perhaps a bandstand or sports courts included.[22] The problem is that the $40 million Lowline may itself end up displacing lower-income Charlestonians.[23] "It [the Lowline] could provide a lot of community amenities," Laura Cantral, former executive director of the Coastal Conservation League, said in 2020. "It also brings risks of gentrification and displacement, and all the things that go along

with that." Councilmember Keith Waring has asked why Lowline
Park is slated to receive more funding than stormwater improvements
and affordable housing initiatives on the East Side; Waring makes
the obvious point that East Side residents don't have the pull that the
Friends of the Lowline does. Substantial funding to build the Lowline
is coming from a special tax district that is supposed to be dedicated
to the East Side of the peninsula.[24]

The city, for its part, has pledged to build new affordable housing
along the Lowline and to make zoning changes that will spur
additional private affordable building in the area.[25] And the planners of the Lowline tried to take flooding into account. Gamble,
of the Eastside Community Development Corporation, is dubious:
"I understand that they want beautiful parks and I understand the
parks, we're going to address the storm water, but if it does not reach
within our community, then we need to come up with a better plan.
You know what I'm saying? I think that's a good plan to have, but
then we need an additional plan, so that we can give our residents
some relief."[26]

Gamble is right. The city's 1984 Master Drainage and Floodplain
Management Plan has provisions for addressing flooding on the East
Side that still haven't been implemented.[27] In April 2022, the city's
Stormwater Manager, Matthew Fountain, updated the City Council's
Committee on Public Works and Utilities on stormwater improvement
efforts on the East Side. "We've cleaned about 10,000 feet of stormwater pipe . . . through the area," Fountain reported. That is the extent
of the city's progress so far. "In a number of areas," he said, "we did have
pretty much complete clogging." Those pipes hadn't been doing much
for the East Side. "There's a lot of debris that accumulates, and a lot
of construction work that's occurred, obviously, in the area," Fountain
explained. Gentrification and development have also been clogging
those East Side pipes.

"We know where the flooding is," he continued. Fountain said that the "outfalls" in the area needed to be larger—basically upsizing the existent pipes. Fountain says it will cost about $10 million to make the pipes under the streets larger to carry more water away. Otherwise, however clean the pipes are, they can't carry enough water to drain the streets out to the Cooper River. He said the city also looked at a number of storage options for water—places to send water to get it off the streets while residents waited for lower tides to drain the area. "Unfortunately," he said, "basically the water table is so shallow in this area, and there's so much water, it's such a large basin, [that] it's very hard to store the water. And so we have to convey it out."

All this means that the East Side has to rely on gravity-driven water systems for drainage. But because the peninsula is so low and flat, these systems won't work during the very high tides or major rainstorms that are coming, and all the water that lands on the spine of King Street will find its way to the lower surfaces of the East Side. Those pipes and drains will be full of water, unmoving. Part of the river. Fountain made this point obliquely, saying, "There will be a future consideration, if we get significant sea level rise over the next twenty to fifty years, of what we do to further improve drainage, as that water starts to not flow out except at low tide cycles." "But this will provide quite a bit more time," he reassured the committee members. There are no plans for a pump station that would power water off the East Side. Fountain said he would be working with his engineers, finalizing the scope of the $10 million pipe-widening plan, and then would come back to council for money to carry the project out. He optimistically suggested that construction might begin "within the next couple of years"[28] and be complete a couple years after that.[29]

Cleaning pipes doesn't help when the pipes are too narrow to carry enough water to make a difference, and gravity-driven drainage doesn't help when there's too much water around. Mayor Tecklenburg asked whether the area was draining any better as a result of the cleanout. Fountain's response was measured. "Every little bit helps," he said, "but it certainly hasn't fixed the problem, is what I'm trying to say." Tecklenburg kept going, looking for good news. "You said with the upsizing [of pipes] that they're proposing, that you showed us, at least for the next couple of decades, you don't believe we'd need a pump station. It would still work by gravity?" Again, Fountain tried to temper the mayor's hopefulness: "It would work at any moderate to low tide period," he said. "It's one of these challenges we have in a lot of the lower-lying areas. That's still a huge improvement versus current condition [with completely clogged pipes], but there would be the potential for a short-term flooding event, basically, during an extreme tide if we also get an extreme rain. Which are typically our hurricane events, right? Our hurricanes or our tropical storms." In other words, Fountain told the City Council and the mayor that when serious storms and tides come, the gravity-driven system on the East Side will no longer work. That moment is fast approaching. It may already be here.

◆

In July 2019, Ramiro Diaz, a landscape architect from New Orleans, made a presentation about the East Side's water issues as part of the Dutch Dialogues process. Climatologists say that rain bombs, high volumes of intense rain over a short period of time, are becoming increasingly common, dropping as much as three-and-a-half inches in an hour. "You combine that with your high tide and you have a big problem," Diaz said. Because the Charleston peninsula is not using many pumps, the only way to keep water from rain bombs from drowning low-lying areas on the peninsula is to ensure that it is stored on the highest ground available. Diaz had a host of suggestions for storage: installing permeable paving stones that allow water into the ground, ensuring there was more storage space underground (he suggested plastic or concrete structures or cells in addition to Charleston's 1850s brick arches), planting more trees with plenty of room for their roots to form water absorbent platforms underground, and installing water channels to move the water. Diaz also suggested storing stormwater runoff on public and open lands, like parks and schools—"places where you intentionally flood and then it can be parks later."

When it came to the East Side in particular, Diaz showed a map of the area that included the idea of "Reintroducing" the "historic creek system" of Vardell's Creek and New Market Creek by bringing them back to the surface and channeling their waters. "Daylighting" these creeks would allow for "fantastic water storage," Diaz said. Right now, he noted, "people only know that [Vardell's Creek] is there when it's flooding. There's this spot right here," he pointed to the corner of the Trident Tech campus, "where the creek expresses itself."

He suggested that the city raise the low streets in the neighborhood, use the school buildings and parks as storage areas, build a water channel ("urban bioswale") along Cooper Street, and generally reintroduce water channels and areas into the neighborhood, which would become a place of boardwalks and water features ("large water squares"). He said that he had met with the Charleston Housing Authority and talked about the water around the public housing areas on the East Side. "We do believe that these lower areas are not only hazardous," Diaz said. "Cars are flooding, and it's a very uncomfortable position. And we walked around there, and it's very evident that there's standing water on this street." Diaz chose his words very carefully. He was certainly suggesting that the creeks needed to be given more room and brought to the surface. And he was certainly recommending creating more room for housing on higher ground.

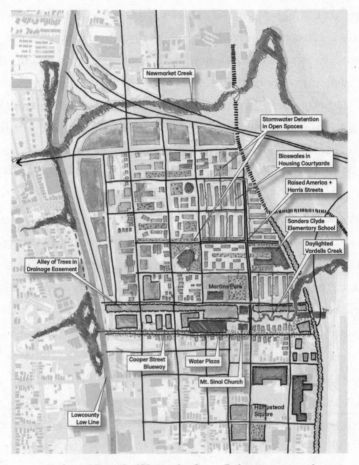

Enlarged Detail of Vision for Green Infrastructure and
Elevated Roadways, created by Waggoner & Ball Architecture/
Environment, from Dutch Dialogues® Final Report, 2019.

As of June 2022, none of these suggestions have been implemented. Development of commercial properties on the higher land just east and north of the East Side is continuing to boom. The too-narrow drainpipes on the East Side have been cleaned out. That, for Charleston, is progress.

◆

The East Side's history is layered with trash. Enslaved trash collectors loaded the carcasses of dead animals and other refuse into carts and dumped it on salt marshes north, west, and east of the city, and one of those areas became the East Side. But there's a middle part of the story—after the dumping but before the sinking—that centers on burning rather than landfill-creation.

In the early twentieth century, public health authorities began agitating for trash incineration, pointing out that rates of typhoid and other diseases in the neighborhoods near the dumps were higher. But siting an incineration plant proved difficult: Roper Hospital didn't want one near it. Nor did the residents of Meeting Street. The city fathers eventually located a vacant lot northeast of the city owned by the local private water and electricity utility, bought the land, and built a modest incinerator plant in 1918. The plant, at what is now the northwest corner of America and Lee Streets, couldn't keep up with the trash generated by the city and had no storage capacity, so workers simply dumped the unburned trash on the nearby marshes each day as they had in the past. This dumping of excess refuse—and all the smells and misery that accompanied it—continued for decades. Finally, in 1932, the city decided to build a larger incinerator plant on a site nearby, bounded by Cooper, East Bay, and Drake Streets. This was a "once more with feeling" move: This second plant had a tall smokestack and much greater capacity than the first, but also couldn't keep up with the daily volume presented for burning. Dumping continued.[30]

By 1943, the smell and awfulness of the marsh dumps was worse than ever. A second matching smokestack was finished in 1944.[31] Then, twelve years later, in 1956, the city decided to go back to wholesale dumping again, but this time in a "modern" fashion by layering earth over each tranche of refuse. The two smokestacks were then taken out of service. By about this time, by 1960, the East Side had become home to many Black Charlestonians and "fell into a state of neglect" over the following decades, according to the *Post and Courier*.[32]

In August 2020, the city announced that the twin 135-foot smokestacks at the east end of Lee Street would be demolished because city engineers had become concerned about the columns' structural integrity.[33] But the brick incinerator plant at America and Lee had been repurposed as a community center in 1979, and had been named in 1992 for St. Julian F. Devine, who had been the first Black member of the Charleston City Council since Reconstruction in 1967.[34] The smokestacks had, over the decades, been embraced by East Side residents as visible, remarkable symbols of their community. Longtime resident Joe Watson called them a "jewel of the East Side."[35] Residents had flagged the deteriorating condition of the smokestacks in 2016, but the city hadn't done anything then, and now, without notice, officials were planning to just knock the columns down.[36] That wouldn't happen in a traditionally white Charleston neighborhood, and Black residents of the East Side knew it.

A brouhaha ensued. Mayor Tecklenburg asserted that funds for rehabbing the smokestacks could be used instead for drainage for the neighborhood and affordable housing, implying that the neighborhood could have drainage or the smokestacks, but not both. Gamble, of the Eastside Community Development Corporation, told the *Post and Courier* that the desire to preserve the smokestacks had united the neighborhood.[37] Preservationist Winslow Hastie said the smokestacks "should not be dismissed as merely trash incinerator chimneys and relics of a bygone industrial era."[38] In the end, the city decided to preserve the columns but said it would need $1.5 million in private funding to do the job.[39]

The story was touching and strange. Residents of the East Side had taken pride in the beauty of smokestacks that might instead have represented callousness. The story had started with enslavement, hundreds

of years of dumping, and unfair treatment—white neighborhoods
had been able to resist having an incinerator near them, after all,
and much of the earth beneath the East Side was made up of fill that
was much looser than the made land below the Battery—but had
arrived in 2020 as a preservation and neighborhood identity narrative.

◆

The East Side of the Charleston peninsula is many things, old and
new. It is the place where Denmark Vesey launched his 1822 fight
for freedom. His church stood at what is now Hanover and Reid on
the East Side. It is the place where David White found refuge in a
Boys and Girls Club that no longer exists. It is the place where wild
gunfire late in the night on Memorial Day, 2022, sent ten people to
the hospital. It is the place where master blacksmith Philip Simmons
created hundreds of wrought iron gates and railings in his shop on
Blake Street, a block and a half from the Hampstead Mall park that
still marks the neighborhood.[40] It is also minutes away from the French
Quarter Inn and the Dewberry, two of the top hotels in the country.[41]

During the public meeting in September 2019 at which the Dutch
water recommendations were rolled out, racial issues went unmen-
tioned. One of the city's consultants did say of the East Side that
"There is some public housing that is regularly flooded." But he did
not suggest that it was government's role to do anything in response.
Instead, he said, "As more affordable housing comes online, you
need to evolve those people, maybe encourage those people to go to
higher ground for their own safety." Finding a safe place to live on
higher ground, from this perspective, appears to be a matter of private, personal initiative ("evolving") rather than the responsibility of
government. Few Black residents of the East Side have any trust that
the rising waters will change this situation. As David White says,

"I just don't see how the city is going to come up with a plan all of a sudden to make sure these people [in public housing] are safely put." Gamble, who grew up in public housing and still lives on the East Side, says, "We've been living with flooding for a long time and we know we still have to."[42]

7

The Upper Peninsula and Michelle Mapp

T he Neck area of Charleston has steadily shifted locations over time. The words "the Neck" have historically meant the part of the Charleston peninsula that isn't on a strictly gridded plan, isn't densely populated, and doesn't feel like part of the historic district. Everything above Broad Street was once "the Neck," a kind of no-man's-land (from the plantation owner's perspective) bounded by the Ashley and Cooper Rivers. Then the southern border of the Neck moved north to Calhoun Street,[1] which was first laid out and called "Boundary Street" in 1769. Today, its boundaries are somewhere above Huger Street, above the Crosstown Freeway, or above Santi's Restaurante Mexicano, depending whom you ask, and east of I-26, a roaring interstate built in the 1960s that now soars high above the upper peninsula on its way into downtown Charleston. From the perspective of a white tourist arriving at the Charleston International Airport, which is actually in the separate city of North Charleston, the Neck is flyover country, a scrappy territory that might (but might not) be glimpsed from above for a moment between baggage claim and the comfort of a luxury hotel on the lower peninsula. Today's Neck is cut through by wide, heavily traveled streets, like Meeting and Morrison, whose construction wiped out many Black homes; those streets feel more like highways. The area is bounded at its upper end, invisibly, by North Charleston.

In the eighteenth century, there were large plantations here, as well as smaller farms and scattered houses.[2]

Map of eighteenth century plantation in the Upper Peninsula, from the Henry A. M. Smith Collection of the South Carolina Historical Society. "Sketch Plan of the City of Charleston and of Charleston Neck showing the lines of the Original Grants in the City and of the Plantations or settlements along the Neck."

Before the Civil War, free Black residents of Charleston found their homes on the relatively surveillance-free Neck. After the Civil War, phosphates were discovered in the earth near the surface of the land in Bear Swamp (now West Ashley, see Chap. 9) and phosphate processing plants and industrial railroad yards set up to serve them emerged on the Neck. Phosphate mining was brutal, backbreaking work; formerly enslaved people resisted it but often found themselves excluded from other employment nearby.[3] On the Neck, the process of refining phosphate rocks into usable material for fertilizing purposes created massive amounts of toxic industrial waste that still affect the area.[4] (As the *Post and Courier* reported in 2019, the contamination these plants produced "gained national attention in the 1990s when shrimp who were exposed to phosphorous started exploding.")[5]

The building of a large Navy base on the former Retreat Plantation on the Neck in 1901 got Charleston's post-Civil War economy back on its feet, employing 1,700 local citizens.[6] The base expanded during World War I and became a major employer of Black Charlestonians. By the mid-twentieth century the phosphate factories had failed and been abandoned, leaving behind their toxic ruin, and the Neck developed a reputation as a blighted, jumbled place where people went to find strip clubs and gambling halls. Then a major economic blow hit the region: The Navy base was shut down in 1996. Twenty thousand direct jobs and another ten to fifteen thousand indirect jobs vanished.[7] Urbanist and developer Vince Graham says that following the base closure, "It just really went to hell, a lot of that whole Neck area."[8]

Today, it is as if Robert Moses won the planning battle in this part of Charleston: the Neck, which was annexed into the city of Charleston in 1976, is utterly car-centric.[9] It has historically been the most socioeconomically vulnerable area in all of Charleston[10] and its residents have been low-income, but the Neck was always sparsely populated and never fully residential. (The Neck was also the home of the ILA building, designed by Harvey Gantt, before the union moved its operations to North Charleston.) All the former industrial high land on the Neck is ripe for development and growth,[11] and is now being rapidly built on.

Although a good deal of the Neck is on higher land, there are also large areas of fill over marshland on the Neck. There is the small African American community of Rosemont, which was sliced through by the construction of I-26 in the 1960s and then again by the building of a port access road to the new State Ports Authority terminal in North Charleston. There is the 300-unit Bridgeview Village low-income housing compound, the single largest low-income housing complex on the peninsula (east of Morrison Drive near the Cooper River).[12] Both of these two are very low areas where Black Charlestonians still live. These places flood frequently.

Map showing annexations/1976 annexation, growth of Charleston.[13]

The Army Corps has concluded that extending its proposed storm surge wall to protect Rosemont and Bridgeview would be economically impractical—the benefits of such a wall would not be worth its cost. The Corps argues that building walls to protect these communities would have substantial impacts on wetlands. It has rejected the idea of raising neighborhood roads. Instead, the Corps is proposing to offer flood-proofing and home-raising measures to residents there.[14] Community members are anxious, and the Southern Environmental Law Center says that the Army Corps proposal "does little more than pay lip service to the needs of" Bridgeview and Rosemont.[15] Meanwhile, polluted tidal waters, the residue of the Neck's industrial past, will continue to wash over these sites.[16] "Rosemont is a historic neighborhood, and we've already given a lot for the greater Charleston area," resident Eduardo Curry II told the *Post and Courier* in 2021. "I really believe that we're not seen as part of the city of Charleston, as we should be."

◆

There is a blocky building on the Neck, much taller than everything around it, marooned between giant boulevards and the interstate. That is the 156-unit Joseph Floyd Manor, home to low-income and developmentally disabled elderly people, which rises thirteen stories above its parking lot.[17] It was once called the Darlington Apartments, and was built in the early 1950s by developer, former State Senator, and former Charleston city councilmember Leonard Darlington Long. In 1979, it was acquired by the Charleston Housing Authority,[18] a business enterprise that gets most of its funding from the Housing and Urban Development agency and is not overseen by either the city or the county council. The residents of the Joseph Floyd Manor live below the poverty line. In 2017, neighborhood advocates joined with artist Mary Edna Fraser to hang a colorful banner all the way down the side of the building bearing a quote from Voltaire: "We argue. Nature acts." The background image on the 100-foot-long banner was Charleston, flooded by 4.5 feet of sea level rise.[19]

We Argue. Nature Acts. banner, "Charleston Airborne Flooded"
Banner for Enough Pie Awakening V: King Tide.

Some people from the Federal Housing Authority came to town, saw the banner, and said it was inappropriately taking a political position. The banner came down.[20] It had been part of an art-based civic discussion about rising tides in Charleston. "We were trying to empower people to not feel hopeless," Cathryn Zommer of nonprofit Enough Pie, which convened the group that put up the banner, said in 2018.

Affordable and public housing in Charleston has a troubled history. In 1934, a federal survey found Charleston's housing facilities to be the worst in the nation. About a fifth of the units had no running water at a time when just 5 percent of housing across the country lacked this amenity. Nearly half the units in Charleston had no indoor toilets, and fully a quarter had no electricity, compared to 18 percent and 8 percent, respectively, of houses in the country. (The situation improved for white residents, but 73 percent of Black households in Charleston still had no indoor toilets and 27.5 percent had no running water as of 1950.)[21] The survey triggered the building of several segregated housing projects in the city, funded by the federal government but built and owned by the city or county. Today, some of those same projects are still standing, and they are home to mostly Black Charlestonians.

Yet even after this survey, the affordable housing picture in Charleston remains awful. Ninety percent of residents making less than $20,000 a year pay more than 30 percent of their income on housing, and one-third of residents making between $50,000 and $75,000 are doing the same. The city would have to open 12,000 more affordable housing units by 2030 to match the demand for them, but nonprofits and developers built less than 2,000 such units in the twenty years between 2000 and 2020.[22] Meanwhile, the median price for a home in Charleston County is above $500,000, which means only 15 percent of households there can afford to buy a home.[23] The city needs eighty more Joseph Floyd Manors, right now, in good condition. It is unlikely that they will appear. If units are built, they are often not built well: The Charleston Housing Authority opened a new 62-unit mixed-income affordable housing development on the East Side in 2020, calling it Grace Homes. By October 2022, the facility was suffering from dramatic structural problems, including cracked foundations, and many tenants were complaining about chronic water issues, infestation by cockroaches and bedbugs, and trash piling up in the hallways.[24] Other recently built buildings put up by the Housing Authority have had severe construction defects.[25] Property managers hired by the Housing Authority routinely filed thousands of eviction cases between 2015 and 2020 as a means to collect late rent.[26]

In 2020, Rep. Wendell Gilliard visited Joseph Floyd Manor in response to residents' complaints and was horrified at the filthy, bug-ridden, rat-infested conditions he found.[27] Mold-coated air vents. Bedbugs and leaks everywhere. Drug dealers making free use of the hallways. The head of the Charleston County Housing Authority, which opened Joseph Floyd as a home for retirees and elderly disabled people in 1981, was fired after these reports came out.[28] A year later, however, residents told the *Post and Courier* that conditions hadn't improved.[29] In the end, the County Housing Authority is likely to decide that it will make sense to sell the building to private developers to be rehabilitated.[30] The idea is that residents would get Section 8 vouchers to find affordable housing elsewhere while the renovation is going on.[31] A 2014 planning document for the Neck area says about 400 new residential units and 700,000 square feet of commercial space could be developed in Joseph Floyd's footprint, and piously recommends that a "variety of housing options" for low-income senior citizens be part of the overall plan.[32] But current residents of the Joseph Floyd Manor pay about $300 per month in rent and are afraid of having nowhere else to go if the building is emptied to be cleaned out.[33] Average monthly rents in Charleston are $1550, an unimaginable amount for them.[34] Even newly opened "afford-able housing" on the peninsula—such as in the roach-infested Grace Homes—is going for at least $1200 a month.[35]

Black residents of Charleston are skeptical about the entire plan. "I think the Joseph Floyd Manor, they want it to die through attri-tion," says Michael Miller, the county's register of deeds. "Because it's so valuable. You think about it, if a developer went in, took over that building and turned half of those rooms into privately owned condos, you could rent some and then you could lease some. That would be a financial goldmine for somebody."[36]

That may be what is happening. In late June 2022, Charleston County Housing and Redevelopment Authority CEO Frank Scott told the *Post and Courier* that the building would be demolished and rebuilt.[37] No one knows what will happen to Floyd Manor's current residents, although Scott says the plan is to "tackle the logistical challenge" of finding temporary housing for those displaced.[38] "The site is more desirable than ever," the paper editorialized.[39] Joseph Floyd Manor is sitting on prime, high, developable land, close to all three of the Neck's wide boulevards (King, Meeting, and Morrison streets) and I-26 on the spine of the Charleston peninsula. There's a reason those streets are there: this is the high ground of the peninsula, undergirded by sand instead of swamp, along which Charlestonians have been traveling for centuries to avoid getting their feet wet.

◆

Michelle Mapp always traveled those streets between her home in North Charleston and the law school in downtown Charleston, traversing the length of the Neck in the process. Mapp knows all about the tragedy of the housing and flooding situation in Charleston: before she made the decision to go to law school so that she could be in a position to change the facts on the ground for Black Charlestonians, she headed the statewide South Carolina Community Loan Fund, managing a dozen staff members and catalyzing hundreds of millions of dollars in loans and grants. Many people feel Mapp, a Black woman with a serenely emphatic manner, should run for office. She's not interested. There's enough to do without having to deal with the nonsense of politics, in Mapp's view.

Mapp was born Michelle Minus in Bad Kreuznach, Germany, where her father Benjamin Minus III was an Army drill sergeant.[40] Her mother, Laretha Johnson, married her father at eighteen and three children were born in short order: Denise in 1967, Michelle in 1969, and then Benjamin IV in 1971. Handling three small children at the age of twenty-two in a foreign country could not have been easy for her mother, but Laretha Johnson Minus somehow managed it. She had a formidable mother herself: Ruth Johnson had raised Laretha along with nine other children on Poinsett Street in Charleston, across Meeting Street from the old city bus station. Laretha had gone to C. A. Brown High School on the East Side, graduating the same year Denise was born and the new Minus trio moved to Germany. Michelle has no memories of Germany; the family returned to living in America when she was four, first at Fort Bragg, in Fayetteville, North Carolina, and then Fort Jackson, in Columbia, South Carolina.

Benjamin Minus III was five years older than Johnson. He grew up on Bogard Street, near where Rev. Darby's AME chapel now stands, and went to Burke High School, class of 1962. He was very intelligent and wanted to be a mathematician. Benjamin was also a very good football player as a student at Burke, and the story in the family is that The Citadel had considered recruiting him. But 1962 was three years before The Citadel admitted Black students. Resistance to desegregation there came from the top, from General Mark Clark, a controversial senior Army officer and The Citadel's president from 1954 to 1965, who denounced *Brown v. Board of Education of Topeka*, saying that it was the Supreme Court's effort to "force indiscriminate racial integration upon the South."[41] It took Clark's retirement to change things, but that happened too late to do any good for Benjamin III.

Michelle's dad was the third oldest of twelve children, and after his father died when Benjamin was still at Burke he felt an obligation to help his mother support the younger Minuses. So he went into the Army instead of college. All his younger brothers and sisters were college educated, and most of them had gone on to get master's degrees or PhDs. Education was crucial for all the Minuses, who have a long history in South Carolina. One of Benjamin's grand uncles, Rev. Daniel Melton Minus, had started the first high school for Black students, Sterling High School in Greenville, a very well-known school later

attended by Jesse Jackson. Benjamin Minus III stressed the importance
of education for his children and was well-respected by his colleagues
and people whom he worked with. Although he was a drill sergeant,
he took it easy on his children; he wanted to decompress from the days
of drilling and was fond of drinking and playing cards.

In 1982, when Michelle was thirteen, the family moved back to
Charleston. Her parents were divorced by then, and Laretha Johnson
and her three children initially stayed with Ruth Johnson on Poinsett
Street. Michelle found the move a cultural shock. She was used to
visiting Charleston; it had been the destination for many summers and
holidays when she was little, and she had spent summers at Hampton
Park with her grandmother and cousins, visiting the animals when
there used to be a zoo there. But there wasn't a lot of segregation in the
Army and in the environments where she had grown up. In Charleston,
things were different. She was put into Rivers Middle School, an all-
African American school on King Street. After about three months,
they took her out. She had never before gone to a school that was all
Black. People said, "You talk differently." All of it bugged her. Her
mom Laretha moved the family to North Charleston. There Mapp
went to Brentwood Middle School, which was integrated, a lot closer
to what she had been used to on military bases.

High school was also in North Charleston, at Garrett High. There
a fine English teacher, Mrs. Teal, took an interest in Michelle Minus.
Mrs. Teal seemed to Michelle like the ideal of a teacher. She had a
huge, soul-stirring belly laugh. Many of the girls at that point had
wanted, at the most, to be teachers. Mrs. Teal, who introduced
Michelle to the power of words and literature, told her she could be an
engineer or a lawyer. Michelle listened hard. Around this same time,
Michelle's dad, the drill master, reinforced this message when he didn't
react well to Michelle saying she wanted to be a journalist or a writer.
Her dad would pound into her head the idea that she would not be

able to support herself that way. "You're a smart student. You should do engineering or math, science, something!" he said.

Michelle had wanted so badly to get out of the state and go to Cornell. She had been admitted there and a number of other places. But Laretha Johnson was by then married to a longshoreman from Mount Pleasant named Freddie Coakley who himself had custody of his four children, all of them born two years apart, the seven children collectively meshing by age like interlaced fingers, and they had formed a strong family. They wanted to be within a car's drive of Michelle and insisted she pick a place in South Carolina. So Michelle had gone to Clemson to study engineering.

There she found a kind of school within a school: there were about 1,200 Black students at Clemson at the time, and they all pretty much knew each other. She was often the only Black student and only woman in her classes. Mapp knew the school's history: after the Civil War, the South Carolina legislature, led by Robert Smalls, had adopted the strongest new state constitutional assertion of the importance of non-discriminatory education for all anywhere in the country, and Black students had entered the University of South Carolina—for the first time—in 1873. The crushing of Reconstruction in South Carolina had been swift, however, and the state stopped funding the University of South Carolina. Instead the state established Clemson Agricultural College, for white males: a college-level segregation academy. It had been set up on John C. Calhoun's Fort Hill Plantation, built in 1825, where hundreds of enslaved people had worked. Calhoun's son-in-law Thomas Green Clemson had owned Fort Hill after Calhoun's death, and willed the land and his fortune to the state to start up Clemson as a land-grant college. Mapp saw the white-columned plantation house that John C. and Floride Calhoun had lived in. It sat at the center of the Clemson campus, and was considered by the college to be a shrine.[42] She knew there had been enslaved people there.

Not one Black student entered Clemson, a public university, until 1963, and it took a class-action lawsuit and the help of the US Supreme Court for that student, future architect and politician Harvey Gantt, to force his way in.[43] South Carolina was one of the last states to desegregate its public schools after *Brown v. Board*. There were no Black faculty at Clemson until the 1970s, and no Black PhD students until 1972. In 1981, Clemson was still lagging when it came to desegregation, and had to implement new programs and activities in order to come into compliance with the Civil Rights Act of 1964, including a five-year desegregation plan.

At Clemson, Michelle Minus began to be more culturally and racially aware. She remembers Jesse Jackson coming to campus, and a group of Black students protesting the student newspaper's generic and stereotyped treatment of Black people in its stories. She remembers that in 1988, her freshman year, the suggestion of an MLK federal holiday (signed into law by President Reagan in 1983 and first observed nationally in January 1986) caused a ruckus at Clemson; students wanted the holiday, but South Carolina did not observe MLK Day until 2000.[44] (Before 2000, South Carolina state employees could choose between celebrating Martin Luther King Jr. Day or one of three Confederate holidays.[45] Today, the choice is between Juneteenth or Confederate Memorial Day.[46]) Michelle experienced a few moments of discrimination, such as when a professor wanted her to take notes instead of actually do a lab exercise, but they seem minor to her now. She took an African American studies class that introduced her to James Baldwin, Howard Thurman, and other great writers; she began to open her eyes. Not that she had been shielded. She just wasn't focused on race.

There's a photograph of her on graduation day 1991 that shows a coiled tiger, the mascot and symbol of Clemson, right over Michelle Minus's head, its huge carved mouth open and snarling, frozen in space. From where she stands clasping her diploma in its purple case in front of her, Michelle can't see the tiger. Her proud mother, Laretha, posed her there, waving her backwards so that Michelle's head was right below the crouching beast's jaw. In the picture, Michelle is smiling confidently, her black mortarboard planted firmly on her head with its tassel placed to the back. Other graduates are wiping the strands of that flimsy tassel out of their faces to the left or right, trying to keep the threads from getting stuck in their mouths. Not Michelle, who folded the rounded white collar of her blouse neatly over her black robe and put on white stockings to bring her look together. Black patent leather ballet flats with bows, too.

Michelle enjoyed her engineering studies at Clemson. She liked the rationality of process and logistics. Industrial engineering sparked her interest when one of her professors talked about the work he had done for Mercedes during his sabbatical. She felt confident that she was just as intelligent as anyone else and could compete with everyone. But after graduating in 1991, right into a recession, she wasn't able to find a job as an engineer doing the kind of work her professor had described. Jobs that seemed so plentiful in the fall of 1987 when she arrived at Clemson dried up while she was there; there were hardly any firms interviewing on campus.

She applied to a graduate program at the University of Tennessee and was accepted as one of the first Ronald E. McNair Post Baccalaureate Achievement Program fellows.[47] It was a summer enrichment program aimed at preparing first-generation, low-income, and underrepresented students for doctoral programs. Most of the participants were Black students, and there were more women than men. Michelle finished the summer program but did not stay on at UT for graduate school. She had good reason: she was walking near campus when a man pulled up in his car, opened the door, and exposed himself to her, telling her to get in the car. Michelle froze; thankfully, a little old woman was cutting the grass nearby. That woman saw what was happening, rolled her lawn mower right towards the guy, and yelled for her husband to come outside. Michelle decided she had seen enough of Tennessee and went back to North Charleston.

The following fall, Michelle arrived in Washington to start a master's program in Engineering Management at George Washington University. There was a lot of 1992 presidential election coverage—those endless overpopulated debates—and news. Michelle got the policy bug, just as she had gotten the engineering bug way back in high school. She also met Marquette Mapp, who was a radioman working for the Navy.

The school had a laundry list of internships available, and Michelle's very first interview was with the Naval Facilities Engineering Command, which promptly hired her to work on Base Realignment and Closure—a process that ended up closing the Charleston Naval Base in the mid-1990s, wiping out one of the key sources of Black employment in the region. It was a massive logistics undertaking that involved building models based on enormous amounts of data about naval facilities. Michelle's role at the time was data input, but she went along for the presentations to Sen. Arlen Specter at the Pentagon. That job went on for a few years. She began to feel far away from her family in the southeast, and they decided to move to Atlanta, where Marquette had grown up. In hindsight, Michelle sometimes wishes she had stayed in DC.[48]

But Atlanta wasn't a bad place for her, and Michelle and Marquette, now married, stayed for several years. Their son Seth was born in Atlanta, and Michelle had a good job in her chosen field, advising Fortune 500 firms on their supply chain and transportation plans, while Marquette began to make his way in corporate America. But then his employer, Nortel Networks, laid off 25,000 people in 2000. Marquette needed employment, quickly, and ended up taking a job in Charleston with defense contractor Eagan McAllister. Michelle, Marquette, and Seth, just four months old, moved back to Charleston in 2001. The frequent travel her job required had gotten to her and she imagined living in Charleston would be ten times better than living in congested Atlanta. She dreamed of being home in the evening with her family, and thought Seth would play in Little League. She believed Charleston would be an idyllic, quieter place where she and Marquette could raise a family, close to Laretha and her intertwined siblings. Michelle decided to become a high school math teacher at R. B. Stall High School in North Charleston.

Now she realizes that, at the time, she did not understand how significantly the school system had changed since her childhood. How much more segregated it had become. She didn't know that there were extreme pockets of poverty hidden in plain view in Charleston. The experience of being a high school teacher brought her up short.

Stall was a Title I high school—meaning that it was eligible for federal aid because the school was serving economically disadvantaged students. Mapp taught mostly first-time sophomores in a program the school called the Freshman and Sophomore Academy. Her students were, on average, nineteen years old, and almost all Black. Mapp began to understand that something had gone wrong for these students that had nothing to do with their innate abilities and potential. From kindergarten through fifth grade, these students did fine. But there seemed to be an invisible hurdle in middle school that caused them to get held back, over and over again. Many of them were incredibly intelligent, bright, and motivated young people. The difference between these older sophomores and other students was, she learned, consistency. She saw that many of her students didn't have a permanent home. They were living in a room in someone's house with the rest of their family. Or maybe their mom was staying with siblings elsewhere but they were with an aunt or uncle to go to school; nothing was fixed or reliable in their lives. She saw children who always went to the back of her classroom, put their heads down on their desks, and fell heavily asleep. Not to take a nap, not because they were a little tired, but because they were exhausted and this was the only place where they could actually sleep. When she sat down and talked to them in a nonjudgmental way, she found they were working full-time jobs when they weren't in the classroom, or that they weren't in a situation where they could rest at night. And there was the young man in her class that everyone called Beats. She thought about him often when she remembered her talented students who were stymied by their circumstances. He was always making music, tapping on the desk, rapping on his chest with his knuckles. He fit no stereotype of a failing Black child; he was really smart. He just hadn't managed to get through high school.

Mapp taught at Stall for two and a half years. Every single one of her students, she felt, wanted to graduate. Maybe some of them had side hustles. But the vast majority showed up every day, determined to get that degree, knowing it was important. There were layers of challenges: The uncertainty of housing near the school was reflected in the troubled community in which the school sat. There wasn't a grocery store or a day care center; all the basic elements that make up a vibrant community were lacking.

The contrast between what Mapp saw in her Stall classroom and her own high school years, and her own life, was jarring. She went to a school that was fifty-fifty Black-white, with a diverse group of teachers, and that single school had athletes, artists, smart kids, and the kids who went behind the building and smoked weed, all in one place. Now there were magnet schools and charter schools and art schools everywhere in the region, and the precarity of life for adults working low-wage jobs was alarming. What you had left were the kids who had challenges in her classroom at R. B. Stall.

Teaching at Stall hooked Mapp on the signal importance of local government, planning and zoning, and community development.

Was anyone going to do anything about what was happening to these children? Was anyone going to ask the hard questions about why these communities were so troubled, why their life was so contingent?

Mapp decided to get another graduate degree, this time in public administration. She stopped teaching in 2003, after the arrival of a second child, a girl she and Marquette named Jordan, and went back to school, this time at the College of Charleston. She decided to dedicate herself to community development, economic development, and housing: without fixing housing costs, larger changes weren't possible. There was such a disconnect between what people could make and what an average house or apartment cost. People simply could not change their conditions in this situation, and because they couldn't make ends meet they kept moving around, getting evicted. This transience was punishing children who were just as talented as any children anywhere.

In 2005, her final year at the College of Charleston, Mapp got a call from one of her professors saying, "There's a graduate of the MPA program, Tammie Hoy, who worked for the city of Charleston in its Department of Housing and Community Development and then left to start a new nonprofit. I think it's a perfect match for what you want to do." At the time, Hoy, a white woman who had grown up in public housing on the South Side of Chicago, had been responsible for working with citizens on options for increasing affordable housing on the Charleston peninsula, and had been considering leaving for Charlotte, North Carolina, to head up a new housing trust fund there. Mayor Joe Riley convinced Hoy to stay, and helped set up the Charleston Housing Trust, whose initial purpose was to provide financing and resources for affordable housing. Hoy, named the founding executive director of the Trust, was looking for an intern who had an interest in housing and community development. During their talk, Mapp enthusiastically said she'd be interested. Mapp became a part-time intern with ten years of work experience and two master's degrees. A year later, after she graduated, she took a full-time job with the Charleston Housing Trust. A few years after that Mapp became Executive Director of the organization, by then renamed the Lowcountry Housing Trust.

In this job, Mapp faced significant legal and financial problems: local governments in the Charleston region didn't make affordable housing a priority and expressed this through their zoning ordinances. Not only that, Mapp's organization, unlike other housing trust funds around the country, couldn't get access to dedicated, reliable funding. In 2007, Lowcountry Housing Trust staff argued that a state deed recording fee should be increased by fifteen cents on every $1,000 and that the money should go to local housing trust funds. Mapp was initially optimistic that people would understand why this fee was a good idea. Housing could be used to pay for housing; dollars thrown off by appreciating housing, captured by appreciating recording fees, could be pooled to build more units that waiters and waitresses and hotel staff could afford. But it was hard to get the public to understand this, to see that creating a system that would benefit a larger society would be a good idea—a better idea than, say, building a single Habitat for Humanity house. People could see the nails and the family touched by the Habitat house. They couldn't see the long-term possibilities of systemic funding for new affordable housing. Realtors and home builders, on the other side, fought hard against this fifteen cent fee, framing it as a tax on their industry. Lowcountry Housing Trust lost this battle.

South Carolina has a system of tax increment financing (TIF) legislation in place, which defines affordable housing as infrastructure that is an appropriate recipient of the money thrown off by appreciating property values in a TIF district. (As you'll recall, any incremental increases in property tax revenues experienced in a TIF district can be devoted in advance to the new roads and infrastructure that the district needs.) But the legislation also requires that in order to be funded the housing had to be owned by the local government. That wasn't attractive to the city of Charleston or North Charleston. Not a lot of local governments around her wanted to be in the housing ownership business.

Faced with these obstacles, Hoy and Mapp decided to morph their organization into a chartered Community Development Financial Institution that would make loans across the state—something more like a bank that would focus on serving the needs of low-income people. Mapp, who had become the organization's Executive Director in 2011, renamed the Lowcountry Housing Trust the South Carolina Community Loan Fund (SCCLF), and went on fighting for support.[49]

Based on her experience teaching at Stall, she knew affordable housing needed to be within an overall functioning community to survive. People told her, "It's great that we now have housing, but there's no grocery store here." Or there was no daycare. Or if a child wanted to buy pencil and paper, there was no drug store, or really any local economic development.

With a staff of just twelve people, she launched loan programs for healthy food enterprises, community facilities, and community-based businesses as well as affordable housing. In the small business area, her group focused on helping local businesses own their underlying real estate, crucial in a place like Charleston that was rapidly gentrifying and where commercial real estate is as unaffordable as housing. The SCCLF funding took away some of the risk of investing in these efforts because its money was often the first into any deal. That allowed Mapp's organization to make possible hundreds of millions of dollars in total development expenditures.

In 2020, the tough COVID year, SCCLF attracted almost $21 million in investment, $16 million of which came from financial institutions and government agencies, provided technical assistance to dozens of entities, and made loans ranging from providing working capital to small businesses navigating the pandemic to multimillion dollar bridge loans for New Market Tax Credits projects.[50] One loan that year, to a community land trust in North Charleston, was particularly noteworthy: the land would never be resold, to avoid gentrification; instead, it would be held in trust for the community while the homes on the land were owned by their residents.

But although she had set these plans in motion at the loan fund, Mapp was already gone by then. At the age of fifty, in firm command of a major statewide financial institution and with two teenagers still at home, she decided to go to law school in 2019.

◆

There were lots of reasons that caused Mapp to make that next move. Mapp was not a political person at Clemson. She had shown up, followed along, and paid attention, but she had not been leading marches. She had felt very peripheral to college activism. But in recent years, working in Charleston, she became much more aware and engaged. So much had happened that needed to be addressed. She never wanted to be an elected official; she was and is a private person. But she could still be a leader, and she thought arming herself with a law degree would make her more effective.

She remembers the June 17, 2015 massacre at Mother Emanuel. She was already in bed when one of her husband's cousins from Atlanta called saying, "Turn on the news. There's been a shooting at a church in Charleston." The news about who was involved trickled in that night. She and her husband knew Reverend Clementa Pinckney and were shocked to hear he had been killed. They got a call about 1:00 A.M. about Tywanza Sanders, one of the victims, who was the son of one of Marquette's coworkers.

The next morning, Michelle was in a car on the way to an event in Georgetown, up the coast from Charleston. The phone rang again, and for the first time she heard the news that Sharonda Coleman Singleton, who was married to one of her high school classmates, had been killed.

She went to Sharonda's wedding; her son Seth had played baseball with Sharonda's son. Then she heard about Depayne Middleton Doctor, who went to church with Michelle and who worked for the city of Charleston in its Housing and Community Development Department. The drumbeat of murder was overwhelming. Unthinkable. Mapp turned around and headed back to Charleston. She was grateful to hear there was a church service to attend. Rev. Darby spoke; it was at Morris AME. She felt better just being with people. But that time, that unbelievable, unfathomable time stayed with Mapp. It was hard to process. She had a sense of anger. But that anger wasn't just about Dylann Roof.

She was angry that the Walter Scott shooting three months before—the shooting of an unarmed fifty-year-old Black man in the back by a white police officer, Michael Slager, aged thirty-three, on the morning of April 4, 2015[51]—didn't spark collective outrage in Charleston. Slager had initially stopped Scott for a nonfunctioning brake light. "Why is it," Mapp says, "that we can understand and see the racism at play and the backstory of Dylann Roof, but we couldn't see or understand that you don't get shot for running away from a traffic stop?" The two events were so close in time. One was a traffic stop for nothing, a kind of daily indignity that then led to a horrifying murder; the other was a massacre. But the daily indignities, the Confederate flags flying, the smooth racism of Charleston was itself traumatizing. "There is all this stuff that exists here that we just overlook," she says.

The governor of South Carolina, Nikki Haley, was asked in October 2014 why the Confederate flag still flew over the capital, and she said it wasn't an issue. "Not a single CEO" had complained about it, she said.[52] She even claimed that South Carolina had overcome its racist past. "But we really kind of fixed all that when you elected the first Indian American female governor," Haley said. "When we appointed the first African American US senator [Tim Scott], that sent a huge message." Horrifying, blind, unthinking. That was just months before the Emanuel shooting finally moved Haley to order, in late June 2015, that the flag be taken down.

That step, removing the flag, felt sheerly political to Mapp. "It was good for business to take the flag down," she says. It was all about economic development—wanting the University of South Carolina to be able to play Duke in Greenville. There was no acknowledgement of what the flag stood for, no acknowledgement that it was put up there in the first place in 1961—a hundred years after the start of the Civil War—to terrorize Black people and declare the state's resistance to the burgeoning civil rights movement.[53] No statement valuing the Black residents of South Carolina as citizens.

Mapp wanted people to understand the meaning of taking that flag down, but that hadn't happened. Daily life for Black people in Charleston was still traumatizing. Thirty-six percent of Black South Carolinians lived below the poverty line—more than twice the 17 percent poverty rate for whites in the state. So many people didn't understand that. All of this was of a piece with the self-narrative of the Charleston region, where white people comforted themselves by pointing out that there was no rioting after Walter Scott's killing. All the forgiveness after Emanuel fit with that pattern, as Mapp saw it. It felt to her like a celebration of Black acquiescence.

Nonetheless, Mapp and her husband shed tears when the flag finally did come down.[54] They were in the car with the kids when they heard the news. She told Marquette, "If you had asked me thirty days ago whether that flag would come down in my lifetime, I would have said, 'No.'"

◆

For Mapp, the drum leading her to law school kept beating. One day in 2017 she went to Jordan's middle school to pick her up. Something was wrong, she could tell. Jordan said, "I'm not going to do well on my social studies test because I refused to answer some questions." Mapp asked what had happened. Jordan said there was a question on the test that read, "If you were a slave, would you rather stay with your master who treats you well, or be a runaway slave?"[55]

Mapp was shocked. "How could a social studies department in 2017 think that it was okay to ask such a question?" she asks. It was mind-boggling.

In Charleston, there are white people with good intentions who want to see things get better, she believes. But there are very few people, white or Black, who are willing to understand what is behind this quotidian, ubiquitous white supremacist attitude. What Dylann Roof had to say was not that different from what politicians often said, was not that different from what was published in certain op-eds by the *Post and Courier*. Roof was not created in a vacuum. No one is asking the hard questions: "What's broken? What happened?" Mapp didn't see changes, she didn't see money flowing to fix broken structures, and she was tired of being invited to events to talk about race in Charleston.

When it comes to the Community Loan Fund she used to lead, she says, "We could have all the resources in the world. We could have the best regulatory environment in the world. But, ultimately, if we want to work our way out of a job, if we really want to change things in South Carolina, that it's going to have to take policy change that moves the world." Mapp decided to go to law school so that she could ask those hard questions and make those policy changes happen.[56] She began classes in January 2019. Today, Mapp is working for the ACLU of South Carolina on reforming eviction law. North Charleston, where she lives, was the eviction capital of the nation as of 2016.[57]

◆

North Charleston hasn't been a city for long. It was formerly a vessel for the spillovers of the commercial and cultural tendencies of the city of Charleston and the peninsula. Now it is the center of gravity for the whole gentrified, congested, and boomtown region. It has a mayor, Keith Summey, who like Joe Riley is a kind of super-incumbent: he has been in office for thirty years. Summey, like Riley, gets credit for building the new North Charleston, which was incorporated in 1972, by turning it into one of the state's top economic engines. And Summey, like Riley, is viewed as doing favors for friendly developers—unconstrained by South Carolina's anemic ethics laws—and not necessarily for North Charleston's Black communities.[58] That's what Michelle Mapp's pastor, Rev. Nelson B. Rivers III, of Charity Missionary Baptist Church in Liberty Hill, says about Summey: "Unfortunately, for my community, we get the short end of the stick."[59]

After its incorporation, North Charleston, like Charleston, grew through romping annexation, swallowing up the naval base, the Air Force base, and the Charleston International Airport, while leaving behind pockets of unincorporated areas, many of them inhabited by Black people. Mapp does not think that happened by accident.

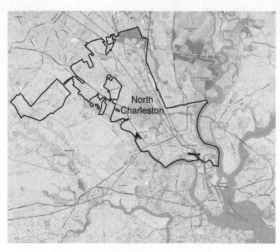

Map of North Charleston.

By the mid-1980s, North Charleston had more than doubled in size and population to 65,000 inhabitants.[60] The city jumped across the Ashley River in 2005 to annex 6,600 acres called Watson Hill, and then turned around to offer developers the chance to build a thousand or more new houses there.[61] In the 1970s and 1980s, North Charleston was the place Black people moved to when the peninsula became prohibitively expensive. It now has about 115,000 residents and sprawls across seventy-seven square miles.[62]

Portions of it are rapidly gentrifying, echoing Charleston's patterns. No city in South Carolina lost more Black residents than Charleston, the state's largest city, between 2010 and 2020.[63] Now North Charleston is, in turn, becoming too expensive.[64] Charleston County lost a larger number of Black residents between 2010 and 2020 than any other county in the state, even though the population of the state had grown substantially.[65]

Michelle Mapp says there are really two North Charlestons: north and south. The southern part is the section that borders on the Neck portion of Charleston, where North Charleston neighborhoods like Chicora-Cherokee, Waylyn, Union Heights, Liberty Hill, and others struggle on, places of poverty and unemployment, populated by Black residents who are mostly living in rental buildings that have seen better days. Union Heights was split in half in the 1960s by the construction of an exit ramp from I-26.[66] These neighborhoods cluster to the right and left of Meeting Street closer to the peninsula, then near Spruill Avenue as you continue to drive north.

In 2005, when Mapp began her internship at the Lowcountry Housing Trust, North Charleston had been made up of seventy percent rental properties—a lot of substandard single-family rental houses, particularly in these southern parts of North Charleston. North Charleston understood that it needed greater density in that southern area, and had moved, slowly, to higher density, multifamily housing. At the time, the pricing pressure hadn't been great, and affordable housing was still possible in North Charleston.

Mapp's mental line between the northern and southern portions of North Charleston lies along Remount Road, named for the shouts of World War I officers commanding soldiers to get back on their horses.[67] At 9:30 A.M. on Saturday, April 4, 2015, Walter Scott, unarmed, was shot five times in the back near Remount Road when he ran away from a police officer who had stopped Scott's car for a broken tail-light. Mapp thinks of Scott every time she sees the "Remount" street sign.

The differences between the two North Charlestons are stark. Mapp lives in the northern, more prosperous and suburban North Charleston, in a mostly white subdivision called Indigo Palms. Like rice, indigo dye was another exploitative eighteenth century Charleston industry. Like the rice plantations, the indigo business was built on the backs of tens of thousands of enslaved Black men. They would soak indigo plants, drain off the juices into fermentation vats, remove the water out of those juices, form and dry scores of blue cakes, pack the cakes into barrels, and get those barrels onto ships bound for England's textile industry, all designed to produce a profit thousands of miles away.[68] Other northern suburban areas of North Charleston include Archdale, Windsor, and Northwoods, home to a giant mall. These are all places where there are many choices of grocery stores, good schools offering scores of AP classes, and twirling cul-de-sacs of solid, four-bedroom houses fronted by garages.

In the southern portion of the city, people are living in food deserts and their neighborhoods are pressed in upon by building sites and new freeways flung up to serve the transit of goods and tourists. The schools are some of the worst in the state. The southern portion has a childhood poverty rate that is sometimes the highest in the state and one of the highest crime rates in the country. There is an eviction for every six renters.[69] The city is planning to displace more than ninety "low-wealth" families in this southern part of North Charleston and spend a billion dollars to widen and extend a freeway.[70] It has already spent many billions of dollars on a new port terminal. What it really needs to do is to build more affordable housing and ensure that the children going to school there learn to read.

North Charleston's southern end always has hopes of revitalization, but that will likely mean displacement for many of its poorest residents. Park Circle, toward the southern portion, was built in 1912 for the diverse community of people working at the city's Navy base.[71] It is now becoming unaffordable, a haven for the professional class, and rents are climbing every month there. The shopping streets right near Park Circle were deserted in the late 1990s after the base closed, but they are now booming with restaurants, breweries, and nightspots. The gentrification pressure in the city of Charleston was so extreme that it had pressed up into Park Circle and other parts of southern North Charleston. The northern region was already wildly expensive and full of million-dollar homes. "We are so far behind the gun in terms of the supply issue on the peninsula," Mapp says. "Why doesn't the paper do an exposé about North Charleston?" Mapp asks.

In 2019, North Charleston advertised itself as among the fifty most affordable places for millennials in the country.[72] Yet its Black residents keep getting evicted. The problem is money: the rents are just too high for people of modest means.[73] Mapp has heard elected officials say they don't want to get involved. "I don't want to get in the housing business. I don't think that's our role,"[74] they will say. She isn't one to argue that the public sector has to own all the housing, but she thinks that the public sector has to set the rules under which the private sector builds. As far as she can tell, that isn't happening, or is happening only incrementally—gaping crevasses of need persist.

The lack of reasonable housing worsens the already horrific congestion problem in the region. "Every time another restaurant opens, and every time another hotel opens, if you don't have housing, you are just exacerbating the transportation issue," Mapp says. "People don't understand that if you are a tourist-dominated peninsula, if the overwhelming majority of people are working in retail, restaurants, hotels, but none of those people can afford to live on the peninsula, they're having to drive or ride a bicycle or ride public transportation to the peninsula from somewhere, and you are going to have traffic problems."

All the municipalities in the state increased their average wage by January 2020 except for Charleston, where the average wage went down. Charleston is more and more becoming a place where huge numbers of minimum wage people are needed to keep the hotels and restaurants going, and many of these are badly paid jobs. There is no way to get around, no transit, and incredibly scarce affordable housing. "We're putting a band-aid on such a huge need," Mapp says, when it comes to housing. "We get excited about a 25 million dollar bond, when in reality it's probably a 250 million dollar issue, or a trillion dollar issue. So we're just barely touching the surface."

This is happening in a context in which the city is talking about a couple of billion dollars to address flooding on the peninsula, but no one is adding to that the money that is going to be needed to build higher, drier, denser, and cheaper.

◆

"We will have to move people," Mapp says. She imagines that intelligent, forward-looking planning would make the high land north of the peninsula the center of the region. Right now, the labels used for that area are Goose Creek, Summerville, Ladson, and North Charleston. If you drive about twenty-five minutes north—in no traffic—from Charleston City Hall up I-26, that's where the center will be, on the high land where Rivers Avenue begins as Highway 78 before it runs gently downhill to the peninsula. That's where the density could be if there was coordinated leadership in the region. That's where, if people were able to work together, there could be public schools and affordable housing and daycare and grocery stores and libraries and public parks, all nestled above the water to come.

She's worried that the region is running out of time. "I've been saying for the thirteen years that I've been here that we're one hurricane away from being a totally different community. And it scares me. I know the number of folk in this community who live in mobile homes still. Who live in substandard housing. I know that we are not creating, despite everyone thinking that we are, I know that we're not creating new housing options that are going to be sustainable for the long term and that are going to be able to withstand the floods. . . . Where will these people go?"

It seems to Mapp that people are waiting for the region to be wiped out by a hurricane to start thinking about changing things. "You think Puerto Rico and the Bahamas would be cautionary tales for us. We don't want to wait until we're wiped out to then try to figure out what this needs to look like," she says. "Who's leading that discussion?"

◆

Cathryn Zommer is a white woman and a former New Yorker who led the Enough Pie nonprofit in 2018 from an office on the Neck. In that capacity, she worked with "a lot of communities of color and diverse communities." She's clear that she doesn't speak for the Neck's residents. She wishes there were other Black people who spoke more strongly for Neck residents. In September 2018, Zommer was invited to join an advisory committee that would be examining Charleston's stormwater guidelines. She looked around the table at the first meeting and saw that there were seventeen people—twelve men and five women, all of them white. "It's unacceptable," she says. "It has to be unacceptable. And yet how do we remedy this scenario. Because if we come back in and there's one or two people of color at the table now, that's tokenism. That should have been addressed before we entered that room."

She is worried about the rapid development of the Neck area: "All this development is going to flood this area even more, and who lives here? This is the last remaining area that has a diverse community. Everyone is moving to North Charleston. People are getting outpriced. So, it's like they're creating the problems, these little cash registers of developers, and yet they're not really sticking around to make sure that the solutions are there."[75]

For several years, there has been a forest of cranes near the Joseph Floyd Manor where I-26 dumps onto the peninsula and Morrison Drive curves upward: nine-story buildings, hundreds of units, big fonts announcing luxury lifestyles, hotels, and apartments with views of the Ravenel Bridge and Charleston Harbor. The Charleston City Paper took to publishing a "crane count" each week; there were nineteen cranes spotted on the higher ground on the peninsula in the first week of May 2021.[76] In the spring of 2022, a new 189-acre mixed-use development right on the Ashley River, a former polluted industrial site running west of I-26, was announced by its Houston-based owner/developer, Clark Davis. He's calling it the Magnolia Project. "You want to start from a strong point, and that's the waterfront," Davis told the Post and Courier. Someday, he hopes, there will be four thousand housing units, more than a million feet of office space, and more than a thousand hotel rooms there. Right now much of the parcel is marshland. The site used to house fertilizer factories and a lumber-treatment plant, belching arsenic and creosote; luxury apartments will someday replace them.[77]

Black residents of Charleston who were priced out of the lower peninsula moved to the East Side, then further up the Neck, then into the southern portion of North Charleston. As the waters rise, it is unclear where they can go next, and the region is not planning ahead. Wherever the ground is high, gentrification and displacement have already arrived or are coming soon, including, now, in North Charleston. Developers are still hoping to make the most money possible from the already damp fringes of the marsh.

8

Upper Lockwood: Gadsden Green, WestEdge, MUSC, and the Future

Rev. Joseph Darby's church, Nichols Chapel, sits on the Charleston peninsula behind a simple wrought iron fence. Its address is 57 Kennedy Street.

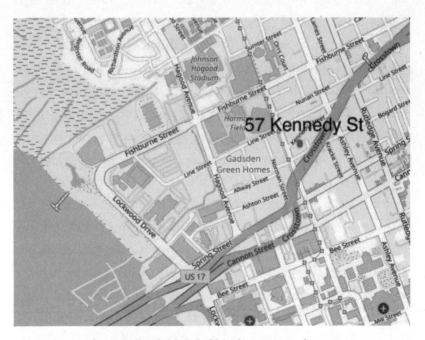

Darby's church/Nichols Chapel map, map of upper west portion of Charleston Peninsula.

Four broad white-bricked steps lead to its double front door, which faces onto a narrow porch framed by two white pillars. In 2020, some of the paint on the wooden pediment above the pillars was peeling, and the glass of the two large front windows on either side of the doors was reinforced with wires set in a diamond pattern. The tan bricks of the church building looked new; a slender white steeple rose up a story from the roof. To the left of the brick steps was a sign bearing the seal of the African Methodist Episcopal Church and the name NICHOLS CHAPEL AME CHURCH in large letters. In somewhat less permanent and smaller lettering, it read, "REVEREND JOSEPH A. DARBY, PASTOR." Below that: "AME STRONG. TRUSTING IN THE LORD." On either side of the church and on either side of Kennedy Street as it made its short, stubby way back east to the Crosstown was a jumble of one-story bungalows with porches, a few of them overgrown with vines and trees, some of them needing a paint job, some of them carefully maintained.

One block north of Nichols Chapel, an entirely different form of housing emerged in late 2020. No one was living there yet. There was raw dirt around the buildings and bedraggled yellow police tape was draped around the boundaries of that dirt. These buildings were all white. Each porch was twelve feet off the ground, above a gray-painted first floor with no function other than to allow water to flow through false shutters designed not to gracefully filter the light of a bright sun but rather to admit a roaring river of surge. The first three buildings appeared to be large single-family homes. Rounding the corner, left onto President Street, which intersects with Kennedy a block south, the buildings appeared to be cookie-cutter postmodernist condominiums: still white, two floors tall, with first floors elevated far above the sidewalk. Each floor had a screened-in porch. Each building was large, uniform, and clearly expensive. By October 2020, these buildings had edged their way onto Kennedy Street as well, and one of them stood white and uninhabited catty-corner from Nichols Chapel. All of this—Nichols Chapel, President Street, Kennedy Street, and the brand-new buildings—is on the West Side of the Charleston peninsula, just above the Crosstown.

This fourth area of Charleston, the West Side, or Upper Lockwood, which is the last location we'll look at on the peninsula, combines every element of Charleston's story: It was the last tidal, marshy area to be filled for development purposes, it has a long and painful racial history, and it features the same extraordinary level of planned development that we saw with the Union Pier project on the lower peninsula. The WestEdge project envisioned for this area, which will eventually include nearly 2,000 apartments, 700,000 square feet of office space, 1,350 hotel rooms, and many other amenities,[1] will realize one of Mayor Riley's most significant plans for the future of his city. The new houses on Line and President Streets were likely built on the expectation that the WestEdge project would bring flooding amelioration and higher property values to the entire area. WestEdge also sits right next to the three-blocks-wide Gadsden Green Homes public housing project, which, like the damp housing projects of the East Side, is one of the few places on the peninsula where low-income Black Charlestonians still live. The trouble is that much of the area, existing and planned, sits on trash and fill. It is profoundly threatened by sea level rise.

◆

In October 2020, Rev. Darby tried to show Nichols Chapel to a visiting cousin. It had been a tough year for Darby. COVID closed his chapel and robbed him of his ability to visit sick and dying members of his flock, which was a painful loss for him. His wife of nearly fifty years, Mary Bright Darby, had suffered for several years with stroke-induced dementia even before the virus struck. Pre-COVID, aides were there to give Darby a weekly break from his wife's care, some time just to sit in his car or in a park and breathe. After the virus arrived, he was on his own, and it was very hard. Mary passed away in August 2020. After a pause, Darby had gone on preaching, meeting his people online and making sure he got a big crowd by setting the service for 11:30 A.M., just a bit later than other churches. With everything the year had brought, he was glad of his cousin's visit and happy to play tour guide.

The two cousins drove east over the Ashley River Bridge to the Charleston peninsula. They left the Crosstown Freeway at Cannon Street, then turned left on President Street. They began heading north until Darby saw that he would have to stop the car. President Street was flooded and closed. He reversed course, got back on the Crosstown, and zoomed east for another few blocks, heading towards the sole exit off that part of the Crosstown, trying to approach Nichols from another direction. The Crosstown makes navigating the streets of the decimated former neighborhood a challenge. Coming back the other way, he could see that the street behind Nichols, Bogard, was also flooded. He pointed out the church about two blocks away to his cousin. That was the church where he had been the pastor for the last eighteen months. He couldn't drive to it. He warned his cousin not to get out of the car. The water was filthy.

Darby hadn't checked the tide charts that afternoon, but most Charlestonians check the tides the way most Americans check the weather as their days begin. Nearly ninety times during 2019, so-called "sunny-day" flooding—water filling the streets when it wasn't raining—brought much of Charleston to its knees, and 2020 flooding was on course to break that record.[2] There were floods before in Charleston's history, but up through the 1980s they happened only a handful of times a year, and usually when a storm was around to strong-arm waves ashore. Now major flooding on days without storms or rainfall was becoming much more frequent and severe. The worst was a king tide, a high tide pulled even higher by a new moon's arrival close to the earth. It was a king tide of more than eight feet—a major flood, two feet above a level that would have caused minor disruption to the city—that kept Darby and his cousin from visiting Nichols Chapel on October 18, 2020.

The *Post and Courier* reported that a tourist visiting Charleston during that same king tide looked up at the sunny sky, confused. "What happened here?" she asked, as she maneuvered around a flooded intersection in downtown Charleston.[3] The harbor water from the Cooper River spilled over the east side of the peninsula onto East Bay Street, flooding most of that major thoroughfare. Along the western side of the peninsula, below Nichols Chapel and the Crosstown, Lockwood Drive had merged with the Ashley River. The water ran in torrents down streets surrounding the Medical District on the edge of that same Ashley River, making it impossible to reach emergency rooms and doctors' offices.

The land on which Nichols Chapel sat, near the corner of President and Kennedy, had been nearly waterfront property in 1804, comparatively dry land sitting near the marshland running in from the Ashley River. Cannon Street, the route Darby had followed to take his cousin to visit Nichols, had its origins in Daniel Cannon's Bridge, built over millponds to allow visitors to enter Charleston from the north. Now almost a mile of man-made land lay between the chapel and the river to the west, and it was settling as the waters were rising.

Darby was right to warn his cousin not to step out of the car on that perfect blue day. Although the state didn't measure water quality, nonprofit environmental firms and journalists had told the public that staggering levels of E. coli were present every time the streets flooded.[4] In 1859, a report commissioned by the Charleston City Council on the yellow fever epidemic of 1858 related a particularly nauseating story. "The entire offal of the city was transported to . . . and deposited along President Street," wrote a committee assigned to study the epidemic. "This street runs through the marsh, so that at every high tide the whole of this sweltering mass was saturated with water and its putrescence dissolved, or suspended, so that when the tide receded, the foul matter was spread over the whole surface of the marsh, where it was left to be acted upon by the summer sun. The result may be easily imagined. But those who realized the actual condition of things from personal observation cannot easily forget the disgusting sight and smell."[5]

◆

Darby remembers when Mayor Tecklenburg came to Nichols Chapel one Sunday in October 2019, when he was running for reelection. The mayor hadn't been to Nichols before. The chapel is a small place and politicians have limited time, Darby graciously acknowledges. But Darby had been the pastor at Nichols since the beginning of 2019, and Darby had a big mouth, so the mayor knew he had to pay a visit. That visit happened on a sunny, dry day.

Darby suggested that Mayor Tecklenburg go out the door to Bogard Street at the back of Nichols Chapel. There he saw what Rev. Darby wanted him to see: running water just five feet to the mayor's right. And not a little bit of water, but water high enough that the mayor's immediate concern was whether he and his team had parked in a dangerous place and whether their cars were flooding. It was a sunny day high tide, and Bogard was a river.

The mayor started talking to his team, standing right there at the door of Nichols Chapel, about what they could do about the flooding. He found out that under the present circumstances, other than bringing in a portable pump, there wasn't very much they could do. The city had improved the drainage on the Crosstown, but that had rerouted the water on the freeway into the Black community by the chapel. The mayor, his team, and Darby could see a river on the street right beside the church, but the Crosstown was dry.

A couple of years later, a sole, very distressed freedman's cottage still sat right across Bogard from Nichol's Chapel. It was rehabbed, listed for sale for $500,000, and eventually rented for $4,000 a month. In the midst of a tropical storm in October 2022, the city sent a truck to pump out the storm drain on Bogard Street outside that house. Rev. Darby was amused. "We'd asked about cleaning that drain for years. But we didn't see the city act until that house was rented to College of Charleston students," he says.[6]

◆

Up through the eighteenth and nineteenth centuries, the upper west side of the Charleston peninsula was mostly marshland used by Black Charlestonians for swimming and fishing.[7] An 1849 map shows a public cemetery up against the soft edges of that marshland.

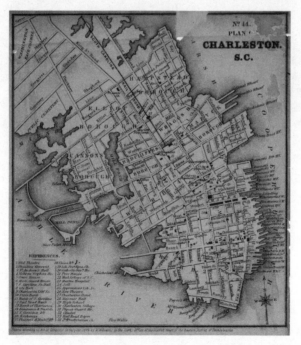

Map of Charleston, "Plan of Charleston, 1849," by Wellington Williams.

Over time, the more solid banks of dirt in the area were used
by small manufacturers for a lumber mill and then a butcher's
district—slaughterhouses, in other words.[8] By the early 1920s, a neighborhood called Fiddler's Green had risen up next to the upper reaches
of the marsh.[9] Because this was a particularly low-lying, marshy,
flood-prone area of the city avoided by white residents, Fiddler's Green
became the place where Black homeowners could afford to buy, and
was home for the largest group of Black property owners of any single
area in the city of Charleston.[10] Those early twentieth century residents
of the West Side were schoolteachers and tradesmen who had become
sufficiently prosperous that they could stop renting on the lower peninsula and start building wealth in the form of property.

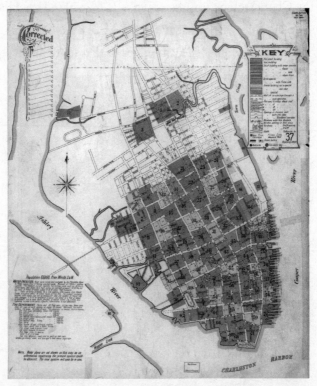

*"Sanborn Fire Insurance Map from Charleston, Charleston County,
South Carolina," by the Sanborn Map Company, 1902.*

On September 29, 1938 a tornado wiped out many Fiddler's Green homes. Housing was already difficult for Black Charlestonians who were being priced out of the lower peninsula, and the tornado made things worse.[11] Mayor Burnet Maybank decided to raze the fifty or so homes still standing on this northerly portion of the West Side and build segregated public housing for Black residents there instead. Black homeowners protested in a letter to Maybank's successor.

49 Norman St.
Charleston, S.C.
March 25th. 1940

Honorable Henry W. Lockwood,
Mayor of the City of Charleston,
City Hall,
Charleston, S.C.

Dear Sir:-

We the undersigned Citizens and Free-holders of the area effected by the proposed low (rent) cost "Housing Project" in the section of Charleston known as "Gadsden Green" South of Line Street, West of President Street and North of Bogard and Alway Streets do most earnestly and honestly protest against this area being used as a Slum-Clearance Project for the following reasons.
This is not a slum district . 2nd. About 75% of the people living in the effected area are either buying or own their homes.
3rd. That a careful survey of all the homes in the effected area show that more than 80 per. cent of the houses are in good repair and the people living in them are respectable , honest hard-working people with respectful connection throughout the City of Charleston among both White and Colored people. A Census of this area will show that more than 50% of the people in this area are Mechanics, Artisans and School Teachers and others who have definite ways of supporting themselves.
4th. That this is the largest group of Colored property owners in any single area in the City of Charleston. If we are forced to give up our homes at this time it will be the greatest tragedy to befall an unfortunate people. With most of our earning power on the wane, we will not be able to go out and face the world again trying to buy homes with sacrifices and privations that we once suffered.
If we give another thought to this situation, there is not another single area in Charleston available to Colored people where so large a group can purchase or build homes, and the few places that are available to our group, are prohibitive in the purchase price.
5th. To go out now and live in rented homes or buy at a higher price than we can sell for, would not be fair to our Children nor to us as it would only leave a flood of mortgages for our children struggle along with.
If you will personally investigate this area, or have an impartial committee do so, you will find the facts as herein stated.
We are also writing Dr. Josiah Smith(Chairman of the Authority) concerning this matter.
We will thank you for any consideration that you give us and anything that you can do about it.

Very Truly Yours, The Citizens of the effected area.

John A. Harris, Secretary for the committee.

Letter from John A. Harris to Mayor Lockwood.

CITIZENS OF THE PROPOSED "GADSDEN GREEN PROJECT" AREA.

1   John B. Howard,   9 Fludd St.
2   Mrs. Willie Ann Michell, 15 Pine St.
3   James Smith, 25 Fludd St.
4   Augustus Parker, 217 Line St.
5   S.B. Chisolm, 6 Fludd St.
7   John Mack, 47 Norman St.
8   Mrs. Katie Pinkney, 6 Alway St.
9   John B. Gadsden, 29 Norman St.
10 Mrs. Viola Harper, 27 Norman St.
11 John H. Green, 31 Norman St.
12 Herman Boone, 14 Fludd St.
13 Oswell Holmes, 45 Norman St.
14 John Dawson, 225 Line St.
15 Thadeus Frasier, 14 Fludd St.
16 John A. Harris, 49 Norman St.
17 Rufus Dingle, 42 Norman St.
18 Herbert Smalls, 44 Norman St.
19 Mary Harrison Truscott, 169 President St.
20 J.R. Logan, 177 President St.
21 Theodore R. Foster, 138 Bogard St.
22 Frank Rollison, 25 Norman St.
23 J.C. Chase, 2 Mayen Ct.
24 Mrs. Josephine Gordon, 8 Lilly St.
25 Paul Richardson, 11 Lilly St.
26 W.M. Felder, 18 Alway St.
27 Mrs. R.A.Y. Ferrett, 4 Pine St.
28 Willie Smith, 11 Fludd St.
29 Mrs. Josephine Williams, 16 Fludd St.
30 Mrs. Emma W. Bailey, 195 President St.
31 Joseph B. Smith, 6 Alway St.
32 Eddie Smalls, 10 Alway St.
33 Mrs. Edith Washington, Line and Norman Sts.
34 Leroy Vanderhorst, 15 Norman St.
35 Mrs. Anna Simmons, 187 President St.
36 Ola F. David, 217 Line St.
37 Mrs. Evelyn Nesbit, 6 Lilly St.
38 Mrs. Marien Washington, 22 Pine St.
    Mrs. Sallie Smalls, 31 Norman St.

Page showing signatories to Harris letter.

—pointing out that there was nowhere else nearby where they could afford to buy or build homes, but the city went ahead.

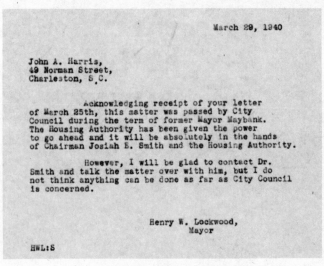

                                        March 29, 1940

John A. Harris,
49 Norman Street,
Charleston, S.C.

        Acknowledging receipt of your letter
of March 25th, this matter was passed by City
Council during the term of former Mayor Maybank.
The Housing Authority has been given the power
to go ahead and it will be absolutely in the hands
of Chairman Josiah E. Smith and the Housing Authority.

        However, I will be glad to contact Dr.
Smith and talk the matter over with him, but I do
not think anything can be done as far as City Council
is concerned.

                        Henry W. Lockwood,
                        Mayor

HWL:S

Mayor Lockwood letter

The west side near what became the Gadsden Green Homes was one of the last tidal waterways on the Charleston peninsula to be filled, covered, and diverted. The city used debris from the tornado to fill the marsh, and named the segregated project Gadsden Green, a nod to Fiddler's Green and to Thomas Norman Gadsden, a white developer from the 1800s who had initially subdivided that marshy area.[12] There is no public record of what happened to the dozens of families and homeowners whose houses were wiped out in the 1940s by the creation of the housing project.

The city expanded the Gadsden Green Homes over the 1950s and 1960s, west and south of modest Black neighborhoods whose buildings echoed the classic Charleston look, if on a small scale: gardens and two-story houses on tree-lined streets. The Gadsden Homes, though, as they sprawled outwards, had none of that streetscape charm. They were unloved barrack-style brick apartments, stark and treeless.

In the mid-1950s, the city decided to dump its trash on marshland nearby, effectively in the backyard of the Gadsden Green Homes.[13] A drainage ditch was dug to get water out from those landfill operations into the Ashley River.[14] The new landfill was unlined, and heavy metals and harmful PCBs leached out into that drainage ditch, which came to be called Gadsden Creek. The creek was fixed in a controlled route, confining what was now a man-made waterway to a sharp-edged "L" shape.

The city reclaimed more land from marshes in the mid-1960s and deeded it to the Charleston Housing Authority, which extended the Gadsden Green Homes atop it.[15] Residents saw the trash heaps and resented them, and hated the rats and flying garbage that they generated. Resident Shirley Chavis and others from the Gadsden Green Homes filed a lawsuit against the city in 1971 to stop the dumping, but nothing came of it.[16] In that same year, the Department of Justice and Army Corps of Engineers also threatened legal action against the city's illegal dumping. In response, the city obtained an after-the-fact permit to dump in Gadsden Creek.

From the perspective of the residents of the Gadsden Green Homes, the dumps blocked their view of the Ashley River, at least from the first floor of the Homes, but they still had a creek to fish from and swim in.[17] Gadsden Creek, that drainage ditch that had been redirected and renamed, ran from the former dumps near the Homes and out to the Ashley River.

Then the roar and concrete of the Crosstown was built in the 1960s, cutting off the Gadsden Green Homes and the surrounding Black neighborhood from the lower portion of the peninsula. Residents were isolated in profound ways. David White's uncle Eric Jackson, who founded Laundry Matters on the East Side and who grew up in Gadsden Green, said in 2021, "I didn't know that I lived on a peninsula until I was in middle school."[18]

The Crosstown itself is a six-lane highway connecting I-26, which runs north to Columbia, with the Ashley River Bridge, which connects the Charleston peninsula to its suburban borough of West Ashley across the Ashley River. In the late 1960s and early 1970s the construction of the Crosstown, which Rev. Joseph Darby drives along every day from West Ashley to reach his church, caused the destruction of 150 homes in a middle-class Black neighborhood around that church—which is why President Street is a stub that runs smack into the roaring highway.[19]

In 1973, the city finally closed the landfill. It then simply built on top of it, putting the central office for the Charleston Police Department where appliances and tires had been thrown. The higher elevation of the police department building, which opened in 1974, caused more water to flow to the Gadsden Green area.[20] The city pressed on. It built a minor league baseball field nearby, the Joe Riley Stadium, and created the ten-acre Brittlebank Park atop the toxic trash running right along the Ashley River.[21] Activist Mika Gadsden noted during one of her 2021 livestream broadcast episodes, "The Joe, the baseball stadium—that location was supposed to be where Trident Tech [College] was going to go. But they broke ground and noticed things were sinking. 'Nah, let's put a stadium there instead,' they said."[22] The pitcher's mound at the Joe is the only thing that's built up high enough to survive a flood.[23]

Map of Septima Clark Crosstown.

Meanwhile, the city's enormous medical district, right smack on the river a few blocks south of the Gadsden Green Homes, was rising.

The Medical University of South Carolina, the VA hospital, Roper St. Francis Hospital for low-income patients, and the Children's Hospital, as well as other researchers and doctors, all needed parking. So the city paved over the marsh that had seeped along near the Homes. The pavement made the flooding worse: the city was taking away ground that could soak up water.[24]

This whole area of the West Side that runs north and east of Lockwood Boulevard—medical buildings, police department, baseball stadium, parking lots, public housing, public park—sits on marsh, graves, and trash, with the low-lying Gadsden Green Homes area on the most toxic loose sludge of all.

Because the trash dumps were so poorly set up and were sitting on loose mud, the land is sinking as the trash decomposes;[25] this area is 120 acres of polluted, toxic landfill on wet, soft marsh. At the same time, the seas are rising quickly. The rains are becoming heavier and more prolonged. The creaky drainage infrastructure in the area is easily overwhelmed. The ditch now called Gadsden Creek is connected to incoming tides, and so high tides can cause it to overflow paved areas along its edges, including Hagood Avenue next to the Gadsden Green Homes.[26] Rain causes even bigger flooding problems. The Gadsden Green Homes, and the streets around them, flood routinely at high tide—particularly when there are king tides, and even more when rain is combined with high tide—bringing mold and misery to residents.

◆

Nichols Chapel is a block and a half away from the Gadsden Green Homes. It was founded in the 1970s as a community church with a strong relationship to Gadsden Green. Just about everyone who lives in Gadsden Green, in a neighborhood known as "Back da Green," is Black, and half live below the poverty line.[27] Most are women and families with young children. They are lucky to have a place in the Homes. There are hundreds more families waiting for placement in public housing in expensive Charleston.[28] Eric Jackson, who grew up in the Homes, was priced out of the peninsula when he came back from the military in 1998. He still believes in the peninsula as a central place for the city's economy, even though he now lives in West Ashley: "We might not be able to live down here, but we'll be able to work and feed our families down here," Jackson says.[29]

Back da Green has declined over the years. Michelle Mapp's paternal grandmother, Susie Minus, lived in Gadsden Green, and when Mapp was a child she often visited her there. The young Michelle loved visiting her grandmother, who lived surrounded by plants and had a soap opera murmuring—*The Young and the Restless!*—all the time. The place was well-kept then and a lady selling candy out of her house lived close by.[30]

Now Gadsden Green is falling apart, dank, and troubled. Few in power seem to care. It seems to Mapp, who saw rapid, wholesale displacement of African American communities and people in North Charleston, that the condition of the Gadsden Green public housing buildings is emblematic of Charleston's attitude towards its Black residents: zero investment for decades benefiting people who had been there all their lives.[31]

◆

In 2004, the Medical University of South Carolina, a state agency that has a large clinical training hospital near the Gadsden Green Homes, was considering moving its operations thirty-five miles

inland, away from its landlocked, constrained location on the historic
Charleston peninsula. Climate change and sea level rise weren't part
of the discussion at the time, but growth was. Mayor Riley and his
team swung into action, rezoning the area for higher density and
far taller buildings at a time when peninsular residents were anxious about anything over sixty feet tall. The city and MUSC's in-
house foundation began working together on a plan to re-envision
the area around the hospital as a research park that could attract
private investment. The initial name for the whole plan was the
Horizon Development, and Mayor Riley's vision was that it would
"link the biomedical research at the Medical University of South
Carolina (MUSC) with job creation," and be a "new live/work
neighborhood on the banks of the Ashley River."[32] The city and
MUSC's foundation pooled their land resources around the hospital, amounting to about twenty acres, and contributed them to
a new entity. This is the origin story of WestEdge: the new entity
was called the WestEdge Foundation.[33] The city also established
a tax increment financing district for the area that it called the
Horizon TIF, and set up the area's zoning so that 15 percent of any
housing built there would have to be "workforce" units that could
potentially serve MUSC's staff. MUSC stayed. The state of South
Carolina was investing in the peninsula, and MUSC was the area's
largest employer, tied to one out of every twelve jobs in the region
and producing $2 billion a year in economic impact.[34]

By 2008 or 2009, sea level rise *was* part of the discussion, and
the city/MUSC project leaders began to understand that WestEdge
would need significant infrastructure investment to protect it from
rising tides over the next fifty years. That included higher roads,
so the new buildings would be above flood levels. Better supported
roads, so they wouldn't sink. Stormwater pipes and sewer pipes

whose supports ran all the way down into the firmer Cooper Marl, so the pipes would stay aligned. Green roofs and gutters and downspouts, so most of the water landing on the development wouldn't be dumped onto its neighbors. Better consolidated soil, topped by a four-foot thick platform, so utility lines could sit on relatively solid ground that ensured their reliable operation. The city worked to ensure that the plans of potential private development partners would generate enough revenue through height, density, and amenities to pay back this infrastructure investment. (The private developers buying the option to develop the land would have to do the work to clean up the pollution that is under their projects.)

WestEdge was trying to figure out how to solve its water problems itself for the next fifty years, and the way to do that was to get money loaned to it through the TIF structure to build substantial dedicated infrastructure to protect the new buildings that the developer would be putting up. By July 2019, this structure had attracted about $350 million in private investment and had resulted in the building of three large commercial buildings.

One of the WestEdge Foundation's key remaining planned fixes is to fill and seal a portion of toxic Gadsden Creek, the heavily polluted drainage ditch that was built between the dumps and the Ashley River. The idea is to replace it with an underground pipe to the Ashley that can be better controlled with tidal gates, and add capacity for storage of storm water.[35] This step will, the WestEdge managers say, resolve the flooding problems now being suffered by the residents of the Gadsden Green Homes. WestEdge also promises to create new wetlands areas—a facsimile of a tidal basin—nearby. It is a complicated plan. It is a plan that avoids the enormous expense and difficulty of actually digging up and removing the toxic landfill in the area.

Maps showing outlines of historic creek beds above archival photographs.[36]

*Closeup of medical district and Gadsden Green Homes. The
line nearest the bridge across the Cooper River is the reshaped
drainage ditch now called the Gadsden Green Creek.*

The Citadel, WestEdge, and the Medical District, marked by author to show location of the Gadsden Green Homes.

WestEdge.

It was at this point in their planning that the WestEdge collaboration ran into a buzzsaw of opposition from the residents of the Gadsden Green Homes. Residents said that continued development of WestEdge would make flooding worse for them.[37] This wasn't news. Rev. Darby remembers one of the older members of his Nichols

Chapel congregation explaining the cause of the flooding. She had seen it coming for years and years. They kept building stuff, and the more they built, the more water problems showed up, she told him. Residents did not believe that covering over water would lead to less flooding.

Nor did residents want to see the creek filled, even though city engineers claimed it was toxic. At a public meeting in 2020, Rev. Darby remembers that a man from the Gadsden Green Homes said, "There ain't no problem with Gadsden Creek. I used to fish in that creek when I was a kid." Someone else said, "You were fishing in a dump." The man replied, "Didn't bother me, fish were good." The residents of Gadsden Green found support in what Frits Palmblom, one of the Dutch landscape architects, said during their visit in July 2019: "We think from the point of view of water management, it's quite problematic to—on the place where you have a natural drainage situation, to replace a natural drainage situation by artificial storage," Palmblom said. "Don't cover it, solve it would be our advice."[38]

Gadsden Green residents were also deeply concerned about displacement: they were convinced that the successful development of WestEdge would in turn raise the value of the land on which the Gadsden Green Homes were built, and the end result would be that some excuse or other would lead to existing residents being evicted. These residents had reason to worry. There was a long history of urban renewal projects on the peninsula leading to displacement of Black Charlestonians—the Ansonborough Homes, the Cooper River Bridge, the Crosstown Freeway. In the case of the Ansonborough Homes, the city had claimed that the soil was too toxic to build on and then had allowed some upscale condos to come in once the public housing was gone.[39] Every time, residents were told that their old housing would be replaced by new houses that they could move into. Every time, those promises hadn't been kept. Now West Side residents are worried that the real plan is to move them out, just as raging gentrification has already pushed out so many Black residents of the East Side.[40]

In September 2020, despite the crushing need for public and affordable housing, the Charleston Housing Authority decided to turn over two Gadsden Green public housing units to the police department for use as a substation, even though there was already a police station nearby.[41] This felt like planning for future condos. It felt like a threat.

As of the preparation of this manuscript, this fight is ongoing. The Southern Environmental Law Center is representing the Friends of Gadsden Green in challenging WestEdge's permit to cap and cover Gadsden Creek.[42]

◆

The WestEdge story helps illustrate a central fault line in the "who pays for what" part of this story. Why doesn't the city of Charleston just spend money itself on widespread water protection for all its citizens? Isn't that what taxes are for? The answer is straightforward: the city runs on a shoestring budget of about $200 million a year and has very little money for extra projects.[43] Raising property taxes would raise more revenue for flooding infrastructure, but public resistance to such a step would be enormous.

So why doesn't the city borrow money from private investors by floating bonds? Couldn't that infusion of money fund a giant infrastructure build—like the one WestEdge is carrying out for the new research park next to MUSC—to protect everyone in the city, including the Gadsden Green Homes and the suburban areas off the peninsula? Isn't there a lot of capital sloshing around America that could be happy with modest, steady, infrastructure-like returns of, say, 4 to 5 percent, that could be covered by increased property taxes if need be? After all, it is usually state and local governments that fund this kind of water-related infrastructure—raising roads, shoring up utilities, and the like.[44]

There are many reasons why going into debt for city-wide infrastructure would be difficult for Charleston. Under South Carolina law, the city would have to get voters' approval if it wanted to incur debt that would exceed 8 percent of the assessed value of all taxable property within its borders.[45] Who wants to go through a referendum? If the city defaulted on its general obligation bond debt service, it would automatically have to raise property taxes. Again, this route would be a nonstarter politically.

But an even more powerful reason for not issuing bonds is that the city can, instead, go the TIF route by borrowing money from, say, the Charleston County School District to fund the building of particular infrastructure that will support private investment in a particular building project. Everybody will get paid back by the increased tax proceeds generated within the area of the project. TIF districts theoretically enable a cash-constrained government to make long-term investments in underdeveloped or blighted areas. The upside of a TIF is that the targeted infrastructure can more easily attract private investment. Private money will be drawn to the possibility of a far higher return than could ever be generated by a municipal bond—a short-term return of, say, 10 percent from work on a development, rather than a long-term return of 3 percent or so from a municipal bond.

The downside is that no one outside that TIF district likely gets equivalent investment in infrastructure. There hasn't been internet access or adequate drainage in Gadsden Green. And, as Michael Miller complained in a previous chapter, the initial funding for the infrastructure is taken from a public source (the school district) rather than borrowed from, say, Wells Fargo. That lowers the cost of capital for the city, but simultaneously limits the scope of the investment while lowering the school district's capacity to serve its students. Finally, as property values climb within the district, which is, after all, the rationale for creating a TIF district in the first place, the risk of displacement of low-income people nearby increases.

Now that the sixty-acre planned development of WestEdge is growing, fiber-optic lines are being put in and there are plans to ensure the area is dry.[46] The WestEdge developer is working on getting stormwater off the streets. Capping and closing the artificial drainage ditch—Gadsden Creek—that runs alongside the old toxic landfill will help manage flooding. Capping and closing the old landfill will help manage toxicity. All this infrastructure work will help drive Charleston's burgeoning "Eds and Meds" economy, because the 25,000 or so doctors, nurses, and students who work in the city's medical district and students at the College of Charleston will have expensive and dry nine-story-tall WestEdge buildings to live in, as well as additional options in new surrounding buildings—like the new townhouses and apartments going up near Nichols Chapel. Life science startups might take root there. There is already a large new supermarket on the ground floor of one of the buildings and a private club/restaurant on the top floor. There's a luxury apartment building called The Caroline that features "unobstructed views of the Ashley River and RiverDogs Stadium."[47] "You know what this wetlands needs?" quips activist Mika Gadsden. "It needs a condo with a rooftop pool. Let's call it The Caroline."[48] Great until it isn't; a water view until you're under it. But no one is talking about actually fixing up the Gadsden Green public housing or shoring up the few houses still owned by Black people in that same area to make them safer for habitation.

◆

Parents taking their kids to school at the Charleston Development Academy Public Charter School, down Line Street in the middle of the Gadsden Green public housing development, "damn near need a canoe to get there" on high tide days, according to Michael Miller, whose daughter went to that school. And the students rap about it:

> *All these tides are flooding our streets . . . / We're on a mission / Not asking permission / Find a solution / For our city's evolution / Gadsden Creek is filled with trash / Now all the flooding is a / Pain in the Ass-phalt . . .*

Rev. Darby has seen President Street turn into a river during heavy rains. When Irma hit in 2017, emergency rescue boats came into Gadsden Green to get people out of there—that's how high the water was. Darby knows that the city is hoping WestEdge tax money coming out of all that shiny new development will help fix some of the flooding issues on the West Side. Maybe the city will fill in the open spaces between the barracks-lines of the Gadsden Green Homes with expensive condominium buildings and use some of the resulting revenues to maintain the existing public housing. Maybe the city will replace the Homes with mixed-income housing. Maybe some of the people who live there will someday be able to move back into those new units.

But Darby firmly believes that, in the end, none of these plans will actually work out for Black people on the West Side who are now living in uncomfortable conditions that are about to get worse. Someday, he hopes, the city will realize how ill-equipped the private sector is to fix public problems or support public values—like equality and dignity—across a poor population. "That's not the private sector's job," he says.[49]

◆

As we've learned, the proposed "general city plan" for the city of Charleston that became the basis for its 1931 Historic Zoning Ordinance envisioned that the swampy area where the Gadsden Green Houses are now would be populated by Black residents, and the sections right next to the Ashley River, where the Medical University of South Carolina (MUSC) is, would be reserved for white residents.[50] And we know that MUSC, the region's only Level One Trauma Center and an R-1 "highest research activity" institution, is doubling down on the peninsula and staying put, even though doctors sometimes have to arrive by boat through filthy, bacteria-filled water, and even though it is a net exporter of talent.[51] In 2019, MUSC opened a new roughly $400 million children's hospital in the Medical District.[52] "We're committed to the peninsula," MUSC CEO Dr. Patrick Cawley told the *Post and Courier*. "We feel good about that. We're not going to leave. Nothing's going to change there."[53] Just what Mayor Riley wanted: continued investment on the peninsula. Charleston is an economic engine for the region and state, and the state, of which MUSC is a part, has an interest in downplaying any threats to its future.

MUSC is run by mostly white people. The Medical University of South Carolina has been viewed with suspicion by Black Charlestonians for decades. In 1969, after almost two years of organizing and protesting against discriminatory working conditions, Black nurses at MUSC, led by Coretta Scott King, went on strike. They fought for four months for the right to bargain collectively.[54] Although MUSC, to end the strike, promised to fix its racist problems and formally apologized in 2015 for its discriminatory behavior back then,[55] the hospital's mostly Black workers still don't have a union contract, and the top-level managers are almost uniformly white.[56] Rev. Darby and the Charleston Area Justice Ministry tried to get MUSC to include money for mobile health units serving low-income Charleston populations in its 2022 budget, but MUSC essentially said "No." It said its execution partner for this proposal, the Fetter Health Care Network, had decided to go in a different direction.[57]

◆

MUSC's buildings in Upper Lockwood are part of a Medical District that includes the Ralph H. Johnson VA Medical Center hospital and Roper St. Francis Hospital. An ordinary thunderstorm can flood many roads around and through that Medical District, making it difficult or impossible for patients or doctors to access buildings there. As the *Post and Courier* puts it, "After every 'frog drowner,' or rain bomb, you'll see more than a dozen cars around MUSC towed because they're often people who are either patients or hospital workers who left their cars parked in the neighborhood, and they couldn't get out in time."[58] Larger storms pose more significant dangers: during Irma in 2017, staff had to be convoyed to the medical district in National Guard vehicles.[59] People have died because they have been unable to get to the emergency room due to flooding.

In November 2021, 332-bed Roper Hospital, one of downtown Charleston's largest employers, announced that it would be moving off the Charleston peninsula after 165 years. The hospital's spokespeople were vague about its reasons, but they did say that they needed to make it possible for patients to more easily access care.

It was clear the flooding was a major element of Roper's decision to move.[60] The *Post and Courier* wrote that the announcement "marks, perhaps, the most visible evidence yet of the major impact climate change has made, and will continue to make, on the coastal city's critical infrastructure."[61] It was significant that Roper didn't alert the city in advance that it would be moving. Apparently its leadership didn't want a repeat of the strong-arming Riley tactics of the early 2000s. Riley's response to the Roper plan was classic: "I think the city of Charleston has been and will continue to make investments so that the city can withstand storms and flooding," he said. "All of the assets in the city, the intellectual and physical assets, are huge, and will stay here."[62]

Hours after Roper's announcement, the Charleston peninsula flooded at high tide, water covering the street next to Roper Hospital. Persistent flooding cost the Medical District $45 million between 2015 and 2020,[63] and those bills will go up: the first six months of 2022 saw more days of flooding than in any year since records began to be kept in Charleston, and there are likely to be 240 such days a year of flooding by 2040.

The city has a plan to build a drainage tunnel underneath the Medical District that will help with its flooding issues, but money for multi-hundred-million-dollar project isn't currently available and planning is still underway.[64] The chances that this tunnel plan, nick-named "Calhoun West," will be successfully implemented any time soon are low.

In July 2022, the *Post and Courier* reported that a giant nearby drainage project begun in mid-2016 called "Spring Fishburne" had fallen ten years behind its original timeline and was tens of millions of dollars over budget. Cascading delays caused by lack of funding and ongoing storms caused the city to take a patchwork, incremental approach to the 500-acre Spring Fishburne project, which was designed to drain the Crosstown freeway as well as low areas around west Calhoun Street. (It was work on Spring Fishburne that caused water to spill from the Crosstown into the street where Rev. Darby's chapel sits, he believes.) Mayor Riley had been optimistic when he applied for $146 million from the federal government in 2009, saying that he believed in the job creation possibilities of the project. But that number amounted to 10 percent of the total funding available, and the city actually received just $10 million for Spring Fishburne.[65] That was an early sign that Spring Fishburne, now planned for completion in 2024 after years of scrambling for drips of additional funding from state sources, would be difficult. It took years to get *$10 million* lined up to direct part of the Medical District's flooding into the Spring Fishburne tunnels while the hospitals wait for Calhoun West to come into being. Calhoun West, the city's largest and most expensive drainage project, doesn't have a detailed project plan yet.[66] It will cost about $500-$600 million to build.[67] That's cosmically expensive for Charleston.

The first phase of the Army Corps-planned seawall, should it ever be funded, will be designed to protect Upper Lockwood and the Medical District from the effects of storm surge (not persistent flooding or rising groundwaters), but that construction won't begin until 2026 at the earliest. City councilmember Mike Seekings says Calhoun West, not the seawall, should be Charleston's top priority: "When you close off the Medical District not one, not two, but 76 or 80 times a year, that's an unsustainable long-term plan for managing the city."[68] Steven Slabbers, the Dutch landscape engineer, doesn't think much of having a giant medical district floating on trash and muck. "Please, take a second or third look at the hospital area," he said in 2019. "Because it doesn't make any sense."[69]

9

Off the Peninsula, Quinetha Frasier & Charlton Singleton

Although tourists would never know it, most of the city of Charleston and almost all its population are not on the historic peninsula itself. These residents won't be protected against storm surge by any wall built to shield the valuable center of the city—and such a wall won't protect against the effects of rapidly accelerating, nonlinear sea level rise, anyway. The people who live in the far-sprawling suburbs of Charleston, many in one of the 127 subdivisions built since 2013, will be on their own. They face increasingly fierce rainstorms, high tides, river flooding, and rising groundwaters. No one is likely to ride to their rescue.

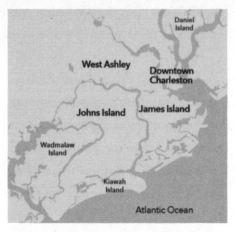

Map of greater suburban Charleston area.

Let's start with forty-four-square-mile West Ashley (named for its location west of the Ashley River) where Charleston's current mayor, John Tecklenburg, lives along with more than half of the residents of Charleston.[1] Where the earliest white settlers in Charleston first made camp is now a state park called Charlestowne Landing, in present day West Ashley.[2] That park is on relatively high land, says Dr. Norman Levine of the College of Charleston: "There's a little sliver of land and a little island that stays there," at six feet of sea level rise.[3] Then those settlers made their ill-fated decision to move to the low-lying peninsula between the Ashley and Cooper Rivers.

Much of the low, marshy area of West Ashley was drained for rice cultivation, then phosphates were extracted from its soils.[4] Its swampland and forest, home to several plantations, remained largely undeveloped until the twentieth century.

Like much of the Charleston peninsula, most of West Ashley was once salt marshes cut through by tidal creeks (today's Church Creek and Stono River), their surfaces dry at low tide and underwater at high tide, the tides pulsing twice a day. Spartina grasses, or cordgrass, the sentinels of southeastern marshes, played an important role in the creation of those marshes. They hung on to sediment when it rolled through, driven by the tides. But these marshes were viewed as the enemy by developers, who filled them up and covered them over to create more land.

Many houses in inner West Ashley, just across the Ashley River from North Charleston and the Charleston peninsula, were built on artificial fill in the 1940s and 1950s, some to house Navy Yard workers, some to absorb white flight from the peninsula.[5] In the 1960s, much of West Ashley was annexed into the city under the leadership of Mayor Gaillard to provide a broader tax basis for the city's operations.[6] Shopping centers, commercial areas, and subdivisions subsequently sprouted up on West Ashley in the 1970s through the 1990s. Since

2001, according to the city, over 2,000 acres in West Ashley have been developed, transformed from marsh and forests to residential areas with impervious surfaces.[7] All this building has compromised the area's ability to absorb rainstorms. Residents have seen flooding increase markedly over the last decade.

Most of the land in West Ashley, as is the case for all of Charleston, is located in a floodplain.[8] The area is now thickly developed, as you can see from this 2020 aerial view:

Aerial map of West Ashley, "NASA Earth Observatory image" by Lauren Dauphin, using Landsat data from the U.S. Geological Survey.

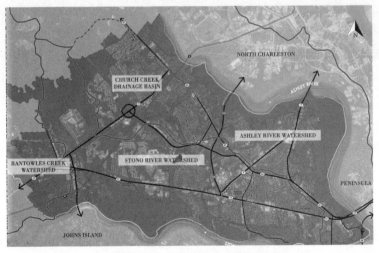

Map of West Ashley watersheds, image created by the City of Charleston.

West Ashley's orientation or geography can be difficult for an outsider to understand. Major roads slicing through the area are highly congested, and the housing subdivisions that lie off those roads are full of inner cul-de-sacs, artificial lakes, and other self-contained elements. There is no particular "downtown" in West Ashley, although the city has extensive plans to centralize and enhance the area's commercial districts.

Confoundingly, not all of West Ashley is actually part of the city of Charleston. There are streets on which some of the houses remain part of the St. Andrews Public Service District, a special purpose area that was created by the state legislature prior to the city's annexation spree. (Before the creation of Charleston County, South Carolina's legislature divided the state into twenty-four Anglican parishes for election and tax purposes; the peninsula was in the parish of St. Philip and what is now West Ashley was in St. Andrews.)[9] These houses get city-like services (sewer, fire, garbage) for which they pay property taxes to the public service district. It all looks the same from the outside, but the color of the garbage cans outside these houses is blue instead of green.[10] Jurisdictional complexity plays a role in the city's challenges.

In 2017, following three historic storms—the Historic Flooding of October 1–5, 2015, Hurricane Matthew in 2016, and Tropical Storm Irma in 2017—that caused horrific flooding near Church Creek in West Ashley, the city commissioned a study of flooding in the 5,000-acre Church Creek drainage area.[11] The city already knew it had major flooding issues in the Church Creek basin, once called Bear Swamp, which used to be mostly marsh and phosphate mines[12] above a very high groundwater table somewhere within five and six feet of the surface.[13] But Church Creek in the modern era isn't continuous. There's a bit of creek visible here and a bit of creek there. It turns out, of course, that Church Creek is still there but has been covered over by development. The city learned that all the overflowing water from the north of the West Ashley Circle was finding its way to the ancient Church Creek levels and rushing out towards the Ashley River. (FEMA had misunderstood the water flows in the area and hadn't predicted this flooding.) There was nowhere for this water to go: Church Creek as it gets near the Ashley River couldn't handle the flow, because its channel is extremely limited—just ten feet wide or so. (Like a "spartina straw," one engineer says.) The city began looking at ways to divert or store water so that it wouldn't all end up flooding the wide area around that narrow channel.

1863 map of Charleston
Church Creek basin is labeled "Bear Swamp."
Image Credit: USGS

1863 map of Charleston Church Creek Basin / Bear Swamp, originally colorized by Waggonner & Ball for Dutch Dialogues® Charleston, has been modified (cropped).

All the flooding was causing misery for the residents of forty-eight low-lying Bridge Pointe townhouses and units in the Church Creek

Basin's Shadowmoss development.[14] These places, all built in the 1980s and 1990s, had chronic flooding problems from the start,[15] and those major storms in 2015, 2016, and 2017 were bringing several feet of water into them over and over again. In 2018, after three years of process, the city received more than $10 million in federal grants that allowed it to buy those homeowners out and demolish their homes.[16]

Mayor Riley's staff may bear some responsibility for these issues. As one former Bridgepointe resident wrote on the *Post and Courier* site, "I lived in Bridgepointe, my heart breaks for my old friends and neighbors, not once did I see the person whose [sic] squarely to blame for this called out! Poor leadership by Mayor Joe! He is the person that allowed this growth even when the Wolpert studies clearly identified the issues, yet the building continued. What's a few elderly folks lives as long as they could grow! We begged him to step in and step up, but all we got were excuses from him and his engineers at the time. The same ones that signed off on development plans from engineering people's whose license had expired! Ask for the hydrology studies [of] shadowmoss residents, good luck, they don't exist! First rule is do no harm, yeah right."[17] A city consultant suggested buying out as many as 350 homes in the Church Creek basin.[18]

The Dutch Dialogues team that visited in July 2019 predicted that 135 homes in the Church Creek area of West Ashley would be lost in three feet of sea level rise by 2050 and another 670 homes needed urgently to be raised or otherwise protected.[19] They urged the installation of an elevated roadway system, recommended that additional wetlands be made available for retention of water, and advised that no one should be allowed to live in the floodplain or in the marshes absent extensive renovations that raised up houses and kept water landing in one place from flooding other properties. Although the city has carried out several drainage projects in West Ashley that were listed in its 1984 Stormwater Master Plan, including in a lower-income suburb named Ardmore that used to be called "Mudmore," and continues to invest in drainage improvements there, none of the transformative steps recommended by the Dutch engineers have happened. "The Dutch Dialogues, yeah, that made some noise," Mika Gadsden said on her online livestream broadcast in mid-2022. "But you can tell that Charleston wasn't going to follow what the Dutch Dialogues [recommended] with actual policy." She said Charleston isn't interested in climate adaptation thought-leadership. "Know what list we make it to the top of?" she asked. "Best city. Some Condé Nast bullshit."[20]

Dr. Levine, who teaches at the College of Charleston, lives in West Ashley, right across the North Bridge from the peninsula. His house is on a bulge of relatively high ground, but houses around him frequently experience flooding. He points to another big problem for the suburbs: Because so many houses were built on fill dirt, and the roads were dug out to provide that dirt as well as drain the land, the roads themselves become water storage places at times of heavy rains and high tides. "That water as it drained away, became less and less powerful," he says, in terms of "being there and being seen as marsh." The people forgot they were living on marsh. In the suburbs, he says, "Every house is built on its own little pad, and these areas of low in between are the roads. In many areas, the roads were designed to move water away from the houses."[21] This means, he says, "The houses can stay up above, but the roads get inundated. And so people can't get in or out."[22]

◆

James Island, another sprawling, congested suburban area, sits across the Wappoo River south and east of West Ashley. Like West Ashley, not all of James Island is part of the city of Charleston: Charleston County, the separate Town of James Island, and the James Island Public Service District all have chunks of territory there.[23]

Science journalist John Tibbetts moved from the peninsula to James Island in 1992. The house he sold there thirty years later sits near an estuarine (meaning an arm of the sea, where it meets a river) salt marsh that historically was a soft extension of the harbor. To facilitate development, the marsh was dredged (the earth below it was dug out) in order to form a man-made lake. That lake now winds through his former neighborhood. "I'm not sure people even realize that man-made lake was a salt marsh," he says. "Basically they're living on the harbor," says Tibbett. "Really our flood exposure is not directly from the harbor," he points out. "It's actually from that remnant salt marsh where [excess] water goes, and it comes up at the end of that lake into my neighborhood." From his perspective, the storms of 2015–17 were "complete game changers." The street a block away from his former house that fronts on the man-made lake "flooded up to the first steps of the porches of four houses along there," about four times during those years. "I was blown away. I couldn't believe it," he says. "It was such a dramatic jump" in water.

Tibbetts thought that the region had time, but starting in 2015 the whole Charleston region suddenly seemed to be "in enormous trouble" from a Category 1 storm that went by thirty miles offshore. Even his own house seemed threatened, as it sits on top of fill dirt that was plopped on the marsh: it's just a hundred yards from the floods he saw in his neighborhood. "And I thought, my God, this is where the flood's going to happen. If it's Charleston, it is going to come right" to James Island, he says. "If a Category 3 hits Kiawah"—the barrier island with the raised golf courses that sits southwest of James Island—"it would blast Charleston to smithereens. And all that water would slosh up to where we are." The storm surge from Irma in 2017 covered a fifth of the buildable land in the Charleston region.[24]

Tibbetts is very worried about the future of homes in the suburbs, including on James Island, that were built from the 1950s through the

1970s. "All those single level houses that are maybe below eight feet" in elevation, he says, "with sea level rise—and there are lots of them still—those are going to be lost. And those people really don't have any recourse. Maybe they will build bulkheads, but they're not going to be able to build them high enough to protect themselves. And many of them aren't going to be able to afford to leave." More than twenty subdivisions were built on James Island during the 1950s alone.[25] Tibbetts believes "that all of those areas in the estuaries, and there are thousands of miles of them in South Carolina alone, are going to be lost." There's a unelevated 1978 house on that flooded street in his former James Island neighborhood that sold in April 2022 for $720,000. "I don't know why somebody would want to pay for that," Tibbetts says. "But a lot of times people don't know."

Tibbetts had to leave his full-time job on the peninsula because the HVAC system in the building he was working in hadn't been maintained. "It created an extreme case of mold," he says, "and so I got sick, very very sick from it." At first he worked from home, but he "didn't recover well enough to really continue." He's now close to recovered, but he retired early, at fifty-nine. He is moving with his wife to Wisconsin. He says that they're moving so that she can be with her family, but it's clear the flooding is a big part of the story. "We can view the future," he says. At some point soon, the riskiness of living on James Island will be fully taken on board by the banking and insurance industries. "I don't know when that collapse is going to happen," he says. He doesn't want to be around when it does.[26]

◆

Also on James Island, nineteen homes within the Willow Walk subdivision, part of the city of Charleston, were built in the 1980s three feet below the then-required FEMA elevation—the so-called "base flood elevation"—without any variance issued by the city beforehand.[27] "Variance" means relief from the elevation requirement. Slab-on-grade, the method was called: Dirt was trucked in to cover the wetness, concrete slabs were poured on top, and a house slapped up for sale—which then, predictably, flooded if any amount of water arrived. The fill, additionally, was taking the place of formerly permeable areas that might have historically stored water, and was instead pushing water into other areas it hadn't been before. The homes in Willow Walk were sold to residents without a certificate of occupancy from the city. After the fact, when the developer pleaded for help, the City Council simply unanimously issued a variance and certificates of occupancy, retroactively blessing the development.[28] During the October 1987 meeting at which the city issued the variance and certificates, Russell Rosen, a member of the city's Board of Architectural Review, said "I certainly hope we don't have a storm that will create a problem." The homes flooded, immediately and frequently, and became uninhabitable. No one was held accountable. One homeowner, Ana Zimmerman, put up a mock advertisement for her house there in February 2019:

"1171 Shoreham Rd., Charleston, SC 29412, 3 beds, 1 bath, 1,237 sq ft. Repetitive Loss Flooded Property. Has an illegal variance issued by the City of Charleston, has an incorrect flood zone on the deed (issued by the City of Charleston). Has an erroneous certificate of occupancy issued by the City of Charleston (this house was never built to code. It is uninhabitable, filled with mold, and noncompliant with federal FEMA standards."[29]

Zimmerman didn't want to sell her house to an unsuspecting buyer. She would have preferred to demolish the place using a FEMA grant, but the bank that held her mortgage wouldn't allow it. Elevating the house was too expensive. She had no choice but to empty out her retirement accounts and pay for another place to live.[30]

The city's encouragement of the Willow Walk development was of a piece with its overall pro-growth mentality in the 1980s and 1990s. Laura Cabiness, the Public Service Director for the city between 1990 and late 2018, told reporter Abigail Darlington in May 2018, "If you're asking me if we're going to stop filling in the floodplain . . . that may have unintended consequences when you're looking at 70 percent of the city and what's available to develop for people to live."[31] In 2019–20, the city made its development standards stricter so that newly built parcels will store and slow water rather than dumping on their neighbors, and outlawed the use of slab-on-grade and fill projects that increase the risk of flooding.[32] But there are thousands of existing houses in the region that were built under the pre-existing, far lower standards.

◆

Johns Island, west of James Island, is vast. It's the fourth largest island on the East Coast, and it used to be mostly rural: Sixty of Johns Island's seventy-six square miles are outside the city's 1999 Urban Growth Boundary, still zoned for rural developments of about one house per acre. At the same time, Johns Island is now the frontier for much of Charleston's continued growth, and its population has doubled over the past decade. Dozens of new subdivisions have been constructed there recently. A key reason for this development is that the island has high land in the form of Pleioscene sand dune structures. Those dunes were deposited on top of the older Cooper Marl of clay and mud the last time sea levels were higher, between 14,000 and 16,000 years ago. One of these narrow dunes now underlies the Maybank Highway, and that is the land the Dutch consultants recommended the city use for dense, interconnected development.

The contrasts on Johns Island are stark. It retains some pockets of peaceful stillness: Johns Island has been home to generations of Black farmers and in the past was populated by mostly Black Charlestonians. But the number of Black residents on Johns Island has plunged in recent years. From 2010 to 2018 Black households on Johns Island declined by 31 percent while white households increased by 64 percent.[33] Some of those Black residents were forced out in "heirs property" disputes. Wary of all forms of white legal process and institutions—including courts and wills—many Black Charlestonians died intestate, assuming that their property was theirs and would be transmitted to their heirs upon their deaths. Today, land known as "heirs' property"— divided by default among potentially hundreds of heirs, making clearing title nearly impossible and FEMA and HUD post-disaster aid unavailable—is estimated to make up more than a third of Southern Black-owned land.[34] Many of those relatives are now living far away from Johns Island and other Sea Islands. Any one of those relatives can force a sale, and real estate developers have successfully exploited this weakness among people who were both distant and unconnected to snatch up large parcels of land. According to ProPublica, African Americans lost about 90 percent of their farmland between 1910 and 1997, and heirs' property disputes and tragedies are woven through the story of Johns Island.

All the strange juxtapositions of Charleston's explosive growth are present on Johns Island. There are strip malls on some of the boulevards, choked with traffic agitating to get elsewhere, as well as dreamy avenues over which mossy oaks bend. Wealthy white homeowners on Kiawah, who now speed over Johns Island by car, are agitating to have the highways on the island widened and the I-526 freeway continued so as to allow them to get directly to and from the airport without having to tangle with secondary roads, just as tourists can get downtown without ever seeing North Charleston or the Neck. But those Johns Island roads even now press into rural areas formerly entirely inhabited by Black residents and pass by occasional roadside fruit and vegetable stands as well as new restaurants. As Johns Island resident Esau Jenkins told the *Post and Courier* in 2021, the island has become "the gateway to Kiawah Island." Johns Island has become a platform for getting Kiawah visitors back and forth smoothly, he said. "That's the bottom line."[35]

The city has adopted a plan to use property taxes paid by the new developments to pay into a dedicated fund for Johns Island infrastructure projects—including drainage and other flood-prevention efforts—that would help maintain the island's green spaces and deal with traffic congestion.[36] Some of the developments over the last ten years away from the high ground of the old dunes have undoubtedly increased the flooding risks on Johns Island. "We have been building on a lot of this low area that should have been considered marginal to begin with," says Dr. Norman Levine of the College of Charleston.[37]

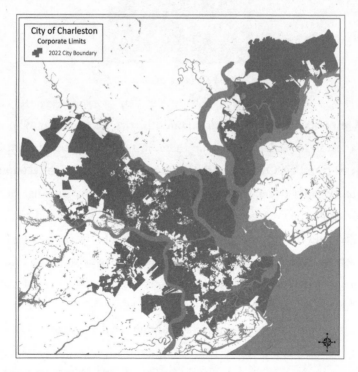

Map of boundaries of City of Charleston; note not all of West Ashley, James Island, or Johns Island is within the city. Created by City of Charleston.

The influx of new subdivisions on Johns Island has spread to unincorporated areas of Charleston County to the west and south, where longtime Black residents live. Drive west from the peninsula, along Route 17, and you will reach Rantowles; bear left, and you'll be on Route 162, which runs through Hollywood and Meggett before reaching Adams Run.

Photograph of Adams Run post office.

Quinetha Frasier, a gregarious midthirties entrepreneur who left Charleston for Atlanta, grew up there, just a short distance from the Adams Run Post Office. She returns frequently. She sees the economic mobility gap between white and Black Charlestonians growing. At the same time, the George Floyd protests during the spring and summer of 2020 and the ensuing international attention to the continuing pain caused by American systemic racism feel overwhelming to Frasier. There are panels and calls and associations and commissions, all focused on "diversity," and she finds having to explain how racism actually affects people's lives across the colonial South exhausting. Frasier suggests having a T-shirt made that has a picture of a blanket on it labeled "DIVERSITY"—tokenism is soothing for people who don't want to acknowledge racism. So many well-meaning white people want to feel comforted that they are Doing the Right Thing. But in the Charleston region, those same people aren't confronting the structures that have left the Gullah Geechee people of the Sea Islands, in particular, in economic despair.

Frasier's ancestors were brought by force to the coasts of Georgia and South Carolina. The white owners of the rice fields there fled their plantations in the face of Union raids at the beginning of the Civil War, leaving their holdings in the care of the enslaved people who had come from rice-growing countries along Africa's West Coast. But even before the owners had left, they had been completely outnumbered by those skilled Africans, who had retained their community traditions and dialects. When the plantation-owners left, Frasier's ancestors remained in tightly knit clusters, raising their own rice. They slowly got wind of the good news that General Sherman's January 1865 Special Field Order Fifteen mandated that this land was theirs. He promised forty acres of land and a surplus Army mule to each freed head of family along the thirty miles of South Carolina coast south of Charleston. But betrayal and painful disappointment followed: President Andrew Johnson reversed General Sherman's order in September 1865. In the decades after that, the Gullah Geechee clawed their way back into land ownership, bartering services, buying parcels outright where they could, forming land cooperatives, and generally doing all they could to hang on.[38] They had a connection to the land that could not be severed, and this feeling of independence and survival tethered to ownership of the earth persists in Frasier's family as it did in the other Gullah people around her. "They did what they had to do to just make it, to live good lives and stay in place," Frasier says.

Frasier is proud of being a Gullah Geechee descendant. "It is the most important thing about me," she says. (The Geechee name is said to have come from the Ogeechee River which empties into the Ossabaw Sound south of Savannah, in turn named for the indigenous native Americans there, and the Gullah creole tongue was born of the need of enslaved West Africans to communicate among their different ethnic groups and be understood by their traders.) Her dad, Reverend Sinclair Frasier, always said, "You are Geechee," and growing up she and her tight-knit friends and family called each other Geechee with pride. Frasier is Geechee because of where she is from, and because her culture was African and the way her people worshipped was African. She has a people and a location, and in her ear she hears a language that blends distinctive African roots with European elements, and African dialect with broken English.

Through all the heirs' property troubles, pockets of Gullah Geechee people have hung on along the coast near Charleston, squeezed by encroaching subdivisions and sometimes living in great material privation, treasuring the beauty of the marshes and cathedral-height trees around them. Frasier's own childhood played out against a complex tapestry of many small settlements on the Sea Islands—Johns Island, Yonges Island, and Wadmalaw Island, among others, each part a tribal area of a kind, with its own habits and name. Her own family's homeplace, where they have been for more than 140 years, is called, variously, Sugar Hill, Yonge's Island, Adam's Run, or Willtown Bluff, and Frasier as a child felt as if she was related to absolutely everyone there. The places of her childhood—Baptist Hill, Sugar Hill, Adams Run, Parkers Ferry, Oakville, Meggett, many names, all within a fifteen mile radius, all in a corridor between Walterboro and Edisto Island—are in an unincorporated part of Charleston County, and her people had little time for or trust in the county government. If someone put up a sign in her region that said, "Come to a meeting with the county government," the people she grew up with thought, "Well, that's the same government that came back after Reconstruction and told us to give them the land back." "Those teeny-weeny communities were resilient," Frasier says. They took care of themselves.

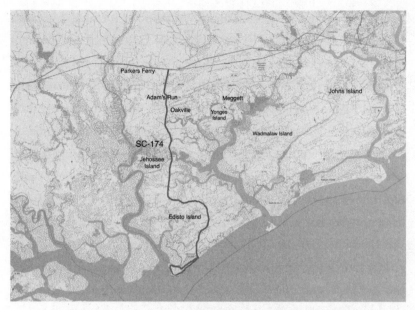

Route 174 running south from Route 17, west of Charleston.

But the lack of connection went both ways: Frasier's community did not get state funding to build public schools until the late
1950s, and her mother, Sadie Joyce Polite, went to the first high
school in the area, the Baptist Hill High School. That school did
not adequately prepare her for the working world. Frasier was born
during her mother's senior year in high school, and her mother resisted
her grandmother's instruction that she quit school. She insisted on
graduating, knowing that she would be better able to help Frasier if
she had a high school diploma. Nonetheless, Sadie Joyce's education
at Baptist Hill was inadequate. She had to take remedial math and
English just to get a job.

Some of Frasier's nineteenth-century West African ancestors planted
rice and fished on Jehossee Island, on a huge plantation that was
owned by William Aiken of Charleston. Frasier's paternal grandfather, Clarence "TC" Frasier, told her that when the plantation and

the warehouse fish processing plant that followed it closed, his father picked up their church on Jehossee Island, block by block, and brought it over to Sugar Hill Road. They called it Mount Zion AME Church.

The land around Frasier's home was beautiful, full of tall trees and tangled bushes, riven by creeks and wetlands. But there was very little paying work there. Although TC Frasier found jobs as a carpenter on Edisto Island, building homes, Frasier's father, Sinclair, struggled and left to join the Army. Troubles with drugs followed, and he eventually returned to the area. He found work as a handyman with a real estate company, but the people there treated him badly because, he felt, he was Black. He left the company and went out on his own.

Her father, Frasier now believes, was depressed. Frasier remembers the combativeness and violence of his relationship with her mother; she now understands that his miserable feeling of stuckness, of lack of agency, fueled those arguments.

On the other side of her family, Sadie Joyce's side, Frasier is proud of her great-grandfather Theodore "Dee" Polite, a short, funny man who never learned to read or write well but forcefully carved his way through life. Frasier has pictures of him holding her hand, the two of them bow-legged and smiling away. Charismatic and playful, Polite found work as a chauffeur for the Arthur Whitney family of Mendham, New Jersey, who had a tradition of coming to the Charleston region for duck hunting. Dee Polite eventually moved his wife Sadie (grandmother of Frasier's mom, for whom Sadie Joyce was named) and five children to Mendham, where Sadie was the housekeeper and Dee the chauffeur on Whitney's gentleman's farm.

When Whitney died, Dee went back to Willtown Bluff driving a snappy red convertible, a gift from Whitney's wife. But the roads near Willtown were so poor that the car couldn't make it the last few miles, and the family had to walk the rest of the way. When they got there, back to their home, they found poverty. The running water, electricity, and modern stove they'd been used to in Mendham didn't exist in Adams Run, and the family lived in a shack with sheets of newspaper on the walls for warmth and an open fire over which Sadie cooked meals. They made the best of it. "Coming back from an estate in New Jersey to a shack without running water or electricity," Frasier says. "Can you imagine?"

Dee Polite returned, he told his son Ted, because he wanted to plant rice. He did, building structures called "trunks" (pronounced "tronks") that let the water in over the seedlings and then drained it out according to a rhythm Polite had known his whole life. He also started a barber shop, the one little store in Sugar Hill, and served as a caretaker for other Northerners' lands, duck ponds, and bluffs. Like Frasier, Dee Polite was an entrepreneur.

Quinetha Frasier also knew poverty. Two of her great-aunts on her dad's side, Mag and Naomi White, lived on Willtown Bluff and were "so freaking poor," she says. They were poor until they died, living in a house that had never been finished and that they could never afford to fully insulate or improve, and their children finally moved away because they were tired of getting flooded out. They just didn't know what to do to make the land useful and keep the water away, so they sold it for close to nothing. And Frasier knew land disputes: her father and his siblings are still disputing over one acre of land in Yonges Island, a marshy area that her great-grandfather Isaiah Frasier, Clarence's dad, was able to buy after World War II and build a house on using Federal Housing Authority money. When her grandparents died, the land was left in their wills to the five siblings, and they couldn't agree what to do with it. At least there was a will; in other places, fifty people owned land that went through the generations without a will in place. At the same time, Frasier saw white people buying up the land around the settlements of her childhood at rock-bottom prices.[39] The asymmetries of cash and capacity in the Charleston region are crushing.

Frasier's mother insisted that Frasier have a better experience than hers in Baptist Hill and sent her to St. Andrew's High School in West Ashley. It was then, riding on the free city bus to West Ashley, looking out the window throughout the long rides between home and school, that confident, charismatic Frasier realized that where she lived was extraordinarily impoverished. Not that she felt poor, personally; her own immediate family might have had a lack of income, but they weren't poor. It was just that the roads and houses and services she saw from the bus were on a whole different level from what she knew at home; so solid and tended for. Once she stepped off the bus at the high school, she also quickly understood that Black people in Charleston looked down on people from the "country," the darker-skinned Gullah Geechee people. They assumed that the dialect meant laziness and ignorance. At home Frasier spoke Gullah all the time.

Frasier felt that disdain and tried to ignore it, joining everything she could: NAACP programs, public speaking training, internships, Girls State, running the news broadcasting show—whatever was available, she signed up for. Dee Polite's daughter, her aunt Marguerite "Meg" Archie-Hudson PhD, took Frasier under her wing and urged her on. Meg was one of the first brilliant darker-skinned Black kids ever to get into Avery Normal School, and successfully went off to Talladega College and a career in politics and education. Eventually she returned to Talladega College as its president.

Frasier kept joining things as a young adult, charging off to Tuskegee University to learn more about her roots and Black history, taking a fundraising job at Talladega College, and then moving back to Charleston to work as a grants developer for the Charleston County Housing Authority. The executive director there, Montez Martin, also encouraged Frasier, pushing her to join Leadership Charleston and the Chamber of Commerce. "Whatever board you could think of," Frasier says, "He made my little Black self join and do it." Frasier started her own Black business group in Charleston, because there wasn't one. As a young adult, Frasier felt like she knew everyone in town. "I was flying high."

Then Montez Martin told her she had to leave Charleston. Frasier was puzzled. He said, "You need to leave and come back, because you're going to hit a ceiling if you don't." So she left for a White House fellowship and an MBA, got training from Wachovia as a salesperson, and then left for Atlanta to start her own consulting company helping other small businesses and nonprofits to write grants. She also got involved with the startup world there. But then it was time to come back to Charleston; Frasier turned thirty-four, and her mother, who was getting divorced from her father for the second time, needed her.

Frasier's deeper awareness of what was really going on in Charleston started then. She got a job raising money for United Way and saw that there were no Black names among the leading donors. The idea that United Way seemed to be designed to categorize white people as the benefactors and Black people as, exclusively, beneficiaries, made no sense to Frasier. Frasier went to the CEO and said, "Let's set up an affinity group that really harnesses the power of Black philanthropy in Charleston." Frasier worked one by one through wealthy Black residents of Charleston, meeting personally with more than seventy-five African American leaders, and persuaded them to become leadership donors for a $2 million fund for education as well as join an African American Leadership Council for the United Way. Frasier did this on the premise, the promise, that the United Way would give that philanthropic group decision-making authority; the Leadership Council would be able to designate that the money be used in unrestricted ways by particular entities.

But the United Way did not keep its promise.[40] It received the gifts but refused to allow the African American Leadership Council to have a say in how the money was spent. Frasier was furious; other groups had been allowed to do this. She decided to stay on, but as an independent contractor rather than an employee. She remained on course to raise that $2 million over three years.

Frasier says she learned some lessons from this experience. Black Americans in Charleston who did manage to attain leadership roles, and there were very few, were unlikely to take risks. They had been there forever; they were entrenched; they were highly unlikely to say to United Way, she says, "Keep your damn word. You said you were going to give us decision making authority." Also, there was a kind of familial, cordial relationship between Blacks and whites as masters and servants that had not gone away in Charleston. When it was a new city, Charleston had followed the Barbados Slave code that required the granting of religious freedom to enslaved people, and slaveowners had allowed for this kind of "freedom:" something of this benevolence remained, she felt.

Frasier remembers white television executive John Rivers speaking to a meeting held after the Mother Emmanuel Nine massacre. "I don't understand what the problem is racially," he told them. "We've always gotten along. My dad used to let our housekeeper come through the front door, and that was in the '80s."

"Out of his own mouth!" Frasier says, shaking her head in wonderment. Other elements compounded the passivity: When it came to the companies offering jobs in Charleston, there were very few Black people moving up in the ranks or being groomed to serve as leaders. And for people from Frasier's own Gullah Geechee community, the economic gaps were even wider and the opportunity to thrive even narrower.

For all these reasons, Frasier decided that although she would stay deeply involved in Charleston, joining the board of Michelle Mapp's South Carolina Community Loan Fund as well as that of the South Carolina chapter of the Nature Conservancy, she could not live in

Charleston full-time. It didn't have the temperature or the speed she needed to fulfill her life's purpose. It was a deeply unfair, status quo place, and it would feel strange for her, someone who had a strong sense of her identity and never felt less-than, to stay. When, pre-COVID, she went to downtown Charleston on Fridays and Saturdays, Frasier could count on two hands how many Black families were there; it was in many ways still the peninsula where, Frasier's father told her, Black people until the late 1970s were not allowed to be downtown after 6 P.M., after dusk. So Frasier made her home in Atlanta.

But Frasier's heart and sense of place remains in Charleston, and she still visits at least twice a month. She wants to somehow connect her Willtown Bluffs community to a better economic future. They have voices, her people, but they have not used them in so long. "It's as if they have laryngitis and forgot they could speak," she says. The gears of development are grinding around them, with subdivisions sweeping down from the Summerville area. They'd been asking for water and sewer lines for eighty years, and now those lines are finally arriving, snaking down Route 17 and up Route 162. But the lines are not coming at the behest of the descendants of the Gullah Geechee. They are being put in to support new enormous subdivisions for white people to live in. These days there are two kinds of places visible from the roads to the Sea Islands near Charleston that pass by Baptist Hill, Church Hill, and Adams Run: either very narrow plots of land on which decaying older homes stand that are lived in by older people or raging developments of giant houses bristling with garages designed for the oversized vehicles of families much richer and whiter than the people from Frasier's childhood.

The land near Adams Run is relatively high ground for Charleston County, higher than the peninsula or the marshy areas surrounding that peninsula, and inland from Edisto Island up Highway 174.[41] That's why the developers are coming. They are hemmed in, to some extent.

The crushing suburbanization of the area is bordered by the Ernest F. Hollings ACE Basin National Wildlife Refuge to the west of Frasier's homeland, where the Ashepoo, Combahee, and Edisto Rivers run to the sea and where development isn't allowed. Development is also constrained by the existing sprawl of marshy Charleston to the east, and by already-built-up Edisto Island fraying its way into the Atlantic to the south. The entire area has been designated an "Opportunity Zone" by Charleston County, which means that developers and investors will get substantial tax advantages by building there, including deferring or avoiding capital gains tax.[42]

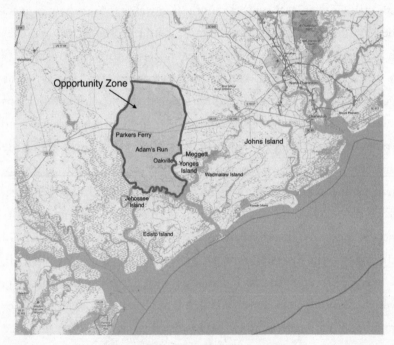

Map of Adams Run/Opportunity zone.

Large houses in cul-de-sacs are about to ooze south into Frasier's childhood region from the harsh new neighborhoods of Summerville and Nexton to the north, anonymous, sprawling, treeless places that are almost wholly white. The county's current zoning overlay plan allows residents to subdivide and sell off their lots at will, as long as the resulting developments are no more dense than one house per acre.[43] These will be expensive houses: in the "Plantation at Stono Ferry" development a few miles to the east, a 2020 house on an acre of land recently sold for nearly $700,000.[44] No affordable housing is permitted to be built in this zone. Very close to the just-about-derelict Adams Run Post Office, along Route 162 heading west towards the Ernest F. Hollings ACE Basin, there's a sign reading, "For Sale, 57+ acres." Highway 162, a two-lane road with little bungalows on its north side and a thick forest of mossy oaks on the left, has just been resurfaced.

It seems to Frasier that the plan is to let the Black people who live there continue on in poverty and dilapidation until they sell out at low prices to the developers who come knocking. And then where will those older communities of people go?

◆

A government program made it possible for Frasier's great-grandparents Dee and Sadie Polite to live out the end of their lives in dignity and comfort. As a young man, long before he became the highest-ranking Black legislator in Congress, Jim Clyburn, working in the 1960s, pushed through an FHA program that set aside land in Adams Run on which people could build brick houses of their own. If they built them, they could keep them; the houses would be theirs. "It was a self-help build program, the first of its kind," Frasier was told.

Afterward, there were ten neat brick one-story houses on Clyburn Road in Adams Run, all with bathrooms inside them—the first time anyone there had indoor plumbing—and Dee Polite's was the first one built. Polite, Frasier's mother's grandfather, then helped the other families build their houses. Each family paid $30 a month for their mortgage. Both sides of Frasier's family were involved: Frasier's paternal grandfather, Clarence Frasier, laid all the framing and woodwork in the homes. It was truly a community program.

Frasier grew up there on Clyburn Road after her parents' marriage had collapsed. She met and knew all her great-grandparents, and they were amazing people, brilliant thinkers. By the time she moved in, together with her mom and her sisters Kimiko and Felicia, nearly twenty years had passed since the house on Clyburn Road had been built and Dee Polite had passed away. Sadie, though, was a powerful sweet-voiced presence, a Grand Matron in the Eastern Stars, the source of discipline as well as cookies and candy. So was Dee Polite's youngest child, William, a smooth, attractive man in his fifties with great shoes who died too young.

Frasier shared a room for four years with her granny, and remembers the feel of the polished wood on the interior walls and the look of the great big old pear tree right behind the house. She remembers a big blue hyacinth bush on the side of the house and an oak tree with a perfect limb for a swing. And Frasier remembers asking, "Granny, how is it that you are always so happy and you stay looking so young?" Her great-grandmother said, "Well, I treat people right and I keep my hand in God's hand."

All of that life, three growing girls, their mom, their smooth uncle, and their great-grandmother, happened in a plain ranch-style house that wasn't more than 900 square feet, "And that was probably a stretch," Frasier says. "Maybe 800." It was possible because Jim Clyburn and the FHA had made it so. Later, when her mom was ready to move out to West Ashley so that Frasier wouldn't have a long bus ride to school, the government had shown up again, offering low-interest loans and down payment assistance aimed at opening up the brick homes of all-white Forest Park, and the neighborhood's park and playground, to Black families like theirs.

So Frasier has hope, generally, for government. She also knows that given the explosive growth of the area, fueled by the arrival of a mostly white population of new people who love the charming ambience they see in photographs, trust is in short supply in Charleston's heterogeneous Black communities. They have seen such displacement, over so many generations, starting with those post-Reconstruction bad guys asking for their land back. "There's a responsibility to educate," Frasier says. When it comes to Adam's Run, and Willtown, and the East and West sides of the peninsula, Black people are not coming to a meeting full of excitement to help government employees think through and plan something they don't understand. Someone needs to explain what is ahead, what the rising waters will mean to people and their communities. At the moment, as far as Frasier can tell, there are critical decisions being made about the region's future without any consensus at all from the Black and lower-income residents who will be affected the most by the disasters to come.

◆

To see the development that is coming to the corridor of Gullah Geechee descendants still living in small settlements off Route 17 west of the peninsula, just drive the other direction, back to the east, and travel along the six-lane Crosstown that cuts its scar across the peninsula. Keep going, passing vestiges of the neighborhoods of Black residents that were marooned by that roaring freeway, and travel across the big, modern Ravenel Bridge to Mount Pleasant. There, as you continue driving, propelled along by incessant traffic, you will find every retail store you can think of in squads of marching strip malls lining broad Johnny Woods Boulevard. Astonishing development has already overwhelmed dozens of the settlements of Black residents and descendants of Gullah Geechee that used to be east of the peninsula along Route 17. Many of these small communities of homes and churches were labeled by their residents for their distance from the Cooper River:

Two Mile community, Four Mile, Six Mile, Seven Mile, Ten Mile, and Fifteen Mile; collectively, "The Miles."[45]

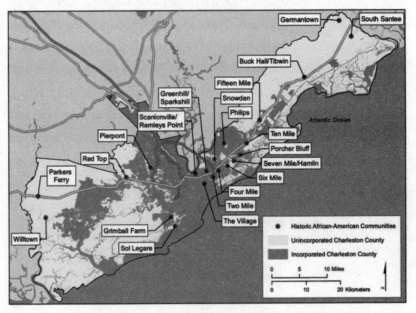

Map showing where Black residents and descendants of Gullah Geechee settled east of the peninsula along Route 17.

Charlton Singleton, a jazz trumpeter and the founder of Grammy-award winning, Charleston-based band Ranky Tanky—their Gullah-influenced album, *GOOD TIMES*, won the award for the "best regional album" in 2020—grew up in Ten Mile.[46] Because there are now so many new, large, two-story houses and subdivisions interlaced with the places Singleton knew as a child, he says, "All of these communities, historically Black communities, are now just literally gone." They've been replaced by housing subdivisions and big box stores.

Singleton's grandfather, whom everyone called Big Daddy, was born on Capers Island in 1892, just off the coast. There was a hurricane in 1898 that forced the family to seek higher ground. "So they basically got on a raft and floated over to the area of the Ten Mile community that we're in," Singleton says. Big Daddy lived to be one hundred years old, "farming and just living the life," according to Singleton, and had ten kids. Singleton's father, Big Daddy's son Charles, was the eighth of them, and met Singleton's mother, Jeannette, when they were in grade school. Charlton Singleton, jazzman, is the fifty-sixth of Big Daddy's fifty-six grandchildren. His title in the family is "Last Grand."

For Singleton, as with Frasier, being Gullah is "just how we live. It's just what you do. It's normal." He goes on: "The way that people talk, the way that people worship, the way that people eat. It's just normal." And he's encountered the same weird reactions that Frasier did about his Gullah accent: "You hear folks say, 'Oh, you talk funny,' or 'you have an accent.'" Sometimes it makes him angry.

His parents—Charles is a retired minister of the Greater Zion AME church, Jeannette is a former school librarian—still live in Ten Mile, but many of their neighbors have sold out to developers. "Maybe a child went off to college," Singleton says. For whatever reason, their neighbors' lives moved elsewhere. "They don't have any plans on moving back. And then, a realtor comes in and says, 'I'll pay you X amount of dollars for that property.' And if you have no reason to come back, and they're going to give you thousands of dollars, or in some cases millions of dollars, for that property, why not take it?"

As recently as 1995, when Singleton took his date MaryJo (now his wife) to his parents' house in Ten Mile to make her a spaghetti dinner, there was just farmland next to Highway 17. "There was nothing out there, nothing," he remembers. MaryJo remembers that dinner too; she was worried because it was all woods, no lights, no nothing. Today, "You can play 18 holes out there. You can literally live in those subdivisions and not leave." There is a Costco, a hospital, a Super Walmart, a big new high school, an enormous subdivision called Parkwest, and crushing, endless SUV traffic. A Home Depot stands where Six Mile used to be. "All of that area used to be nothing but Black communities and small little houses, like maybe a few houses on the road," Singleton says. His parents' house is still there, but they built a big fence around it so as not to look out of place next to the shiny two-story houses with their own "border-wall-looking fence things" that Singleton says the developers put in next door. Today in the Ten Mile community there's a cluster of grand new houses called Bees Crossing. They are stark gray and the trees haven't had time to grow back in near them.

Singleton wishes the influx of new people had understood what they were doing. "They uprooted families," he says. They paid for houses and land, but often not enough to allow those families to go find another place to live in the region. "And it ain't cheap around here," he says. For Singleton, money doesn't capture the values of community and pride that he grew up with. "Charleston being a tourist town," he says, "it's all about heads in beds." He goes on: "And the money that you offer—thank you for the million dollars that you just paid me. I appreciate that. However, I think it's really kind of interesting that now you're going to sell that same property for 15 million." The house-flippers who came in didn't pay attention to the erasure of The Miles. "Families are gone," he says. "I understand it's growth, but it's still hard to fathom. It's just hard to see that."

Unlike Frasier, Charlton Singleton is staying. He sees the loss of identity, the tourist culture, and the arrival of hordes of white people who plan to live in large, square houses. He's been pulled over by a white cop while he was driving near his parents' house and made to wait while being questioned for half an hour ("Have you been stopped before?" the officer asked), only to be told that he's got a missing license plate light—at two o'clock on a summer afternoon. He knows that incident happened because, he says, "I'm a Black man in a nice car." He remembers how bad the water tasted when he was growing up and how hard Black communities had to beg for sewer service. But, he says, "It's always going to be home. And while Charleston has its issues racially, it'd be hard for me to imagine actually living someplace else. Because it's home. Because it's what I know. It has what I need, what my family needs. I figure my parents have always been here. That's all what I need to know. Their parents. There's no need for me to pick up and leave, this is my home, I got to deal with it. It's just like any family, you got crazy shit in your family, but you still love them and you got to deal with it."

◆

White people who dream of Charleston's restaurants and charm are probably thinking about the peninsula, the narrow spit of land between the Ashley and Cooper Rivers. Development has certainly been extensive there, and there are always cranes up above the streets busily putting together new luxury apartments and new hotels. But the development story that covered West Ashley and James Island, that is creeping across Johns Island, that erased most of the Gullah Geechee settlement that shaped Charlton Singleton, that is marching towards wiping out Quinetha Frasier's past in Adam's Run—that story is one of outright suburban sprawl. One new white resident of this sprawl, someone who had moved to the area four months before, said during an online public meeting about Charleston's comprehensive plan during October 2020 that she was very surprised by what she was experiencing: "I must say what I read about Summerville and the Charleston area and the charm and the restaurants and the shopping . . . I really haven't seen any of that." She went on: "The amount of housing, the traffic, it's just not what I expected."[47]

Both Ten Mile and Adam's Run may be slightly less risky for development right now because they are both on relatively higher ground compared to the peninsula. After all, there is a market craving these new houses: People from all over the country, particularly from major metro areas like New York, Atlanta, and Charlotte, are coming to Charleston to buy homes, and they are not as worried about flooding and rising water issues as they should be. Homebuyers generally don't have access to the information that government agencies and commercial real estate firms do.

But if you were planning for the Charleston region of 2050 and beyond, you would not build there and you would not want people to move there. Tick off the dangers: storm surge, sea level rise, chronic flooding, groundwaters rising, risk to drinking water—it's all about to get much more dangerous beginning no later than 2050. The wall of water brought by a Category 3 hurricane will reach a thousand houses in West Ashley alone, and almost everything within Adam's Run and Ten Mile. Hugo (1989) flooded everything below ten feet in elevation, even though it didn't hit Charleston directly; Irma (2015) reached everything below seven feet. We know that everything below ten feet of elevation will be chronically threatened by both tidal flooding and stormwater flooding by 2050.

◆

The overall story of the areas of Charleston that are not on the peninsula is one of explosive development huddled near the water's edge on a coastal plain that is truly low. The Gullah Geechee descendants who remain in the places where Frasier and Singleton grew up are likely to be displaced by water if they haven't already been displaced by development. There is no plan to protect them or the people who have built houses where they used to live. Over the next couple of decades, the already-difficult flooding the area is experiencing will intensify and accelerate. No amount of denial or boosterism will protect Charleston from what will happen next.

When this hot real estate market inevitably softens, when the quantum of risk is finally reflected in the region's housing prices, it will become even more difficult than it already is to come up with the local tax revenue needed to build and rebuild drainage and infrastructure. The soaring rates of development across the region, including in the former Black settlement areas that mean so much to Frasier and Singleton, is generating some additional tax revenue to use to pay for adaptation. But the city will have to pay far more to protect that increased development—if it planned to carry out that kind of work in the first place, which it doesn't. Local governments will be forced to limit or defer any such capital investment, although they will obviously keep prioritizing the peninsula's tourist attractions. As the years go on, more disasters will strike, and richer white inhabitants will pick up and leave, so that even thinking about infrastructure as a category of spending will become impossible. The region's local governments will stop being able to pay their utility bills as their long-term fiscal capacity diminishes. The system will crumble; consistent power and affordable utility services will become things of the past; the region will become less safe as it becomes more saturated.

When life becomes unpleasant, wealthier people will have choices, as they always do. They will be able to get out, absorb their losses, and start over elsewhere. But the poorer residents of the region, many of whom are Black, will have nowhere to go. That will leave whoever is still there in City Hall with a sharply diminished ability to attract wealth and economic development in an environment in which they will need that support more than ever, and at a time when the population they will need to serve is needier and more desperate than it has ever been. It is an impossible equation, a nightmarish swirl.

10

Muddling Through and
Managed Retreat

"Only avoidance and relocation can remove coastal risks
for the coming decades, while other measures only delay
impacts for a time, have increasing residual risk or per-
petuate risk and create ongoing legacy effects and virtually
certain property and ecosystem losses (high confidence)."

—*IPCC Sixth Assessment Report:
Impacts, Adaptation, and Vulnerability (2022)*

R ight now, the extremely rare is becoming commonplace. In the
1980s, the average time between billion dollar climate disasters
in the US was about eighty-two days. Today, it is about eighteen
days.[1] The federal government spends billions each year recovering
from increasingly common coastal disasters. By mid-century, taxpayers
will be spending at least $15 billion a year on coastal recovery. A
couple of decades after that, we will be laying out at least $50 billion
yearly.[2] As a country, and like many countries around the globe, we
have created a stunning moral hazard: the more valuable a particular
coastal development is, the more likely it will be rebuilt or protected
using federal funds.

Over the next several decades, we will gradually wake up to the reality that we cannot stabilize our shorelines and somehow keep everyone in place. Incrementally, painfully, it will become apparent that every expensive, heroic shoreline project we build has an expiration date that is measured, at most, by a decade or two. The rising seas are more powerful than we are. Will our awakening to this fact be accompanied by the wisdom needed to do things differently?

Think of Charleston as sitting in a basin of water. A bathtub. As long as the bathtub has seven feet or less of water in it, life in the Holy City continues peacefully along.[3] Tourists fly in and out, never seeing the Neck or the car-choked suburbs, and enjoy ample desserts and cocktails. They've heard from *Travel + Leisure* that the city "expresses the perfect balance of Southern charm, knockout food and drinks, and walkability,"[4] and they're pleased with what they find. The grand new buildings of the Union Pier and Magnolia developments rise up, filled with gleaming apartments. Retirees flock to the area—thirty-three new residents move there every day—and pay top dollar for homes that still cost less than those in Westchester County. All is superficially just fine, at least for a white person with means to buy a place to live, if you don't mind sitting in traffic and you shut your eyes to the city's ongoing racism. If you are Black and live in Charleston, the legacy of the city's past lingers on in a hundred small ways, day after day, whatever the water level is.

But as soon as more than seven feet of water is in the bathtub, the picture changes. Just half a foot more can make a major difference. As Steven Taylor of the National Weather Service puts it, "When we start to get close to seven feet, all the drainage is full of sea water, and so any kind of rain has nowhere to go." That's why, Taylor says, "downtown Charleston has such a threat for flooding when it rains."[5] Or when it doesn't rain but a high tide comes in over seven feet. Even now, increasingly common flooding over seven feet in Charleston makes life unpleasant in many parts of the city.[6] Roads are closed, first floors of houses flood, medical buildings are hard to reach. What will happen as the seas rise?

Imagine Charleston twenty-five years from now, in 2047 or so. By then, as the air warms around the globe—imagine the Earth has a thick electric blanket around it that is very gradually heating up—many increasingly powerful storms ever more heavily loaded with rain and wind will have ravaged the peninsula and its outlying areas over and over again.

Walls of rain and wind from storms won't be the only problems, though. Rising seas and the moon wobble will combine to bring more water into the bathtub. As Dr. Philip R. Thompson told the *New York Times* in July 2021 about the moon wobble, "It's important to realize that at the mid-2030s point, where the switch flips and the natural cycle seems to amplify the rate of sea level rise, then we are going to see a rapid change."[7] The La Niña conditions that have been in place for the last few years will also, inevitably, shift, bringing still more water onshore.[8] As Dr. William Sweet, a leading oceanographer with NOAA's National Ocean Service, puts it, the moon wobble and the presence of La Niña have "helped take the foot off the accelerator" in recent years, slowing the frequency of floods.[9] When these phases end, the groundwater table beneath the sandy soil of Charleston will rise even more rapidly and even more water will flow over the mostly flat territory of the city far more often. Another two feet of water will be surrounding and landing on Charleston by 2050.[10]

There will be water pooling in backyards and roads because it is seeping upward, water spilling over soft creek banks into neighborhoods because the rivers are rising, and water sitting on streets that cannot drain effectively after storms because they sit too low for a gravity-driven system to work. No one knows exactly how much more water will be in the basin, but the region is so precarious already that it won't take much to make things far worse than they already are.

NOAA has said that the flooding Charleston has been experiencing as of the early 2020s, high tide flooding that even now brings the city to its knees and closes roads, will be two to three times more frequent by 2030, and five to fifteen times as frequent by 2050.[11] That's a lot. Norman Levine, the professor at the College of Charleston, thinks the number of flood days in 2040 will be "close to 240 days" a year, based on tide gauge data from the Charleston Harbor.[12] Flooding with a tidal height that puts six feet of water onto the land of the city of Charleston will be common in the latter part of this century, he believes.[13] Those very frequent days of flooding will likely be accompanied by gradual saltwater intrusion into freshwater aquifers serving the city, straining drinking water supplies. Let's not forget that every degree of global warming means the air carries seven percent more water, making for increasingly heavy and increasingly frequent downpours that sit stolidly in one place, dumping enormous amounts of rain. The risks of extreme rainfall are accelerating at the same time the tides are rising.[14]

Each summer's hurricane season causes dread for those of the city's residents who remember Hugo and haven't been lulled into complacency by the last few relatively quiet years. More severe storms accompanied by larger surges will be increasingly common in the coming years. It's also grueling to be in Charleston during the summer and fall, because the city now experiences about twenty-two more days with hotter-than average temperatures than it did fifty years ago.[15] Summers are longer and hotter these days. Temperatures start soaring well into the nineties in May.

Imagine the morning after just one flooding event. Imagine the oppression of waking to a world in which everything is wet and you cannot leave where you are. Think of the pounding heat and the stink of your muddy possessions. Buildings and structures around you will be damaged. Food and fresh water supplies will be difficult to secure.

Now imagine many such mornings, until they run together in your mind in a haze of uncertainty and damp.

There is a substantial risk that areas in Charleston that are already flooding today will be worse off in 2047. The East Side gravity-driven stormwater system is designed to deal with very ordinary storms and tides; pummeling rain bombs and king-level tides will swamp drains there. Unless something dramatic happens that protects the Gadsden Green public housing units from flooding, residents there may also be experiencing miserable deluges even more often than they do now. Thousands of residents of West Ashley and James Island, perched now next to wetlands and marsh, may be flooded more frequently as well.

Existing social conditions in Charleston will likely be amplified by this exponential rise in sea levels by 2047. As the risks confronted by the area become more obvious, houses that were the hopes of their not-well-off owners, their sole real investments for retirement, may very swiftly lose value and become impossible to either insure or sell. The mortgages burdening those owners will implacably remain in place. Those not-rich owners may be stuck with homes that will often literally be underwater. Renters will look around for less risky places to stay and may end up either having to commute even farther to their jobs or leaving the region altogether, worse off than they were before. Fetid floods may be a constant in the lives of residents in public housing units on the peninsula.

The economic collapse of the housing market, should it happen, would drive a cascade of other collapses in utilities and public services as well as businesses. This would happen because those who have choices and bank accounts and second homes would leave in a steady, invisible stream. "Similar environmental hazards can produce very different decisions to move or not to move," says Dr. Elizabeth Ferris of Georgetown University's Institute for the Study of International Migration. The "possibilities for someone with the means to move are quite different than those who are less fortunate economically."[16]

The bathtub will not stop filling in 2047. The risks of these things happening will continue to increase. The bathtub will likely be filling faster and faster as the years go by. By 2070, when a child born today is middle-aged, there is a substantial risk that there will be at least four more feet of water sloshing over Charleston. Maybe six. This would mean that most of the peninsula would be chronically inundated. But more than the peninsula would be affected: Repetitive flooding will be particularly devastating for homes that are in what the Dutch called the "Wet Zone" in their 2019 report—land under six feet of elevation. Dr. Levine has looked at the parcel-level data for the city and has figured out that most of the pieces of land that will be affected by chronic "wet zone" inundation are residential. In effect, houses in the City of Charleston are buffering businesses, which generally sit on higher land. Many high-priced houses, worth $600,000 or more, are in this wet residential group in Charleston—perhaps 27,000 of them.[17] Those people probably have other sources of income and would be able to rescue themselves. But there are about 20,000 residential parcels in Charleston's "wet zone" that are worth $300,000 or less,[18] and for those people most of their personal wealth is in their home.[19] This analysis doesn't account for renters or people in public housing, many of whom in Charleston are Black. Even without taking into account the risk of even more rapid mid-century sea level rise stemming from melting glaciers or a weakening Gulf Stream, the risks of displacement are high and getting higher. "You're going to have retreat through disaster attrition," Dr. Levine says.[20] Charleston is one of the communities most vulnerable to inundation in the US, up there with New Orleans and Cape Coral, Florida.

The spine of King Street will remain above the waves, and so will the sand dunes of Johns Island. Much of the eastern portion of West Ashley may be wet all the time; the same thing may happen on James Island. North Charleston will survive.

Given these real and growing risks to human flourishing, there is—just barely—time to be wiser. Norman Levine argues that after about 2032, the city's ability to make choices about its future will narrow sharply: "It's going to be much, much harder," he says. Looking at this future is like "looking down that railroad track and seeing that little light," according to seasoned scientist Bob Perry. When he talks to skeptics, he says, "We all know that train is coming. By gosh, we got to get off the track." There are many things Charleston could do to be prepared for the moment that train rolls through. "We're leaving and we're not coming back," says Perry.[21] He's talking about Charleston.

Abby Levine, Norman Levine's wife, keeps asking her husband, "'Why haven't we sold our house yet?" Their house sits on relatively higher land in West Ashley. "She's wanted out of the house for years."[22] But he loves his house and his short commute to his job at the College of Charleston. They wouldn't be able to afford anything less than forty-five minutes away, and that distance seems impossible to him. He doesn't have an alternate plan. At the same time, Levine feels it is in some sense his destiny to try to deliver the truth about what is actually going on in Charleston.

What is actually going on is that Charleston, like almost all coastal cities, doesn't have a firm plan to protect its residents from the chronic, debilitating flooding that will arrive in the next few decades. The problem is growing: There are platoons of recent arrivals who don't understand deep in their bones how risky their situation is. South Carolina real estate law requires that the fact of prior flooding claims be disclosed to buyers, but not the amount of those claims.[23]

It might be a good time for Norm and Abby Levine to sell their house. John Tibbetts, the science journalist, made it to Minneapolis in mid-2022. "No, the people aren't getting it" in Charleston, he says. "It's absolutely the opposite. People are running toward the water. They're not running away from it at all." The real estate market in Charleston, he says, is "insane."[24]

◆

In September 2020, consultants hired by the city of Charleston told the public that all the land in the city that is less than ten feet in elevation is both in the FEMA "100-year" floodplain (subject to flooding from rainfall, tides, and storm surges *already* predicted by FEMA to have a 1 percent chance of occurring each year) as well as subject to the risk of additional, less frequent, but more powerful storm surges. They also said that what used to be thought of as a "500-year" storm (flooding that FEMA believes has a 0.2 percent chance of happening each year) is now happening on the "100-year" timetable.[25] (FEMA is notorious for understating risks to US properties. As Elizabeth Rush said in an April 2022 opinion piece for the *New York Times*, "Nearly twice as many properties face danger from potential inundation as FEMA predicts—a 1 percent chance of flooding in a given year—according to a group of experts at the First Street Foundation in New York City.")[26] They made clear that even the small part of the city of Charleston that is above ten feet in elevation, those portions between ten-to-twenty feet, was also largely subject to flood risk and violent storm surges.

They showed pictures that demonstrated there was very little land on the peninsula that was high enough that it could be built on safely. James Island also had little safe land. Johns Island had a little more buildable land (above those ancient sand dunes) and the Cainhoy Peninsula, to the east above historic Charleston, had the most. Joshua Robinson, a landscape engineer based in Charleston, made the point bluntly: "Because of these flooding risks from the ocean, tidals, surge, and storm surge risks, it's going to become a better idea to move into the higher ground."[27]

During that same session, the consultants also suggested identifying areas that could accommodate the migration of marshland upland (as existing marshes are drowned by rising sea levels) and keeping those areas as "natural" as possible. Some of the maps they showed indicated that the East Side of the peninsula, where David White runs Laundry Matters, could be turned into marsh. "Some land is going to have to be reserved going forward so that the marshes can migrate to do all the wonderful things that they do," consultant Dale Morris said.[28]

After the formal presentation, Morris took questions from the online audience. He read one aloud: "Why isn't retreat one of the planning strategies that were identified?" He equivocated, briefly, saying the team wasn't done with its analysis, and then said, "But we will say that there are a lot of other places that are similarly situated to Charleston, where they have started to devise a retreat strategy." There it was, out on the table. "How do you retreat wisely and fairly?" Morris asked. "I don't think there's an easy answer to that question," he said. He went on: "That would not be for us [the consultants] to suggest. It's for the city and the citizens to start to ponder."[29]

◆

Imagine if planning for a carefully staged departure from the coastal edge of the Charleston region were actually happening. There would be an announcement that over the next ten years, say, a host of incentives allowing for a modest but fair return on their investments in their homes would encourage people to move. These announcements would be accompanied by frank, clear disclosures about the high-risk nature of these areas.

Right now, it is very difficult for ordinary consumers to get access to good data about the risk profile of particular residential properties. The Town of East Hampton, New York issued a report in mid-2022 making clear that, absent extraordinary and wildly expensive protective efforts, by 2070 the town would be transformed "into a series of islands" due to rapidly rising sea-levels.[30] It is difficult to imagine Charleston publishing similar information.

Relocation packages would be created; a raft of government tax and credit levers would incentivize the construction of new homes in safer areas. These new residential districts would be dense, be well-served by transit, and include ample amounts of truly affordable houses. The land left behind once residents voluntarily left would be turned into protected marshland and parks, the very things that will help slow flooding further inland. It is very difficult to persuade anyone to leave their home if they believe that their land will be snapped up and developed for a profit the moment they depart and not left to be allowed to return to protective marshland.

Policy makers would also announce that after the first ten years, the incentives would be lower, perhaps far lower, so as to encourage early decision-making. Coastal regions like Charleston (and many other places) would need to pay much more attention to actually engaging meaningfully with communities, including with faith-based groups and nonprofits—not just looking for buy-in to existing plans, or placating groups by featuring leading nonoppositional members of those communities. This planning will require genuine partnerships tasked with creating funded plans that acknowledge the equity and environmental justice issues implicated by relocation.[31] So far, managed retreat has been a piecemeal thing, carried out by small towns acting alone.

We urgently need to shift to strategic efforts that include sociocultural as well as physical factors and involve the whole country. As Professor A. R. Siders of the University of Delaware, a leading academic in the emerging field of managed retreat, says, "A substantial amount of innovation and work—in both research and practice—will need to be done to make strategic, managed retreat an efficient and equitable adaptation option at scale."[32] We need to pay attention to the social costs of displacement, and plan ahead to avoid cruelty and harm.

What we really need is federal leadership and national planning—and funding—for withdrawal from coastal regions. Alice Hill of the Council on Foreign Relations believes we need a national adaptation plan: "The plan on the national level would at a minimum help prioritize our federal investments. We'll send signals to state, local governments and the private sector as to where we are going to make sure that we are building resilience and areas where maybe it isn't cost effective for the federal government to be involved any more."[33] We need, she says, to "measure our progress" as well. "Should we invest in beach renourishment, or do we build a seawall, or do we help these communities relocate altogether? Without a national adaptation plan, it's very difficult to do that."[34]

The residents of Doggerland likely didn't plan very far ahead for their departure. But they had neither our tools of democratic governance nor our ability to predict and visualize the changes that are about to happen so rapidly. We should face our need to withdraw rather than hide from it.

Even if the nation isn't yet thinking seriously about large-scale strategic withdrawal, some Charleston residents are. During the September 2019 public meeting at which the Dutch Dialogue recommendations were presented, William Hamilton, executive director of Best Friends Lowcountry Transit, asked the key question: "Do we have places that we can put people where they can get to work and where they'll be safe from hurricanes and flooding?" Mark Wilbert, at the time the city's emergency manager, agreed with Hamilton that finding suitable places for people to live would be important. But he did not suggest that the city had a plan in mind or planned to develop one. Hamilton pressed on: "Everybody's great on theory with affordable housing and transit, but we got to find a place to build it, a real place." Mayor Tecklenburg cut him off with a polite, low "Thank you," and ended the Q&A session. Hamilton appears to be a known quantity at public meetings, and the mayor didn't seem to want to hear more from him.

That exchange captured a central problem with Charleston's ability to take on its flooding risks: The city's leadership does not like the idea of radical changes, and likes the idea of radical changes prompted by its Black residents even less. That tendency comes from the top. Mayor Tecklenburg is an amiable man, but he is not one to want to rock the boat. As Charleston Activist Network director Mika Gadsden told the *Charleston City Paper*, "I just don't have any faith in this current city council, this current mayor."[35]

As Michelle Mapp puts it, "This is that cultural DNA part of Charleston. There's a reluctance to focus on the negative. We always want to put a positive spin on things. But I think that what we are sorely lacking right now is for someone to acknowledge the negatives." If the city doesn't address the threats facing it, she says, "All of the things that we see as being positives and being the accolades [of] this wonderful place to live are going to go away."[36]

◆

So far, Charleston's efforts to take on both its flooding risks and its history of cruelly unfair treatment of its Black residents have been incremental. The city apologized for its central role in slavery in 2015, but the resolution to do so was adopted by a vote of 7–5.[37] It took down the menacing statue of John C. Calhoun towering above Marion Square in June 2020, but only when it felt it had no choice; until then, the city dodged the issue by taking the position that it was not legally permitted to remove it.[38] In 2021, the City Council refused to accept a 545-page report from a committee on equity, inclusion, and racial conciliation that it launched following the murder of George Floyd and charged with "eliminat[ing] the vestiges of Jim Crow and slavery in our City."[39] The city's Equity, Inclusion, and Racial Conciliation Manager quit in April 2022, citing the personal attacks that had been made against her because of the recommendations that had been made by the committee. Charleston then created a temporary "Human Affairs and Racial Conciliation Commission" that was barred from setting up reparations or removing Confederate war memorials on public property.[40] That renamed commission has faced a concerted campaign against it. The position of Equity, Inclusion, and Racial Conciliation Manager has not been filled as of the preparation of this manuscript in late 2022. During July 2022, the City of Charleston put up a plaque noting its role in whipping enslaved people on their owners' behalf. "For an added cost," Emma Whalen of the *Post and Courier* wrote, "city employees would literally throw salt on the wounds."[41] Mayor Tecklenburg cried during the ceremony.

Charleston is completely unlikely to take on the issue of "strategic withdrawal" or "managed retreat": When asked about retreat, Mayor Tecklenburg says, "Not on my watch."[42] Councilmember Mike Seekings agrees. "I'm not ready to retreat or even think about retreat," he says. "If the projections are wrong and they're wrong on the low side, maybe we're making an error, but I do believe that this is manageable," he adds. Then he reflects: "But if we get run over, we get run over. If we do, then the whole East Coast of the United States has got a problem."[43]

Retreat will be an unquestionably difficult process. Not everyone will want to leave. Quinetha Frasier says that the people she knew growing up, the ones who are still there, will want to stay, because they love their homes and their homeland. Money to move may not matter to them. They may be highly suspicious of any buyout offer: Queen Quet, the queen of the Gullah Geechee people, said in 2018 that her people would resist efforts to buy them out. "We will do nothing of the sort," she said. They have been betrayed far too many times by government. Until it was clear that all the very wealthy and overwhelmingly white denizens of Hilton Head, Fripp Island, Kiawah, Seabrook, Sullivan's Island, and the Isle of Palms were also being bought out and told to move away and go inland, any approach by government aimed at encouraging the Gullah Geechee people to move would, she suspected, be nothing but a front put up by developers to build shiny huge houses on the land that her people left. "Because you are not going to approach the Gullah Geechees and tell us you're doing something in our best interest," she said to a white interviewer. "You've never worked in our interest. You've always worked in your own interests."[44] Michelle Mapp is sympathetic to these concerns, and worried that long-term planning and leadership to address them is in short supply.

Resistance to departures will be significant. And that's why every level of government needs to hunt under all the policy couch cushions for every possible lever, incentive, and plan that could remove support for dangerous coastal living while building up that support equitably and fairly in safer places.

The kind of aggressive, coordinated planning needed in the Charleston region will require strong mayors who can collaborate and plan ahead. "It really is a three-county region, of Berkeley, Dorchester, and Charleston County," Mapp says, "And any solutions that we try to figure out are going to have to be regional solutions. Especially if you look at the projected growth of the region, where people are going to be living, where we have the ability to move people."[45]

But the mayors of the largest cities in the region, North Charleston, Summerville, and Charleston, are all older white men who have been around forever (Mayor Summey of North Charleston and Mayor Ricky Waring of Summerville) or are the proteges of men who have been around forever, in the case of Tecklenburg. A kind of complacent cheerfulness has taken hold, at the same time that the context for the region, its tragic failures in housing, flood planning, and transit, is deteriorating rapidly. "We pay for really good experts and then we don't do what they tell us to do," Mapp says.[46]

As we've heard, Mapp imagines that intelligent, forward-looking planning would make the high land north of the peninsula the center of the region. The city is talking about a couple of billion dollars to address flooding on the peninsula, but no one is adding to that the money that will needed to build higher, drier, denser, and cheaper places in Summerville. "What's that price tag?" Mapp says. "Why isn't that part of the billion dollars that we're talking about investing just to shore up and do anything we need to do to protect against the water?" No one understands the scope of the long-term capital investment needed to change the status quo in Charleston when it comes to how people live and where they live, she thinks. Taking this step of moving people would be a fundamental shift for a lot of Charleston residents. "What's that decision point that says, 'Hey, we've been impacted by X number of hurricanes,' or, 'We have been flooded so many times, we're going to now move somewhere else,'" she says. "Where do I go? Where do I recreate the sense of community that I've had here for generations?"

This will be particularly painful, she knows, for the Black communities in the region. "Many of the places that we hold dearest in the African American community are probably some of the places that are most environmentally vulnerable in terms of water. What happens to that history? Right now, all the discussions about housing and the future are so very reactive."

As far as Mapp can tell, all the politicians in the region seem to say the same things and to be determined to keep the status quo in place. "We're going to just continue to get what we already got. And that's not what we need," she says.[47] When candidates for office do emerge in the region, they tend to be backed by single-issue groups. The Coastal Conservation League will back someone who opposes new highways and is thinking about conservation, but that person will never mention housing and equity and transportation. No one seems to be thinking comprehensively, much less planning ahead. There is a big job ahead to persuade the three-county region of 800,000 people that it needs planning for future dense, affordable development on high, dry ground.[48] The elders can argue all day long about one issue at a time, but where is the next generation of planners and zoning people, engineers and environmentalists who are really going to grapple with this mess?

To move the Charleston region into a new phase, to somehow keep its natural beauty protected while creating, in advance, welcoming places to which people can move, will require very strong leadership. It will require leaders who can withstand lawsuits by developers when they get kicked out of the floodplain, and who can make residents understand that everyone is in this dangerous boat together. Residents need to stop opposing the new, dense construction that will be necessary in the right places. And regional leaders will need to attract and wrangle billions of dollars to get this done. They will need to encourage the federal government to hugely expand its efforts to swiftly buy out individual coastal homeowners and assist renters in high-risk areas. Those buyouts and payments will avoid even greater flood insurance payouts and disaster relief costs in the future. All of these programs should give priority to low-income residents.

Once in a while, people with this broad view do show up. Then they are often run out of town. Vince Graham, a New Urbanist developer who grew up in Beaufort, was appointed chair of the state infrastructure bank in 2017.[49] He started asking hard questions about whether it really made sense to extend the I-526 beltway around Charleston and down towards Kiawah rather than invest in affordable housing and everything else the region needed. "And they shut him down and they got him out of there," Mapp remembers. "That's what happens. Anyone who comes along and starts asking the hard questions, the common sense questions, the economic questions, very quickly, they are attacked. They are undermined. They are moved out of those positions." Who is coming up who would understand that these issues all fit together? "Maybe Marvin Pendaris," the state representative from North Charleston, Mapp says. "Maybe Clay Middleton, who works for the City of Charleston." Someone, she says, "has to step forward and say, 'Let's think about this differently.'"

In mid-2022, activist and founder of the Charleston Activist Network Mika Gadsden stepped forward, saying she plans to run for mayor of Charleston in 2023.[50] She tied the threads together on her livestream broadcast: Mayor Riley, who Gadsden calls "Developer Riley," had set in motion, "damn near thirty years ago," a vision and plan for Charleston that was not sustainable. "It's not sustainable to live here," she said. "It's not sustainable to rent here." Her own apartment in West Ashley had begun leaking dramatically, cascades of water falling from the ceiling. "And these issues are really what are driving me to run for mayor."[51] Gadsden's presence in the race may shake things up. Or it may not, given the reigning complacency of the region.

Mapp continues to believe that Charleston has the potential to get this transition right, and more broadly that the city can represent what could be when it comes to race in America. She is not giving up. "If Charleston can change," she says, "the South can change. If the South can change, America can change."

◆

"Managed retreat" is not a new idea. Dozens of communities across the country that were sick of flooding—all much smaller than Charleston—have managed to pick up and move, relocating displaced residents to a new place and hoping to keep their social fabric intact. One Midwest town, Soldiers Grove, Wisconsin, was flooded time after time by the Kickapoo River. The U.S. Army Corp of Engineers proposed the construction of an expensive levee whose maintenance costs alone would exceed the town's tax receipts. Instead, in the 1970s, Soldiers Grove chose to relocate its downtown outside the river's floodplain.[52] Valmeyer, Illinois did the same thing in the 1990s, moving all of its residential, commercial, and religious structures out of harm's way. Some people left after the move but most stayed on, and the flooding had gotten so bad that people had already started leaving anyway. Those who relocated claimed their community had stayed intact in the new place.[53] There are examples of strategic withdrawal from Oklahoma, Tennessee, North Carolina, Alaska, Wisconsin, and Louisiana. The head of the German FEMA counterpart, Ralph Tiesler, says that areas that flood "should not be resettled due to climate change and the acute threat of storms and flood." He does not rule out the possibility that there will be climate refugees within Germany in the future.[54]

Even some Dutch experts, who come from a country that markets itself as a global leader on armoring coastlines and pumping out water from land back into the sea, have begun to talk about needing to redirect residential construction away from the coast. Dutch research scientists say that walls built to protect Rotterdam and Amsterdam will be adequate until 2050, but not necessarily afterward.[55] Here is Maarten Kleinhaus, professor of physical geography at Utrecht University, quoted in early 2020: "If you have children now, you are talking about people who may be losing their land. Who will soon no longer be Dutch, because there is no more the Netherlands. That's what we're talking about."

Marjolijn Haasnoot, a leading Dutch researcher in water management, says "The models now assume that it"—rapidly accelerating sea level rise—"will really start around 2050. My children will be the same age as I am now. It's not as far away as we think."[56] Haasnoot, a lead author for the IPCC, has been at Deltares, a quasi-independent Dutch research organization that is closely tied to the Dutch government, for about thirty years.[57] She emphasizes that the science is clear that a rise of two meters (six and a half feet) in sea levels by 2100 cannot be ruled out, and she has steadily pushed to get Dutch civil servants to plan in light of the risks to safety this uncertainty creates.[58] (Before Haasnoot's work, the Dutch had been planning on a rise of 85 centimeters, or less than three feet, by 2100.)[59]

Hasnoot says retreat is "unavoidable in low-lying coastal areas." She understands that retreat is framed as "giving up," but argues that "seeing withdrawal as a serious option and considering it in conjunction with other social goals and developments can lead to favorable outcomes in the long run."[60] She says retreat can be better than the status quo: "If you think about where you want to build new developments such as infrastructure, if you take the time, make people aware of the risks [of staying] and consult with communities about other residential areas, if you map out such a path in decades, it can be more attractive than staying." Where sunny day flooding is appearing on the streets, as it is in Charleston, "It is better to make a different decision now, and be clear about it." For Haasnoot, the uncertainty of the speed at which the seas will rise, in combination with the extreme weather that is increasingly pummeling low-lying areas, means that life in the thickly populated Ranstad area—like life in Charleston—could get dicey within the next few decades.[61] For Haasnoot, this uncertainty dictates that planning and action must happen now.

Haasnoot points out that doing nothing, by contrast, will harm the poorest. Why? Because after brief evacuations for frequent punishing rainstorms and floods, poorer people will simply return and get flooded out all over again. Without planning ahead for dry options in other places that include infrastructure and offices and places to live, without having the socio-economic infrastructure to support them there, she says, "there is no reason for those people to stay elsewhere." Haasnoot is concerned that lack of planning for places less-rich people can go will further exacerbate economic inequality. "The gap between rich and poor will widen."[62]

◆

In 2020–21, as required by state law, Charleston developed a "comprehensive plan" that was designed to guide the city for its next ten years. There were some real moments of innovation and recognition in the plan: It said clearly that the city would be guided by a "water first" philosophy; it recommended for the first time that future zoning and development be shaped by the elevation at which new buildings were being constructed; it called out the traditionally Black settlement areas within the city's limits that it said deserved special consideration; it expressly noted the vast economic disparities between Black and white residents and the demographic shifts in different areas of the city; and it focused acutely on the affordable housing crisis confronting the region. The plan presented the public with the data about how little of Charleston's land area could or should be built upon in the future and how far water is expected to slosh inland when storms hit.

But the people working on the plan kept reassuring the public that it operated at a "thirty-thousand foot level." In fact, planning manager Christopher Morgan took pains to make everyone understand that the act of creating a comprehensive plan would not change a thing. The idea was that the plan would make recommendations that might be integrated someday into zoning, stormwater regulations, taxation, and other rules and policies. It would "set the tone for the direction the city is going at," Morgan said.[63]

In creating the 2021 comprehensive plan, the city announced that it would "provide real solutions informed by every one of our citizens." It said that consultants would "compile firsthand accounts from residents" about the flooding and rainstorms that were rapidly getting worse.[64] But as far as Rev. Joseph Darby knows, the outreach from the city to its Black community was not significant. He isn't an arrogant man, but as an NAACP officer and community leader, he believes he would know about any real effort on the city's part to find out what Black residents of Charleston had on their minds. "No one asked me for my views," he says.

An August 2020 public Zoom meeting aimed at getting input for the comprehensive plan about the Charleston peninsula, hosted by the city, seemed to bear out Darby's concerns. At least half of the twenty or so people attending were city employees or consultants. The city played a short video for the group that touted Charleston's "diverse cultural fabric" and called for residents to get involved. Consultant Thetyka Robinson of the Asiko Group set up a breakout room in order to have residents answer anodyne questions about Charleston—including "What do you like most about your community?" There was a retired white woman who had recently relocated to the Charleston peninsula from New Jersey because of the walkability of the city and "the restaurants, the art." Robinson's microphone stopped working for the rest of the breakout session. The attendees kept going as she listened. A white, male, ten-year resident of the East Side chimed in to say he had concerns that the East Side was "treated much differently than all the other neighborhoods on the Peninsula." He went on: "It seems like the East Side is often forgotten about by the city." He'd seen "things being placed on the East Side that wouldn't, by no means, pass muster in any other neighborhood." He thought that a better quality of life for residents would require all neighborhoods to be treated equally and not forgotten about. "Let's make [Charleston] a great place for people to live, not just visit," he said staunchly. It was a very polite, white, and mild meeting. There were no Black residents in attendance other than the consultants.

Eric Jackson, who grew up in Gadsden Green, was hired by the city to do outreach to the Black community in connection with the Comprehensive Plan. He said later that there were other comprehensive plan meetings exclusively with Black Charlestonians—"because we know sometimes their voices get lost in these meetings"—that brought about thirty Black voices into the planning process. He was proud of this work.[65] Still, even with these special efforts the numbers were tiny.

◆

Charleston's 2021 plan didn't change the status quo. It didn't create new mandates. It didn't set up subsidies or incentives to help people move out of the way of danger or smooth their transitions away from their mortgage obligations. It didn't suggest regional action to create high, dry, affordable places to which residents could move in the future. Those actions will happen, if they do, years in the future, and whether they happen will be dependent on confounding crosswinds of politics and leadership at every level of government. Even the incremental step of having the city take land elevation into account when zoning for *future* residences and commercial buildings—much less when dealing with the safety risks posed to people by inhabiting current dwellings—will become a political firestorm if developers decided to mount substantial objections.

In November 2021, before Jacob Lindsey left his job as Boulder's city planner and moved back to Charleston to take on the job of shepherding the Union Pier redevelopment project through the city's permitting process, he said, "Maybe Charleston just ends up like New Orleans, with crumbling infrastructure, very precariously balanced in its region, and kind of muddling through, with the potential for a major disaster event to really impact the place or wipe a significant part of it off the map."[66]

"Muddling through" captures the current state of things in Charleston well. It's not that the city is inactive. It has a spray of plans to drain and pump out the peninsula. It has spent years talking with the Army Corps of Engineers about a plan to build a storm surge wall around the peninsula in slow stages, focusing initially on protecting Eds, Meds, and tourism.[67] It has substantially strengthened its storm-water management requirements. It has commissioned a comprehensive water plan that is aimed at coordinating these disparate efforts and ensuring projects are prioritized and complementary—even if it hasn't allocated enough money to ensure the plan can actually be written.[68]

Maybe the city will manage to come up with a holistic series of pumps to join up with the seawall and continually pump the peninsula dry. That might be done, at an extreme cost, with great organization and technical competence, all of which would have to be contracted for by City Hall. But it is unclear where money to pay for the large engineering fixes the city contemplates—hundreds of millions, perhaps a billion, for draining and pumping, billions for the seawall—will come from, or if they will work: As currently planned, unless it is redesigned at great expense to the city to handle flooding from sources other than hurricanes—groundwater seeping upwards, rainstorms pounding downwards—the seawall will have the single narrow function of blocking surges of water driven by hurricanes.

It will certainly be obsolete for that function within a few years, because it is designed to handle only a modest amount—less than two feet—of sea level rise.[69] The Army Corps representative in Charleston, Wes Wilson, said candidly that anything more forward-looking would be too expensive to survive Congressional review.[70] Hurricane Hugo's highest points at its landfall in 1989 had centered on McClellanville, forty miles up the coast, not Charleston, and the Army's suggestion that the wall would protect against another Hugo wasn't premised on a direct hit from a storm of Hugo's size,[71] much less the future storms that will probably exceed Hugo's height. At most, the wall seems to be aimed at moderate storm surge, because the Corps is planning on about 1.43 feet of sea level rise over fifty years. Even Charleston has gone up to three feet by 2070 in its own planning, and that is conservative. The wall will be useless, pretty quickly.

The wall, plus any pumps Charleston can afford, won't protect the rest of Charleston, where most of its citizens live. "The flip side of that logic," says Lindsey, "is that all the other distributed areas where . . . all the other shorelines, where there's the high-value ranch homes and all that stuff, those are going to be unprotected. There's not really a way to do it. You can't really harden all the shorelines. They're going to have to retreat from those areas, and I don't think there's a way around that."[72] As we know, as currently planned, the wall won't reach the East Side for decades, won't improve day-to-day life for the residents of the Gadsden Green Homes, won't cover Rosemont or Bridgeview on the Neck, and won't protect any lower-income people, Black or white, living in the suburbs.

Nonetheless, the city is pressing hard for the Army Corps's storm surge seawall.[73] The project has a great estimated benefit-to-cost ratio—one of the highest in the country, because of the value of the Medical District and the College of Charleston buildings—which makes it more likely that Congress will approve it. The costs associated with planning and building it will mostly be covered by the federal government, with just 35 percent left for the city to cover (not that it's clear where the city's share will come from).[74] Such a deal! But people rarely discuss the fact that all the costs of operations and maintenance for the wall, all the money involved in opening and closing the zillions of gates set into the wall when storms threaten, and keeping those gates working, will be borne by the city.[75] Forever.

The city wants to be ready with its plans for a wall for the peninsula so that after a big, destructive storm, it will be ready to attract federal funding. This may seem strange, but that is the plan: the city believes that it is unrealistic to expect any money unless and until it is wiped out by a major storm.[76]

Along these same logical lines—first disaster, then help—the hope for fixing the insufficiencies of the wall in the future—its short stature, its lack of connection to any pumping system that will be needed to deal with other sources of water that aren't hurricanes—is that the wall after it is built will be overtopped by a storm. That overtopping water will then just sit inside the wall, because most of the peninsula has a gravity-driven drainage system that won't have the ability to pump the water back out over the wall into the rivers. Then the Army Corps, the city believes, will be faced with a "design exceedance" in its own plans and will be obliged to put in pumps to mitigate the damage caused by the insufficiencies of its own wall.[77] See how this works?

It isn't necessarily the city of Charleston's fault that it is pursuing these disaster-driven directions when looking for funding, nor that it is prioritizing its most valuable commercial and institutional buildings rather than the lives of all of its residents, much less prioritizing the safety of its least-well-off people. At every level of government, we have focused as a country on disaster recovery rather than proactive planning. As Alice Hill of the Council on Foreign Relations puts it: "What instead we do right now is we wait for the bad thing to happen, the disaster to happen and then we pour massive amounts of money into those communities." Billions are spent following disasters, and US federal and local governments usually rationalize this spending—to the extent they do—based on benefit/cost ratios like the one shaping the conversation in Charleston. Because the federal government's spending is driven by post-disaster, bang-for-the-buck reasoning, the city is pleading for the thing it believes it will most likely be funded by Congress: a hugely expensive wall that won't help most of Charleston's residents or protect against the kinds of flooding routinely being suffered through by the city. Meanwhile, the drumbeat of accelerating sea level rise is getting louder. "We are, as a nation, deeply unprepared for the types of extremes that are hitting us, just now, much less those in the future," says Hill.[78]

◆

The problems start long before a disaster strikes. FEMA does administer programs ($5 billion worth in fiscal 2021) that spend money in advance on lessening the effects of flooding on residents,[79] but it insists that any funded project have benefits directly attributable to improved flood protection that outweigh their costs. Intangible or difficult-to-quantify benefits like ensuring minority or low-income populations are fairly treated and thrive in the long run are difficult to fit within this conceptualization.[80] "FEMA's mitigation programs may sustain or even exacerbate existing social vulnerability," says academic author Kelly McGee.[81]

The Army Corps, as we've seen, is tasked with protecting "national assets," not residences, from future destruction by storm surges, and its proposed projects—about fifty of them in 2021–2022[82]—compete for congressional funding. The benefit/cost ratio of a particular project is a crucial element of its competitive viability. This approach, similarly, doesn't focus on equity or rescuing people who don't have the resources to rescue themselves.

The city of Charleston knows that most of its territory, and perhaps all of it, is in risky flood-prone terrain, but only very recently has it begun edging toward requiring that new buildings not be put in places that are likely to be completely uninhabitable in a few decades. It should be applauded for even talking about elevation-based zoning. In most parts of the country, Rob Moore, director of the Water and Climate Team at the Natural Resources Defense Council, says, "We're putting houses in places that are already at risk today and are going to be even more vulnerable tomorrow." There are thirty states in the US[83] where current homeowners have no obligation to inform buyers about past flood damage.[84] At least South Carolina requires such disclosure, even though the dollar amount of those claims doesn't have to be. And at least Charleston is considering limiting future building in low-lying areas.

Charleston should be applauded not only for talking about genuine future flooding risks to its entire region but also for seeking out many sources of information in addition to FEMA's maps. Many of these maps are decades out of date. There are many Americans who don't know what their real risks are, or know at most whether their house is "in" or "out" of a FEMA-designated floodplain, as if water will stop when it reaches a dotted line on a map. FEMA's maps "really under-inform people about the flood risks that they face," says Rob Moore. A national flood risk assessment by the First Street Foundation found in 2020 that the number of properties in the US that had a 1 percent annual risk of flood (the "100-year" flood) was about 70 percent higher than FEMA's maps showed—14.6 million instead of 8.7 million properties at risk.[85] At least 80 percent of the commercial properties and houses damaged during Hurricanes Harvey and Irma (2017) were outside FEMA's floodplains.[86]

FEMA's maps are also incomplete. "FEMA's flood maps don't take into account how flooding is going to change in response to climate change, how is extreme rainfall going to change flood patterns, [or] how sea-level rise is going to change flood patterns," says Rob Moore.[87] This is an enormous problem: As Prof. A. R. Siders of the University of Delaware puts it, "The FEMA maps aren't the end-all of risk com-munication. We need something better than that to help people under-stand the risk that they face not only today but 30 or 40 years down the road. If you're buying a home with a 30 year mortgage, you need to know if that home is going to be literally underwater, pardon the pun, in 30 years."[88] Not only that, but the concerns of developers and local governments worrying about continued property tax revenues have often taken precedence over safety concerns when it comes to FEMA's mapping work. Although the maps are static—in the sense that they don't take into account predicted risks—challenges to proposed maps from people and officials in richer areas often lead to houses being removed from FEMA floodplain designations.[89] These inadequate maps, originally intended to be used only for insurance purposes, are not standardized. Consultants, not the government, generate the data for FEMA in different parts of the US. Different consultants provide different maps. This leads to mixed messages and confusion. Earthquake data, by contrast, is a government product. Coastal sea level rise? It feels as if it can be gamed by anyone with money.

Charleston has had its struggles with FEMA's requirements in the past, particularly during the Riley era, but recently it has been trying to comply with or exceed the agency's standards. This is important, because FEMA sets required minimum standards for local ordinances that have to be in place in order for residents to be able to buy flood insurance. (Banks can't give mortgages to houses in the FEMA-designated floodplains without flood insurance in place.)[90] Without flood insurance, people whose houses are damaged by water have to rely on FEMA grants, which are tiny and difficult to access.

The trouble is that the flood insurance structure in the US is a mess and FEMA's standards are hopelessly low. It may be, in fact, that the availability of flood insurance for risky coastal locations creates a moral hazard by encouraging homeowners to assume they will be bailed out by the federal government no matter where they live.

Of the eighty-eight million houses at some risk of flooding in America, in 2020 just 3.7 million homeowners paid for federal flood insurance through FEMA's heavily subsidized National Flood Insurance Program (NFIP),[91] created in 1968. (There is some private flood insurance available, but many insurers exited following the Great Mississippi Flood of 1927 and NFIP holds most of the existing policies.)[92] Low-income homeowners in floodplains are far less likely to have flood insurance than wealthier residents,[93] even if they hold mortgages; enforcement of flood insurance requirements is low. NFIP is widely seen as a hopelessly underfunded and badly administered program. It is more than $20 billion in the red, and such a political hot potato that it keeps being reauthorized by temporary extensions—nineteen times since the end of 2017—to keep it from vanishing altogether, because Congress can't agree on the fundamental restructuring the program clearly needs.[94] Overhaul of the program seems unlikely. R. J. Lehmann of the International Center for Law & Economics told E&E News in June 2022, "I continue to be skeptical that there's much movement for significant reform in Congress," adding, "The voices that are opposed are much louder and more organized than the voices for reform."[95]

Charleston cannot possibly believe that flood insurance will rescue those of its residents who happen to have it. NFIP as currently structured is focused on providing assistance with rebuilding homes where they are (up to a maximum of $250,000 in payouts, which is less than half the value of a typical Charleston-region home),[96] and won't pay to eliminate flood risk by allowing people to move to higher ground. FEMA's standards are so low, so unresponsive to the increasing severity and frequency of floods, storms, and hurricanes, that its work is arguably creating more risk than it is avoiding.

The "moral hazard" element of NFIP is clear in Charleston: as of 2020, the city was home to 700 residences that flooded repeatedly, a number that amounts to about a third of all such homes in South Carolina and is higher than that for any other community in the state.[97] Homes there have been repaired over and over again at federal expense following storms.

NFIP is rolling out a revision to its premium system called "Risk Rating 2.0" that will, over time, price flood insurance premiums based on the individual flooding experience of particular properties rather than solely on FEMA's maps. Eventually, rates will rise to be in line with expected losses. Existing policyholders are protected by statute from premium increases over 18 percent per year. The trouble is that there is no cap on how swiftly rates will go up for people who don't already have insurance from NFIP, and most of those homeowners are lower-income.[98] This may mean that lower-income homeowners in the

Charleston region, people who don't pay for their houses in cash, won't be able to afford flood insurance. And, "if you don't buy flood insurance because it seems too expensive," says *New York Times* climate reporter Christopher Flavelle, "you're unlikely to have the savings you need to recover if your house gets destroyed."[99]

How about federal help for buying people out of chronically flooded houses? FEMA does have a Hazard Mitigation Grant Program that allocates money for buyouts, under which the federal government reimburses cities 75 percent of the cost of buying out a "repetitive flood" house; HUD also has a buyout program. Nashville used these programs to buy out more than 400 homes and vacant lots between 1998 and 2019. The owners got market value for their homes, and the city got wet land that could be used as parks.[100] Birmingham, Alabama, used these programs to buy out 735 properties in a chronically flooded area.[101]

As we saw in Chapter 9, Charleston similarly bought out forty-five homes in the Shadowmoss neighborhood of West Ashley. South Carolina is near the top of the list of states getting flooding buyout support from the federal insurance program.[102] (Members of the public can't find out exactly where those properties are or whether the number of repetitive flooding properties has grown since then; that information isn't available without making an open records request of the federal government.)[103]

The problem is that these programs are tiny and usually take more than five years to work through their process—and the request itself needs to be triggered by a disaster. The Shadowmoss application took four years to be processed.[104] During those four years, the neighborhood went through several agonizing floods. The Birmingham process took twenty years.[105]

These waits are forever from a desperate homeowner's perspective. What should they do? Wait for possible buyout funding to show up? Rebuild their house yet again on their own? Sell to a real estate speculator who wants to flip the house and not disclose its history? Given the slowness of the buyout process, the low buyout amounts that are offered, and the hot coastal real estate market in the US, many homeowners are turning down buyout offers.[106] They're reasoning they'll never find replacement properties in the same community that they can afford. In Charleston, where the price of a typical house climbed more than 30 percent between 2021 and 2022 alone, homeowners may make this same short-term calculation under the current program.

If FEMA buyouts continue at their current pace, they'll be able to get to about 130,000 more houses over the next ninety years.[107] But there are something like thirteen million Americans in coastal areas who will need buyouts by 2051 in light of accelerating sea level rise.[108] The current program has ad hoc distributional impacts: The counties who apply for and get FEMA buyout funding tend to be wealthier and whiter, but the residents who are actually bought out tend to be rural and poorer, Prof. Siders has found.

FEMA's current buyout program does not offer any help to people in public housing or renters.[109] Nearly all of the residents of Charleston's public housing units, almost all of which are in frequently inundated areas, are Black.[110]

There is no chance that FEMA's current program has the capacity to help everyone who needs it. And there is no chance that Charleston has either the money or the will right now to help people move out of harm's way. But it seems clear that, given the risks that already exist and that are likely to rapidly accelerate no later than 2032, it would make sense for the people living on or near the Charleston Peninsula, including on Kiawah Island—where a billion dollars changed hands in the form of real estate deals during 2021[111]—to make plans to pick up and move elsewhere, notwithstanding the bizarrely hot real estate market in the area. The people on Kiawah will be irritated by this, but they'll smoothly, invisibly find their way out, buoyed up above the waves by plump checking accounts and networks of connections. There are golf courses in other locations, even if the wide, flat, ten-mile-long beach enjoyed by those on Kiawah is irreplaceable. What will happen to the low-income Black residents of Charleston on the East Side, on the Neck, and in the Gadsden Green Homes? What will happen to the not-so-rich people in the suburbs, both Black and white? What's needed is a region-wide strategic withdrawal program assisted by coordinated governments at all levels, not a series of one-off buyouts.

◆

For Charleston, the alternative to planning ahead is to continue muddling along upholding the status quo. The risk is that the status quo may be about to change, drastically, as the banks, insurers, and credit rating agencies begin raising alarms about the slow-rolling cataclysm facing Charleston. The mispriced risk of sea level rise is presenting tempting opportunities for investors. The collapse that may be ahead will likely be precipitous, and Black and lower-income residents will be harmed the most by its consequences.

Here's how this could happen. When an individual takes out a mortgage from a bank, that mortgage does not stay with the bank. Instead, it is packaged with other loans and sold as part of a tranche, or pool, to government sponsored entities (GSEs) like the Federal Home Loan Mortgage Corporation (Freddie Mac), the Government National Mortgage Association (Ginnie Mae), or the Federal National Mortgage Association (Fannie Mae). Those GSEs design financial instruments for sale that are based on those loan tranches. Those instruments are then sold as "securities" to investors. The investors are buying bonds that entitle them to a share of the cash eventually paid by the borrowers, the individuals, on their mortgages. Through this process, a nontradeable asset, the mortgage, is magically transformed into a tradeable thing. Other financial actors help in this process. A credit rating agency rates the "bond," and sometimes someone will guarantee the bond, which reduces the risk of the security being sold. In this instance, when we're talking about mortgages, the "bond" is called a "mortgage-backed security." The buyer of the bond gets a government guarantee that he'll be paid whether or not the original individual defaults on his mortgage.

After many mortgage-backed securities defaulted during the Great Recession, US taxpayers, who back the GSEs, had to bail them out. To shift the risk of this happening again away from the public sector (and thus the taxpayer), Freddie Mac in 2013 established something independent of mortgage-backed-securities called a credit risk transfer (CRT). A CRT is also a security based on a pool of loans, but they have no collateral standing behind them. Because they are risky for an investor, they pay a higher rate of interest; the GSEs pay that interest to investors, as well as "principal" that is actually a portion of the guarantee fee the GSEs are paid monthly to guarantee the mortgage. If the pool of loans incurs losses—begins to include defaults—that exceed a threshold that has been set in advance, the value of the CRTs is reassessed, or "written down," to reflect this loss, and the GSE's obligation to pay that lost portion of its guaranteed fee to investors in the form of "principal" is lessened or removed altogether. This means that when there are losses, it is the investors in the CRTs who have the exposure, rather than the GSEs themselves. COVID led the credit rating agencies to downgrade a number of these vehicles, but the CRT market is still booming as of mid-2022.[112]

If all of this is reminding you of the complexity of the synthetic securities ("credit default swaps") based on residential mortgages that, when residential foreclosures began happening in waves in 2007, simultaneously created a crisis in liquidity that led to the Great Recession of 2008, you are in the right ballpark of anxiety. The lobbyists supporting greater uses of CRTs claim that they provide more diverse sources of capital for the GSEs and thus, inevitably, better mortgages for consumers because the cost of capital goes down across the system. But the same optimistic assessment of the strength of actually junky mortgage pools back in 2007 that led to the crisis then is present in the frothy CRT marketplace now. It is not clear that Fannie or Freddie is adequately factoring in the disastrous risks of extreme climate change for coastal residential real estate.

Just ask Dave Burt, who while he was at Cornwall Capital in New York City was one of the few investing consultants who predicted the 2008 housing crash. Burt has started a new investment research firm called DeltaTerra, and he has developed a model he calls Klima.[113] His thesis is that the GSEs are mispricing climate risk. "I believe we are experiencing a similar value bubble today driven by the market's failure to consider the increasing risk of damages resulting from climate change," Burt says.[114] He estimates that "rationalization" of climate risk mispricing—in other words, everyone waking up and realizing that the risks of inundation are not actually being reflected in housing prices or tax rates or insurance premiums or maintenance costs or mortgage rates—could begin in the next couple of years and lead to losses ranging up to $1.9 trillion in a short time.[115] In the process, all those credit risk transfer bonds could perform really badly. All of this leads to "a compelling opportunity to generate climate driven-alpha while climate risk mispricing persists."[116] Translated: if someone creates a securitized bet that these CRT bonds will pay off, and then you bet against that bet, you stand to make an amazing amount of money. (Paying off bets of this magnitude is what triggered the subprime mortgage crisis.)

Burt points in particular to credit risk transfer bonds based on coastal residential real estate that is in a "special flood hazard area" that has been mapped by FEMA. (Just about all of Charleston falls in this category.) He predicts that many millions of homes in America will be affected by this mispricing and that their value will drop by between 20 and 40 percent. When it becomes too expensive to insure a home, or adapt it by raising it, homeowners who can afford it will move. Many low- and medium-income homeowners will default on their mortgages, Burt predicts. Lots of coastal properties that are in areas that FEMA hasn't mapped yet (or hasn't recognized as risky when they actually are) will be profoundly affected. There might be even greater losses if there is "a less orderly correction in which market participants anticipate a failure to effectively mitigate the impacts of global warming."[117] In other words, a panic.

As Burt puts it, "A lot of real estate is massively overpriced and there's a lot of [climate] risk associated with that and the big risk is another foreclosure crisis."[118] It's 2007 all over again: The window of mispricing is bound to shut soon. "We believe that this capital markets mispricing could be just as damaging financially to homeowners as actual acute flooding events."[119]

When the bubble bursts and the crash comes, and the wealthier people of Charleston pick up and leave, abandoning their houses, it is the poorer residents who will be stuck there with increasingly inadequate and unsupported infrastructure. Increasingly salty drinking water. Increasingly fetid and disease-ridden streets. There are already cholera spores in the water around Charleston.[120]

◆

Roughly a fifth of the planet, coastal places where three billion people now live, could be extremely uncomfortable or even unlivable by 2070.[121] The world is not ready for this. The majority of Americans who live in coastal counties—52 percent of us—are not ready for this.[122] Something like thirteen million people may be on the move in the US as those coastal counties flood over the next few decades.

Charleston's lack of preparation is clearly not unique. But we can predict that the catastrophic effects of climate change in Charleston will lead to a large movement of people, many of whom will be Black and low-income. For much of coastal America, Charleston is a bellwether. If we continue to muddle ahead as we are now, that migration is likely to be panicked, forced, miserable, and unfair. Neither local governments in the US nor the federal government have grappled with how to deal with making that migration work on a large scale. It would be a good idea to plan ahead as a nation, starting right now, for this future.

The map of Charleston will likely be substantially changed by the coming storms. We do not know how quickly this will happen. But we now have the capacity to ensure that this transition is deliberate and thoughtful. Passivity and delay in response to uncertainty are actively harmful choices. As Charleston resident William Hamilton asked, "Have you all been able to identify locations on high ground, where we can build high density, affordable communities for the people that are going to be forced away from the sea, before the rich people out at the beaches discover that they want to own North Charleston and get away from the ocean?" So far, he hasn't been answered. He deserves an answer. More pointedly, the question Charleston and its past raises for the US deserves a strong, affirmative response. What is the role of government if not to ensure that everyone has the opportunity to be safe and thrive in dignity?

When Michelle Mapp thinks of her grandmother, Ruth Johnson, Mapp knows her grandmother would be proud of her. Ruth Johnson has left this planet, but Mapp says, "I think I would want her to know that the love that she invested in me is paying dividends." She pauses, tearing up. "That what she taught us about loving one another is with me. And I'm going to do my damndest to teach that to my children and share that with the world." Charleston, and every coastal city, just barely has time to absorb that lesson and turn it into action.

Acknowledgments

So many people have helped me during the years I have been exploring Charleston and the subjects of this book. I am grateful to Jack Hitt, a son of Charleston, for launching me down this path six years ago, and to Kevin Baker for launching me toward Jack. The Very Rev. Kurt Dunkle introduced me to Charlestonians who generously talked to me about their beloved city. Darren Walker, Frank Rich, Ron Suskind, and Yochai Benkler got me going on this project, and Ted Widmer and John Schwartz provided crucial thoughtfulness when I most needed it. Caroline Mauldin was a warm and gracious presence in my life who introduced me to her generation in Charleston.

Todd Shuster and Justin Brouckaert of Aevitas Creative Management, my agents, believed that this was a book I could and should write even before I did. I am so grateful to them. Clay Risen's calm editorial eye was essential to this project, and I cannot thank him enough.

As a professor, I'm lucky to have a home at Harvard Law School. I'm grateful to Martha Minow for many things, and especially for her unwavering belief in me. Annette Gordon-Reed's graciousness in providing the foreword to this volume remains one of the single kindest acts by a colleague I have ever experienced. The Harvard University Center for the Environment, led by Dan Schrag and James Clem, has been central to my becoming a climate writer. This book would not have come into being without HUCE's support, and I was fortunate to meet Jesse Keenan, A. R. Siders, and John Macomber at HUCE events. I have benefited enormously from the help of sterling research assistants over the years, including the marvelous Becca Ellison,

Ariel Silverman, Madeline Kitch, and Cooper Knarr. Alex Harper, Kathryn Mueller, Lauren O'Brien, Mia Gettenberg, Mohammad Zia, Noelle Graham, Sarah Hannigan, Will Lindsey, and Jason Bell were members of a Fall 2018 reading group that played a substantial role in getting this project off the ground. Steven Trothen and Samantha Burke have been wonderful assistants to me over the years I have been at Harvard.

Many people helped me in big and small ways during the years I was carrying out interviews for this book. None of them is responsible for any failings of this project; many likely don't agree with my conclusions. They met with me, consented to be interviewed by me, gave me advice, steered me in different directions, or made introductions, among other things. It is impossible to name them all, but I would like to single out Tony Bartelme, Dana Beach, Jenny Brennan, Dan Burger, Laura Cabiness, Thomas Cabiness, Laura Cantral, Polly Carpenter, Jason Crowley, Cathryn Davis, Chris DeScherer, Piet Diercke, Dennis Dowd, Steve Dudash, Carol Fishman, Matt Fountain, Albert George, Vince Graham, John Hagerty, Winslow Hastie, Alice Hill, Eric Jackson, Alex Jones, KJ Kearney, Mayor Billy Keyserling, Betsy LaForce, Norm Levine, Jacob Lindsey, Michael Maher, Madeleine McGee, Michael Miller, Paul Moravec, Dale Morris, Phil Noble, Bob Perry, Jeff Peterson, Prof. Bernard Powers, Prof. Simon Richter, Elizabeth Sarnoff, Mike Seekings, Charlton Singleton, Steven Slabbers, Gus Speth, John Tibbetts, William Sweet, Mayor John Tecklenburg, Steve Warner, Joannes Westerink, Spencer Wetmore, Mark Wilbert, David White, Carolee Williams, and Andrew Wunderley. I am more grateful than I can say to Rev. Joseph Darby, Quinetha Frasier, and Michelle Mapp.

Thanks to everyone at Pegasus Books for bringing this book into the world. Thanks especially to Jessica Case for her belief in this project. I am grateful to Elizabeth Shreve for making sure its message is heard.

This book is dedicated to Mitchell, a son of Waynesboro, GA. He was the soul of wisdom and thoughtfulness throughout, understood I needed to spend time in Charleston, was quietly supportive as draft followed draft, and read the final version with a clear eye and sharp pen.

Image Credits

p. 33　　　　　A complete description of the Province of Carolina in three parts: 1st, the improved part from the surveys of Maurice Mathews & Mr. John Love; 2nd, the West part by Capt. Tho. Nairn; 3rd, a chart of the coast from Virginia to Cape Florida by Edward Crisp, Thomas Nairne, John Harris, Maurice Mathews, and John Love has been modified (cropped) and is in the public domain. The image was accessed through the Library of Congress, Geography and Map Division at https://www.loc.gov/item/2004626926.

p. 35　　　　　"Historic Charleston on a map, showing original high tide water lines, fortifications, boroughs, great fires, historic information, etc.," by Alfred O. Halsey, 1949. From the collections of the South Carolina Historical Society. Used by permission.

p. 36　　　　　Charleston City Plan, designed by Mary Mac Wilson, licensed under Creative Commons license PD-US, accessed through https://www .charlestoncityplan.com.

p. 60　　　　　Photograph of John C. Calhoun by Matthew Brady, 1849, retrieved from Wikipedia, used under PD-US.

p. 62　　　　　Plan of the City and Neck of Charleston, S.C. 1844, used by permission, David Rumsey Map Collection, David Rumsey Map Center, Stanford Libraries.

p. 67　　　　　Scan of Olmsted Associates Records by Olmstead Associates. Accessed through LOC, used under PD-US, https://www.loc.gov /item/mss5257101529/.

pp. 68-69　　　Excerpt from Morris Knowles plan, showing "white residency districts" and "negro residency districts." Accessed through LOC, used under PD-US, https://www.loc.gov/resource/mss52571.mss52571-02 -088_0355_0435/?sp=10&st=single&r=-0.023,0.064,1.188,0.488,0.

pp. 70-71　　　Morris Knowles, Inc., Report of the City Planning and Zoning Commission, upon a Program for the Development of a City Plan with Specific Studies of Certain Features Thereof, 2 July 1931. "[U] ndeveloped sections adjoining the Ashley River will be reserved

as white residences sections by developers through the use of deed
covenants. . . . [R]esidence property east of King Street and north
of Laurens Street may ultimately become negro sections. Such
development generally will be advantageous and should be encouraged
when and as necessary."

p. 89   Summary of population by race on Charleston's peninsula, 1890–2020.

p. 118   Map of the lower peninsula. Contains information from
             ©OpenStreetMap contributors at openstreetmap.org, which is made
             available under the ODC Attribution License found at openstreetmap
             .org/copyright.

p. 121   Western edge of lower Charleston peninsula, including Colonial
             Lake. Contains information from ©OpenStreetMap contributors
             at openstreetmap.org, which is made available under the ODC
             Attribution License found at openstreetmap.org/.

p. 123   Public domain map with overlays by the City of Charleston; black line
             shows reclamation of 47 acres and division into 191 lots; dotted line is
             the Low Battery.

p. 124   Photo of Low Battery flooding. Photo taken September 11, 2017,
             copyright Jared Bramblett. Used by permission.

p. 129   Map of Union Pier Terminal and The Cooper, contains information
             from ©OpenStreetMap contributors at openstreetmap.org, which
             is made available under the ODC Attribution License found at
             openstreetmap.org/copyright.

p. 134   Outline of Union Pier Redevelopment Project superimposed on 1788
             "Ichnography of Charleston, South-Carolina : at the request of Adam
             Tunno, Esq., for the use of the Phœnix Fire-Company of London,
             taken from actual survey, 2d August 1788," available from the
             Library of Congress at https://www.loc.gov/resource/g3914c.ct00042
             3/?r=0.198,0.094,0.865,0.355,0.

p. 143   The East Side of the Charleston modern map, contains information
             from ©OpenStreetMap contributors at openstreetmap.org, which
             is made available under the ODC Attribution License found at
             openstreetmap.org/copyright.

p. 144   Appletons' general guide to the United States and Canada. Part II.
             Western and Southern States. New York: D. Appleton and Company,
             Charleston 1885. Accessed through the University of Texas Libraries,
             in the public domain. Modified to show current-day outline of the East
             Side. https://maps.lib.utexas.edu/maps/historical/charleston_1885.jpg.

p. 162   Enlarged Detail of Vision for Green Infrastructure and Elevated
             Roadways, created by Waggoner & Ball Architecture/Environment,
             from Dutch Dialogues® Final Report, 2019. Used by permission.
             ("Dutch Dialogues" is a registered trademark of Waggoner & Ball.)

p. 168   Map of eighteenth century plantation in the Upper Peninsula, from
             the Henry A. M. Smith Collection of the South Carolina Historical

Society. "Sketch Plan of the City of Charleston and of Charleston
Neck showing the lines of the Original Grants in the City and of
the Plantations or settlements along the Neck." Used by permission.
Everything above Line Street was originally "the Neck."

p. 170   Map showing annexations/1976 annexation, growth of Charleston.
                Courtesy of Charleston County Public Library.

p. 172   We Argue. Nature Acts. banner, "Charleston Airborne Flooded"
                Banner for Enough Pie Awakening V: King Tide. Used by permission
                of artist Mary Edna. Accessed through https://maryedna.com
                /installations/charleston-airborne-flooded/.

p. 191   Map of North Charleston. Contains information from
                ©OpenStreetMap contributors at openstreetmap.org, which is made
                available under the ODC Attribution License found at openstreetmap
                .org/copyright.

p. 199   Darby's church/Nichols Chapel map, map of upper west portion of
                Charleston Peninsula. Contains information from ©OpenStreetMap
                contributors at openstreetmap.org, which is made available under the
                ODC Attribution License found at openstreetmap.org/copyright.

p. 205   Map of Charleston, "Plan of Charleston, 1849," by Wellington
                Williams, licensed under PD-US, accessed through Wikimedia
                Commons at https://commons.wikimedia.org/wiki/File:1849_map
                _of_Charleston,_South_Carolina.peg.

p. 206   "Sanborn Fire Insurance Map from Charleston, Charleston County,
                South Carolina," by the Sanborn Map Company, 1902, licensed under
                PD-US. Modified to show current location of Gadsden Green. Map
                retrieved from the Library of Congress, https://www.loc.gov/item
                /sanborn08124_003/. Fiddler's Green map.

p. 207   Letter from John A. Harris to Mayor Lockwood. From the Mayor
                Henry W. Lockwood Mayoral Papers, City of Charleston, South
                Carolina, Records Management Division. Used by permission.

p. 208   Page showing signatories to Harris letter. From the Mayor Henry
                W. Lockwood Mayoral Papers, City of Charleston, South Carolina,
                Records Management Division. Used by permission.

p. 208   Mayor Lockwood rejection letter/housing. From the Mayor Henry
                W. Lockwood Mayoral Papers, City of Charleston, South Carolina,
                Records Management Division. Used by permission.

p. 211   Map of Septima Clark Crosstown, contains information from
                ©OpenStreetMap contributors at openstreetmap.org, which is made
                available under the ODC Attribution License found at openstreetmap
                .org/copyright.

p. 216 (2 images)   Maps showing outlines of historic creek beds above archival
                photographs. ©Coastal Conservation League, used by permission.

p. 217   Closeup of medical district and Gadsden Green Homes,
                OpenStreetMap data used under the Open Database License, see

Endnotes

1. Charleston and Its Global Cousins

1   Vince Gaffney, Anniversary Professor of Landscape Archaeology at the University of Bradford, "Doggerland," interview by Melvyn Bragg, *In Our Time*, BBC, June 27, 2019, audio, https://www.youtube.com/watch?v=wcubRlMqaEs.

2   Andrew Curry, "Europe's Lost Frontier," *Science*, January 30, 2020, accessed June 20, 2022, doi: 10.1126/science.abb0986.

3   "Geodigest." 2021. *Geology Today* 37 (2): 42–56. https://doi.org/10.1111/gto.12342.

4   "Howick House," International Association of Archaeological Open-Air Museums, accessed June 20, 2022, https://exarc.net/venues/howick-house-uk.

5   This book takes as a given the accepted scientific finding that humans primarily caused the global warming we are now seeing. In 2020, Earth was about 2 degrees F (1.1 degrees C) warmer than it was early in the industrial era. NASA, Goddard Institute for Space Studies, Surface Temperature Analysis, at https://data.giss.nasa.gov/gistemp/. IPCC's Fifth Assessment stated, "It is extremely likely that human influence has been the dominant cause of the observed warming since the mid-20th century." IPCC, 2013: Summary for Policymakers. In: Climate Change 2013: The Physical Science Basis. Contribution of Working Group I to the Fifth Assessment Report of the Intergovernmental Panel on Climate Change [Stocker, T.F., et al. (eds.)]. Cambridge University Press, Cambridge, United Kingdom and New York, NY, USA, p.17. As Dr. Michael Oppenheimer puts it, "[T]he accumulation of greenhouse gases (such as carbon dioxide) in the atmosphere as a result of human activity (largely related to fossil fuel combustion to provide energy) is the primary cause of the observed global warming," and "Changes in heat, precipitation and sea level are attributed with medium or high confidence to the greenhouse gas buildup." Testimony of Dr. Michael Oppenheimer, Princeton University, at the Committee on Science, Space, and Technology, US House of Representatives, March 12, 2021, On Climate Change Science.

6   C40 Climate Leadership Group, "Sea Level Rise and Coastal Flooding," n.d., www.c40.org/what-we-do/scaling-up-climate-action/adaptation-water/the-future-we-dont-want/sea-level-rise/.

7   Mihai Andrei, "Doggerland—the land that connected Europe and the UK 8000 years
     ago," *ZME Science*, February 1, 2021, accessed June 20, 2022, https://www.zmescience
     .com/other/feature-post/doggerland-europe-land/.

8   Norman Levine, PhD Director, Santee Cooper GIS Laboratory and Lowcountry
     Hazards Center and Associate Professor in the Department of Geology and
     Environmental Geosciences, College of Charleston, May 1, 2019 presentation to
     Dutch Dialogues team in Charleston, South Carolina.

9   Sweet, William V., Benjamin D. Hamlington, Robert E. Kopp, Christopher P. Weaver,
     Patrick L. Barnard, David Bekaert, and William Brooks, "Global and Regional Sea
     Level Rise Scenarios for the United States: Updated Mean Projections and Extreme
     Water Level Probabilities Along U.S. Coastlines," 2022, *National Oceanic and
     Atmospheric Administration*, *National Ocean Service*, NOAA Technical Report NOS 01.

10   Compared to 2000 levels. Global sea levels rose by 2.5mm per year in the 1990s,
     3.4mm in the 2000s, and now in the 2020s sea level is rising at about 4.5mm per
     year. If this accelerating rate of growth continues, and it appears likely to given the
     high emissions track the world is now on, and ice sheet processes trigger nonlinear
     rise, we could see 2-3 meters (5-10 feet) of rise by 2100. John Englander, *Moving To
     Higher Ground* (Boca Raton: The Science Bookshelf, 2021), 54-55. As the IPCC put
     it in 2019, "a rise of two or more metres [by 2100] cannot be ruled out. . . . Even if
     efforts to mitigate emissions are very effective, [Extreme Sea Level] events that were
     rare over the last century will become common before 2100, and even by 2050 in
     many locations. Without ambitious adaptation, the combined impact of hazards like
     coastal storms and very high tides will drastically increase the frequency and severity
     of flooding on low-lying coasts." Michael Oppenheimer et al., "Sea Level Rise and
     Implications for Low-Lying Islands, Coasts and Communities," in IPCC Special
     Report on the Ocean and Cryosphre in a Changing Climate, eds. H.-O. Pörtner et
     al. (Cambridge, UK and New York, NY, USA: Cambridge University Press, 2019),
     321-445. According to NOAA, "About 2 feet (0.6 meters) of sea level rise along the
     U.S. coastline is increasingly likely between 2020 and 2100 because of emissions to
     date. Failing to curb future emissions could cause an additional 1.5–5 feet (0.5–1.5
     meters) of rise for a total of 3.5–7 feet (1.1–2.1 meters) by the end of this century."
     Sweet, William V., Benjamin D. Hamlington, Robert E. Kopp, Christopher
     P. Weaver, Patrick L. Barnard, David Bekaert, and William Brooks, 2022: Global
     and Regional Sea Level Rise Scenarios for the United States: Updated Mean
     Projections and Extreme Water Level Probabilities Along U.S. Coastlines. NOAA
     Technical Report NOS 01. National Oceanic and Atmospheric Administration,
     National Ocean Service, Silver Spring, MD, 111 pp. https://oceanservice.noaa.gov/
     hazards/ sealevelrise/noaa-nos-techrpt01-global-regional-SLR-scenarios-US.pdf;
     see also Katharine Hayhoe et al., "Our Changing Climate," in Impacts, risks, and
     Adaptation in the United States: Fourth National Climate Assessment, Volume II,
     eds. D. R. Reidmiller et al. (Washington, DC, USA: U.S. Global Change Research
     Program, 2018), 72-144 (projecting "extreme" level of sea-level rise by 2100 at 2.4 meters,
     or 7.8 feet). NOAA is confident that there will be 4 feet of SLR by 2075 and

6 feet by 2092 in Charleston County. NOAA Coastal County Snapshots, based on projections from the 2022 Sea Level Rise Technical Report for the Charleston, SC tide gauge. Uncertainty in projections beyond 2050 is based in large part on the fate of the ice sheets in Greenland and Antarctica, as discussed below. The East Coast of the US has already experienced 1.5 to twice as much sea level rise as the global average. Oppenheimer 2021 testimony.

11   "NOAA report: Sea levels on track to rise more than a foot by 2050," *Fox4Now News*, https://www.fox4now.com/wftx-weather-stories/noaa-report-sea-levels-on-track-to -rise-more-than-a-foot-by-2050.

12   "Joint NASA, NOAA Study Finds Earth's Energy Imbalance Has Doubled," June 15, 2021, https://www.nasa.gov/feature/langley/joint-nasa-noaa-study-finds -earths-energy-imbalance-has-doubled.

13   James Hansen, Makiko Sato and Reto Ruedy, "Global Temperature in 2021," https ://mailchi.mp/caa/global-temperature-in-2021.

14   "The probability of low-likelihood, high-impact outcomes increases with higher global warming levels (high confidence). Abrupt responses and tipping points of the climate system, such as strongly increased Antarctic ice-sheet melt and forest dieback, cannot be ruled out (high confidence)." IPCC, 2021: Summary for Policymakers. In: *Climate Change 2021: The Physical Science Basis. Contribution of Working Group I to the Sixth Assessment Report of the Intergovernmental Panel on Climate Change* [Masson-Delmotte, V., P. Zhai, A. Pirani, S.L. Connors, C. Péan, S. Berger, N. Caud, Y. Chen, L. Goldfarb, M.I. Gomis, M. Huang, K. Leitzell, E. Lonnoy, J.B.R. Matthews, T.K. Maycock, T. Waterfield, O. Yelekçi, R. Yu, and B. Zhou (eds.)].

15   Emily Williams, "Despite Pandemic, Charleston Tourism Had Bigger Impact in 2021 Than Before COVID," *Post and Courier*, March 30, 2022.

16   AFP, "Millions Stranded, Dozens Dead as Flooding Hits Bangladesh and India," *Phys.org*, May 21, 2022, https://phys.org/news/2022-05-millions-stranded-dozens -dead-bangladesh.html.

17   Adam Piore, "Cities Brace for Apocalyptic Flooding As New Age of Super Storms Dawns," *Newsweek*, May 11, 2022, https://www.newsweek.com/2022/05/27/cities -brace-apocalyptic-flooding-new-age-super-storms-dawns-1705402.html.

18   Fiona Harvey, "Pakistan Floods 'Made up to 50% Worse by Global Heating,'" *Guardian*, September 15, 2022, https://www.theguardian.com/environment/2022 /sep/15/pakistan-floods-made-up-to-50-worse-by-global-heating.

19   Tristan McConnell, "The Maldives is Being Swallowed by the Sea. Can it Adapt?" *National Geographic*, n.d, www.nationalgeographic.com/environment/article /the-maldives-is-being-swallowed-by-the-sea-can-it-adapt.

20   "Water-Related Hazards Dominate Disasters in the Past 50 Years," *World Meteorological Organization*, July 23, 2021, https://public.wmo.int/en/media /press-release/water-related-hazards-dominate-disasters-past-50-years.

21   Jeff Berardelli, "How Climate Change is Making Hurricanes More Dangerous," *Yale Climate Connections*, July 8, 2019, https://yaleclimateconnections.org/2019/07 /how-climate-change-is-making-hurricanes-more-dangerous/.

22 Richard Davies, "Côte d'Ivoire—Torrential Rain Triggers Deadly Floods in Abidjan, *Floodlist*, October 22, 2021, floodlist.com/africa/cotedivoire-floods-abidjan -october-2021.

23 Nimi Princewill, "Africa's Most Populous City is Battling Floods and Rising Seas. It May Soon be Unlivable, Experts Warn," CNN, last modified August 1, 2021, www.cnn.com/2021/08/01/africa/lagos-sinking-floods-climate-change-intl-cmd /index.html.

24 Egypt Today staff, "Alexandria Has Witnessed Heavy Torrential Rains, Floods Since 2015: Governor," *Egypt Today*, November 4, 2021, www.egypttoday.com /Article/1/109552/Alexandria-has-witnessed-heavy-torrential-rains-floods-since -2015-Governor.

25 "Europe Flooding Deaths Pass 125, and Scientists See Fingerprints of Climate Change," *New York Times*, last modified September 7, 2021, www.nytimes.com/live /2021/07/16/world/europe-flooding-germany; Peter Yeung, "In Hamburg, Surviving Climate Change Means Living with Water," *Bloomberg*, December 18, 2021, www .bloomberg.com/news/features/2021-12-18/how-hamburg-learned-to-live-with -rising-water.

26 "State of Climate in 2021: Extreme Events and Major Impacts," *World Meteorological Organization*, October 31, 2021, https://public.wmo.int/en/media/press-release /state-of-climate-2021-extreme-events-and-major-impacts.

27 Prime Minister Lee Hsien Loong, "National Day Rally 2019," Transcript of speech delivered at the Institute of Technical Education College Central, August 18, 2019.

28 John Englander, *Moving To Higher Ground* (Boca Raton: The Science Bookshelf, 2021), 98; Sebastian Weissenberger and Chouinard Omer, *Adaptation to Climate Change and Sea Level Rise : The Case Study of Coastal Communities in New Brunswick, Canada* (Dordrecht: Springer Netherlands: Imprint: Springer, 2015), 9 ("IPCC estimates have often been considered too conservative, in that they do not take into account a possible acceleration of ice sheet melt"); As Dr. Michael Oppenheimer puts it, "In a high emissions scenario that could lead to global warming in excess of 9 degrees F (5 degrees C) above recent temperatures, sea level rise is expected to reach 9-16 inches by mid-century and 24-43 inches by year 2100. . . . However, sea level rise is not distributed uniformly around the world. Many local effects cause place-to-place variations of +/-30%. As it happens, the northeast US coast has already experienced sea level rise of 1.5-2.0 times the global average." Testimony of Dr. Michael Oppenheimer, Princeton University, at the Committee on Science, Space, and Technology, US House of Representatives, March 12, 2021, On Climate Change Science.

29 M. Haasnoot et al., "Adaptation to Uncertain Sea-Level Rise; How Uncertainty in Antarctic Mass-Loss Impacts the Coastal Adaptation Strategy of the Netherlands," *Environmental Research Letters* 15 (3): 34007 (Large ice loss could "rapidly increase [sea-level rise] in the second half of this century . . . The magnitude and rate of this rise depends strongly on the global and regional temperature change, altered oceanographic dynamical patterns near Antarctica, and the corresponding response of the Antarctica ice cap, which are all closely linked to greenhouse gas emissions.")

30   "Third of Antarctic Ice Shelf Area at Risk of Collapse as Planet Warms." University
      of Reading, April 8, 2021, www.reading.ac.uk/news/2021/research-news/pr855740;
      Kristin Pope, "What the Latest Science Says About Antarctica and Sea-Level Rise,"
      Yale Climate Connections, February 23, 2022; John Englander, *Moving to Higher Ground*,
      at 28.

31   As NOAA senior oceanographer Dr. William Sweet puts it, "[W]e know, through
      the geological record in the past, there have been abrupt and very rapid increases of
      sea level." Dr. William Sweet, interview by Peter Ravella and Tyler Buckingham, *The
      American Shoreline Podcast*, March 27, 2022, https://www.coastalnewstoday.com
      /podcasts/unpacking-the-noaa-2022-sea-level-rise-technical-report-with-dr-william
      -sweet. *See also* Englander, *Moving to Higher Ground*, at 33.

32   Brian McNoldy, "This Supermoon has a Twist—Expect Flooding, but a Lunar Cycle
      is Masking Effects of Sea Level Rise," *The Conversation*, Academic Journalism Society,
      April 23, 2021, theconversation.com/this-supermoon-has-a-twist-expect-flooding-but
      -a-lunar-cycle-is-masking-effects-of-sea-level-rise-158412. ("During those years [post
      2025], the rate of sea level rise is effectively doubled in places like Miami,' says Brian
      McNoldy, an atmospheric scientist at the University of Miami.")

33   As Norman Levine of the College of Charleston puts it, "Now we have potential for
      increased extremes [caused by the mood wobble] during a time period when we're
      seeing this increased expected rise as well." Interview with Norman Levine, July 21,
      2021.

34   Rolf Schuttenhelm, "Sea Level Rise is Bigger Than We Think, and the Netherlands
      Doesn't Have a Plan B: In face of Rising Sea Levels the Netherlands 'Must Consider
      Controlled Withdrawal,'" February, 2019, translated from Dutch to English by UvA
      Talen and Robert Smith Translations (citing studies supporting the worst-case-
      scenario of a rise in sea levels of 292 centimeters, or 9.6 feet, by 2100, and stating "This
      upper limit is almost three times what scientists thought possible just a decade ago."),
      https://www.vn.nl/rising-sea-levels-netherlands/.

35   Gilbert Felongco, "Sea-Level Rise 'May Cross Two Meters By 2100," SciDev.Net,
      October 12, 2022, https://phys.org/news/2022-10-sea-level-meters.html. Michael
      Oppenheimer and his colleagues have been nudging planners to take these risks on
      board, saying in a 2019 paper that a faster disintegration of the Antarctic ice sheet
      would make at least six and a half feet (two meters) of sea level rise likely by 2100;
      Oppenheimer and his coauthors emphasized that "The consideration of such high-end
      scenarios is important for longterm coastal risk management, in particular in densely
      populated coastal zones." Perhaps counterintuitively, ice losses in Antarctica are
      particularly felt along the East Coast of the United States, because of gravitational
      responses: "As the mass of the ice sheet shrinks, its gravitational attraction weakens,
      and water congregates farther from it." New York City Panel on Climate Change,
      2019 Report, Chapter 3: Sea Level Rise, March 15, 2019, https://doi.org/10.1111
      /nyas.14006. Scientists have consistently *underestimated* the risks from melting of the
      West Antarctica Ice Sheet. Naomi Oreskes, Michael Oppenheimer, Dale Jamieson,
      "Scientists Have Been Underestimating the Pace of Climate Change," *Scientific
      American*, August 19, 2019, https://blogs.scientificamerican.com/observations

/scientists-have-been-underestimating-the-pace-of-climate-change/ ("When new
observations of the climate system have provided more or better data, or permitted us
to reevaluate old ones, the findings for ice extent, sea level rise and ocean temperature
have generally been worse than earlier prevailing views.") In 2019, Oppenheimer and
others stated, "We find it plausible that [sea-level rise] could exceed 2 m by 2100 for
our high-temperature scenario, roughly equivalent to business as usual. This could
result in land loss of 1.79 M km2, including critical regions of food production, and
displacement of up to 187 million people. A [sea-level rise] of this magnitude would
clearly have profound consequences for humanity." Bamber, J. L., Oppenheimer, M.,
Kopp, R. E., Aspinall, W. P., & Cooke, R. M. (2019). Ice sheet contributions to
future sea-level rise from structured expert judgment. Proceedings of the National
Academy of Sciences of the United States of America, 116(23), 11195–11200. https
://doi.org/10.1073/pnas.1817205116. From the NOAA 2022 report: "Considering low
-confidence ice-sheet processes and high emissions pathways with warming
approaching 5°C, probabilities rise to about 50%, 20%, and 10% of exceeding
1.0 m, 1.5 m, or 2.0 m of global rise by 2100, respectively. These processes are unlikely
to make significant contributions with 2°C of warming, but how much warming
might be required to trigger them is currently unknown." In October 2021, sea level
expert Sybren Drijfhout of the official Dutch agency KNMI substantially increased
his sea level rise estimates for the Netherlands' North Sea coast, saying: "The current
calculations have an upper limit of 1 meter 20 in the year 2100. If ice loss in Antarctica
accelerates, it could be even higher, up to 2 meters by the end of the century."
"KNMI: Sea Level Rise off the Dutch Coast Threatens to Accelerate Sharply," NU.nl,
October 25, 2021, https://www.nu.nl/klimaat/6163142/knmi-zeespiegelstijging-voor
-nederlandse-kust-dreigt-fors-te-versnellen.html.

36   Justin Gillis, "The Sea Level Did, in Fact, Rise Faster in the Southeast U.S.," *New York
Times*, August 9, 2017 (seas rose six times faster in southeast 2011-2015 than global
average); NCA4, chap. 19: "This recent global rate increase, combined with the local
effects of vertical land motion (sinking) and oceanographic effects such as changing
ocean currents, has caused some areas in the Southeast to experience even higher local
rates of sea level rise than the global average."

37   "In Harm's Way, Hurricane Ida's Impact on Socially Vulnerable Communities,"
NOAA National Centers for Environmental Information, May 5, 2022; IPCC,
2022: *Summary for Policymakers* [H.-O. Pörtner, D.C. Roberts, E.S. Poloczanska,
K. Mintenbeck, M. Tignor, A. Alegría, M. Craig, S. Langsdorf, S. Löschke,
V. Möller, A. Okem (eds.)]. In: *Climate Change 2022: Impacts, Adaptation, and
Vulnerability. Contribution of Working Group II to the Sixth Assessment Report of the
Intergovernmental Panel on Climate Change* [H.-O. Pörtner, D.C. Roberts, M. Tignor,
E.S. Poloczanska, K. Mintenbeck, A. Alegría, M. Craig, S. Langsdorf, S. Löschke,
V. Möller, A. Okem, B. Rama (eds.)]. Cambridge University Press (small islands
and lowland coastal areas are most vulnerable to sea-level rise resulting from climate
change and present the most urgent need for investment in capacity building and
adaptation strategies; climate change disproportionately affects those with limited
resources and minorities).

38 Thomas Frank, "Flooding Disproportionately Harms Black Neighborhoods," *Scientific American*, June 2, 2020.

39 Id.

40 In Harm's Way, at 18.

41 Maya K Buchanan et al, "Sea level rise and coastal flooding threaten affordable housing," *Environmental Research Letter*, 15 124020/2020.

42 Adam Voiland, "Rising Seas in Charleston," *NASA Earth Observatory*, January 11, 2021, https://earthobservatory.nasa.gov/images/147761/rising-seas-in-charleston.

43 Less than 5 percent of the land within the Urban Growth Boundary of the City of Charleston is above thirty feet above sea level. Just fifteen square miles or so of the City of Charleston is over twenty feet in elevation. "Most of the land [in the city] is occurring in this kind of range up to about 15, 15, 18 feet." Jacob Lindsey, speaking at Water Lab meeting, Sept. 23, 2020.

44 "Charleston Harbor, SC Tide Events by Year (7.0 ft MLLW or higher)," https://www.weather.gov/images/chs/coastalflood/chts1_yearly_70.png.

45 "There are already internal climate change refugees in the United States. Today, at least 17 communities, mostly Native American or Native Alaskan, are in the process of relocating for climate related reasons. Even if climate change is arrested in its tracks, it is estimated that 414 cities and towns will have to relocate. The only relocation program currently being run by the federal government is the moving of Isle de Jean Charles in Louisiana. Not a buyout program, this effort aims to move the 99 residents together to another location at a cost of $48 million. Even with this small number of people, it is a complex and daunting task." *Promoting American Energy Security by Facilitating Investments and Innovation in Climate Solutions, Before the Senate Environment and Public Works Committee*, March 23, 2022 (statement of Raymond Mabus, former secretary of the Navy).

46 There is evidence that incremental "climate-proofing" infrastructure adaptation steps can actually increase the vulnerability of coastal residents: "We argue in this article that these policies have already and likely will continue to exacerbate the negative consequences of positive feedbacks in coastal real estate markets in the United States— and are likely to exacerbate the negative consequences of positive feedbacks in other coastal real estate markets worldwide as these regions simultaneously continue to grow and begin to address the looming threat of sea level rise." Real estate markets condition their investments on the reduced risk, driving markets in unsafe areas ever higher. A. G. Keeler, D. E. McNamara, and J. L. Irish, "Responding to sea level rise: Does short-term risk reduction inhibit successful long-term adaptation?" *Earth's Future* 6, 618–621 (2018), https://doi.org/ 10.1002/2018EF000828.

47 Katharine J. Mach and A. R. Siders, "Reframing Strategic, Managed Retreat for Transformative Climate Adaptation," *Science* 372 (6548), 1294-1299 (2021), DOI: 10.1126/science.abh1894.

48 Quoted in Polly Mosendz and Eric Roston, "Unlimited Sand and Money Still Won't Save the Hamptons," *Bloomberg*, Oct. 29, 2021, https://www.bloomberg.com/graphics/2021-hamptons-real-estate-beach-climate-proofing/. During an interview with Krista Tippett on March 3, 2022, Colette Pichon Battle, a climate

activist and lawyer, said that the head of FEMA told her during a meeting at the White House that "The disaster process in this country is designed for the middle class." Colette Pichon Battle, interview by Krista Tippett, *On Being with Krista Tippett*, March 3, 2022, https://onbeing.org/programs/colette-pichon-battle-placed -here-in-this-calling/#transcript.

49   Chris Iovenko, "Dutch Masters: The Netherlands Exports Flood-Control," *Earth Magazine*, August 31, 2018, https://www.earthmagazine.org/article/dutch-masters -netherlands-exports-flood-control-expertise. As Prof. Simon Richter of the University of Pennsylvania puts it, "The fact of the matter is the Dutch are all over the United States. Anywhere there's a coastal city that is dealing with the challenges of rising sea level and subsidence, whether it's Boston, New York, Norfolk, or Miami or New Orleans or Houston or San Diego, or the Bay Area, believe me, the Dutch are already there." "The Divergent Climate Futures of Jakarta & Amsterdam," *Climate Week at Penn*, April 6, 2021, https://www.youtube.com/ watch?v=we4Quj8X-Ik.

50   "Keeping Retreat on the Table in the Safest Delta in the World," *Climate Week at Penn*, presentation by Prof. Simon Richter, June 26, 2021, https://www.youtube.com /watch?v=ysOQAc5RHkc.

51   Rolf Schuttenhelm, "Sea Level Rise is Bigger Than We Think, and the Netherlands Doesn't Have a Plan B: In face of Rising Sea Levels the Netherlands 'Must Consider Controlled Withdrawal,'" *Vrij Nederland*, February, 2019, translated from Dutch to English by UvA Talen and Robert Smith Translations, https://www.vn.nl/rising-sea -levels-netherlands/. Prof. Simon Richter has persuasively presented the steps of this Dutch change of heart in several presentations and posts, and I am indebted to him. You can follow his work on Twitter: @Poldergeist3.

52   Steven Slabbers, interview by the author, July 3, 2019.

53   "Keeping Retreat on the Table in the Safest Delta in the World," *Climate Week at Penn*, presentation by Prof. Simon Richter, June 26, 2021, https://www.youtube .com/watch?v=ysOQAc5RHkc. Haasnoot quoted in Schutterhelm article, n. [50]: "What is certain, says Haasnoot, is that a wait-and-see approach will not be the best strategy. 'Every measure will require time. And now is the time to think about it and come up with a good plan—so that we can also implement it in time. When it comes to sea level policy, you need to be able to deal with uncertainties. You can't simply wait until you know exactly what is going to happen. By the time you know for certain, it's already happening—and what's more, it could be happening much too fast.'"

54   Credit again to Prof. Simon Richter of the University of Pennsylvania, who has written and spoken extensively about this topic. The article, supra n. [50], appeared in February 2019 in a publication called *Vrij Nederland* (Free Netherlands).

55   "Exploration Deltares—Strategies for Adaptation to High and Accelerated Sea Level Rise," *National Delta Program Documents*, September 30, 2019, 21 (in Dutch, translation by Prof. Simon Richter), https://www.deltaprogramma.nl/documenten /publicaties/2019/09/30/verkenning-deltares—-strategieen-voor-adaptatie-aan-hoge -en-versnelde-zeespiegelstijging#:~:text=Eind%20september%202019%20heeft%20 Deltares,spelen%20op%20een%20toekomstige%20zeespiegelstijging.

56   Haasnoot quoted in Schutterhelm article, n. [50].

57   Marjolijn Haasnoot, Judy Lawrence, Alexandre K. Magnan, "Pathways to Coastal Retreat:
      The Shrinking Solution Space For Adaptation Calls For Long-Term Dynamic Planning
      Starting Now," *Science*, 372 (6548), 1287-1290 (2021), DOI: 10.1126/science.abi6594.

58   "Delta Commissioner's advice: take the climate of the future into account when
      building housing," *National Delta Program News*, December 6, 2021, https://www
      .deltaprogramma.nl/nieuws/nieuws/2021/12/06/advies-deltacommissaris-houd-bij
      -woningbouw-rekening-met-het-klimaat-van-de-toekomst ("In the advice, for which
      Sweco, Defacto, Deltares and Ecorys have provided data, the Delta Commissioner
      calls on the central government and the region to reserve space in advance for measures
      required in the event of a future sea level rise of 2 meters in the North Sea.")

59   Steven Slabbers, interview with author, July 4, 2019.

60   Bas Button and Martine Wool Bag, "'We Cannot All Live Together in the Randstad,"
      FD.nl, May 17, 2022 (interview with Hugo de Jonge, minister for spatial planning);
      Prof. Simon Richter interview with author, July 12, 2022.

61   Laura Cantral, interview with author, October 27, 2020.

62   Benjamin H. Strauss et al., "Unprecedented threats to cities from multi-century sea
      level rise," *Environmental Research Letter* 16, 114015 (2021).

63   Bill Chappell, "Jakarta Is Crowded And Sinking, So Indonesia Is Moving Its Capital
      To Borneo," NPR, August 26, 2019, https://www.npr.org/2019/08/26/754291131
      /indonesia-plans-to-move-capital-to-borneo-from-jakarta.

64   "The Divergent Climate Futures of Jakarta & Amsterdam," Climate Week at Penn,
      April 6, 2021, presentation by Prof. Simon Richter, https://www.youtube.com/watch
      ?v=we4Quj8X-Ik.

65   Prof. Simon Richter interview with author, July 12, 2022.

2. Charleston's Natural Environment

1   Walter J. Fraser, Jr., *Charleston! Charleston! The History of a Southern City* (Columbia,
      South Carolina, 1991), 2.

2   Fraser, *Charleston! Charleston!*, 4.

3   Fraser, *Charleston! Charleston!*, 4.

4   There were more than two dozen distinct groups of Indigenous people living in South
      Carolina's Lowcountry during the sixteenth, seventeenth, and eighteenth centuries.
      According to Nic Butler of the Charleston County Public Library, at least three of
      these communities, the Stono, Kiawah, and Etiwan people (associated with the Stono,
      Ashley, and Cooper Rivers, respectively), were present when English colonists began
      settling around Charleston Harbor. By about 1751, the vast majority of Indigenous
      people around Charleston had been driven out or annihilated. Nic Butler, "The First
      People of the South Carolina Lowcountry," Charleston County Public Library, https
      ://www.ccpl.org/charleston-time-machine/first-people-south-carolina-lowcountry.

5   Fraser, *Charleston! Charleston!*, 6.

6   Fraser, *Charleston! Charleston!*, 4, 7.

7   Fraser, *Charleston! Charleston!*, 7.

8   Fraser, *Charleston! Charleston!*, 11.

9   Fraser, *Charleston! Charleston!*, 5.

10 Fraser, *Charleston! Charleston!*, 9.

11 Fraser, *Charleston! Charleston!*, 10.

12 Christina Rae Butler, *Lowcountry at High Tide: A History of Flooding, Drainage, and Reclamation in Charleston, South Carolina* (Columbia, South Carolina, 2020), 3.

13 I am indebted to Christina Rae Butler for her marvelous study of landfill practices in Charleston, *Low Country at High Tide*. If you have any interest in this subject, you must read her book.

14 Butler, *Low Country at High Tide*, 67, 91.

15 Nic Butler, "Hampstead Village: The Historic Heart of Charleston's East Side," Charleston County Public Library, https://www.ccpl.org/charleston-time-machine /hampstead-village-historic-heart-charlestons-east-side.

16 Adam Parker, "Charleston, Johns Island undergoing huge demographic shift among Blacks, Whites," *Post and Courier*, May 28, 2021.

17 Sammy Fretwell, "30 years after Hugo tore it down, SC coast builds back in the danger zone," *The State*, September 21, 2019.

18 "Land Elevation & Flood Risk (Within UGB)," shown during City of Charleston City Plan Water Lab meeting on September 23, 2020.

19 "City Land Elevation (Within UGB)," shown during City of Charleston City Plan Water Lab meeting on September 23, 2020. "Minor" flooding of 7 feet above "mean low lower water" in Charleston, which closes some roads and maroons people in their homes, happened 89 times in 2019 and 68 times in 2020, and "moderate" flooding of 7.5 feet, which closes many roads and floods properties, happened 26 times in 2019 and 22 times in 2020. National Weather Service, Coastal Flood Event Database, https ://www.weather.gov/chs/coastalflood. NOAA is predicting that moderate flooding in 2050 will be as frequent as minor flooding was in 2020. *Sea Level Rise Technical Report*, February 2022, 60. According to Flood Factor, 62 percent of properties in Charleston County are at risk of flooding, and this number is projected to increase to 85 percent by 2030. https://riskfactor.com/county/charleston-county/45019_fsid/flood.

20 "Critical Land & Water Levels," shown during City of Charleston City Plan Water Lab meeting on September 23, 2020.

21 "Land Elevation & Flood Risk (Within UGB)," shown during City of Charleston City Plan Water Lab meeting on September 23, 2020.

22 Eli Flesch, Updating FEMA Flood Maps Critical But Costly, Experts Say, Law360, November 10, 2022.

23 Andy Sternad, Waggoner & Ball, at Water Lab meeting, September 23, 2020.

24 All of these statements are from the Dutch Dialogues Final Presentations meeting held in Charleston on July 19, 2019.

25 Steven Slabbers, interview with author, July 19, 2019.

26 All of these statements are from the Dutch Dialogues Final Report, September 2019.

27 Michelle Mapp, interview with author, October 18, 2018.

28 Michelle Mapp, interview with author, October 18, 2018.

29 David White, interview with author, November 10, 2020.

30 Rev. Joseph Darby, interview with author, November 16, 2020.

31 Rev. Joseph Darby, interview with author, November 16, 2020.

32 John Tibbetts, interview with author, May 11, 2022.

33 Jenny Brennan, interview with author, October 9, 2018.

34 John Tibbetts, email to author, May 6, 2022.

35 Norman Levine, interview with author, October 9, 2018.

36 Even without a high tide, if our swirl even comes close to Charleston it will be highly destructive. John Tibbetts, the science journalist, was alarmed to see water coming up to the steps of houses near his on James Island when a Category 1 hurricane went by, thirty miles offshore. John Tibbetts, interview with author, May 11, 2022.

37 Bob Perry, interview with author, October 12, 2018.

38 Henry Fountain, "Ida strengthened quickly into a monster. Here's how," *New York Times*, August 29, 2021.

39 For up-to-date flooding information for Charleston, see https://www.weather.gov/chs /coastalflood.

40 From February 15, 2022 NOAA report: "In short, assuming continuation of current trends and summarized at the national level, a flood regime shift is projected by 2050, with moderate HTF occurring a bit more frequently than minor HTF events occur today, and major HTF events occurring about as frequently as moderate HTF frequencies occur today."

41 Jeff Goodell, "'The Fuse Has Been Blown,' and the Doomsday Glacier Is Coming for Us All," *Rolling Stone*, December 29, 2021.

42 "Thwaites Glacier Facts," *CIRES*, Accessed June 15, 2021, thwaitesglacier.org/about /facts; Rachel Ramirez, "The ice shelf holding back the 'Doomsday glacier' could shatter within the next five years, scientists warn," CNN, December 14, 2021; Becky Oskin, "Antarctica Meltdown Weakens Earth's Gravity," *Live Science*, *Future US*, October 1, 2014, www.livescience.com/48099-antarctica-melting-earth-gravity -changes.html.

43 Stephanie Krzywonos, "There Is No 'Doomsday Glacier': What We Can Learn from the Thwaites Glacier Panic," sierraclub.org, Oct. 18, 2022, https://www.sierraclub.org /sierra/there-no-doomsday-glacier-thwaites.

44 Noel Gourmelen et al., "Channelized Melting Drives Thinning Under a Rapidly Melting Antarctic Ice Shelf," *Geophysical Research Letters* 44 (19), (October 2017): 9796–9804, https://doi.org/10.1002/2017GL074929; Hongju Yu et al., "Retreat of Thwaites Glacier, West Antarctica, over the Next 100 Years Using Various Ice Flow Models, Ice Shelf Melt Scenarios and Basal Friction Laws," *The Cryosphere* 12 (12), (December 2018): 3861–76, https://doi.org/10.5194/tc-12-3861-2018.

45 Timothy M. Lenton et al., "Climate Tipping Points—Too Risky to Bet Against," *Nature* (London) 575 (7784), (November 2019): 592–95, https://doi.org/10.1038 /d41586-019-03595-0; Martin Siegert, *Sea Level Change* (London: Imperial College London, 2015.)

46 Robert M. Deconto et al, "The Paris Climate Agreement and Future Sea-Level Rise from Antarctica," *Nature* (London) 593 (7857), (2021): 83–89, https://doi.org/10.1038 /s41586-021-03427-0.

47 Lydia Smears and Pablo Gutiérrez, "The Strange Science of Melting Ice Sheets: Three Things You Didn't Know," *Guardian*, Guardian News & Media, September 12,

2018, https://www.theguardian.com/environment/ng-interactive/2018/sep/12/greenland-antarctic-ice-sheet-sea-level-rise-science-climate.

48 Dr. William Sweet, NOAA, interview with author, June 26, 2019; *see also* NOAA February 2022 *Sea Level Rise Technical Report*. Michael Oppenheimer et al., "Sea Level Rise and Implications for Low-Lying Islands, Coasts and Communities," in IPCC *Special Report on the Ocean and Cryosphere in a Changing Climate*, eds. H.-O. Pörtner et al. (Cambridge, UK and New York, NY, USA: Cambridge University Press, 2019), 321-445.

49 Paul Voosen, "Ice Shelf Holding Back Keystone Antarctic Glacier Within Years of Failure," *Science*, December 13, 2021, www.science.org/content/article/ice-shelf-holding-back-keystone-antarctic-glacier-within-years-failure.

50 Jeff Goodell, "'The Fuse Has Been Blown,' and the Doomsday Glacier Is Coming for Us All," *Rolling Stone*, December 29, 2021 ("Even if we cut carbon emissions to zero tomorrow, warm water will continue to flow beneath the ice sheet for decades, destabilizing the ice and further pushing the glacier toward eventual collapse").

51 Sweet, William V., Benjamin D. Hamlington, Robert E. Kopp, Christopher P. Weaver, Patrick L. Barnard, David Bekaert, and William Brooks, "Global and Regional Sea Level Rise Scenarios for the United States: Updated Mean Projections and Extreme Water Level Probabilities Along U.S. Coastlines," 2022, National Oceanic and Atmospheric Administration, National Ocean Service, NOAA Technical Report NOS 01 ("With an increase in average global temperature of 2°C above preindustrial levels, and not considering the potential contributions from ice-sheet processes with limited agreement (low confidence) among modeling approaches, the probability of exceeding 0.5 m rise globally (0.7 m along the CONUS coastline) by 2100 is about 50%. With 3°–5°C of warming under high emissions pathways, this probability rises to >80% to >99%. The probability of exceeding 1 m globally (1.2 m CONUS) by 2100 rises from <5% with 3°C warming to almost 25% with 5°C warming. Considering low-confidence ice-sheet processes and high emissions pathways with warming approaching 5°C, probabilities rise to about 50%, 20%, and 10% of exceeding 1.0 m, 1.5 m, or 2.0 m of global rise by 2100, respectively.")

52 "Third of Antarctic Ice Shelf Area at Risk of Collapse as Planet Warms," University of Reading, April 8, 2021, www.reading.ac.uk/news/2021/research-news/pr855740; Jeff Goodell, "'The Fuse Has Been Blown,' and the Doomsday Glacier Is Coming for Us All," *Rolling Stone*, December 29, 2021; Sweet et al. 2022 NOAA report.

53 Helen Ekker, "Antarctica expedition to increase knowledge about Thwaites glacier melt risk," *NOS*, January 22, 2022, https://nos.nl/artikel/2414068-antarctica-expeditie-moet-kennis-over-smeltrisico-thwaites-gletsjer-vergroten.

54 Hongju Yu et al., "Retreat of Thwaites Glacier, West Antarctica, over the Next 100 Years Using Various Ice Flow Models, Ice Shelf Melt Scenarios and Basal Friction Laws," *The Cryosphere* 12 (12), (December 2018): 3861–76, https://doi.org/10.5194/tc-12-3861-2018.

55 Council on Foreign Relations, "The Growing Risk of Climate Tipping Points," comments of Peter Cox, February 4, 2022.

56 Paul Voosen, "Ice Shelf Holding Back Keystone Antarctic Glacier Within Years of Failure," *Science*, December 13, 2021, www.science.org/content/article/ice-shelf

-holding-back-keystone-antarctic-glacier-within-years-failure; Helen Ekker, "Antarctica expedition to increase knowledge about Thwaites glacier melt risk," *NOS*, January 22, 2022, https://nos.nl/artikel/2414068-antarctica-expeditie-moet-kennis -over-smeltrisico-thwaites-gletsjer-vergroten.

57   IPCC, 2021: Summary for Policymakers. In: *Climate Change 2021: The Physical Science Basis*. Contribution of Working Group I to the Sixth Assessment Report of the Intergovernmental Panel on Climate Change [Masson-Delmotte, V., P. Zhai, A. Pirani, S.L. Connors, C. Péan, S. Berger, N. Caud, Y. Chen, L. Goldfarb, M.I. Gomis, M. Huang, K. Leitzell, E. Lonnoy, J.B.R. Matthews, T.K. Maycock, T. Waterfield, O. Yelekçi, R. Yu, and B. Zhou (eds.)]. Cambridge University Press, Cambridge, United Kingdom and New York, NY, USA, pp. 3–32, doi:10.1017/9781009157896.001.

58   Brandon Specktor, "The Gulf Stream Is Slowing to a 'Tipping Point' and Could Disappear," *Live Science*, March 3, 2021, www.livescience.com/gulf-stream-slowing -climate-change.html.

59   Tal Ezer, "Regional Differences in Sea Level Rise Between the Mid-Atlantic Bight and the South Atlantic Bight: Is the Gulf Stream to Blame?" *Earth's Future* 7 (7), (2019): 771–83, https://doi.org/10.1029/2019EF001174; Tony Bartelme, "A Powerful Current Just Miles from SC Is Changing. It Could Devastate the East Coast," *Post and Courier*, September 5, 2018, www.postandcourier.com/news/special_reports /a-powerful-current-just-miles-from-sc-is-changing-it-could-devastate-the-east -coast/article_7070df22-67fd-11e8-81ee-2fcab0fd4023.html.

60   David Fleshler, "The Gulf Stream is slowing down. That could mean rising seas and a hotter Florida," *South Florida Sun-Sentinel*, August 2, 2019, https://www.sun-sentinel .com/news/florida/fl-ne-gulf-stream-climate-change-20190802-mblbzlj4xbdm3j54 xazbfg4kgq-story.html.

61   Johannes Westerink, interview with author, May 2, 2019.

62   David Fleshler, "The Gulf Stream is slowing down. That could mean rising seas and a hotter Florida," South Florida Sun-Sentinel, August 2, 2019, https://www .sun-sentinel.com/news/florida/fl-ne-gulf-stream-climate-change-20190802 -mblbzlj4xbdm3j54xazbfg4kgq-story.html.

63   Jim Morrison, "Flooding Hot Spots: Why Seas Are Rising Faster on the U.S. East Coast," *Yale E360*, April 24, 2018.

64   Norm Levine, interview with author, October 30, 2019.

65   William Sweet, interview with author, June 26, 2019.

3. Rev. Joseph P. Darby and the History of Charleston

1   Charleston (SC), *Digest of the Ordinances of the City Council of Charleston, from the Year 1783 to July 1818: To which are Annexed, Extracts from the Acts of the Legislature which Relate to the City of Charleston*, (United States: A.E. Miller, 1818).

2   Bernard Powers, *Black Charlestonians: A Social History, 1822-1885* (Fayetteville, Arkansas: 1994), 3 (between 1803 and 1807 "it is estimated that forty thousand Africans were brought to the city" of Charleston).

3   "The Importation and Sale of Enslaved People," *Massachusetts Historical Society*, https ://www.masshist.org/features/endofslavery/trade.

4   Ethan J. Kytle and Blain Roberts, *Denmark Vesey's Garden: Slavery and Memory in the Cradle of the Confederacy* (New York: The New Press, 2018), 14.

5   Kytle and Roberts, *Denmark Vesey's Garden*, 17.

6   Kytle and Roberts, *Denmark Vesey's Garden*, 18-19.

7   Powers, *Black Charlestonians*.

8   Christopher Dickey, *Our Man in Charleston: Britain's Secret Agent in the Civil War South* (New York: Broadway Books, 2015), 19.

9   Robert Behre, "The Citadel's Early Story," *Post and Courier*, Mar. 25, 2018.

10   Walter Edgar, *South Carolina: A History* (Columbia, South Carolina: 1998), 350.

11   Christina Rae Butler, *Lowcountry at High Tide: A History of Flooding, Drainage, and Reclamation in Charleston, South Carolina* (Columbia, South Carolina: 2020), 101.

12   Walter J. Fraser, Jr., *Charleston! Charleston!: The History of a Southern City* (Columbia, South Carolina: 1989), 285.

13   Stephanie Yuhl, *A Golden Haze of Memory: The Making of Historic Charleston* (Chapel Hill, North Carolina: Univ. of North Carolina Press, 2005), 6-7.

14   Yuhl, *Golden Haze of Memory*, 12-13.

15   Yuhl, *Golden Haze of Memory*, 130.

16   Yuhl, *Golden Haze of Memory*, 133.

17   Yuhl, *Golden Haze of Memory*, 132.

18   Yuhl, *Golden Haze of Memory*, 134.

19   Yuhl, *Golden Haze of Memory*, 132, 134.

20   Available through Library of Congress, https://www.loc.gov/resource/mss52571 .mss52571-02-088_0355_0435/?sp=71&st=single&r=-0.337,0.031,1.701,0.699,0.

21   In May 2020, a young Black activist named Mika Gadsden, a Gullah Geechee descendant whose father was born and raised on Wadmalaw Island, got into a scuffle on Twitter with Kathryn Dennis, a descendant of John C. Calhoun and one of the stars of "Southern Charm." A nail salon owner announced that she wanted to host a boat parade for President Trump; Gadsden tweeted in response, "In Charleston you learn, fairly quickly, that the face of White Supremacy resembles that of the boutique-owning, gatekeeping glitterati." Dennis then taunted Gadsden, eventually sending her multiple monkey emojis. Gadsden had publicized the conversation, making clear that she viewed Dennis's communication as part of a pattern of racism in Charleston: Dennis, to her, personified the pretty face of hate. Dennis apologized, but three members of the cast quit in protest and a Mount Pleasant clothing boutique, Gwynn's, severed its relationship with Dennis. "Southern Charm" is roundly hated by many Black Charlestonians, including David White, the young man who runs Laundry Matters on the East Side; it presents Charleston as a romantic, all-white paradise of elaborate meals and wealth, the visual Confederate Disneyland, in Darby's words, that has brought so much touristic attention.

22   Adam Parker, "Membership Controversy Roils Charleston Rifle Club after Black Candidate is Blackballed," *Post and Courier*, updated September 15, 2020, www .postandcourier.com/features/membership-controversy-roils-charleston-rifle-club -after-black-candidate-is-blackballed/article_a44b8e4a-e9d1-11e8-a012-3734d3 cd4808.html. A Black member was finally admitted in September 2020. Adam Parker,

"Charleston Rifle Club admits its first Black member after drawn-out controversy," *Post and Courier*, Sept. 16, 2020.

23   Jennie Lightweis-Goff, "Charleston Is a Small Place: Literature and Tourism in a Season of Horror," *South: A Scholarly Journal* 50:1 (Fall 2017).

24   Matthew Vann and Erik Ortiz, "Walter Scott Shooting: Micahel Slager, Ex-officer, Sentenced to 20 Years in Prison," *NBC News*, NBC Universal, updated December 9, 2017, www.nbcnews.com/storyline/walter-scott-shooting/walter-scott-shooting -michael-slager-ex-officer-sentenced-20-years-n825006.

25   Steve Bailey, "Charleston's annexation wars are over—the suburbs won," *Post and Courier*, April 7, 2018.

26   Steve Bailey, "Charleston's annexation wars are over—the suburbs won," *Post and Courier*, updated September 14, 2020, www.postandcourier.com/opinion/commentary /charleston-s-annexation-wars-are-over-the-suburbs-won/article_abcc813c-380c -11e8-bff1-37f34766ba1b.html.

27   Vince Graham, interview with author, December 5, 2018.

28   FEMA Aug. 2018 report, at https://bloximages.newyork1.vip.townnews.com /postandcourier.com/content/tncms/ass ets/v3/editorial/f/c4/fc4325b4¬c135¬11e8¬930 1¬5313b3a52c32/5baaf287153c9.pdf.pdf.

29   Steven Emerman, "Commentary: Why development has not improved drainage in Charleston," *Post and Courier*, August 2020.

30   Abigail Darlington, "While Charleston works on clearing up FEMA's concerns, one neighborhood left in limbo," *Post and Courier*, January 30, 2019; Steve Bailey, "How a James Island neighborhood was destined to flood," *Post and Courier*, April 28, 2018.

31   Chloe Johnson and Stephen Hobbs, "Charleston failed to properly identify flood damages, leaving homes and buyers unprotected," *Post and Courier*, June 29, 2019.

32   Abigail Darlington, "Little-known federal law keeps buyers from finding out if a home routinely floods," *Post and Courier*, August 9, 2018.

33   Michael Miller interview with author, December 28, 2020.

34   Vince Graham interview with author, December 5, 2018.

35   "Hurricane Hugo," *Storm of the Century Magazine*, September 1989, www.weather.gov /media/ilm/climate/Hugo/Hugo-Storm_of_the_Century.pdf.

36   Brian Hicks, *The Mayor: Joe Riley and the Rise of Charleston* (Charleston, South Carolina: Evening Post Books, 2015) at 3848; Paul Bowers, "What if Joe Riley had never been elected mayor?," *Charleston City Paper*, December 24, 2013.

37   Norman Levine, interview with author, October 9, 2018.

38   Project was the renovation of the Gaillard Municipal Auditorium, which had first opened in 1968. "Riley-era construction in 2012 unearthed 36 graves of enslaved people on the site." https://www.ccpl.org/charleston-time-machine/searching -history-gaillard-graves.

39   Costar insight: Charleston Claims Title As Nation's Fastest-Growing Apartment Market: Multifamily Pipeline Suggests 2021 Will Be Another Big Year for South Carolina's Lowcountry Region, Jan. 25, 2021. South Carolina was the second-fastest growing state east of the Mississippi between 2010 and 2020, second to Florida. Although the US as a whole became substantially more racially and ethnically diverse

during that decade, South Carolina's racial makeup has stayed about the same due to the large influx of non-Hispanic white people moving to the state. Most of that growth has happened in coastal regions of the state, with Charleston's outlying suburbs growing enormously. David Slade, "The 2020 census shows South Carolina and the nation have been growing differently," *Post and Courier*, August 15, 2021.

40   Caitlin Byrd, "Historic SC city fears losing authenticity. Will outsiders drown out Charleston natives?," *The State*, October 28, 2021.

41   1900 census: U.S. Census Bureau. "Composition and Characteristics of the Population For Cities of 25,000 or More." Volume III. Population, Reports by States, with Statistics for Counties, Cities, and Other Civil Division: Nebraska-Wyoming, Alaska, Hawaii, and Porto Pico. Table II. Accessed August 11, 2022. https://www2.census .gov/library/publications/decennial/1910/volume-3/volume-3-p5.pdf; 1910 census: U.S. Census Bureau. "Composition and Characteristics of the Population For Cities of 25,000 or More." Volume III. Population, Reports by States, with Statistics for Counties, Cities, and Other Civil Division: Nebraska-Wyoming, Alaska, Hawaii, and Porto Pico. Table II. Accessed August 11, 2022. https://www2.census.gov/library /publications/decennial/1910/volume-3/volume-3-p5.pdf; 1920 census: U.S. Census Bureau. "Age, For Cities of 10,000 or More: 1920." 1920 Census: Volume 3. Population, Composition and Characteristics of the Population by States. Table 8. Accessed August 11, 2022. https://www2.census.gov/library/publications/decennial /1920/volume-3/41084484v3ch08.pdf; 1930 census: U.S. Census Bureau. "Population by Color, Nativity, and Parentage, For Cities of 25,000 to 100,000: 1930 and 1920." 1930 Census Volume 3. Population, Reports by States. Table 27. Accessed August 11, 2022. https://www2.census.gov/library/publications/decennial/1930/population-volume-3/10612982v3p2ch07.pdf; 1930 census: U.S. Census Bureau. "Population by Color, Nativity, and Parentage, For Cities of 25,000 to 100,000: 1930 and 1920." 1930 Census Volume 3. Population, Reports by States. Table 27. Accessed August 11, 2022. https://www2.census.gov/library/publications/decennial/1930/population -volume-3/10612982v3p2ch07.pdf; 1940 census: U.S. Census Bureau. "Composition of the Population, For cities of 10,000 to 100,000: 1940." 1940 Census Volume 2. Table 31. Accessed August 11, 2022. https://www2.census.gov/library/publications /decennial/1940/population-volume-2/33973538v2p6ch4.pdf; 19 U.S. Census Bureau. "Composition of the Population, For cities of 10,000 to 100,000: 1940." 1940 Census Volume 2. Table 31. Accessed August 11, 2022. https://www2.census .gov/library/publications/decennial/1940/population-volume-2/33973538v2p6ch4.pdf; 1950 census: U.S. Census Bureau. "General Characteristics of the Population, For Standard Metropolitan Areas, Urbanized Areas, and Urban Places of 10,000 or More: 1950." 1950 Census of Population: Volume 2. Characteristics of the Population. Table 34. Accessed August 9, 2022. https://www2.census.gov/library/publications /decennial/1940/population-volume-2/33973538v2p6ch4.pdf; 1960 census: U.S. Census Bureau. "Characteristics of the Population for Standard Metropolitan Statistical Areas, Urbanized Areas, and Urban Places of 10,000 or More: 1960." 1960 Census: Population, Volume 1. Characteristics of the Population, Part 1-57. Table 21. Accessed August 11, 2022. https://www2.census.gov/library/publications/decennial

/1960/population-volume-1/37749999v1p42ch3.pdf; 1970 census: U.S. Census Bureau. "General Population Characteristics: 1970." 1970 Census of Population: General Population Characteristics. https://www2.census.gov/library/publications /decennial/1970/pcp1/02605992ch02.pdf; 1980 figures: Slade, David. "Racial Shift: Charleston Peninsula's Makeup Reverses in 30 Years, With Blacks Leaving for Suburbs, Area Becoming Two-Thirds White." *Post and Courier.* March 28, 2011. https://www.postandcourier.com/news/racial-shift-charleston-peninsulas-makeup -reverses-in-30-years-with-blacks-leaving-for-suburbs-area/article_69581977-ef00 -5f6c-b969-edb7104344bb.html; Barbato, Lauren. "What Are the Racial Demographics of Charleston?" Bustle. June 18, 2022. https://www.bustle.com/articles/91226-what -percentage-of-charleston-is-black-theres-been-a-radical-shift-in-the-citys-racial -demographics; 1990 figures: "Racial Profile by Neighborhood." City View, April 1996. South Carolina Vertical File: The Charleston Peninsula. South Carolina History Room at Charleston County Public Library; 2000 figures: U.S. Census Bureau. Population Demographics, 2000. Prepared by Social Explorer. (Accessed Aug 9, 2022), https ://www.socialexplorer.com/tables/C2010_PL94/R13167059; 2010 figures: U.S. Census Bureau. Population Demographics, 2010. Prepared by Social Explorer. (Accessed Aug 9, 2022), https://www.socialexplorer.com/tables/C2010_PL94/R13167059; 2020 figures: https://www.socialexplorer.com/tables/C2010_PL94/R13167059.

42   Bernard Powers interview with author, April 13, 2018.

43   Jenna Schiferl, "College of Charleston founded 250 years ago as one of the oldest universities in the US," *Post and Courier,* April 24, 2021.

44   Video: https://www.live5news.com/2020/06/16/live-groups-call-repeal-heritage-act -removal-calhoun-statue/.

45   Video: https://www.live5news.com/2020/06/16/live-groups-call-repeal-heritage-act -removal-calhoun-statue/.

46   In June 2018, Charleston's City Council voted to apologize on the city's behalf for its role in slavery. The resolution was initially greeted with disbelief by some Council members, and five of them voted against it. Four of those five were white people who represented the majority-white West Ashley region of Charleston. Abigail Darlington, "Why Charleston's slavery apology barely passed City Council," *Post and Courier,* June 24, 2018; Abigail Darlington, "Vote on Charleston's slavery apology reveals just how divided City Council is on race," *Post and Courier,* June 20, 2018.

47   There's a story here—the law was presented as a "compromise" and the flag was indeed taken off the dome of the capitol. But it was left standing on the Capitol grounds next to a statue of a Confederate soldier until it was finally removed following the Emanual massacre in 2015. It took the horrific deaths of the Emanuel Nine for that flag to be taken off the statehouse grounds in Columbia.

48   Interview of Bernard Powers, Understand SC, June 25, 2020.

49   Fleming Smith, "Marion Square owners oppose moving Calhoun Monument, others say it's not far enough," *Post and Courier,* June 18, 2020.

50   After a rally in Marion Square in August 2017 calling for the Calhoun statue to be taken down, Mayor Tecklenburg said taking it down was difficult due to the Heritage Act. He proposed having the city's History Commission draft text for a plaque that

would aid in contextualizing the monument. The vote on the resulting draft, which both condemned and praised Calhoun, was deferred on Jan. 9, 2018 and no further action was taken. In 2019, another rally focused on asking that the statue be taken down. Tecklenburg told the *Post and Courier* that he wasn't sure organizers "understand the Heritage Act is somewhat of a controlling factor here in South Carolina." Mikaela Porter, "'It's art activism': Charleston artists gather at Calhoun monument, urge its removal," *Post and Courier*, May 17, 2019, https://www.postandcourier.com/news/it-s-art-activism-charleston-artists-gather-at-calhoun-monument/article_adc13c2a-7817-11e9-84f5-aba85f1a5ad9.html.

51 Mika Gadsden broadcast, May 19, 2021.

52 Mika Gadsden broadcast, June 8, 2021.

4. Charleston and Water, 2016–2022

1 If you are interested in the details of Charleston's colorful history of filling and draining over the centuries, Christina Rae Butler's recent wonderful book, *Lowcountry at High Tide: A History of Flooding, Drainage, and Reclamation in Charleston, South Carolina* (Columbia, South Carolina: Univ. of South Carolina Press 2020), is both authoritative and highly readable.

2 Butler, *Lowcountry at High Tide*, 191; Davis & Floyd, Inc., "Master Drainage and Floodplain Management Plan for City of Charleston, South Carolina," May 1984, https://www.charleston-sc.gov/1513/Storm-Drainage-Mapping.

3 Jason Crowley, Communities & Transportation Senior Program Director, Coastal Conservation League, interview with author, October 11, 2018. ("Market Street always flooded like crazy because it was a creek that was filled in. The Calhoun East Tunnel project right here, another one that worked really well.")

4 Robert Behre and Abigail Darlington, "Charleston's 34-Year-Old List of Drainage Projects Not Quite Half Done After $239 Million," *Post and Courier*, September 9, 2017.

5 Charleston's 34-year-old list of drainage projects.

6 Robert Behre and Abigail Darlington, "Charleston's 34-Year-Old List of Drainage Projects Not Quite Half Done After $239 Million," *Post and Courier*, September 9, 2017. South Carolina pays some of the lowest residential property taxes in the country. "Charleston also ranks first in the nation for property tax on apartments as compared to residential homes. Renters effectively pay three times more in property tax than homeowners, in part because renters pay for school operations and homeowners don't." Ted Pitts, "Commentary: Renters, businesses also hit hard by SC's flawed property tax laws," *Post and Courier*, October 24, 2019.

7 Jason Crowley interview with author, November 13, 2020. The Calhoun East project did help the southern part of the East Side, which is not really the East Side—it's Mazyck-Wraggborough. "East Side is further to the north and it doesn't really do anything for them."

8 Laura Cabiness interview with author, July 13, 2018. Until November 16, 2018, Cabiness was director of Charleston's Public Service Department, "the city's highest-ranking engineer who guides decisions about drainage and flood prevention," according to the *Post and Courier*.

9   Riley's team managed to get small drainage projects, like Calhoun East (2001, $15.8 million) and Market Street (finished 2018, $30 million), and several projects in West Ashley, done or at least underway before he left office at the end of 2015. Presentation to Charlestowne Neighborhood Association, March 12, 2018, 11.

10 Tony Bartelme and Doug Pardue, "Rain bombs and rising seas: Area leaders fail to take serious action in face of rising threats from above and below," *Post and Courier*, October 9, 2015.

11 Laura Cabiness interview with author, July 13, 2018.

12 John Tibbetts interview with author, May 11, 2022.

13 Bob Perry interview with author, October 12, 2018. In 2011, Bob Perry, now retired, was the Director of the Office of Environmental Programs of the South Carolina Department of Natural Resources, which is primarily responsible for managing the state's land and water conservation and marine and wildlife resources, and the editor of the proposed climate report. *The State* obtained a draft copy of the report, which had taken more than a year to write, and published it. Sammy Fretwell, "Secret Climate Report Calls for Action in SC," *The State*, February 24, 2013. The DNR later released the final report.

14 Bob Perry interview with author, October 12, 2018.

15 Bob Perry interview with author, October 12, 2018; Sammy Fretwell, "Ex-Wildlife Chief Warns of Climate Change in SC," *The State*, February 27, 2013.

16 McMaster shines in debate with Warren in SC governor runoff, Jun. 26, 2018.

17 Bruce Smith, "As world talks climate, Charleston fights flooding, sea rise," *Spartanburg Herald–Journal*, December 8, 2015 (Riley quoted saying work completed, underway, planned has price tag of about $250 million; city budget about $150 million). Mayor Riley interview with author, February 22, 2018.

18 12 18 2015 Sea Level Strategic Plan.

19 Winslow Hastie, president and CEO of Historic Charleston Foundation, interview with author, July 17, 2019 ("Sure we had some rain events, we had some storms, we were doing pretty well. We had a nice long run. So when you're mayor and those aren't issues that you're hearing about in your constituency, then frankly why would you focus on it? . . . No one had a clue, they didn't even know what storm water even was. It was all kind of working okay, so don't ask any questions."); Jason Crowley interview with author, October 11, 2018 ("Some of the [water] issues of the Riley administration that was going for 40 years. There was a lot of stuff that was sort of swept under the rug of, 'We'll get to that later. Things are good.'").

20 "Historic Flooding-October 1-5, 2015," National Weather Service, National Oceanic Atmospheric Administration, accessed June 24, 2022, www.weather.gov/chs /HistoricFlooding-Oct2015.

21 "Torrential Rainfall in north, South Carolina Leaves at Least 12 Dead," *Al Jazeera America*, October 5, 2015, http://america.aljazeera.com/articles/2015/10/5/torrential -rainfall-in-south-carolina.html.

22 Bill Chappell, "Hurricane Matthew Makes Landfall in S.C.; 'Serious Inland Flooding' Reported," NPR, October 8, 2016, www.npr.org/sections/thetwo-way/2016/10 /08/497167154/large-part-of-s-c-coast-faces-storm-surge-of-6-9-feet-from-hurricane -matthew.

23   John Tibbetts interview with author, May 11, 2022.

24   "Mayor Tecklenburg Sworn Into Office," *Daniel Island News*, January 13, 2016, http ://www.thedanielislandnews.com/news/mayor-tecklenburg-sworn-office.

25   Jamie Lovegrove, "The other Tecklenburg: brother of Charleston mayor advises Pelosi as she becomes speaker," *Post and Courier*, February 17, 2019.

26   Dean Livingston, "Tecklenburg: Orangeburg Connection," *Times and Democrat*, 2001 (republished November 27, 2015).

27   January 6, 2019 video at 46:20, singing his own composition after saying this.

28   ABC News 4, "Mayor Tecklenburg Removed as Woman's Conservator After Unapproved Estate Loans," July 10, 2018, https://abcnews4.com/news/local/mayor -tecklenburg-removed-as-womans-conservator-after-unapproved-estate-loans. Tecklenburg disagreed with the court's action, saying, "I've done nothing but look after the best interest of my former neighbor, who I love, and did my best to add to her resources and save her money wherever I could."

29   Mikaela Porter, "Preliminary audit finds no 'self-dealing' by Charleston Mayor John Tecklenburg," *Post and Courier*, July 15, 2019. The audit was triggered by city councilmember Harry Griffin, who was running for mayor at the time. Mikaela Porter, "Candidate for Charleston mayor moves to audit Tecklenburg over his new business cards," *Post and Courier*, May 15, 2019.

30   John Tecklenburg interview with author, April 13, 2018.

31   "Dutch Dialogues" is a registered trademark of Waggoner & Ball, an architecture and environment firm based in New Orleans that has been active in consulting with coastal cities and in facilitating connections between Dutch engineering professionals and American cities.

32   John Tecklenburg interview with author, April 13, 2018.

33   Author's recollection.

34   Rev. Joseph Darby interview with author, March 8, 2019.

35   "Supplemental Funding Projects," U.S. Army Corps of Engineers, accessed June 24, 2022, www.sac.usace.army.mil/Missions/Civil-Works/SupplementalFunding/.

36   U.S. Department of the Army, Corps of Engineers, "Charleston Peninsula Coastal Storm Risk Management Study," April 2022, www.sac.usace.army.mil/Portals/43 /docs/civilworks/peninsulastudy/Final%20FR-EIS/ChsPenStudy%20FR-EIS _April%202022%20-%20Signed.pdf?ver=M1f4onDB8qXVUsVlyRm5Rw%3d%3d.

37   To generate this ratio, the Army Corps performs an economic analysis that involves running models of "synthetic storms" topped by synthetic waves against buildings whose elevations have been estimated, figuring out what the functions of those buildings are, estimating their property values over the next 50 years, and then stating what damages will be averted if the wall is in place. Professor Rob Young, Western Carolina University, expert in coastal geology and director of the Program for the Study of Developed Shorelines, presentation to Pensacola CivicCon, May 9, 2022, https://www.pnj.com/story/news/civiccon/2022/05/10/rob-young-discusses-climate -change-civiccon-pensacola/9707956002/.

38   "An Update: Our Vulnerability Has Heightened," The Charleston 3×3 Army Corps Citizens Advisory Committee, May 2022, www.charleston-sc.gov/DocumentCenter

/View/31840/3×3-Advisory-Committee-Peninsula-Study-Comprehensive-Update
-5922?bidId=.

39   The city's view is that it will be providing nonstructural contracts and water studies for
      Rosemont and Bridgeview Village, making those areas "get the same level of protection
      as the wall would provide, just in a different way." Dale Morris, Chief Resiliency
      Officer, September 21, 2021 webinar. The Army Corps asserts a variety of different
      reasons for not including Rosemont and Bridgeview within the wall: Bridgeview is
      not receiving a sea wall because "Large areas of marsh wetland and an adjacent large,
      historic cemetery would make construction of a wall for this community impracticable,"
      and the Rosemont neighborhood will because "construction of a wall in this area is
      constrained due in part by potential marsh wetland impacts, and the proximity of
      homes in this area being built very close to the shoreline." U.S. Department of the
      Army, Corps of Engineers, "Charleston Peninsula Coastal Storm Risk Management
      Study," April 2022.

40   The city is asserting that "the net cost to the city will likely be closer to $250 million
      after subtracting the value of land-use credits the city will receive for enabling
      the structure to be built on city property." "An Update: Our Vulnerability Has
      Heightened," The Charleston 3×3 Army Corps Citizens Advisory Committee,
      May 2022, www.charleston-sc.gov/DocumentCenter/View/31840/3x3-Advisory
      -Committee-Peninsula-Study-Comprehensive-Update-5922?bidId=.

41   The Army's suggestion that the proposed wall would protect against another
      Hurricane Hugo is not premised on a *direct hit* from a storm of Hugo's size. Hugo's
      highest points at its landfall in 1989 centered on McClellanville, not Charleston.
      Future storms will likely exceed Hugo's height. The Corps is planning on just 1.43 feet
      of sea-level rise over 50 years. Even the City of Charleston is planning on 3 feet over
      50 years, and that is conservative. As Charleston's Chief Resilience Officer, Dale
      Morris, put it in February 2022, "And again, that 12 foot [height for the wall] is
      probably okay in year one to 10 of the structure's surge life. But because we don't
      know how quickly sea levels are rising, it's just a guess right now. We're probably
      going to need that resilience [of nature-based features, living shorelines], that extra
      resiliency for more friction in the out years, in year 40. So in 2070 or 2080." City of
      Charleston City Council Meeting, February 15, 2022, https://www.youtube.com
      /watch?v=xRhED81vZjg.

42   No construction of any phase of the project begins until design and construction
      of the previous phases is completed. The Charleston wall project, if approved by
      Congress, would begin with planning for Phase 1. This planning phase (called PED,
      for Preconstruction Engineering and Design) for Phase 1 is estimated to be complete
      in 2032. Wes Wilson, Army Corps of Engineers, February 18, 2021. Only then would
      construction begin: Phase 1 construction, which will likely take 7 years, is aimed at
      protecting the Medical District, with a wall running from the Coast Guard Station,
      near the intersection of Murray Boulevard and Tradd Street, to behind the Joe Riley
      Stadium, all along the Ashley River. Phase 2 will be the Lower and Upper Batteries—
      again, likely 3-7 years of planning followed by 7 years of construction. Because the city
      will not want to pay its share of design and construction costs for any later phases until

it absolutely has to, and because design of later phases will not start until construction of the previous phases is done, it could be decades before the city would get to any later phases of the project—phases beyond protecting the Medical District and the Batteries, the most valuable areas of the peninsula. Not until Phase 3 would the planning begin for the Eastside—again, 3-7 years of planning followed by 7 years of construction. Phase 4 is Wagener Terrace. Thirty or forty years could go by before the city got through all four phases of the Army Corps plan, if it ever did. As councilmember Mike Seekings said on February 28, 2021 during a public meeting about the Army Corps plan, "One of the things that was not really focused on tonight, but if we go through all four phases of the Army Corps of Engineers project, we're looking at thirty to forty years down the road."

43 City staff often feel that crucial activities are greatly underfunded and that they are underpaid. Fully a quarter of them express that feeling each year by leaving. Government worker morale in the City of Charleston is "brutally low," according to Councilmember Mike Seekings. "Every four years we have 100 percent turnover." Mike Seekings interview with author, November 17, 2021.

44 "Fast Facts 2022," City of Charleston, accessed June 24, 2022, www.charleston-sc.gov /DocumentCenter/View/31238/FAST-FACTS-2022.

45 NOAA Predicts Above-Normal Atlantic Hurricane Season." National Oceanic Atmospheric Administration, NOAA, accessed June 24, 2022, www.noaa.gov /news-release/noaa-predicts-above-normal-2022-atlantic-hurricane-season.

46 Norm Levine interview with author, October 9, 2018.

47 Rev. Joseph Darby interview with author, May 28, 2019.

48 Rev. Joseph Darby interview with author, March 8, 2019.

49 The Vera Institute of Justice found that in 2018, "In Charleston, South Carolina, Black people were arrested at a rate 4.29 times higher than white people. For nonviolent, nonserious incidents, Black people were arrested at a rate four times higher than white people. "What Policing Costs: Charleston, SC," *Vera Institute of Justice*, accessed June 24, 2022, www.vera.org/publications/what-policing-costs-in-americas-biggest -cities/charleston-sc.

50 Gregory Yee, "Charleston Police Say They've Changed Since May 2020 Rioting; Report Details How," *Post and Courier*, February 23, 2021.

51 Gregory Yee and Mikaela Porter, "13 Hours: How the George Floyd protest and rioting changed Charleston," *Post and Courier*, Aug. 29, 2020.

52 Tariro Mzezewa and Kim Severson, "Charleston Tourism Is Built on Southern Charm. Locals Say It's Time to Change," *New York Times*, August 12, 2020.

53 Edward M. Gilbreth, "What was really behind the shocking Charleston violence?" *Post and Courier*, June 4, 2020.

54 Jennifer Berry Hawes, "After Emanuel and Walter Scott shootings, Charleston stayed nonviolent. What changed?" *Post and Courier*, June 1, 2020.

55 Jack Jenkins and Elana Schor, "Activism cuts into the political might of S.C. black church," Associated Press, February 28, 2020.

56 Adam Parker and Rickey Ciapha Dennis Jr., "Black Church is an Essential Community Pillar That Has Been a Target Over The Centuries," *Post and Courier*, January 16, 2022.

57　The Charleston Area Convention & Visitors Bureau, also known as the CVB or Explore Charleston, which is headed by the powerful Helen Hill, was the subject of investigative reporting by *Frontline* and the *Post and Courier* in a September 2022 piece. About a third of accommodations tax revenues (a two percent state tax on hotel room stays) are funneled to designated marketing organizations that are allowed to spend the money only on promoting tourism. But Explore Charleston, which received nearly $8 million in fiscal 2021-22 from accommodations tax receipts and has an overall yearly budget of $24 million, is not required to make public how that money is spent, and Helen Hill does not want to say. "Do I want my competition in another state to know [what the money is spent on]? Probably not," she told the newspaper. The journalists dug up CVB's required yearly nonprofit tax filings, which revealed the group has paid *Travel + Leisure* more than $8 million and Condé Nast (publisher of *Condé Nast Traveler*) $6.7 million since 2015. Both magazines have routinely named Charleston the top city and small city in the US for visitors. Explore Charleston in 2021 "credited its work with having more than a $10 billion [yearly] economic impact on the Greater Charleston area." Briah Lumpkins and Doug Pardue, "Charleston's tourism machine: Lack of scrutiny, accountability keeps public in dark about millions of taxpayer dollars spent every year," *Post and Courier*, Sept. 23, 2022.

58　Mika Gadsden twitch.tv broadcast, May 12, 2021.

59　Mika Gadsden twitch.tv broadcast, May 12, 2021.

5. The Lower Peninsula and Jacob Lindsey

1　Vince Graham interview with author, December 5, 2018.

2　This story was told to me by journalist and author Jack Hitt, an extraordinary son of Charleston. The rooms were brought to the Minneapolis Institutes of Art, and a 1931 article about the acquisition by Harold Stark explains why Fox jumped out the window and why his broken leg was important to history: "It was a custom in Tory Charleston when the port was served that the guests might do justice to the host's choice cellar. Marion, who was of a temperate turn of mind, sought the only means of escape. He was taken to his country house to recuperate and by this stroke of Fate was not in Charleston when the English took his city, and was at liberty to organize his attacks from the swamp that were so annoying to the British." Stark loved the exhibit: "[O]ne feels the atmosphere of an interior that has survived from that rich and lively period of Charleston in its aristocratic days, at the time of the Revolution, when eighteenth-century English life was carried to the Colonies in the full measure of its sophistication and intellectual accomplishment." Harold Stark, "The Colonial Rooms at the Minneapolis Institute," *The American Magazine of Art* 23:3 (September, 1931), 183-90. It is this haze of aristocracy, or some dim invented memory of it, that still brings white tourists downtown.

3　Brian Hicks, *The Mayor: Joe Riley and the Rise of Charleston* (Charleston, South Carolina: Evening Post Books, 2015), 633 (Kindle edition).

4　Brian Hicks, *The Mayor*, 636.

5　Holly Roberts, "Learn About LaBrasca's Pizzeria, Which Claims to be the First Restaurant in Charleston To Serve Pizza," *Charleston, The City Magazine*, February 2022, https://charlestonmag.com/features/learn_about_labrasca_s_pizzeria_which_claims _to_be_the_first_restaurant_in_charleston_to.

6   John Tibbetts, interview with author, May 11, 2022.

7   Butler, *Lowcountry at High Tide*, 66.

8   Nic Butler, "A Brief History of the High and Low Battery Seawalls, Part 1," Charleston Public Library, October 26, 2017, https://www.ccpl.org/charleston-time-machine /brief-history-high-and-low-battery-seawalls-part-1.

9   Nic Butler, "A Brief History of the High and Low Battery Seawalls, Part 1," Charleston Public Library, October 26, 2017, https://www.ccpl.org/charleston-time-machine /brief-history-high-and-low-battery-seawalls-part-1.

10   Nic Butler, "A Brief History of the High and Low Battery Seawalls, Part 2," Charleston Public Library, November 2, 2017, https://www.ccpl.org/charleston-time-machine /brief-history-high-and-low-battery-seawalls-part-2.

11   City of Charleston, "Low Battery Restoration Project," accessed June 27, 2022, https ://storymaps.arcgis.com/stories/bc6e1790933b4c018a52dca8c1daec6a.

12   Nic Butler, "A Brief History of the High and Low Battery Seawalls, Part 2," Charleston Public Library, November 2, 2017, https://www.ccpl.org /charleston-time-machine/brief-history-high-and-low-battery-seawalls-part-2.

13   Robert Behre, "Two houses, two very different solutions to one big problem," *Post and Courier*, March 19, 2022.

14   Conversation with Latonya Gamble, hosted by the Avery Research Center and the Lowcountry Action Committee, May 6, 2021.

15   Jacob Lindsey, interview with author, October 11, 2018.

16   Of the cities with more than 50,000 residents in South Carolina, Charleston will experience the highest frequency of days of extreme heat—as many as 65 days a year with a heat index above 100. Kristina Dahl et al., "Killer Heat in the United States: Climate Choices and the Future of Dangerously Hot Days," Union of Concerned Scientists, July 2, 2019, https://www.ucsusa.org/resources/killer-heat-united-states-0; Bo Petersen, "'Too hot to believe' extreme days to get more frequent in SC, study says," *Post and Courier*, August 4, 2019.

17   David Wren, "Firm hired to prep Charleston port's Union Pier for sale shows interest as buyer," *Post and Courier*, April 16, 2022.

18   John Fritteli and Jennifer Lake, "Terminal Operators and Their Role in U.S. Port and Maritime Security," *Congressional Research Service* 7-5700, April 10, 2007. The South Carolina State Ports Authority is organized as an agency or instrumentality of the state government, and therefore enjoys immunity from suit under the U.S. Constitution. See *Federal Maritime Comm'n v South Carolina Ports Authority*, 535 US 743 (2002). A strike at the Cigar Factory nearby prompted the state to take over operation of the port in order to avoid unionization.

     There is a renovated four-story cigar factory at 701 East Bay Street in Charleston. It was built as a textile mill in 1881, a 240,000 square foot, five-story, cotton-weaving Victorian behemoth, making it part of South Carolina's economic development after the Civil War. It was repurposed a couple of decades later for cigar manufacturing, and operated until the 1970s as an American Tobacco Company plant, mostly providing poor jobs for poor people rolling out, at peak production, 1.5 million cigars a day. In the 1940s, managers segregated the floors of the factory by race, and African

Americans worked in the poisonous ammonia-stinking atmosphere of the basement, stemming tobacco leaves, while whites worked upstairs making the cigars. Wages were about 45 cents an hour. On October 22, 1945, over a thousand cigar factory workers walked off the job, organized by the Food, Tobacco, Agricultural, and Allied Workers Union (FTA-CIO), demanding back pay and a 25 cent hourly raise. Most were African American women, but some black men and white workers joined the strike, protesting rampant discrimination and bad treatment.

Striker Lucille Simmons sang "We will overcome, and we'll win our rights someday" to end each day on the picket line; it was a work song, a spiritual, sung slowly.

The strike went on for five months, and resulted in only modest gains for the strikers and even more modest advances in interracial relations in Charleston. Pete Seeger, meanwhile, changed the lyrics of the workers' song to "We Shall Overcome," Martin Luther King made it a central hymn of the civil rights movement, and President Lyndon Johnson co-opted the phrase two decades later in calling for voting rights legislation.

The factory stopped producing cigars in 1973, but the building stayed up and stumbled along through various guises over the years. It was empty as of 2009, when the recession ended redevelopment plans, and then roared back into life in 2014 when a group of developers bought the building for $24 million and put $55 million in to fix it up. Now you can eat at Mercantile and Mash, an enormous wood-lined foodie-cum-networking food hall and coffee shop that anchors the southern wing of the former factory, or get a pedicure at a place that describes itself as Charleston's "first ethical and nontoxic nail salon," or buy a one-of-a-kind Charleston antique from a design collective, or go to see a personal trainer, or slurp oysters.

The Cigar Factory's neighborhood often floods, even on sunny days without rain, when tides rise nearby. So does the street it is on, East Bay Street, which runs parallel to the Cooper River.

19   Dana Beach interview with author, July 12, 2018. On March 17, 1947, the City of Charleston gave title to the Columbus Street Terminal, Union Piers 1 & 2, Union Public Warehouse, Adgers Wharf and 1 Vendue Range to the South Carolina State Ports Authority.

20   The South Carolina Ports Authority is just one of several large public authorities that wield tremendous, unaccountable power in the state. These authorities, which have their own streams of revenue and are thus isolated from any public or political influence (remember Robert Moses and his very lucrative, unaccountable Triboro Bridge Authority) are nearly impervious to democratic processes. Take the Santee Cooper, which is the state's very large public electric utility. It has historically offered concessions and advantages to private sector companies. Then, the private sector companies that get those deals become deeply beholden to the legislators who get them these perks, and the government officials become deeply intertwined with the fates of the private customers. Dana Beach interview with author, July 12, 2018.

21   David Wren, "Charleston ports agency starts process to sell key waterfront site," *Post and Courier*, March 17, 2020; Greg Hambrick, "Port, city begin Union Pier redevelopment," *Charleston Citypaper*, October 8, 2009.

22   Emily Williams, "Charleston Place buyer now a partner in waterfront hotel project downtown," *Post and Courier*, December 10, 2021.

23   David Wren, "Charleston ports agency starts process to sell key waterfront site," *Post and Courier*, March 17, 2020.

24   Patrick Hoff, "Port Entitles Section of Union Pier for Redevelopment," *SC Biz News*, March 18, 2020, https://scbiznews.com/news/distribution-logistics/78164/.

25   John McDermott, "Charleston's surging real estate values helped sweep Carnival out to sea," *Post and Courier*, May 29, 2022.

26   David Wren, "Carnival cruise ship to leave Charleston in late '24 for Union Pier redo," *Post and Courier*, May 25, 2022.

27   City Council Workshop, "Update on U.S. Army Corps of Engineers' Coastal Flood Risk Management Study for Charleston Peninsula," February 15, 2022.

28   The mechanism that allows this is called Tax Increment Financing. The City of Charleston has established a number of TIF districts over the years. The idea is that issuing a public bond—another way to generate revenues—would produce a far lower percent return than private developers require to commit to invest, and its proceeds would have to be spread across the entire city rather than the narrow district in which the new buildings sit. This is the central problem of infrastructure—it should generate no more than a six or seven percent return. But distant investors want a far higher rate of return than those bonds make possible.

29   David Wren, "Carnival cruise ship to leave Charleston in late '24 for Union Pier redo," *Post and Courier*, May 25, 2022.

30   "Our Team," Lowe, accessed June 27, 2022, https://lowe-re.com/who-we-are/team/.

31   Butler, *Lowcountry at High Tide*, 148.

32   David Wren, "Firm hired to prep Charleston port's Union Pier for sale shows interest as buyer," *Post and Courier*, April 16, 2022.

33   "Our Watershed," *Charleston Waterkeeper* 2014, at 8.

34   Emily Williams, "Rising tides take Charleston to the brim, threatening businesses— even when it's sunny," *Post and Courier*, October 19, 2020.

35   Joint City Council—Planning Commission Meeting, June 30, 2021.

36   David Wren, "Firm hired to prep Charleston port's Union Pier for sale shows interest as buyer," *Post and Courier*, April 16, 2022.

37   David Wren, "Union Pier contract draws private groans from developers, praise from ports agency," *Post and Courier*, June 28, 2022; Emma Whalen, "Charleston leaders want input on what to do with 70-acre waterfront port property," *Post and Courier*, August 26, 2022.

38   Steve Bailey, "Can Jacob Lindsey and Lowe accomplish the impossible on Union Pier?," *Post and Courier*, April 16, 2022.

39   1788 map of Union Pier, from Historical Assessment of Proposed Renovations to Union Pier Terminal, September 2015, report prepared for the SCPA by Brockington and Associates, Inc., Cultural Resources Consulting.

40   Emily Williams, "Rising tides take Charleston to the brim, threatening businesses— even when it's sunny," *Post and Courier*, October 19, 2020.

41   John McDermott, "Charleston's surging real estate values helped sweep Carnival out to
      sea," *Post and Courier*, May 29, 2022.

42   1996 Downtown Plan, p. 74: "FEMA flood plain regulations: The new, restrictive
      flood plain regulations will perhaps have the greatest impact along the Cooper River
      waterfront. Because all the [planned] development is new, most active uses will
      [have to] be elevated above grade, potentially creating an inhospitable pedestrian
      environment. One option is to elevate the height of all the streets up to the level
      required by FEMA, in order that active uses be at street level. While this might be an
      expensive option, the cost must be weighed against the impact of FEMA [limitations
      on building in floodplains as of 1996] on the livability, aesthetics and atmosphere, and
      therefore its sustainability as an attractive place for residents and visitors." This was at
      a time when FEMA's maps didn't take into account sea level rise or increased rainfall.
      Riley: "We must always seek to find opportunities to preserve forever our citizens'
      access to the water's edge." Council Chamber meeting, January 26, 1999, about Union
      Pier.

43   Michael Maher interview with author, July 19, 2019.

44   For all the fuss about Charleston being a "seaside American treasure," no water is
      visible from much of the eastern side of the lower peninsula.

45   David Slade, "Union Pier design gets changes: Terminal entrance, parking-lot plan to
      soften impact," *Post and Courier*, June 1, 2011.

46   City Council meeting, July 20, 2021. Seekings went on to call it "undeveloped,
      unzoned raw property. It's an incredible opportunity for the city, this region, for the
      private sector." Mike Seekings interview with author, November 17, 2021.

47   David Wren, "Union Pier contract draws private groans from developers, praise from
      ports agency," *Post and Courier*, June 28, 2022.

48   Mike Seekings interview with author, November 17, 2021. The SCPA issued this
      statement following the negotiation: "After direct and positive communications
      with the U.S. Army Corps of Engineers Charleston District and the South Carolina
      Ports Authority since the draft report release, the South Carolina ports authority is
      optimistic a realignment can and will be achieved, before the U.S. Army Corps of
      Engineers Chief's report is approved, that will not have a negative impact on maritime
      operations at Columbus Street Terminal or diminish property values at Union Pier
      Terminal." City Council meeting, October 12, 2021.

49   Charleston Regional Hazard Mitigation Plan, at 188; David Wren, "Charleston's port
      kept its top 10 spot despite tough 2020," *Post and Courier*, May 9, 2021.

50   Dale Morris, October 21, 2021 City Council workshop, Army Corps plan.

51   Dale Morris, February 15, 2022 City Council workshop: "At some point that wall
      height will be insufficient. Okay. You are anticipat[ing] a 12 foot surge and you get a
      13 foot surge. Irma was 9.9 feet. Hugo was 10 feet. So this wall, this structure would
      protect against that. Wonderful. What happens if you get a 14 foot surge? Well, two
      foot coming over the top or one foot coming over the top of the water—coming over
      the top of the wall. That's something. And then if you normally have overland drainage
      for gravity, that wall has now created a bathtub. So you're impounding water.

The Army Corps of Engineers has to put pumps in there to mitigate those things, to mitigate that extra flooding. Okay. So those pumps now become an important resilience feature for us that if we can link that into the current drainage system, then we have additional resiliency. . . . And keep in mind that if the water comes over 12 feet, that's just a design exceedance and you have to have that pumping there to do that."

52   John McDermott, "Charleston's surging real estate values helped sweep Carnival out to sea," *Post and Courier*, May 29, 2022; Post and Courier editorial staff, "Editorial: Continue the remarkable momentum with SC ports," *Post and Courier*, June 25, 2022 ("The new Hugh K. Leatherman Terminal, only the second terminal built by the State Ports Authority since its creation in 1941, eventually can be expanded to the approximate size of the Wando terminal—work that the authority hopes to finance not with borrowing but largely with proceeds from the sale of Union Pier.").

53   Black men had more political power in South Carolina than in any other state in the South between 1867 and 1876. Ted Reed and John J. Yurechko, *Kenny Riley and Black Union Labor in the Port of Charleston* (Jefferson, North Carolina: McFarland & Company, 2020), 68.

54   Reed and Yurechko, *Kenny Riley*, 81.

55   Reed and Yurechko, *Kenny Riley*, 81.

56   Michael Thompson, "Working on the Dock of the Bay: Labor and Enterprise in an Antebellum Southern Port," Univ. of SC Press, 2015, at 2.

57   Reed and Yurechko, *Kenny Riley*, 109.

58   David Wren, "Charleston's waterfront an economic lifeline, source of pride for generations of families," *Post and Courier*, September 5, 2021.

59   Associated Press, "Union seeks Biden admin's help in Charleston port dispute," November 1, 2021 ("with only 1.7 percent of its workforce represented by organized labor groups in 2021, according to data from the U.S. Bureau of Labor Statistics (BLS)").

60   Eli Poliakoff, "Charleston's Longshoremen: Organized Labor in the Anti-Union Palmetto State," Harvard thesis, 2022. Nikki Hailey, the state's governor from 2011 to 2017 and a perennial almost-national figure, once said, "I wear heels, and it's not for a fashion statement. It's because we're kicking the unions every day." Reed and Yurechko, *Kenny Riley*, 172.

61   SCPA, "Historical Assessment of Proposed Renovations to Union Pier Terminal," 2015, at 30.

62   Tom Horton, "Charleston port of call for Wallenius-Wilhelmsen M/V Turandot," *Post and Courier*, May 22, 2020; Liz Segrist, "Automotive drives commerce at Columbus Terminal," *Charleston Regional Business Journal*, June 14, 2017; John McDermott, "Last cranes come down at Columbus St.," *Post and Courier*, October 30, 2016.

63   David Wren, "BMW's SC plant remains nation's top car exporter, sending $9.6B in SUVs to foreign market," *Post and Courier*, March 2, 2020.

64   Naida Hakirevic Prevljak, "SCPA officially opens Hugh K. Leatherman terminal," *Offshore Energy News*, April 12, 2021.

65   Michelle Mapp, interview with author, August 19, 2021.

66   ILA's claim is that ILA gets jurisdiction under that contract over crane drivers and yard workers at any new facility opened in the South Atlantic. Peter Tirschwell,

"Charleston port offers ILA path to resolve Leatherman dispute," *The Journal of Commerce*, February 22, 2022.

67 Reed and Yurechko, Kenny Riley, 169.

68 Kim Link Wills, "South Carolina Ports defends hybrid labor model," *American Shipper*, January 7, 2021.

69 Post and Courier editorial staff, "Editorial: Save Charleston's Longshoreman's Hall," *Post and Courier*, December 21, 2021.

70 Brian Hicks, "Nation's capital of the slave trade, Slavery in Charleston: A chronicle of human bondage in the Holy City," *Post and Courier*, April 9, 2011.

71 City Council workshop, February 15, 2022, Dale Morris paraphrasing Jim Newsome, CEO of SPA: "[Union Pier] is going to provide, if developed appropriately, and as we imagine now, tremendous amount of economic value and housing and other things for the city. So why wouldn't you protect that? [with the wall] And Jordi's boss [Jim Newsome] is fond of saying, 'Who knows what the future of transportation looks like in 25 years? Will we be exporting BMWs and Volvos from that facility? No one knows.' So the future uses of Columbus Terminal may also change over the license, so let's make sure we get that protected. That's massive. And it was important that we get it done."

6. The East Side and David White

1 Susan Millar Williams, "East Side History Series: Vardell's Creek," Trident Technical College, October 26, 2016, https://ttcpalmernews.blogspot.com/2016/10/east-side -history-series-vardrells-creek.html.

2 For thorough treatments of the East Side's demographics and history, see Dale Rosengarten et al., "Between the Tracks: Charleston's East Side During the Nineteenth Century," The Charleston Museum and Avery Research Center, September 1987; Bernard E. Powers, Jr., *Black Charlestonians: A Social History, 1822–1885* (Fayetteville, Arkansas: University of Arkansas Press, 1994).

3 Jason Christopher Grismore, "Public Housing on Peninsular Charleston, South Carolina: A History of Subsidized Housing," 2009 master's thesis, https://tigerprints .clemson.edu/historic_pres/2.

4 Adam Parker, "'America Street' documentary explores issues facing Charleston's East Side community," *Post and Courier*, October 27, 2019.

5 Adam Parker, "'America Street' documentary explores issues facing Charleston's East Side community," *Post and Courier*, October 27, 2019.

6 Abigail Darlington, "Charleston's plan for vacant East Side site falls apart, Harvard experts step in," August 8, 2018.

7 Conversation with Latonya Gamble hosted by the Avery Research Center and the Lowcountry Action Committee, May 6, 2021.

8 Stephen Hobbs and Rickey Ciapha, "How flooding intensifies the Charleston region's racial and wealth inequities," *Post and Courier*, September 22, 2020.

9 Adam Parker, "Hampstead Mall on Charleston's East Side gets a makeover, becomes new common ground," *Post and Courier*, November 16, 2021.

10   Christine Rae Butler, *Lowcountry at High Tide: A History of Flooding, Drainage, and Reclamation in Charleston, South Carolina* (Columbia, South Carolina: University of South Carolina Press, 2020), 99.

11   Shamira McCray, "Tuberculosis, other potential human pathogens in Charleston waterways, C of C study finds," *Post and Courier*, May 28, 2022; Tony Bartelme and Glenn Smith, "Charleston's Floodwaters Carry Dangerous Levels of Bacteria Even When It's Sunny," *Post and Courier*, October 1, 2020.

12   On April 11, 2022, Stormwater Manager Matthew Fountain reported to the city's Public Works and Utilities Committee that the city had cleaned out 10,000 feet of stormwater pipe on the East Side, saying "We did have pretty much complete clogging in a number of areas." Without spending at least $10 million to replace the existing pipes with higher-capacity channels, flooding in this area will remain chronic: "We saw that the existing system probably can only handle maybe what we call a one year or two year storm [lighter storms that are expected to be frequent] without upsizing." Even with the upsizing, Fountain predicted that heavy rainstorms at times of high tides would still overwhelm a gravity-driven drainage system today on the East Side, and rising sea-levels in the future will wipe out any gravity-driven system on the peninsula. "There will be a future consideration if we get significant sea level rise over the next 20 to 50 years of what we do to further improve drainage as that water starts to not flow out except at low tide cycles, but this [upsizing] will provide quite a bit more time," Fountain said.

13   Abigail Darlington, "Charleston's plan for vacant East Side site falls apart, Harvard experts step in," *Post and Courier*, August 8, 2018.

14   Conversation with Latonya Gamble hosted by the Avery Research Center and the Lowcountry Action Committee, May 6, 2021.

15   David Slade, "All public housing in Charleston to be replaced or renovated in sweeping initiative," *Post and Courier*, May 2, 2021. ("Existing complexes and buildings with a combined 1,407 apartments will either be extensively renovated or demolished in order to build larger buildings on the same properties.")

16   David Slade, "Huge rent increases have Charleston-area residents questioning if they should move," *Post and Courier*, Oct. 8, 2022.

17   Kalyn Oyer, "'It's too dark in here': Black nightclub DJs in Charleston speak up about discrimination," *Post and Courier*, June 17, 2020.

18   David White interview with author, November 10, 2020.

19   Michael Miller interview with author, December 28, 2020.

20   Laura Cantral interview with author, October 27, 2020.

21   "Charleston approves $250,000 for design, engineering and surveying of Lowline park," *Post and Courier*, Apr. 15, 2021.

22   https://www.counton2.com/news/local-news/lowcountry-lowline-would-create-new -park-walking-space-in-the-middle-of-downtown-charleston/.

23   Lillian Donahue, "City, Developers Look to Protect Neighborhoods Along Lowcountry Lowline," *Live 5 News*, Gray Television, March 12, 2021, https ://www.live5news.com/2021/03/12/city-developers-look-protect-neighborhoods -along-lowcountry-lowline/.

24 "Potential millions spent on Charleston park could limit East Side stormwater fixes,"
    Post and Courier, Mar. 26, 2021.

25 Lillian Donahue, "City, Developers Look to Protect Neighborhoods Along Lowcountry
    Lowline," *Live 5 News*, Gray Television, March 12, 2021, https://www.live5news.com
    /2021/03/12/city-developers-look-protect-neighborhoods-along-lowcountry-lowline/.

26 A Conversation with Latonya Gamble hosted by the Avery Research Center and the
    Lowcountry Action Committee, May 6, 2021.

27 Laura Cantral interview with author, Oct. 27, 2020.

28 Matt Fountain and City of Charleston Committee on Public Works and Utilities, 4112022.

29 Matt Fountain presentation to City of Charleston Committee on Public Works and
    Utilities, April 11, 2022.

30 Nic Butler, "A Trashy History of Charleston's Dumps and Incinerators," Charleston
    County Public Library, September 4, 2020, https://www.ccpl.org/ikipedia-time
    -machine/trashy-history-charlestons-dumps-and-incinerators.

31 Nic Butler, "A Trashy History of Charleston's Dumps and Incinerators," Charleston
    County Public Library, September 4, 2020, https://www.ccpl.org/ikipedia-time
    -machine/trashy-history-charlestons-dumps-and-incinerators.

32 "Pair of fragile smokestacks on Charleston's East Side are saved," *Post and Courier*, Nov.
    7, 2021.

33 Mikaela Porter, "Few Attend Monday Night Meeting on East Side About Smokestacks
    Future," *Post and Courier*, updated October 13, 2020, https://www.postandcourier.com
    /news/few-attend-Monday-night-meeting-on-east-side-about-smokestacks-future
    /article_de44f77e-0736-11eb-bcb6-2745b269b0e0.html.

34 Nic Butler, "A Trashy History of Charleston's Dumps and Incinerators," Charleston
    County Public Library, September 4, 2020, https://www.ccpl.org/ikipedia-time
    -machine/trashy-history-charlestons-dumps-and-incinerators.

35 Mikaela Porter, "Few Attend Monday Night Meeting on East Side About Smokestacks
    Future," *Post and Courier*, updated October 13, 2020, https://www.postandcourier
    .com/news/few-attend-Monday-night-meeting-on-east-side-about-smokestacks
    -future/article_de44f77e-0736-11eb-bcb6-2745b269b0e0.html.

36 Mikaela Porter, "East Side Residents Urge Charleston Officials to Preserve
    Deteriorating Smokestacks," *Post and Courier*, updated January 14, 2021, https://www
    .postandcourier.com/news/east-side-residents-urge-charleston-officials-to-preserve
    -deteriorating-smokestacks/article_3701cd3c-07fb-11eb-97db-5b86d7f603b6.html.

37 Editorial Staff, "Editorial: Don't Rush Decision on Smokestacks," *Post and Courier*,
    updated December 15, 2020, https://www.postandcourier.com/opinion/editorials
    /editorial-don't-rush-decision-on-smokestacks/article_9a007e94-0a60-11eb-8efc
    -ab8b73fe561a.html.

38 Winslow Hastie, "Commentary: Charleston's East Side Smokestacks Matter. Here's Why,"
    Post and Courier, updated July 9, 2021, https://www.postandcourier.com/opinion
    /commentary/commentary-charlestons-east-side-smokestacks-matter-heres-why
    /article_f3cee134-3edd-11eb-a2ae-0fd6976c4528.html.

39 David Slade, "Task Force Calls For Saving Historic East Side Smokestacks; Funding
    an Issue," *Post and Courier*, July 2, 2021, https://www.postandcourier.com/news

/task-force-calls-for-saving-historic-east-side-smokestacks-funding-an-issue
/article_7ca8d7d8-5691-11eb-afff-d7fa30a5f1ef.html.

40   Adam Parker, "Hampstead Mall on Charleston's East Side gets a makeover, becomes
      new common ground," *Post and Courier*, November 16, 2021.

41   Simone Jasper, "These South Carolina hotels rank among the nation's best, report finds.
      Here's why," *The State*, May 24, 2022.

42   Conversation with Latonya Gamble hosted by the Avery Research Center and the
      Lowcountry Action Committee, May 6, 2021.

7. The Upper Peninsula and Michelle Mapp

1   Nic Butler, "Grasping the Neck: The Origins of Charleston's Northern Neighbor,"
      Charleston County Public Library, August 24, 2018, https://www.ccpl.org/ikipedia
      -time-machine/grasping-neck-origins-charlestons-northern-neighbor; Nic Butler,
      "Squeezing Charleston Neck, From 1783 to the Present," Charleston County
      Public Library, August 31, 2018, https://www.ccpl.org/ikipedia-time-machine
      /squeezing-charleston-neck-1783-present.

2   John Beaty and Ralph Bailey, *A Historic Architectural Resources Survey of the Upper
      Peninsula Charleston, South Carolina* (Charleston: Brockington and Associates,
      Inc., 2004), 19. Everything above "Line Street" on this map, marked in green as
      within the "Survey Universe," is today's Neck area. Note how much of the Neck is
      marshland.

3   Chloe Johnson and Robert Behre, "SC's Forgotten Phosphate Industry Spurred
      Transformations at Home and Worldwide," *Post and Courier*, June 22, 2019, https
      ://www.postandcourier.com/news/scs-forgotten-phosphate-industry-spurred
      -transformations-at-home-and-worldwide/article_59cc13be-71d8-11e9-b6c6
      -c7d09b5f2b43.html.

4   Nic Butler, "Squeezing Charleston Neck, From 1783 to the Present," Charleston
      County Public Library, August 31, 2018, https://www.ccpl.org/ikipedia-time
      -machine/squeezing-charleston-neck-1783-present.

5   Chloe Johnson and Robert Behre, "SC's Forgotten Phosphate Industry Spurred
      Transformations at Home and Worldwide," *Post and Courier*, June 22, 2019, https
      ://www.postandcourier.com/news/scs-forgotten-phosphate-industry-spurred
      -transformations-at-home-and-worldwide/article_59cc13be-71d8-11e9-b6c6
      -c7d09b5f2b43.html ("Those familiar with Charleston lore might suspect the EPA
      took notice of the Ashley River waterfront after the problem with spontaneously
      combusting shrimp in 1992. That's when a man who had been shrimping along the
      river was driving home across the old Cooper River bridge and noticed smoke coming
      from his cooler. The reason? The shrimp had been exposed to phosphorous in the muck
      along the riverbed, near a chemical plant, and phosphorous spontaneously can catch
      fire when exposed to oxygen."); David Slade, "Addressing a Century of Pollution: $100
      Million and Countless Tons of Dirt Leave the Ashley Riverfront Cleaner, Safer," *Post
      and Courier*, May 10, 2014, https://www.postandcourier.com/news/special_reports
      /addressing-a-century-of-pollution-100-million-and-countless-tons-of-dirt-leave-the
      -ashley/article_cff48040-e737-5e04-bc80-89325daaf457.html.

6   Brian Hicks, "Hicks: Charleston's Early 1900s Renaissance Brought Success . . . And
     Violence," *Post and Courier*, December 13, 2020, https://www.postandcourier.com/350
     /hicks-charlestons-early-1900s-renaissance-brought-success-and-violence/article
     _99848afe-3b62-11eb-bb08-ab92515fc5a8.html. The base was established on land that the
     Olmstead brothers of Massachusetts (Frederick Law Olmstead's children) had envisioned
     for the City of Charleston as a majestic regional park, to be called Chicora Park and
     connected to downtown Charleston by trolley. Pres. Theodore Roosevelt visited the park
     and then the federal government bought the site from the city of Charleston for use as a
     new naval base.

7   Steve Warner, at the time the Charleston Regional Development Alliance's chief
     strategist, now asssistant vice president at Clemson University, interview with author,
     December 4, 2018.

8   Vince Graham interview with author, December 5, 2018.

9   Robert Moses spoke at the College of Charleston's commencement ceremony in 1968.
     Vince Graham interview with author, December 5, 2018.

10   Cathryn Zommer, Enough Pie, interview with author, October 9, 2018.

11   Jason Crowley, Coastal Conservation League, interview with author, October 11, 2018.

12   David Slade, "Bridgeview, the Largest Affordable Apartment Complex in Charleston,
     Has Been Sold," *Post and Courier*, February 19, 2021, https://www.postandcourier
     .com/business/real_estate/bridgeview-the-largest-affordable-apartment-complex-in
     -charleston-has-been-sold/article_c4505d64-7242-11eb-bece-1b775f03b973.html.

13   Nic Butler, "Squeezing Charleston Neck, From 1783 to the Present," Charleston County
     Public Library, August 31, 2018, https://www.ccpl.org/ikipedia-time-machine
     /squeezing-charleston-neck-1783-present.

14   U.S. Department of the Army, Corps of Engineers, "Charleston Peninsula Coastal
     Storm Risk Management Study," April 2022, www.sac.usace.army.mil/Portals/43
     /docs/civilworks/peninsulastudy/Final%20FR-EIS/ChsPenStudy%20FR-EIS
     _April%202022%20-%20Signed.pdf?ver=M1f4onDB8qXVUsVlyRm5Rw%3d%3d.

15   Chloe Johnson, "One Community Outside Charleston's Proposed Flood Wall is
     Anxious About Army Corps Plan," *Post and Courier*, November 20, 2021, https://www
     .postandcourier.com/environment/one-community-outside-charlestons-proposed
     -flood-wall-is-anxious-about-army-corps-plan/article_cc3ba158-46f1-11ec-9a7f
     -3f51e7194e86.html.

16   Chloe Johnson, "One Community Outside Charleston's Proposed Flood Wall is
     Anxious About Army Corps Plan," *Post and Courier*, November 20, 2021, https://www
     .postandcourier.com/environment/one-community-outside-charlestons-proposed
     -flood-wall-is-anxious-about-army-corps-plan/article_cc3ba158-46f1-11ec-9a7f
     -3f51e7194e86.html.

17   Jocelyn Grzeszczak, "Plans Have Begun to Tear Down, Replace Charleston's
     Joseph Floyd Manor, CEO Says," *Post and Courier*, June 22, 2022, https://www
     .postandcourier.com/news/plans-have-begun-to-tear-down-replace-charlestons
     -joseph-floyd-manor-ceo-says/article_153d159e-f08e-11ec-98fb-9f3f73f05e02.html.

18   Editorial Staff, "Editorial: At Joseph Floyd Manor, Killing Bedbugs Looks Like the
     Easy Part," *Post and Courier*, June 14, 2020, https://www.postandcourier.com/opinion

/editorials/editorial-at-joseph-floyd-manor-killing-bedbugs-looks-like-the-easy-part
/article_752fdcce-aa69-11ea-8827-8f28df551899.html.

19   Mary Edna, "Charleston Airborne Flooded," Accessed July 5, 2022, https://maryedna
      .com/installations/ikipedia-airborne-flooded/.

20   Mary Edna Fraser, artist, says "This 100-foot banner "Charleston Airborne Flooded"
      hung on the exterior of the Joseph Floyd Manor in Charleston SC. The project was part
      of an art- and event-based civic discussion about rising sea levels, which Mary Edna
      helped organize in collaboration with nonprofit Enough Pie, called Awakening V:
      King Tide. The art shows flooding of 4.5 feet on the Charleston coastline by the year
      2020, as predicted by NOAA. The batik image was photographed and printed locally,
      and includes a quote by Voltaire, "We argue. Nature acts."; Cathryn Zommer interview
      with author, October 9, 2018.

21   College of Charleston, "The State of Racial Disparities in Charleston County, 2000–
      2015" (2017), 11.

22   Editorial, "New data clarify Charleston's affordability crisis; something has to give,"
      Post and Courier, Jan. 16, 2021.

23   Editorial staff, "More Work Needed on Housing Help in Charleston County," *Post and
      Courier*, July 2, 2022.

24   Emma Whalen, "New affordable housing complex, Grace Homes, facing structural
      concerns, tenant complaints," *Post and Courier*, October 4, 2022.

25   Emma Whalen, "New affordable housing complex, Grace Homes, facing structural
      concerns, tenant complaints," *Post and Courier*, October 4, 2022.

26   Emma Whalen, "New affordable housing complex, Grace Homes, facing structural
      concerns, tenant complaints," *Post and Courier*, October 4, 2022.

27   Alexis Simmons, "Charleston County Leaders Calling For Major Changes at Senior
      Public Housing Building," *Live5News*, Gray Television, May 20, 2020, https://www
      .live5news.com/2020/05/20/ikipedia-county-leaders-calling-major-changes
      -senior-public-housing-building/.

28   Gregory Yee, "At Joseph Floyd Manor, Housing Agency Head Fired as Officials Move
      to Help Residents," *Post and Courier*, May 28, 2020, https://www.postandcourier.com
      /business/real_estate/at-joseph-floyd-manor-housing-agency-head-fired-as-officials
      -move-to-help-residents/article_8719f3b6-a118-11ea-90c2-47e5cb58053d.html.

29   Jocelyn Grzeszczak, "Mold, Pest Problems Persist at Joseph Floyd Manor a Year After
      Inspection, Residents Say," *Post and Courier*, November 1, 2021, https://www
      .postandcourier.com/news/mold-pest-problems-persist-at-joseph-floyd-manor-a-year
      -after-inspection-residents-say/article_9478ea24-366a-11ec-98db-1b3a4246cbf7.htm.

30   Gregory Yee, "Funding Issues at Charleston's Joseph Floyd Manor Could Soon be
      Resolved," *Post and Courier*, July 16, 2021, https://www.postandcourier.com
      /news/funding-issues-at-charlestons-joseph-floyd-manor-could-soon-be-resolved
      /article_1a507f24-e3e9-11eb-8a4f-5f2e1471b252.html; Jocelyn Grzeszczak,
      "Charleston's Floyd Manor Gets Upkeep, Repairs 1.5 Years After Failed Livability
      Inspection," *Post and Courier*, February 14, 2022, https://www.postandcourier.com
      /news/charlestons-floyd-manor-gets-upkeep-repairs-1-5-years-after-failed-livability
      -inspection/article_1ab27dde-8077-11ec-8661-c7283e69eeca.html.

31   The nickname for this kind of scheme is "Rental Assistance Demonstration" or
      RAD project. The Federal Housing Authority is encouraging the privatization of
      public housing along these lines. Editorial staff, "Time to plan for renovating or
      replacing Joseph Floyd Manor," *Post and Courier*, January 2, 2021. Criticism of RAD
      is widespread. The City of Charleston is planning to convert all of its public housing
      into privately managed properties, making tax credits available to developers for use in
      building and renovating public housing. David Slade, "All public housing in Charleston
      to be replaced or renovated in sweeping initiative," *Post and Courier*, May 2, 2021,
      https://www.postandcourier.com/business/real_estate/all-public-housing-in
      -charleston-to-be-replaced-or-renovated-in-sweeping-initiative/article_d7aa9a52
      -93dd-11eb-842d-63dd1fa73cf9.html.

32   Partnership for Prosperity, A Master Plan for the Neck Area of Charleston and
      North Charleston, (Charleston: Berkeley-Charleston-Dorchester Council of
      Governments, 2013), 92, http://www.neckprosperity.org/uploads/2/5/0/5/25050083
      /draftreport_131206_web.pdf ("Community meetings [for this plan] were sparsely
      attended, raising concerns about whose voices were included and whether the real
      planning agenda was to develop prime real estate, with the Neck's African American
      residents displaced as economic collateral damage.")

            Arlene Goldbard. "Prototyping Cultural Democracy Series Part 2: conNECKted:
      Imaginings for Truth and Reconciliation." U.S. Department of Arts and Culture.
      August 14, 2018. https://usdac.us/news/2018/7/23/prototyping-cultural-democracy
      -series-part-2-conneckted-imaginings-for-truth-and-reconciliation.

33   Gregory Yee, "At Charleston's Newest Affordable Housing, Some See High Costs,
      Others See Signs of Hope," *Post and Courier*, October 22, 2020, https://www
      .postandcourier.com/news/at-charlestons-newest-affordable-housing-some-see-high
      -costs-others-see-signs-of-hope/article_32a06e20-147f-11eb-b28e-d313a7c77e63.html.

34   Jocelyn Grzeszczak, "Plans have begun to tear down, replace Charleston's Joseph Floyd
      Manor, CEO says," *Post and Courier*, June 22, 2022.

35   Gregory Yee, "At Charleston's Newest Affordable Housing, Some See High
      Costs, Others See Signs of Hope," *Post and Courier*, October 22, 2020, https
      ://www.postandcourier.com/news/at-charlestons-newest-affordable-housing
      -some-see-high-costs-others-see-signs-of-hope/article_32a06e20-147f-11eb-b28e
      -d313a7c77e63.html.

36   Michael Miller interview with author, December 28, 2020.

37   Editorial staff, "Editorial: Welcome Progress at Joseph Floyd Manor," *Post and Courier*,
      June 23, 2022.

38   Jocelyn Grzeszczak, "Plans have begun to tear down, replace Charleston's Joseph Floyd
      Manor, CEO says," *Post and Courier*, June 22, 2022.

39   Editorial staff, "Editorial: Welcome Progress at Joseph Floyd Manor," *Post and Courier*,
      June 23, 2022.

40   Mapp, Michelle, "Interview by Kieran W. Taylor, 10 April, 2017," Lowcountry Digital
      Library, The Citadel Archives & Museum, February 2, 2013.

41   Alex Macaulay, "The Modern Period," Transcript of speech given at the Presidential Inaugural Celebration, Western Carolina University, April 20, 2006, https://www.citadel.edu/root/ceitl-programs/88-info/info-home/history/2396-the-modern-period.

42   Clemson University, "Clemson Commencement Program, May 1988," (Clemson Commencement Programs. 205. https://tigerprints.clemson.edu/ikip_programs/205; "History," Clemson University, Accessed July 5, 2022, https://www.clemson.edu /about/history/timeline.html.https://tigerprints.clemson.edu/cgi/viewcontent.cgi ?article=1205&context=ikip_programsfm.

43   "History," Clemson University, Accessed July 5, 2022, https://www.clemson.edu /about/history/timeline.html.

44   NCC Staff, "How the Martin Luther King Jr. Birthday Became a Holiday," *Constitution Daily*, National Constitution Center, January 17, 2022, https://constitutioncenter.org /blog/how-martin-luther-king-jr-s-birthday-became-a-holiday-3.

45   See https://en.wikipedia.org/wiki/Martin_Luther_King_Jr._Day.

46   Editorial staff, "Editorial: Juneteenth Deserves State Holiday Status," *Post and Courier*, June 19, 2022.

47   Kenneth Chatman, "A Study of The University of Tennessee Ronald McNair Post Baccalaureate Achievement Program: Factors Related to Graduate School Enrollment for First Generation, Low-Income and Under-represented College Students," PhD diss., University of Tennessee, 1994, https://trace.tennessee.edu/utk_graddiss/4375.

48   Mapp, Michelle, "Interview by Kieran W. Taylor, 10 April, 2017," Lowcountry Digital Library, The Citadel Archives & Museum, February 2, 2013.

49   Ordinary banks, which are required by the Community Reinvestment Act to show that they are serving the needs of their communities, get credit under that Act for investing money with Community Development institutions at below-market rates. As traditional banks have consolidated, Community Development Financial Institutions have stepped up to receive funds and make safe, affordable credit available to areas that are not served by the banking industry. That's the role that Mapp's organization filled, taking money from foundations, high-wealth individuals—whoever she could reach that was interested—and then applying each year to the Treasury Department for up to $2 million in matching funds.

50   South Carolina Community Loan Fund. *2020 Annual Report: Investing in Community*, Accessed July 5, 2022. https://sccommunityloanfund.org/wp-content/uploads/2021 /04/SCCLF_Annual_Report_2020.pdf.

51   See https://en.wikipedia.org/wiki/Killing_of_Walter_Scott. "On April 4, 2015, a White officer, Michael Slager, stopped a 50-year-old Black man, Walter Scott, because of his car's faulty brake light. During the encounter, Scott ran away and shortly thereafter a physical altercation ensued between the two men, which included struggling over the officer's Taser. As Scott fled, Slager fired his handgun eight times, hitting Scott in the back five times. A bystander's recorded the shooting on his cell phone—video that contradicted Slager's account of the shooting and resulted in him being fired and tried for murder. A mistrial was declared after the jury deadlocked in the state trial in late 2016. In the subsequent federal trial in May 2017, Slager pleaded guilty to a civil rights charge and currently awaits sentencing." Angela S. Lee, Ronald Weitzer, and Daniel E. Martínez. "Recent Police Killings in the United States: A

Three-City Comparison." *Police Quarterly* 21, no. 2 (June 2018): 196–222. https://doi
.org/10.1177/1098611117744508.

52   Luke Brinker, "Nikki Haley: It's OK to Have the Confederate flag at the Statehouse
      Because Not 'a Single CEO' Has Complained," *Salon*, Salon.com, October 15, 2014,
      https://www.salon.com/2014/10/15/nikki_haley_its_ok_to_have_the_confederate
      _flag_at_the_statehouse_because_not_a_single_ceo_has_complained/.

53   Justin Worland, "This is Why South Carolina Raised the Confederate flag in the
      First Place," *Time*, TIME USA, June 22, 2015, https://time.com/3930464/south
      -carolina-confederate-flag-1962/.

54   Michelle Mapp interview with author, November 4, 2020.

55   Michelle Mapp interview with author, November 4, 2020.

56   Market-based solutions needed, Nov. 4, 2020. Racism definitely on the ballot in 2020.
      But she still sees so many glimpses of goodness. We can still believe in humanity.
      Charleston County new sheriff is important.

57   Quoctrung Bui and Emily Badger, "In 83 Million Eviction Records, a Sweeping and
      Intimate New Look at Housing in America," *New York Times*, the New York Times
      Company, April 7, 2018, https://www.nytimes.com/interactive/2018/04/07/upshot
      /millions-of-eviction-records-a-sweeping-new-look-at-housing-in-america.html.

58   Paul Bowers and Brenda Rindge, "Mayor Summey's Reign in North Charleston a
      Boon for Developers, Friends, and Other Allies," *Post and Courier*, August 26, 2017.

59   Paul Bowers and Brenda Rindge, "Mayor Summey's Reign in North Charleston a
      Boon for Developers, Friends, and Other Allies," *Post and Courier*, August 26, 2017.

60   City of North Charleston, "Population & Demographics," Accessed July 5, 2022.
      https://www.northcharleston.org/residents/community/primenorthcharleston/the-data
      /population-demographics/.

61   Hannah Alani, "North Charleston Proceeding With More Annexation in West Ashley;
      Likely to Spark Charleston Lawsuit," *Post and Courier*, December 12, 2017, https://www
      .postandcourier.com/news/north-charleston-proceeding-with-more-annexation-in-west
      -ashley-likely-to-spark-charleston-lawsuit/article_8b55c084-df5c-11e7-acfe-43a8c
      94005f7.html; Schuyler Kropf, "North Charleston finalizes Watson Hill annexation," *Post
      and Courier*, May 15, 2011, https://www.postandcourier.com/north-charleston-finalizes
      -watson-hill-annexation/article_96de49b0-d0cf-51b0-87b3-c5ad1ff7d2c3.html.

62   United States Census Bureau, "Quick Facts: North Charleston City, South Carolina,"
      U.S. Department of Commerce, Accessed July 5, 2022, https://www.census.gov
      /quickfacts/fact/table/northcharlestoncitysouthcarolina/PST045221.

63   David Slade and Adam Parker, "Census Shows Charleston City and County Losing
      Black Residents," *Post and Courier*, August 21, 2021, https://www.postandcourier.com
      /news/census-shows-charleston-city-and-county-losing-black-residents/article
      _4487b478-fb96-11eb-90a6-db21b50594fd.html.

64   Rickey Ciapha Dennis Jr., "As North Charleston Booms With New Apartments, Many
      Unaffordable to Average Residents," *Post and Courier*, April 18, 2021, https://www.postand
      courier.com/business/real_estate/as-north-charleston-booms-with-new-apartments
      -many-unaffordable-to-average-residents/article_78542ba0-9710-11eb-84b7
      -d3ef7772ec7e.html.

65   David Slade and Adam Parker, "Census Shows Charleston City and County Losing Black Residents," *Post and Courier*, August 21, 2021, https://www.postandcourier.com/news/census-shows-charleston-city-and-county-losing-black-residents/article_4487b478-fb96-11eb-90a6-db21b50594fd.html.

66   Rickey Ciapha Dennis Jr., "North Charleston neighborhood split by I-26 could be reconnected with affordable housing," *Post and Courier*, August 25, 2022.

67   North Charleston Heritage Corridor, "North Charleston," Arcadia Publishing, Accessed July 5, 2022, https://www.arcadiapublishing.com/Products/9780738513904.

68   Nic Butler, "Indigo in the Fabric of Early South Carolina," Charleston County Public Library, August 16, 2019, https://www.ccpl.org/charleston-time-machine/indigo-fabric-early-south-carolina.

69   Matthew Desmond, *Evicted: Poverty and Profit in the American City* (New York: The Crown Publishing Group, 2016).

70   Rickey Ciapha Dennis Jr., "Mitigations For Billion-Dollar Road Plan in North Charleston Include Affordable Housing," *Post and Courier*, November 6, 2020, https://www.postandcourier.com/news/mitigations-for-billion-dollar-road-plan-in-north-charleston-include-affordable-housing/article_15e154b0-1fa7-11eb-81ce-13c245f811f6.html.

71   "Park Circle History," ParkCircle.com, Accessed July 5, 2022, https://www.parkcircle.com/about.

72   Warren L. Wise, "North Charleston Among Top 50 Most Affordable Places For Millennials in U.S., Study Says," *Post and Courier*, July 20, 2019, https://www.postandcourier.com/business/real_estate/north-charleston-among-top-50-most-affordable-places-for-millennials-in-u-s-study-says/article_03966db0-aa3f-11e9-837c-13addcea7f9a.html.

73   Rickey Ciapha Dennis Jr., "As North Charleston Booms With New Apartments, Many Unaffordable to Average Residents," *Post and Courier*, April 18, 2021, https://www.postandcourier.com/business/real_estate/as-north-charleston-booms-with-new-apartments-many-unaffordable-to-average-residents/article_78542ba0-9710-11eb-84b7-d3ef7772ec7e.html.

74   Rickey Ciapha Dennis Jr., "As North Charleston Booms With New Apartments, Many Unaffordable to Average Residents," *Post and Courier*, April 18, 2021, https://www.postandcourier.com/business/real_estate/as-north-charleston-booms-with-new-apartments-many-unaffordable-to-average-residents/article_78542ba0-9710-11eb-84b7-d3ef7772ec7e.html.

75   Cathryn Zommer interview with author, October 9, 2018.

76   Staff Reports, "Crane Count, 7/4: 16 Cranes Dot the Peninsula," *Charleston City Paper*, https://charlestoncitypaper.com/charleston-crane-count/.

77   Warren Wise, "Charleston's long-envisioned Magnolia project inks deal with Atlanta developer," *Post and Courier*, June 10, 2022.

8. Upper Lockwood: Gadsden Green, WestEdge, MUSC, and the Future

1   "About WestEdge: A Transformational Development," WestEdge Charleston, West Edge, https://www.westedgecharleston.com/plan/.

2   Coastal Flood Event Database," National Weather Service, National Oceanic and
    Atmospheric Administration, https://www.weather.gov/chs/coastalflood.

3   Glenn Smith and Fleming Smith, "High Tide Floods Downtown Charleston Streets
    Sunday, With More Flooding Expected Monday," *Post and Courier*, October 18, 2020,
    https://www.postandcourier.com/news/high-tide-floods-downtown-charleston
    -streets-sunday-with-more-flooding-expected-monday/article_72d58858-115b-11eb
    -a1c9-572df5d29fa1.html.

4   Tony Bartelme and Glenn Smith, "Charleston's Floodwaters Carry Dangerous Levels
    of Bacteria Even When It's Sunny," *Post and Courier*, October 1, 2020. https://www
    .postandcourier.com/rising-waters/charlestons-floodwaters-carry-dangerous-levels-of
    -bacteria-even-when-its-sunny/article_1e4536a0-0353-11eb-8304-7fb4057a8d15.html.

5   Evan R. Thompson, "The Historical Reason Charleston's Streets Flood," *Charleston
    City Paper*, August 21, 2013, charlestoncitypaper.com/the-historical-reason-why
    -charlestons-streets-flood/.

6   Rev. Darby email to author, Nov. 15, 2022.

7   Adam Parker, "The Debate Over Charleston's Gadsden Creek Flooding-Remediation
    Plan Heats Up," *Post and Courier*, May 7, 2022, https://www.postandcourier.com
    /news/the-debate-over-charlestons-gadsden-creek-flooding-remediation-plan
    -heats-up/article_a766bf34-cba3-11ec-8d80-7f81117ab38a.html.

8   Allston McCrady, "Development is Threatening a Downtown Wetland and Concerned
    Citizens are Sounding the Alarm. Can Gadsden Creek be Saved?" *Charleston City Paper*,
    July 10, 2019, https://charlestoncitypaper.com/development-is-threatening-a-downtown
    -wetland-and-concerned-citizens-are-sounding-the-alarm-can-gadsden-creek-be-saved/.

9   Allston McCrady, "Development is Threatening a Downtown Wetland and Concerned
    Citizens are Sounding the Alarm. Can Gadsden Creek be Saved?" *Charleston City
    Paper*, July 10, 2019, https://charlestoncitypaper.com/development-is-threatening-a
    -downtown-wetland-and-concerned-citizens-are-sounding-the-alarm-can-gadsden
    -creek-be-saved/.

10 Stephen Hobbs and Rickey Ciapha Dennis Jr., "How Flooding Intensifies the
    Charleston Region's Racial and Wealth Inequities," *Post and Courier*, September 22,
    2020, https://www.postandcourier.com/rising-waters/how-flooding-intensifies-the
    -charleston-regions-racial-and-wealth-inequities/article_7a5f724c-afc6-11ea-b878
    -2795af874a5b.html.

11 Stephen Hobbs and Rickey Ciapha Dennis Jr., "How Flooding Intensifies the Charleston
    Region's Racial and Wealth Inequities," *Post and Courier*, September 22, 2020, https
    ://www.postandcourier.com/rising-waters/how-flooding-intensifies-the-charleston
    -regions-racial-and-wealth-inequities/article_7a5f724c-afc6-11ea-b878-2795af874a5b.html.

12 Stephen Hobbs and Rickey Ciapha Dennis Jr., "How Flooding Intensifies the
    Charleston Region's Racial and Wealth Inequities," *Post and Courier*, September 22,
    2020, https://www.postandcourier.com/rising-waters/how-flooding-intensifies-the
    -charleston-regions-racial-and-wealth-inequities/article_7a5f724c-afc6-11ea-b878
    -2795af874a5b.html.

13 "A Timeline of Abuses Against Gadsden Creek and the Gadsden Green Community,"
    Friends of Gadsden Creek, Accessed July 7, 2022, https://static1.squarespace.com

/static/5c71bd8493a632103f202be3/t/5f70e5104278c74ee0e44b37/1601234197133
/Illustrated+Timeline_Color_092720.pdf.

14   Adam Parker, "The Debate Over Charleston's Gadsden Creek Flooding-Remediation
      Plan Heats Up," *Post and Courier*, May 7, 2022, https://www.postandcourier.com
      /news/the-debate-over-charlestons-gadsden-creek-flooding-remediation-plan
      -heats-up/article_a766bf34-cba3-11ec-8d80-7f81117ab38a.html.

15   Allston McCrady, "Development is Threatening a Downtown Wetland and Concerned
      Citizens are Sounding the Alarm. Can Gadsden Creek be Saved?" *Charleston City
      Paper*, July 10, 2019, https://charlestoncitypaper.com/development-is-threatening-a
      -downtown-wetland-and-concerned-citizens-are-sounding-the-alarm-can-gadsden
      -creek-be-saved/.

16   "Reports," Friends of Gadsden Creek, Accessed July 7, 2022, https://friendsofgads
      dencreek.com/research.

17   Chloe Johnson, "Gadsden Creek Becomes a Flashpoint in Charleston Discussion on
      Environmental Justice," *Post and Courier*, July 17, 2020, https://www.postandcourier
      .com/news/gadsden-creek-becomes-a-flashpoint-in-charleston-discussion-on
      -environmental-justice/article_8a40ece8-c5e9-11ea-b50e-df363e8bef92.html.

18   Eric Jackson interview with author, November 13, 2020.

19   Adam Parker, "Why are Highways Built to Run Through Black Communities?
      SC Faces a Historic Dilemma Again," *Post and Courier*, October 17, 2020, www
      .postandcourier.com/news/local_state_news/why-are-highways-built-to-run-through
      -black-communities-sc-faces-a-historic-dilemma-again/article_576f3fce-0976-11eb
      -a46c-635e6fad5d38.html.

20   Stephen Hobbs and Rickey Ciapha Dennis Jr.,"How Flooding Intensifies the
      Charleston Region's Racial and Wealth Inequities," *Post and Courier*, September 22,
      2020, https://www.postandcourier.com/rising-waters/how-flooding-intensifies-the
      -charleston-regions-racial-and-wealth-inequities/article_7a5f724c-afc6-11ea-b878
      -2795af874a5b.html.

21   Allston McCrady, "Development is Threatening a Downtown Wetland and Concerned
      Citizens are Sounding the Alarm. Can Gadsden Creek be Saved?" *Charleston City
      Paper*, July 10, 2019, https://charlestoncitypaper.com/development-is-threatening-a
      -downtown-wetland-and-concerned-citizens-are-sounding-the-alarm-can-gadsden
      -creek-be-saved/.

22   Mika Gadsden twitch.tv livestream, Oct. 11, 2021.

23   Norm Levine interview with author, July 21, 2021.

24   Allston McCrady, "Development is Threatening a Downtown Wetland and Concerned
      Citizens are Sounding the Alarm. Can Gadsden Creek be Saved?" *Charleston City
      Paper*, July 10, 2019, https://charlestoncitypaper.com/development-is-threatening-a
      -downtown-wetland-and-concerned-citizens-are-sounding-the-alarm-can-gadsden
      -creek-be-saved/.

25   Chloe Johnson, "Gadsden Creek Becomes a Flashpoint in Charleston Discussion on
      Environmental Justice," *Post and Courier*, July 17, 2020, https://www.postandcourier
      .com/news/gadsden-creek-becomes-a-flashpoint-in-charleston-discussion-on
      -environmental-justice/article_8a40ece8-c5e9-11ea-b50e-df363e8bef92.html.

26 Stephen Hobbs and Rickey Ciapha Dennis Jr.," How Flooding Intensifies the Charleston Region's Racial and Wealth Inequities," *Post and Courier*, September 22, 2020, https ://www.postandcourier.com/rising-waters/how-flooding-intensifies-the-charleston-regions -racial-and-wealth-inequities/article_7a5f724c-afc6-11ea-b878-2795af874a5b.html.

27 Chloe Johnson, "Gadsden Creek Becomes a Flashpoint in Charleston Discussion on Environmental Justice," *Post and Courier*, July 17, 2020, https://www.postandcourier .com/news/gadsden-creek-becomes-a-flashpoint-in-charleston-discussion-on -environmental-justice/article_8a40ece8-c5e9-11ea-b50e-df363e8bef92.html.

28 Stephen Hobbs and Rickey Ciapha Dennis Jr., "How Flooding Intensifies the Charleston Region's Racial and Wealth Inequities," *Post and Courier*, September 22, 2020, https://www.postandcourier.com/rising-waters/how-flooding-intensifies-the -charleston-regions-racial-and-wealth-inequities/article_7a5f724c-afc6-11ea-b878 -2795af874a5b.html.

29 Eric Jackson interview with author, November 13, 2020.

30 Michelle Mapp interview with author, August 19, 2021.

31 Michelle Mapp interview with author, August 19, 2021.

32 January 2015 Riley "State of the City" address, at 3.

33 As of 2020, which is the most recent Form 990 on file, The WestEdge Foundation is a 501(c)(3) nonprofit that is managed by a 12-member board. Four members are appointed by the city, four by MUSC, and there are four at-large members. Michael Maher is the CEO of the WestEdge Foundation. The WestEdge Foundation received $2.9 million in TIF funding in 2017 and $18.6 million in TIF funding in 2020.

34 City Council Workshop, Peninsula Coastal Flood Risk Management Study, Feb. 18, 2021.

35 Abigail Darlington, "Charleston's WestEdge Development Promising to Fix the Area's Flooding Problem," *Post and Courier*, July 20, 2018, https://www.postandcourier .com/news/charlestons-westedge-development-promising-to-fix-the-areas-flooding -problems/article_75d2b94e-8937-11e8-b934-4f72d04ac229.html.

36 The archival photos used to create these images can be found at https://aerialphotos .library.sc.edu/.

37 Abigail Darlington, "Charleston's WestEdge Development Promising to Fix the Area's Flooding Problem," *Post and Courier*, July 20, 2018, https://www.postandcourier.com /news/charlestons-westedge-development-promising-to-fix-the-areas-flooding-problems /article_75d2b94e-8937-11e8-b934-4f72d04ac229.html.

38 Dutch Dialogue Charleston final presentations, July 19, 2019.

39 Stephen Hobbs and Rickey Ciapha Dennis Jr., "How Flooding Intensifies the Charleston Region's Racial and Wealth Inequities," *Post and Courier*, September 22, 2020, https://www.postandcourier.com/rising-waters/how-flooding-intensifies-the -charleston-regions-racial-and-wealth-inequities/article_7a5f724c-afc6-11ea-b878 -2795af874a5b.html.

40 Rev. Rosalyn Brown, speaking as a guest on Mika Gadsden Apr. 1, 2022 livestream trwitch.tv broadcast.

41 Harve Jacobs, "New Police Substation Opening at Charleston Housing Complex with History of Crime," *Live5News*, Gray Television, August 4, 2020, https://www

.live5news.com/2020/08/04/new-police-substation-opening-housing-complex-with
-history-crime/.

42   Hearing Set to Begin in the Fight for Gadsden Creek," South Carolina Environmental
      Law Project, June 3, 2022, https://www.scelp.org/news/hearing-set-to-begin-in
      -the-fight-for-gadsden-creek.

43   City of Charleston, 2022 Approved Budget & Capital Improvement Plan, John
      J. Tecklenburg, Charleston: City of Charleston, 2021, https://www.charleston-sc.gov
      /DocumentCenter/View/31429/City-of-Charleston-Budget---2022.

44   Christine Sgarlata Chung, "Rising Tides and Rearranging Deckchairs: How Climate
      Change Is Reshaping Infrastructure Finance and Threatening to Sink Municipal
      Budgets," 32 *Envtl. Law Review* 165, 179 (2020).

45   Article X, Section 14, SC Constitution.

46   Rhiannon D'Angelo, "Charleston's Vikor Scientific Set to Transform Healthcare From
      New WestEdge Headquarters," *WestEdge News*, WestEdge, February 17, 2020, https
      ://www.westedgecharleston.com/news/charlestons-vikor-scientific-set-to-transform
      -healthcare-from-new-westedge-headquarters/.

47   Caroline Apartments, "Caroline Apartments: Luxury Apartments," Accessed July 7,
      2022, https://www.livecarolineapartments.com/caroline-charleston-sc/.

48   Mika Gadsden, Oct. 11, 2021.

49   Rev. Joseph Darby interview with author, November 16, 2020.

50   maps of proposed racial distribution, under Comprehensive Plan tab. From Morris
      Knowles, Inc., Report of the City Planning and Zoning Commission, upon a Program
      for the Development of a City Plan with Specific Studies of Certain Features Thereof,
      July 2, 1931.

51   Steve Warner, then the chief strategist for the Charleston Regional Development
      Alliance, interview with author, December 4, 2018 (only Tier 1 institution and net
      exporter of talent).

52   Mary Katherine Wildeman. "MUSC has Taken on About $1 Billion in Expansion
      Projects. Here's How They're Affording it." *Post and Courier*, February 15, 2019,
      https://www.postandcourier.com/business/real_estate/musc-has-taken-on-about-1
      -billion-in-expansion-projects-heres-how-theyre-affording-it/article_c5bcf490-3127
      -11e9-94f0-3bb6549d6756.htm.

53   Lauren Sausser and Chloe Johnson, "Roper Hospital Plans Historic Move Off
      Charleston Peninsula, Citing Flooding, Other Issues," *Post and Courier*, November 3,
      2021, https://www.postandcourier.com/news/roper-hospital-plans-historic-move-off
      -charleston-peninsula-citing-flooding-other-issues/article_784ad6ae-3c9c-11ec-93ee
      -77672af5ce24.html.

54   Mike Elk, "South Carolina Hospital Accused of Tarnishing Legacy of Coretta
      Scott King," *Guardian*, Guardian News & Media, January 15, 2018, https://www
      .theguardian.com/us-news/2018/jan/15/medical-university-south-carolina-musc
      -coretta-scott-king-strike.

55   Adam Parker, "MUSC Sorry for Past Discrimination," *Post and Courier*, August 13,
      2015, https://www.postandcourier.com/archives/musc-sorry-for-past-discrimination
      /article_2bc867e4-f899-5359-ad14-c619573e77a8.html.

56 Mike Elk, "South Carolina Hospital Accused of Tarnishing Legacy of Coretta Scott King,"
    Guardian, Guardian News & Media, January 15, 2018, https://www.theguardian.com
    /us-news/2018/jan/15/medical-university-south-carolina-musc-coretta-scott-king-strike.

57 Adam Parker, "CAJM Nehemiah Action Eyes Gadsden Creek, Housing Fund,
    Mobile Clinics, Student Discipline," *Post and Courier*, April 5, 2022, https://www
    .postandcourier.com/news/cajm-nehemiah-action-eyes-gadsden-creek-housing-fund
    -mobile-clinics-student-discipline/article_0bb458d2-b4fe-11ec-b7da-235eba7b38c0.html.

58 Brooks Brunson and J. Emory Parker, "Interview with Chloe Johnson and Tony
    Bartelme on Flooding," *Understand South Carolina*, Podcast audio, August 20, 2019,
    https://understand-sc.simplecast.com/episodes/flooding-da7n0za_.

59 Tony Bartelme and Glenn Smith, "Here's Your Future: A Tropical Storm Surge Sends
    Charleston an Urgent Message," *Groundswell Charleston*, September 17, 2017,
    http://groundswellcharleston.org/news/heres-your-future-a-tropical-storm-surge
    -sends-charleston-an-urgent-message/.

60 Daniel Chang and Lauren Sausser, "Hurricane Ian shows that coastal hospitals aren't
    ready for climate change," *Post and Courier*, Oct. 23, 2022 ("Flooding, even after heavy
    rain and high tide, is one reason Roper St. Francis Healthcare—one of three systems in
    Charleston's downtown medical district—announced plans to eventually move Roper
    Hospital off the Charleston peninsula after operating there for more than 150 years.");
    Tony Bartelme and Glenn Smith, "Here's Your Future: A Tropical Storm Surge Sends
    Charleston an Urgent Message," *Groundswell Charleston*, September 17, 2017, http
    ://groundswellcharleston.org/news/heres-your-future-a-tropical-storm-surge-sends
    -charleston-an-urgent-message/.

61 Lauren Sausser, "Roper Hospital Plans Historic Move Off Charleston Peninsula,
    Citing Flooding, Other Issues," *Post and Courier*, November 3, 2021, https://www
    .postandcourier.com/news/roper-hospital-plans-historic-move-off-charleston
    -peninsula-citing-flooding-other-issues/article_784ad6ae-3c9c-11ec-93ee
    -77672af5ce24.html.

62 Lauren Sausser, "Roper Hospital Plans Historic Move Off Charleston Peninsula,
    Citing Flooding, Other Issues," *Post and Courier*, November 3, 2021, https://www
    .postandcourier.com/news/roper-hospital-plans-historic-move-off-charleston
    -peninsula-citing-flooding-other-issues/article_784ad6ae-3c9c-11ec-93ee
    -77672af5ce24.html.

63 Chloe Johnson and Mary Katherine Wildeman, "Plagued by some of Charleston's
    Worst Flooding, Hospitals in Charleston's Medical District Plan to Stay," *Post and
    Courier*, September 25, 2020, https://www.postandcourier.com/rising-waters/plagued
    -by-some-of-charlestons-worst-flooding-hospitals-in-medical-district-plan-to-stay
    /article_c5c68a86-ac0b-11ea-82c0-a786e28291d3.html.

64 "Calhoun West/Beaufain Drainage Improvement Project," Charleston SC, Accessed
    July 7, 2022, https://www.charleston-sc.gov/1676/Calhoun-West-Drainage
    -Improvement-Projec ("The Calhoun West/Beaufain basin contains the Medical
    University of South Carolina (MUSC), the College of Charleston, Roper Hospital,
    and many businesses and residences that are impacted by frequent flooding. Flooding
    of streets poses many problems including restricting access to hospitals, diverting

traffic around accumulated water, and damage to vehicles parked along flooded streets. Calhoun Street is one of the principal east/west vehicular corridors through the City. It also has a significant amount of pedestrian traffic due to the locations of MUSC, Roper Hospital, and the College of Charleston. Economic impacts, both direct and indirect, may be significant. The City of Charleston is currently conducting a study for improving drainage in the Calhoun West/Beaufain drainage basin and alleviating many of the existing drainage problems. Ultimately, the project will increase the capacity of the stormwater collection and conveyance system as well as provide means to convey stormwater directly into the Ashley River during storms and tidal events via pumping systems." . . . Based on the 1984 Master Drainage Plan (MDP), this approximately 300+ acre basin bounded by King Street, Cannon Street, and Beaufain Street has only one primary outfall to the Ashley River, a four-foot wide box culvert under Calhoun Street.

65 Emma Whalen, "Tunnel Trouble: Charleston's Spring-Fishburne Drainage Project is Years Behind, $44 million Over Budget," *Post and Courier*, July 8, 2022, https://www .postandcourier.com/tunnel-trouble/charlestons-spring-fishburne-drainage-project-is -years-behind-44m-over-budget/article_31143344-f32a-11ec-b39f-03e1f9f6bf8c.html.

66 Ray Llerena, "Charleston receives updates on Calhoun West Drainage project for peninsula flooding," *Live5News*, April 11, 2022.

67 Ray Llerena, "Charleston receives updates on Calhoun West Drainage project for peninsula flooding," *Live5News*, April 11, 2022.

68 Jordan Cioppa interview with Mike Seekings, *Counton2News*, WCBD, November 6, 2021.

69 Steven Slabbers interview with author, July 4, 2019.

9. Off the Peninsula, Quinetha Frasier & Charlton Singleton

1   "Fast Facts 2022," City of Charleston, Accessed June 24, 2022, www.charleston-sc .gov/DocumentCenter/View/31238/FAST-FACTS-2022.

2   "Charles Towne Landing: State Historic Site," South Carolina Parks, South Carolina Department of Parks, Recreation & Tourism, Accessed July 10, 2022, https ://southcarolinaparks.com/charles-towne-landing.

3   Dr. Norman Levine interview with author, Ocobert 9, 2018.

4   "Church Creek Drainage Basin," Charleston, SC, Accessed July 10, 2022, https ://www.charleston-sc.gov/2636/Church-Creek-Drainage-Basin.

5   Dover, Kohl & Partners, Plan West Ashley, Charleston: Dover, Kohl & Partners, December 28, 2017, https://static1.squarespace.com/static/5612e13ae4b0c 37386e86b7e/t/5b7b00b18a922da69258fe70/1534787780354/PLAN+WEST+ASHL EY+THE+FULL+REPORT.pdf.

6   Nic Butler, "Squeezing Charleston Neck, From 1783 to the Present," Charleston County Public Library, August 31, 2018, https://www.ccpl.org/charleston-time -machine/squeezing-charleston-neck-1783-present.

7   Dover, Kohl & Partners, Plan West Ashley, Charleston: Dover, Kohl & Partners, December 28, 2017, https://static1.squarespace.com/static/5612e13ae

4b0c37386e86b7e/t/5b7b00b18a922da69258fe70/1534787780354/PLAN+WEST+AS
HLEY+THE+FULL+REPORT.pdf.

8   Abigail Darlington, "Charleston Allows More Floodplain Developments Than Other
     Coastal Cities," *Post and Courier*, May 29, 2018, https://www.postandcourier.com
     /news/charleston-allows-more-floodplain-developments-than-other-coastal-cities
     /article_0d73aa5a-57a7-11e8-9c1d-13724320a1b3.html.

9   Nic Butler, "Parishes, Districts, and Counties in Early South Carolina," Charleston
     County Public Library, June 4, 2021, https://www.ccpl.org/charleston-time-machine
     /parishes-districts-and-counties-early-south-carolina.

10   Editorial Staff, "Editorial: Charleston Should Gobble up West Ashley Doughnut
     Holes, All of Them," *Post and Courier*, November 27, 2021, https://www.postand
     courier.com/opinion/editorials/editorial-charleston-should-gobble-up-west-ashley
     -doughnut-holes-all-of-them/article_72e36144-4c9c-11ec-a315-f7c478b965b3.html.

11   "Church Creek Drainage Basin," Charleston, SC, Accessed July 10, 2022, https
     ://www.charleston-sc.gov/2636/Church-Creek-Drainage-Basin.

12   Charleston's 34-year-old list of drainage projects not quite half done after $239 million,
     Sept 9, 2017.

13   Robert Behre and Abigail Darlington, "Charleston's 34-year-old List of Drainage
     Projects Not Quite Half Done After $239 Million," *Post and Courier*, Updated
     September 9, 2017, www.postandcourier.com/news/charlestons-34-year-old-list-of
     -drainage-projects-not-quite-half-done-after-239-million/article_77a09ea0-9278
     -11e7-aba2-6f65d7bc0420.html; Norman Levine interview with author, July 26, 2019.

14   Abigail Darlington, "Charleston's Use of Federal Grants to Raze Flood-Prone
     Properties Part of a National Trend," *Post and Courier*, October 25, 2017, https://www
     .postandcourier.com/news/charlestons-use-of-federal-grants-to-raze-flood-prone
     -properties-part-of-a-national-trend/article_46ff6332-b995-11e7-988e-bfc5a27300a2.html.

15   Johns Island Overview, governing mag.

16   Charleston's use of federal grants to raze flood-prone properties part of a national
     trend, Oct 25, 2017; Charleston begins mass demolition of 32 frequently flooded West
     Ashley townhomes, Jul. 10, 2019. Oct 24, 2017: CHARLESTON, S.C. (WCIV)—
     The City of Charleston has been approved for a multimillion dollar FEMA grant to
     buy and demolish 35 town homes in a flood plagued West Ashley community.

     The homes are located in the Bridgepointe Town Homes community within
     Shadowmoss Plantation inside what city leaders says is a Special Flood Hazard Area.
     There have been at least four major flooding events in the Bridgepointe community in
     the last two years.

     City leaders proposed the buyout to FEMA in 2015 following the thousand year
     flood and smaller flooding events in years prior.

     The FEMA grant will cover 75 percent of the properties' appraised value, which
     is about $2.4 million of the project's $3.2 million estimated purchasing and demolition
     costs.

     Charleston City Councilman Dean Riegel says the state will be picking up the
     remaining 25 percent of the tab, which is roughly $817,000.

Afterward, the properties will be returned to green space, and the city will maintain ownership and https://abcnews4.com/archive/shadowmossresidentshopefemawillbuyout floodedhomeletthemmove.

17 Abigail Darlington, "Development About to Restart in One of Charleston's Most Flood-Prone Regions," *Post and Courier*, Sept. 6, 2018 (online comment by Don Bartlett).

18 Mikaela Porter, "Charleston Begins Mass Demolition of 32 Frequently Flooded West Ashley Townhomes," *Post and Courier*, July 10, 2019, https://www.postandcourier.com /news/charleston-begins-mass-demolition-of-32-frequently-flooded-west-ashley -townhomes/article_9378654e-a28a-11e9-9cdf-4b2aa9211e78.html.

19 Statement of Robbert de Kooning, Dutch Dialogue final presentations, July 19, 2019.

20 Mika Gadsden twitch.tv episode, July 27, 2022, https://www.twitch.tv/videos /1544214950.

21 Dr. Norman Levine interview with author, October 9, 2018.

22 Dr. Norman Levine interview with author, October 9, 2018.

23 Abigail Darlington, "Charleston Has Just Months to Begin Untangling a Decades-Old Fiasco on James Island," *Post and Courier*, May 19, 2017, https://www.postandcourier .com/news/charleston-has-just-months-to-begin-untangling-a-decades-old-fiasco-on -james-island/article_da236362-35b9-11e7-8519-a36005d08b14.html.

24 Norman Levine interview with author, October 9, 2018.

25 Brigitte Surette, "James Island and Its Neighborhoods: The Best of Everything With a Down-to-Earth Vibe," *Post and Courier*, September 19, 2020, https://www.postand courier.com/business/james-island-and-its-neighborhoods-the-best-of-everything -with-a-down-to-earth-vibe/article_9ff18496-f68e-11ea-b76a-13613b7d647d.html.

26 John Tibbetts interview with author, May 11, 2022.

27 Steve Bailey, "How a James Island Neighborhood Was Destined to Flood," *Post and Courier*, April 28, 2018, https://www.postandcourier.com/opinion/commentary/how -a-james-island-neighborhood-was-destined-to-flood/article_bd3b74bc-47b3-11e8 -aa19-e7d4831c6408.html; Abigail Darlington, "Residents Asking Feds to Investigate Charleston for Failure to Protect Against Flood Risks," *Post and Courier*, July 23, 2018, https://www.postandcourier.com/news/residents-asking-feds-to-investigate -charleston-for-failure-to-protect-against-flood-risks/article_1f8b1786-8e80-11e8 -bb5e-5f4152cd6a01.html.

28 Steve Bailey, "How a James Island Neighborhood Was Destined to Flood," *Post and Courier*, April 28, 2018, https://www.postandcourier.com/opinion/commentary/how-a -james-island-neighborhood-was-destined-to-flood/article_bd3b74bc-47b3-11e8 -aa19-e7d4831c6408.html; Abigail Darlington, "While Charleston Works on Clearing Up FEMA's Concerns, One Neighborhood Left in Limbo," *Post and Courier*, January 30, 2019, https://www.postandcourier.com/news/while-charleston-works-on-clearing -up-femas-concerns-one-neighborhood-left-in-limbo/article_40d7c02c-2329-11e9 -bb79-6f27f3b8fb82.html.

29 About two years later, as of Aug. 30, 2021, this house was under contract for 185K. The ad on Zillow read: "Hard to find a home like this on James Island! Charming 3 bedroom/1 bath home. Full privacy fence with large shed out back. Good size deck. Bright, open and airy."

30 Steve Bailey, "How a James Island Neighborhood Was Destined to Flood," *Post and Courier*,
    April 28, 2018, https://www.postandcourier.com/opinion/commentary/how-a-james-island
    -neighborhood-was-destined-to-flood/article_bd3b74bc-47b3-11e8-aa19-e7d4831c6408
    .html; Abigail Darlington, "While Charleston Works on Clearing Up FEMA's Concerns,
    One Neighborhood Left in Limbo," *Post and Courier*, January 30, 2019, https://www
    .postandcourier.com/news/while-charleston-works-on-clearing-up-femas-concerns-one
    -neighborhood-left-in-limbo/article_40d7c02c-2329-11e9-bb79-6f27f3b8fb82.html.

31 Abigail Darlington, "Charleston Allows More Floodplain Developments Than Other
    Coastal Cities," *Post and Courier*, May 29, 2018, https://www.postandcourier.com
    /news/charleston-allows-more-floodplain-developments-than-other-coastal-cities
    /article_0d73aa5a-57a7-11e8-9c1d-13724320a1b3.html.

32 Robert Behre, "Behre: Charleston Tackles a Tricky Task: Making Development
    Improve Drainage," August 22, 2020, *Post and Courier*, https://www.postandcourier
    .com/opinion/commentary/behre-charleston-tackles-a-tricky-task-making-development
    -improve-drainage/article_b35c4bca-e279-11ea-ad75-2778ec61f17f.htm.

33 Adam Parker, "Charleston, Johns Island Undergoing Huge Demographic Shift Among
    Blacks, Whites," *Post and Courier*, May 28, 2021, https://www.postandcourier.com
    /news/local_state_news/charleston-johns-island-undergoing-huge-demographic-shift
    -among-blacks-whites/article_265e2680-bf2d-11eb-b772-0bb9e5a926b0.html.

34 Lizzie Presser, "The Reels Brothers Spent Eight Years in Jail for Refusing to Leave It,"
    ProPublica and *The New Yorker*, July 15, 2019, https://features.propublica.org
    /black-land-loss/heirs-property-rights-why-black-families-lose-land-south/.

35 Adam Parker, "Charleston, Johns Island Undergoing Huge Demographic Shift Among
    Blacks, Whites," *Post and Courier*, May 28, 2021, https://www.postandcourier.com
    /news/local_state_news/charleston-johns-island-undergoing-huge-demographic-shift
    -among-blacks-whites/article_265e2680-bf2d-11eb-b772-0bb9e5a926b0.html.

36 Andrew Brown, "Charleston Wants Special Tax on New Development on Johns Island to
    Fund Infrastructure," *Post and Courier*, May 27, 2021, https://www.postandcourier.com
    /business/real_estate/charleston-wants-special-taxes-on-new-development-on-johns
    -island-to-fund-infrastructure/article_fe7194d8-be35-11eb-81a8-07d701dc3202.html.

37 Norman Levine interview with author, October 9, 2018.

38 New South Associates, Charleston County Historic Resources Survey Update
    (Charleston: New South Associates, 2016), 26-27.

39 Quinetha Frasier interview with author, Sept. 8, 2020.

40 Quinetha Frasier interview with author, Sept. 8, 2020.

41 See https://elevation.maplogs.com/poi/adams_run_sc_usa.225941.html.

42 SC Opportunity Zone, Accessed July 11, 2022, https://scopportunityzone.com/.

43 Charleston County, Parkers Ferry Community Overlay Zoning District, Charleston:
    Charleston County, 2017, 10.

44 Realtor.com, "5143 Timber Race Course," Accessed July 11, 2022, https://www.realtor
    .com/realestateandhomes-detail/5143-Timber-Race-Crse_Hollywood_SC_29449
    _M55516-20817.

45 New South Associates, Charleston County Historic Resources Survey Update (Charleston:
    New South Associates, 2016), 64.

46   Drew Tripp and WCIV Staff, "Charleston's Ranky Tanky Wins Grammy for Best
     Regional Album in American Roots Music," *ABC News 4*, Sinclair Broadcast
     Group, January 26, 2020, https://abcnews4.com/news/local/charleston
     -ranky-tanky-grammy-2020-best-regional-album-in-american-roots-music.
47   South Carolina Coastal Conservation League, "Shape the Future—Comprehensive
     Plan Engagement Session," (Session held over Zoom, October 29, 2020).

10. Muddling Through and Managed Retreat

1   Statement of Secretary of Commerce Gina Raimondo, Department of Commerce press
     briefing, June 29, 2022.
2   Statement of White House Deputy National Climate Advisor Ali Zaidi, Department
     of Commerce press briefing, June 29, 2022.
3   This is a simplification. The National Ocean Service calculates the average of the
     lowest low tides in Charleston across a long period of time (at the moment, 1983-
     2001), calls that average Mean Low Lower Water (or MLLW), and then labels high
     tides according to how much higher they are than that MLLW value. So, for example,
     on July 6, 2022, the two high tides were 5.05 feet at 1:01 A.M. and 4.81 feet at 1:49
     P.M.—about five and four feet, respectively, above MLLW. Any tide in Charleston
     Harbor that is 7 feet or higher above MLLW is called a "minor" flood and is tracked
     in the National Weather Service's coastal flood event database. "Minor" floods in
     Charleston trigger alerts by the National Weather Service, and cause flooding around
     the peninsula (Lockwood Drive, Wentworth and Barre, Fishburne and Hagood,
     and Morrison Drive). As tides approach 7.5 ft MLLW, more roads can become
     impassable and closed. Other impacts of flooding are felt near area beaches including
     Isle of Palms, Sullivan's Island, Folly Beach, Kiawah Island, and Edisto Island. For
     our purposes, anything over 7 feet is a flood. In 2019, there were 89 "minor" floods in
     Charleston. "Major" coastal flooding in Charleston is 8 feet: "Widespread flooding
     occurs in Downtown Charleston with numerous roads flooded and impassable and
     some impact to structures." There were seven "major" floods in Charleston in 2019 (the
     most per year since records began in 1921), and four in 2021—all in October, which
     was a record month since 1921. As water levels rise, NOAA is saying that there will
     be a category shift by 2050: currently "moderate" floods (26 in 2019, 22 in 2020, 8 in
     2021) will be happening as often as "minor" floods do now (89, 68, 46 in 2019, 2020,
     and 2021 respectively).
          Somewhat confusingly, NOAA also provides "flood" numbers for localities
     around the country "based on a certain height, which is normalized for apples to
     apples comparisons around the country," (per William Sweet on August 2, 2022), and
     says that Charleston experiences "flooding" when water is 0.57m, or 1.9 feet, above
     MHHW—the average of the highest high tides over the same period.
          In Charleston, MHHW is 5.6 feet above MLLW, see https://tidesandcurrents
     .noaa.gov/datums.html?id=8665530. This means that NOAA doesn't count a "flood" in
     Charleston unless it is 7.5 feet—the "moderate" marker used by the National Weather
     Service, which is higher than the 7 foot "minor" marker that triggers NWS alerts and
     deep concern in Charleston.

That's why NOAA's annual "flood" numbers for Charleston (7 in 2021, predicted 5-9 in 2022) are so much lower than the number of floods that Charlestonians are actually experiencing (46 in 2021). But it also means that NOAA's prediction of 70-90 "floods" in Charleston by 2050 is truly alarming. https://tidesandcurrents.noaa.gov /HighTideFlooding_AnnualOutlook.html.

4   In 2022, *Travel + Leisure* named Charleston the No. 1 travel destination in the U.S. for the tenth year in a row. Condé Nast Traveler had already named Charleston the best city to visit in the country for ten years running, beginning in 2010—Aspen broke the city's streak in 2021. Charleston has been named a World's Best Hall of Fame honoree by *Travel + Leisure*. Warren Wise, "Charleston named No. 1 city in US for 10th straight year by *Travel + Leisure* magazine," *Post and Courier*, July 12, 2022.

5   Emma Whalen, "King Tides, rain bring more flooding threats as Charleston seeks broader mitigation strategy," *Post and Courier*, July 11, 2022.

6   "Coastal Flood Event Database," National Weather Service, Accessed June 24, 2022, www.weather.gov/chs/coastalflood.

7   Jacey Fortin, "How the Moon 'Wobble' Affects Rising Tides," *New York Times*, the New York Times Company, July 16, 2021, https://www.nytimes.com/2021/07/16 /science/moon-wobble-rising-tide-sea-level.html.

8   La Niña "affects prevailing winds on the East Coast" which bring storm tracks more inland, according to Dr. William Sweet of NOAA. Dr. William Sweet, "NOAA State of High Tide Flooding and Outlook," press conference, August 2, 2022.

9   Dr. William Sweet, "NOAA State of High Tide Flooding and Outlook," press conference, August 2, 2022.

10   The National Oceanic and Atmospheric Administration (NOAA) recently issued new estimates of future sea level rise concluding that the rate of sea level rise along the American coasts is accelerating and is likely to rise as much over the next 30 years (i.e., about 1.3 feet by 2050 in the "Intermediate" scenario) as it has over the last 100 years. Sea level rise averaging as high as 1.7 feet around the coastline is possible over this period and could reach as high as 2.2 feet in some places. Charleston will likely be in the higher bands of sea-level rise. NOAA, "Global and Regional Sea Level Rise Scenarios for the United States," February 2022, https://aambpublicoceanservice.blob.core.windows.net /oceanserviceprod/hazards/sealevelrise/2.0-Future-Mean-Sea-Level.pdf.

11   Christopher Flavelle, "New Data Shows an 'Extraordinary' Rise in U.S. Coastal Flooding," *New York Times*, the New York Times Company, July 14, 2020, https ://www.nytimes.com/2020/07/14/climate/coastal-flooding-noaa.html.

12   Norman Levine interview with author, Nov. 15, 2021.

13   Norman Levine interview with author, Nov. 15, 2021.

14   Rolf Schuttenhelm, "Reconstruction of a flood in Limburg: A climate disaster can strike anywhere," NU.nl, July 14, 2022, https://www.nu.nl/nu-klimaat/6211837 /reconstructie-watersnood-in-limburg-een-klimaatramp-kan-overal-toeslaan.html.

15   John Ramsey, "SC Summers Keep Getting Longer and Hotter, Especially At Night," *Post and Courier*, July 26, 2022.

16   Eric P. Schwartz, Elizabeth Ferris, Abraham Lustgarten, Kanta K. Rigaud, "The Next Great Wave: Human Migration and Climate Change," (Silberstein Family

Annual Lecture on Refugee and Migration Policy delivered on Zoom, Council on Foreign Relations, June 13, 2022, https://www.cfr.org/event/next-great-wave-human -migration-and-climate-change).

17   Norman Levine interview with author, Nov. 15, 2021.

18   Norman Levine interview with author, Nov. 15, 2021.

19   John C. Weicher, "The Distribution of Wealth in America Since 2016," Research Institute for Housing America, Dec. 2021.

20   Norm Levine, Jul. 21, 2021.

21   Bob Perry interview with author, October 12, 2018.

22   Norman Levine interview with author, November 15, 2021.

23   Editorial Staff, "Editorial: Finally, SC Moves to Protect Homebuyers," *Post and Courier*, December 11, 2019, https://www.postandcourier.com/opinion/editorials/editorial-finally -sc-moves-to-protect-homebuyers/article_baf81372-1c50-11ea-ae72-5f1d8b2a0494.html.

24   John Tibbetts interview with author, May 11, 2022.

25   City of Charleston Water Lab meeting, Sept. 23, 2020. The flooding in New York City that drowned people living in Queens basements during the fall of 2021 was caused by the remnants of Hurricane Ida, and was classified by experts as a 500-year flood. Superstorm Sandy was also a 500-year event, just nine years before. Southeast Texas saw 500-year floods for five straight years beginning in 2015.

26   Elizabeth Rush, "I Would Have Never Bought This Home if I Knew It Flooded," *New York Times*, April 11, 2022.

27   City of Charleston Water Lab meeting, Sept. 23, 2020.

28   City of Charleston Water Lab meeting, Sept. 23, 2020. In September 2020, Dale Morris was working with landscape architects Waggoner & Ball on an engagement with the city that was an outgrowth of their 2019 Dutch Dialogues® process in Charleston. In September 2021, Dale Morris joined the City of Charleston staff as the city's Chief Resilience Officer. Sarah Haselhorst, "Rising seas are trouble for Charleston's booming community. This method may prevent disaster," *The State*, August 10, 2022, https://www.thestate.com/news/state/south-carolina/article 264170451.html. Earlier in his career, Morris worked for the Netherlands Embassy, ending his time there in 2018 as senior economist and director of the embassy's Dutch Government's Water Management and Adaptation work in the U.S.

29   Water Lab question time with Dale Morris, Sept. 23, 2020.

30   GZA GeoEnvironmental, Inc., "Town of East Hampton Coastal Assessment and Resiliency Plan," April 2022, at i & 28.

31   "Global Change Research Needs and Opportunities for 2022-2031." Washington, DC: The National Academies Press. https://doi.org/10.17226/26055 (Box 4.1, "Integrating Case: Managed Retreat for Coastal Communities").

32   "Global Change Research Needs and Opportunities for 2022-2031." Washington, DC: The National Academies Press. https://doi.org/10.17226/26055 (Box 4.1, "Integrating Case: Managed Retreat for Coastal Communities").

33   CFR meeting, Alice Hill, Sept. 13, 2021.

34   CFR meeting, Richard Haass, Katherine Mach, Arun Majumdar, Alice Hill, Oct. 14, 2021. The Coastal Flood Resilience Project, a coalition of nonprofit

organizations working for stronger programs to prepare for coastal storm flooding and rising sea level in the US, has been active in pressing for a national adaptation plan and federal leadership in this crucial area. See https://www.cfrp.info.

35 Staff Reports, "Skepticism and Hope for Equity Impacts of Charleston 10-Year Plan," *Charleston City Paper*, September 8, 2020, https://charlestoncitypaper.com /skepticism-and-hope-for-equity-impacts-of-charleston-10-year-plan/.

36 Michelle Mapp interview with author, Sept. 27, 2019.

37 Brigit Katz, "Charleston, South Carolina, Formally Apologizes for Its Role in the Slave Trade," *Smithsonian Magazine*, June 20, 2018, https://www.smithsonianmag .com/smart-news/charleston-formally-apologizes-its-role-slave-trade-180969415.

38 Andy Shaun and Seanna Adcox, "Calhoun Statue Not Protected by SC Monument Law Deemed Constitutional by State AG," *Post and Courier*, June 25, 2020, https ://www.postandcourier.com/politics/calhoun-statue-not-protected-by-sc-monument -law-deemed-constitutional-by-state-ag/article_94a836f0-b72a-11ea-8d9d-6b4c11 8135de.html.

39 Emma Whalen, "Charleston race conciliation commission buckling under weight of compromise," *Post and Courier*, Jan. 30, 2022.

40 Stephen Hobbs, "New Charleston commission focused on racial equity begins work amid hope, suspicion," *Post and Courier*, July 17, 2022.

41 Emma Whalen, "Charleston Puts up Plaque Where Slaves Were Beaten, Punished," *Post and Courier*, July 29, 2022.

42 Mayor Tecklenburg interview with author, May 3, 2021.

43 Mike Seekings interview with author, November 17, 2021.

44 Queen Quet interview with author, July 26, 2018.

45 Michelle Mapp interview with author, October 10, 2018.

46 Michelle Mapp interview with author, October 10, 2018.

47 Michelle Mapp, Sept. 27, 2019.

48 Population Data," Charleston County Development, Charleston County Economic Development, Accessed July 13, 2022, https://www.charlestoncountydevelopment.org /data-center/population-data/.

49 Diane Knich, "Gov. Henry McMaster Replaces Vince Graham as Chair of S.C. Infrastructure Bank Board," *Post and Courier*, March 1, 2017, https://www.postand courier.com/news/gov-henry-mcmaster-replaces-vince-graham-as-chair-of-s -c-infrastructure-bank-board/article_98e03f30-fea3-11e6-bce6-4f6328852aa7.html.

50 Mika Gadsden Confirms She Plans to Run for Mayor of Charleston," *Holy City Sinner*, May 28, 2022.

51 Mika Gadsden broadcast, July 12, 2022; Emma Whalen, "Charleston mayoral candidates report first fundraising numbers for 2023 election," *Post and Courier*, July 14, 2022.

52 "The Solar Village," Soldiers Grove, Accessed July 13, 2022, http://soldiersgrove.com /history/the-solar-village-2/.

53 Rachel Hellman, "A Midwestern Town Moved Uphill to Survive the Elements. Can Others Do the Same?" *Guardian*, Guardian News & Media, August 21, 2021, https://www.theguardian.com/us-news/2021/aug/21/valmeyer-illinois-town-moved -uphill-escape-flooding.

54 "Some Areas are No Longer Inhabitable," *Tagesschau*, July 13, 2022, https://www
.tagesschau.de/inland/gesellschaft/klimawandel-deutschland-unbewohnbar-101.html.

55 Rutger Bregman, "A Letter to All Dutch People: Climate Change Threatens the
Survival of Our Country," January 28, 2020 (quoting seven identified Dutch scientists:
"I was amazed at how candidly they speak about the scenario in which we have to give
up large parts of the Netherlands.")

56 Rutger Bregman letter, 28 January 2020.

57 Prof. Simon Richter interview with author, July 12, 2022.

58 Prof. Simon Richter interview with author, July 12, 2022.

59 Prof. Simon Richter interview with author, July 12, 2022.

60 Marjolijn Haasnoot, "Climate Adaptation, but how?" *Leeuwarder Courant*, June 5,
2021, https://lc.nl/friesland/Klimaatadaptatie-maar-hoe-26866606.html.

61 Prof. Simon Richter interview with author, July 12, 2022.

62 Arjen Schreuder, "Climate researcher: 'Now think about retreating if sea levels rise,"
NRC.NL, June 17, 2021, https://www.nrc.nl/nieuws/2021/06/17/denk-erover-na
-wegwezen-de-zeespiegel-stijgt-a4047783?t=1655993611.7.

63 City Plan meeting, Peninsula, August 25, 2020.

64 Mikaela Porter, "Flooding, Affordable Housing a Focus For Charleston's 10-Year Plan,
Public Meetings Start Thursday," *Post and Courier*, August 19, 2020, https://www
.postandcourier.com/news/flooding-affordable-housing-a-focus-for-charlestons
-10-year-plan-public-meetings-start-thursday/article_b6e98bb6-e177-11ea-bf18
-df0d642f458c.html.

65 Eric Jackson interview with author, November 13, 2020.

66 Jacob Lindsey interview with author, November 16, 2021.

67 February 17, 2022 City Council workshop (Dale Morris: "I've said very clearly, phase
one of PED is going to show us the flexibility that the Corps of Engineers can provide
to us because we will go from Joe Riley Stadium, the bottom of the Citadel, across
Joe Riley, down to the Coast Guard station.

There we have—that creek in front of Joe Riley Stadium. We have Brittlebank
Park, which is soft, some nature-based features, a softer type of surge structure
there. Come—there is the complex medical district which needs the highest level
of protection, the strongest level, all redundancy possible there, because we need to
protect that. Coming down the Lockwood Corridor to help Harleston Village and
South of Broad communities. So we're going to see there, in that process, how creative
we can be and how flexible the Corps of Engineers is going to be." If PED for Phase
One starts in 2023, construction for Phase One will begin in 2027.)

68 Mike Seekings comment at City Council meeting, February 2022.

69 Robinson Design Engineers Op-Ed.

70 Wes Wilson, Feb. 2022 City Council workshop: "So we looked at a seven foot wall,
a nine foot wall, and a 12 foot wall. And anything above a 12, we realized we had
to make some modifications to bridges, I-26. And at that point we kind of just
quantitatively ruled it out. So we did a quantitative assessment on the seven, nine,
and twelve, and to maximize our net benefits, which is our national economic and
development plan, we selected the 12 foot wall. The incremental benefits go up

drastically, the higher wall you go, the elevation. And the costs are just a small fraction of that because a lot of the costs have to do with the mobilization, getting the contractor on site, and then the piles in the ground." Dale Morris conceded that the wall is likely too short in the long run: "And again, that 12 foot is probably okay in year one to 10 of the structure's surge life. But because we don't know how quickly sea levels are rising, it's just a guess right now. We're probably going to need that resilience, that extra resiliency for more friction in the out years, in year 40. So in 2070 or 2080."

71   Wes Wilson slide: "Justification for height of wall," Feb. 18, 2021.

72   Jacob Lindsey interview with author, November 16, 2021.

73   John Ramsey, "As Charleston sea wall plan heads through Congress, local doubts linger," *Post and Courier*, July 16, 2022, https://www.postandcourier.com/environment /as-charleston-sea-wall-plan-heads-through-congress-local-doubts-linger/article _529ea92c-fca3-11ec-a327-a3ecfc994d25.html.

74   Dale Morris, Feb. 18, 2021: "Yeah. I mean, it . . . as valuable as all of our homes are, they [laughs] don't touch the value of a big corporation or whatever, or of a big port structure or of historical facilities, right? So the Corps of Engineers, isn't involved in protecting, whatever, neighborhoods. Wagener Terrace might be an exception, right, because of its integration with the rest of the peninsula. The Corps of Engineers is really protecting national economic assets. Mayor: Yeah. Hospitals, colleges, universities, right."

75   Mark Wilbert, Apr. 29, 2020.

76   Wilbert Apr. 29: "Should we be subject to a major storm here in Charleston, particularly on the peninsula and it was time to rebuild. It would be important to have this study all completed and signed. It would be very quick at that point, historically to go ahead and get it through for quick approval and maybe have it done after a storm."

      Winslow Hastie talking about Dale: "But unfortunately my dear friend Dale Morris, who I do believe is also on this webinar. He forbadingly has said, a lot of times, unfortunately you don't start . . . You don't see a penny until you get another big storm and then the flood gates open. And let's hope that doesn't have to happen. But a lot of times that is sort of where you get people's attention."

      Andy Sternad: "This means that if a study is approved and it's sitting on the shelf, ready to be funded at the federal level and a major disaster strikes, that plan may suddenly happen and be federally funded all at once, rather than over this five, eight, 10 year cycle that is laid out right now. It means it's especially more important to get the factors right in the plan at every stage, just in case."

77   Dale Morris, Feb. 2022: "At some point that wall height will be insufficient. Okay. You are anticipat[ing] a 12 foot surge and you get a 13 foot surge. Irma was 9.9 feet. Hugo was 10 feet. So this wall, this structure would protect against that. Wonderful. What happens if you get a 14 foot surge? Well, two foot coming over the top or one foot coming over the top of the water—coming over the top of the wall. That's something. And then if you normally have overland drainage for gravity, that wall has now created a bathtub. So you're impounding water. The Army Corps of Engineers has to put pumps in there to mitigate those things, to mitigate that extra flooding. Okay. So those pumps now become an important resilience feature for us that if we can link that into the current drainage

system, then we have additional resiliency. So, in the Army Corps version of the world, this is dealing with surge, but if we can create those connections—and this is something that Matt and I and others have talked about, and some other good engineers—if we can do that, then we are going to help to manage, or create some resiliency for our system."

78   Alice Hill CFR lecture, September 13, 2021.

79   Steve Hallo, "NFIP Senior Exec Talks Hurricane, Flood Response," *Property Casualty 360*, ALM Global, September 7, 2021, https://www.propertycasualty360 .com/2021/09/07/fema-exec-talks-hurricane-flood-response/?slre turn=20220614184135.

80   Kelly McGee, A Place Worth Protecting: Rethinking Cost-Benefit Analysis under FEMA's Flood-Mitigation Programs, 88 U. CHI. L. REV. 1925, 1941 (2021).

81   Kelly McGee, "A Place Worth Protecting: Rethinking Cost-Benefit Analysis Under FEMA's Flood-Mitigation Programs," *University of Chicago Law Review* 88, no. 8 (2021): 1925–70.

82   https://www.usace.army.mil/Media/News-Releases/News-Release-Article-View /Article/2476138/us-army-corps-of-engineers-releases-work-plan-for-fiscal-2021-civil -works-appro/.

83   Rob_Moore_NRDC_final.

84   NRDC, "Buyer Beware: In 21 States Home Buyers Don't Have to Be Informed About Past Flood Damages," August 16, 2018, https://www.nrdc.org/media/2018/180816-0.

85   First Street Foundation. The First National Flood Risk Assessment: Defining America's Growing Risk. PDF file. 2020. https://assets.firststreet.org/uploads /2020/06/first_street_foundation__first_national_flood_risk_assessment.pdf.

86   Blackrock. Also https://riskcenter.wharton.upenn.edu/lab-notes/riskratingburt/.

87   *America Adapts* podcast, June 6, 2022.

88   "Everything you wanted to know about Managed Retreat but were afraid to ask (with Dr. AR Siders), *America Adapts* podcast, November 11, 2019, https://www .americaadapts.org/episodes/everything-you-wanted-to-know-about-managed-retreat -but-were-afraid-to-ask-with-dr-ar-siders?rq=siders.

89   Devin Lea and Sarah Pralle, "To Appeal and Amend: Changes to Recently Updated Flood Insurance Rate Maps," *Risk, Hazards & Crisis in Public Policy* 13, no. 1 (2022): 28–47, https://doi.org/10.1002/rhc3.12222; Kate Duguid and Ally Levine, "RPT-From New York to Houston, Flood Risk For Real Estate Hubs Ramps Up," Reuters, June 29, 2020, https://www.reuters.com/article/usa-floods-real-estate-idINL1N2E60IU.

90   A Special Flood Hazard Area is an area of land that would be inundated by a "flood" having a 1% or greater probability of occurring in any given year (i.e. "base flood" or "100-year flood"). On average, there is a 26% probability of experiencing a 100-year flood during a 30-year mortgage. That is nearly 30 times the probability of a fire loss over the period. To address flood risk for most residential and smaller commercial loans and satisfy the mandatory insurance requirement, borrowers and banks have historically relied on the NFIP, which enables the purchase of insurance at subsidized rates."

91   "Conversations About Risk Rating 2.0, Part III," Risk Management and Decision Processes Center, the Wharton School, June 4, 2022, https://riskcenter.wharton .upenn.edu/lab-notes/riskratingburt/.

Communities that adopt floodplain management practices that exceed the minimum requirements of the NFIP can get a discount for their residents who buy flood insurance. Community Rating System (CRS), a voluntary incentive program. AXIOS What's Next newsletter, "Flood Pains," Jun. 17, 2022.

92   National Research Council. 2015. Affordability of national flood insurance program premiums: Report 1. Washington, DC: National Academies Press.

93   Conversations About Risk Rating 2.0, Part III," Risk Management and Decision Processes Center, the Wharton School, June 4, 2022, https://riskcenter.wharton .upenn.edu/lab-notes/riskratingburt/.

94   "[T]he NFIP has been reauthorized 19 times since the end of 2017, with some extensions as short as a few weeks." Micah Guiao, "NAMIC calls for Reform to National Flood Insurance Program," *Insurance Business Magazine*, Key Media, May 26, 2022, https://www.insurancebusinessmag.com/us/news/catastrophe/namic-calls-for -reform-to-national-flood-insurance-program-407447.aspx

95   Thomas Frank, "Biden admin: Stop flood Insurance for New, Risky Homes," *E & E News*, Politico, June 13, 2022, https://www.eenews.net/articles/biden-admin-stop -flood-insurance-for-new-risky-homes/?utm_source=newsletter&utm _medium=email&utm_campaign=newsletter_axioswhatsnext&stream=science.

96   When your Local Building Department Says You Need to Rebuild to Higher Standards, FEMA Flood Insurance May Help." FEMA. U.S. Department of Homeland Security, November 16, 2021. https://www.fema.gov/fact-sheet/when -your-local-building-department-says-you-need-rebuild-higher-standards-fema-flood. According to Zillow, as of August 8, 2022 the value of a typical home in Charleston went up by more than 30 percent between 2021 and 2022 and is $520, 311. Zillow.com, "Charleston Home Values," https://www.zillow.com/charleston-sc/home-values/.

97   Abigail Darlington, "Charleston Adopts New Flood Prevention Rules—Mostly to Avoid Federal Penalty," *Post and Courier*, September 25, 2018, https://www .postandcourier.com/news/charleston-adopts-new-flood-prevention-rules-mostly-to -avoid-federal-penalty/article_9feb6b66-c0d9-11e8-a7b8-57b938f2407b.html.

98   Conversations About Risk Rating 2.0, Part III," Risk Management and Decision Processes Center, the Wharton School, June 4, 2022, https://riskcenter.wharton .upenn.edu/lab-notes/riskratingburt/.

99   Somini Sengupta, "Climate Forward" newsletter, *New York Times*, August 5, 2022.

100 John Schwartz, "As Floods Keep Coming, Cities Pay Residents to Move," *New York Times*, the New York Times Company, July 6, 2019, https://www.nytimes.com/2019 /07/06/climate/nashville-floods-buybacks.html.

101 FEMA, Acquisition, Evaluation, and Analysis: Acquisition Successes in Birmingham, PDF file, February 24, 2011, https://www.hsdl.org/?view&did=9869.

102 Chloe Johnson and Stephen Hobbs, "SC Got $1B in Flood Payments, But New Data Still Won't Say If Your Home Flooded," *Post and Courier*, June 12, 2019, https://www .postandcourier.com/business/real_estate/sc-got-b-in-flood-payments-but-new-data -still/article_7716a2be-8d0c-11e9-968d-db487666a877.html.

103 Chloe Johnson and Stephen Hobbs. "Fixed For Failure: How Flood Insurance Keeps Dangerous Homes Standing In SC." *Post and Courier*. May 20, 2020.

104 Rob Moore, "As Climate Risks Worsen, U.S. Flood Buyouts Fail to Meet the Need,"
     Yale Environment 360, Yale School of the Environment, January 23, 2020, https://e360
     .yale.edu/features/as-climate-risks-worsen-u.s.-flood-buyouts-fail-to-meet-the-need.

105 FEMA, Acquisition, Evaluation, and Analysis: Acquisition Successes in Birmingham,
     PDF file, February 24, 2011, https://www.hsdl.org/?view&did=9869.

106 Ben Finley, "Housing market slows retreat from rising seas, bigger storms," Associated
     Press, June 18, 2022.

107 Rob Moore, "As Climate Risks Worsen, U.S. Flood Buyouts Fail to Meet the Need,"
     Yale Environment 360, Yale School of the Environment, January 23, 2020, https
     ://e360.yale.edu/features/as-climate-risks-worsen-u.s.-flood-buyouts-fail-to
     -meet-the-need. FEMA was sharply criticized by the DHS OIG in Sept. 2020 for
     its implementation of its "severe repetitive loss" program: it doesn't have good data
     about the properties, and doesn't provide equitable nor timely relief to applicants.
     FEMA concurred with this evaluation and promised to mend its ways. "FEMA Is
     Not Effectively Administering a Program to Reduce or Eliminate Damage to Severe
     Repetitive Loss Properties," DHS OIG, Sept. 8, 2020.

108 Porter, J. R.; Shu, E.; Amodeo, M.; Hsieh, H.; Chu, Z.; Freeman, N., "Community
     Flood Impacts and Infrastructure: Examining National Flood Impacts Using a High
     Precision Assessment Tool in the United States," *Water* 2021, 13,3125. https://doi
     .org/10.3390/ w13213125, at 9: "at a high level, impacts to residential properties
     are expected to increase by 10% over the next 30 years with 12.4 million properties
     exposed today (14%) and 13.6 million at risk of flooding in 2051 (16%). Additionally,
     2.0 million miles of road (23%) are at risk today and are expected to increase by 3%
     over the next 30 years. Commercial properties are expected to see a 7% increase in
     the risk of flooding from 2021 to 2051, with 918,540 at risk today (20%) and 984,591 at
     risk of flooding in 30 years (21%). Currently, 35,776 critical infrastructure facilities are
     at risk today (25%), increasing to 37,786 facilities by 2051 (26% with a 6% increase in
     risk). 71,717 pieces of social infrastructure facilities are at risk today (17%), increasing
     to 77,843 by 2051 (19% and an increase of 9% over that time period)."

109 According to Prof. Siders, renters who are forcibly displaced by their landlords' decision
     to be bought out by the federal government are compensated under the Uniform
     Relocation Act. Those benefits are sharply time-limited, however. Prof. A.R. Siders
     interview with author, March 2, 2021.

110 Stephen Hobbs and Rickey Ciapha Dennis Jr., "How Flooding Intensifies the Charleston
     Region's Racial and Wealth Inequities," *Post and Courier*, September 22, 2020.

111 Warren L. Wise, "Kiawah Island Sales Topped $1B in 2021," *Post and Courier*, January 15,
     2022, https://www.postandcourier.com/business/real_estate/kiawah-island-sales
     -topped-1b-in-2021/article_feb23842-6125-11ec-8c5b-0f0ca10e79f2.html.

112 Freddie Mac, "Freddie Mac Credit Protected $828 Billion of Single-Family Mortgages
     in 2021," *Global News Wire*, February 25, 2022, https://www.globenewswire.com/en
     /news-release/2022/02/25/2392553/0/en/Freddie-Mac-Credit-Protected-828-Billion
     -of-Single-Family-Mortgages-in-2021.html; Federal Housing Finance Agency, Credit
     Risk Transfer Progress Report, PDF file, 2021, https://www.fhfa.gov/AboutUs
     /Reports/ReportDocuments/CRT-Progress-Report-4Q21.pdf.

113 Delta Terra Klima, "Climate Risk Analysis Report Measures Flooding and Wildfire Risk in U.S. Single-Family Property Market and CRT Bond Market," July 27, 2021, https://www.deltaterracapital.com/news-research/klima-report-2021.

114 Dave Burt, Dave Burt Written Testimony, PDF File, March 2020, https://www.schatz .senate.gov/imo/media/doc/DaveBurtWrittenTestimony.pdf.

115 Press release, "DeltaTerra's Klima™ Report Estimates $1.2 Trillion–$1.9 Trillion of Climate-Driven Value Loss Across 17 Million Single-Family Homes," PRWeb, July 28, 2021, https://www.prweb.com/releases/climate_risk_analysis_report _measures_flooding_and_wildfire_risk_in_u_s_single_family_property_market_and _crt_bond_market/prweb18097494.htm.

116 Press release, "DeltaTerra's Klima™ Report Estimates $1.2 Trillion–$1.9 Trillion of Climate-Driven Value Loss Across 17 Million Single-Family Homes," PRWeb, July 28, 2021, https://www.prweb.com/releases/climate_risk_analysis_report_measures _flooding_and_wildfire_risk_in_u_s_single_family_property_market_and_crt_bond _market/prweb18097494.htm.

117 DeltaTerra, Measuring Climate Risk in Real Estate Capital Markets, U.S. Single-Family Market, 2021, Klima Climate Risk Report Summary.

118 Patrick Kearns, "This 'Big Short' investor is betting against mortgage market again," *Inman*, November 4, 2019, https://www.inman.com/2019/11/04/this-big-short -investor-is-betting-against-mortgage-market-again/.

119 "Conversations About Risk Rating 2.0, Part III," Risk Management and Decision Processes Center, the Wharton School, June 4, 2022, https://riskcenter.wharton .upenn.edu/lab-notes/riskratingburt/.

120 Shamira McCray, "Tuberculosis, other potential human pathogens in Charleston waterways, C of C study finds," *Post and Courier*, May 28, 2022.

121 Abrahm Lustgarten, environmental reporter for ProPublica, Jun. 11 2022 CFR meeting.

122 NOAA (National Oceanic and Atmospheric Administration). 2013. National coastal population report: Population trends from 1970–2020. Washington, DC: NOAA.

Index